Henry Creswicke Rawlinson

England And Russia in the East

A Series of Papers on the Political and Geographical Condition of Central Asia

Henry Creswicke Rawlinson

England And Russia in the East
A Series of Papers on the Political and Geographical Condition of Central Asia

ISBN/EAN: 9783744760706

Printed in Europe, USA, Canada, Australia, Japan

Cover: Foto ©ninafisch / pixelio.de

More available books at **www.hansebooks.com**

ENGLAND AND RUSSIA IN THE EAST.

A SERIES OF PAPERS ON

THE POLITICAL AND GEOGRAPHICAL CONDITION
OF CENTRAL ASIA.

BY

MAJOR-GEN. SIR HENRY RAWLINSON,
K.C.B., F.R.S.,
PRESIDENT OF THE ROYAL GEOGRAPHICAL SOCIETY,
AND MEMBER OF THE COUNCIL OF INDIA.
(Formerly Envoy and Minister at the Court of Persia.)

WITH MAP.

LONDON:
JOHN MURRAY, ALBEMARLE STREET.
1875.

PREFACE.

THIS little volume, which is intended as a sort of Manual for students of the Eastern question, comprises five papers on the recent history and political condition of Central Asia, and one on its Geography, three of these papers being reprints from Periodical Reviews, and three being original.

To justify the reproduction of the three papers to which I have alluded and which relate both to the affairs of Persia and of Central Asia, it might be sufficient to point out that the events of the last few years, and the giant strides which Russia is now making in the East, have revived public interest in the subject, imparting indeed fresh importance to the history of the earlier period, and to the facts and opinions which were formerly put on record regarding it. But these are not the only arguments that have induced me to issue this volume in its present form. I have further considered : firstly, that the "Calcutta Review" of 1849, which contains the article on Persia—the only corrected summary that has ever been drawn up of our political relations with that country—has been long out of print ; and secondly, that the late Lord Strangford, who, as it is well known, had made a special study of the affairs of Central Asia, strongly recommended the "Quarterly Review" articles of 1865 and 1866 for republication, shortly after their appearance, as the most convenient method of informing the public upon a difficult subject and drawing their attention to the encroachments of Russia in the East.* I believe then, that I am only meeting a real and pressing requirement in adding to

* See "Pall Mall Gazette" of January 7th, 1868.

the new essays which are contained in this volume, a few of my earlier papers upon Persia and Central Asia, appending at the same time to such papers a series of notes, the object of which is to show in how far former speculation has been verified by events, and generally to bring up to the present day our information on the various subjects that are discussed.

It may now be convenient to state briefly of what materials the volume is composed. Chapter I., which was published in India in 1849, contains a review of our relations with Persia from the commencement of the century to the accession of the reigning Shah. It shows how we sought at first to employ Persia in scourging the Afgháns; how we afterwards, in defence of Indian interests, wrestled with France for the Persian alliance; and how the country subsequently, being neglected by England, yielded to the sustained pressure of Russia, till it became, so to speak, a mere instrument in that power's hands. In Chapter II., which has been written for this work, the political history of Persia is continued to the present time, recent events of interest, such as the settlement by arbitration of her Eastern frontier, and the establishment of the Indo-European telegraph, together with the Reuter concession and the Shah's visit to Europe, being duly recorded and explained. The political affairs of a second-rate Oriental power like Persia, which are discussed in these opening chapters in considerable detail, cannot be expected, under existing circumstances, to prove of an engrossing interest to English readers; but it may be well to remember that the country is so placed geographically, midway between Europe and India, that it can hardly fail to play an important part in the future history of the East; and that the condition of its people, therefore, and the temper of its Government are entitled to the attention of thoughtful inquirers, in a degree altogether disproportioned to the space which the dominions of the Shah occupy on the map of the world, or the rank which Persia holds in the scale of nations. The Persia of to-day is not, it is true, the Persia of Darius, nor even is it the Persia of Shah Abbas the Great; but it is a country, which, for good or for ill, may powerfully affect the fortunes of Great Britain's Empire in the East, and which requires, therefore, to be studied by our Statesmen with care, with patience, and, above all, with indulgent consideration.

The third chapter, which is reprinted from the "Quarterly Review" of October, 1865, contains a fair statement, taken from the most authentic sources, of Russia's progress in the East, from the time of her first crossing the Kirghiz Steppe to her establishment in Tashkend, which has ever since been the head-quarters of her power in Central Asia. When this article first appeared the Russian Press complained of its being written in a hostile spirit, but did not attempt to impugn the accuracy of the facts recorded, which, nevertheless, were of so startling a nature when duly brought before the public, as to raise serious doubts amongst us of the intentions of Russia, and to awaken us, at any rate, to a sense of the impending gravity of the position. I take some credit to myself that at so early a period as 1865 I forecasted the development of Russian power in Central Asia very much as it has since occurred, and that I then suggested the policy, to which I now recur, of proceeding, on the approach of real danger, to man the outposts of our Indian Empire at Herát and Candahar, in order to prevent their falling into the hands of the enemy.

Chapter IV., which is principally devoted to the geography of Central Asia, and to a record of English and Russian discovery in that region, also carries on the political narrative to the capture of Khojend. This article appeared in the "Quarterly Review" of October, 1866.

The next paper, forming Chapter V., is of a more confidential character. It is an amplified version of a speech on Central Asian affairs, which I had intended to address to the House of Commons in the summer of 1868, but which I was prevented by an accident from delivering. It embodies a survey of the political position, which was held at that time respectively by Russia and England in the East; and it points to the necessity of replacing the old policy of "masterly inaction" by creating, without loss of time, a direct barrier in Afghanistán against further Russian encroachment. This paper has never been published, though it was communicated at the time to the authorities in India, and may have thus had some share in influencing their decision to support Shír Alí Khan at Cabul.

And the series is closed with Chapter VI., which deals with the later phases of the Central Asian question, and brings up the outline narrative of events to the present day. Many very important subjects, bearing on the future relations between England and Russia in the East, are here discussed; but the essential feature of the chapter, and indeed of the whole volume, is the principle which it inculcates at the close of the argument, that if Russia should overstep certain limits in her approach to India, she must be checked by an armed resistance, even at the risk of producing war between the two countries. Herát, which has been justly named "the key of India," must, in my view, be secured against Russian occupation at all hazards, even though it should be necessary to march a force from India for its protection. But it must not be supposed that such a programme, bold as it may seem in these halcyon days of general repose, is really of a warlike tendency. On the contrary, it is put forward essentially in the interests of peace. It may be remembered that we drifted into the Crimean war because the nation uttered an "uncertain sound" when appealed to on behalf of Turkey, and Russia thus thought she might press forward with impunity. On the present occasion, it is hoped that the sound will not be uncertain, but that the public voice will declare our resolution to fight for the safety of Herát, in which case, to use her own expressive language, Russia "will think seven times "* before she prosecutes her enterprise against the Turcomans of Merv.

* See Extract from Grigorief's letters,' p. 271 of this volume.

A few additional words seem to be required in explanation of the two serious questions of responsibility and authority involved in this publication. Occupying as I do at present a seat in the Council of India, I may be supposed by some to speak on Eastern matters with official authority, and in fact to represent the views of the Government; but this would be entirely an erroneous assumption. The Council of India has no executive powers. It is a purely consultative body, in which every man has his own opinion, and communicates it, when asked, to the Secretary of State, who is alone responsible for administrative action. In my own case, for instance,— as the result of forty years' continuous observation of the course of political affairs in Central Asia, fortified by a large personal experience in Persia, in Afghanistán, and in India,—I have formed a very decided opinion, which I have repeatedly brought before the public, and in which I am supported by the judgment of late Sir Justin Sheil,* who was for ten years our Minister at Teherán, that in the event of Russia's approach to Herát, it will be indispensable to the safety of India that we should resume our military occupation of Western Afghanistán; but I have no reason whatever for believing that such views are shared by the responsible officers of the Crown, either in India or in England. The arguments in favour of such a course are put forward on my individual responsibility, and with a view of eliciting discussion, not as foreshadowing the policy of the Government.

Again, in regard to my narrative of passing events, and the criticism I have sometimes expressed on the proceedings of Government as well as of individuals, it should be clearly understood that I do not speak in my official capacity, nor do I rely upon official records; but on the contrary, that I have formed independent opinions from personal communication with the actors in the scenes described, as well as from information obtained through the press in Russia and in India,

* See Appendix to Lady Sheil's "Life in Persia."

and especially through an extensive correspondence which I maintain with gentlemen, both European and native, in India, in Persia, and at St. Petersburg. The feeling of the age is against all secrecy as tending to mislead and to confuse; and in ordinary affairs, perhaps, it may be admitted that publicity and an appeal to the common sense of mankind, are the safest guides to follow: but on the other hand there can be no doubt that in dealing with suspicious and half-instructed orientals, indiscreet revelations, or even premature discussion, may cause an infinity of mischief; and in noticing, therefore, certain current topics of high interest, such as the Afghán succession, the arrest of Yacúb Khan, and our future relations with Cabul, if I have thought it necessary to employ a certain reserve, and to refrain from passing any definite opinion, I trust my motives will not be misunderstood.

It only remains to explain why I venture to think that my views regarding the occupation of Herát are more appropriately addressed to the British public than to the Indian. Notwithstanding, then, that the expenses of the last Afghán war, which was brought on mainly through Russian intrigue, were, as in the case of all other Indian wars, except those beyond sea, defrayed exclusively from Indian revenues, I submit that the defence of India against Russia is a question of Imperial rather than of local policy, and that if it should be necessary, therefore, to arrest the progress of Russia towards the Indus by marching a British force to the extreme Afghán frontier, the Home Government must, at the very least, share the expense with the Indian Government. I will not go the length of saying that India, whose public debt does not amount to two years' revenue, is too poor to defend herself, but the principle seems to me undoubted, and should, I think, be acknowledged from the outset,—adding as it would a very important element of strength to our Indian Empire—that in any contest between India and a European enemy, whether involving actual war or mere preliminary field operations, the

Imperial Treasury must be liable at least in the same degree as the Indian Treasury. If this view meets with general approval, it will not only give additional security to India, but will obtain from Indian economists a more attentive consideration than has been hitherto vouchsafed, for those active measures of defence beyond the frontier, which I conceive, under certain circumstances, a sound policy would require.

LONDON, *January*, 1875.

P.S.—The map of Central Asia which I have been fortunately able to obtain for the illustration of this volume, was compiled by the late Mr. Arrowsmith, the first of British geographers, and occupied the greater part of his time during his declining years. It has been rendered more complete by recent additions from English and Russian surveys, and is probably the most accurate delineation, on a small scale, of the vast regions of Central Asia that is now to be obtained. For the political coloured boundaries, which do not profess to be throughout rigidly correct, I am myself responsible.

H. C. R.

THE MAP OF CENTRAL ASIA WILL BE FOUND AT THE
END OF THE VOLUME.

	COLOURED
Russian Empire with her new acquisitions	*Green*
British India	*Red*
Persia	*Yellow*
Afghanistán	*Buff*
Smaller Independent States	*Uncoloured*

CONTENTS.

CHAPTER I.

OUR POLITICAL RELATIONS WITH PERSIA.

(*Reprinted, with Notes, from " Calcutta Review," Vol. XII., Art. I.*, 1849.)

PAGE

1. Opening of relations with Persia at the close of the last century.—2. Captain Malcolm's mission and treaty, 1800.—3. War between Russia and Persia, 1802—1806 ; and opening of relations with France, General Gardanne being appointed minister in 1807.—4. Appointment of Sir Harford Jones by the Crown and of General Malcolm by the Government of India to be Minister in Persia. Malcolm's retirement and Sir H. Jones's treaty, 1807-1811.—5. Our interests in Persia and the policy adopted in support of them.—6. Sir Gore Ouseley's embassy, 1811, and definitive treaty, 1813.—7. Treaty of Teheran, concluded by Messrs. Morier and Ellis, 1814.—8. Summary of our relations with Persia, from 1814 to Russian treaty of Turcoman-chäi in 1828.—9. Modification of the treaty of Teheran, by Sir J. Macdonald, 1829.—10. Origin and explanation of Persian designs upon Herát.—11. State of affairs in Persia, to the death of Futteh Ali Shah in 1834.—12. Our relations with Court of Teheran from accession of Mahomed Shah to the raising of the siege of Herát, June 23, 1838.—13. Suspension of our relations with Persia, and Sir J. McNeill's return to England. Expedition to the Persian Gulf and Afghan war, 1838-1841.—14. Reconciliation with Persia, and retirement from Afghanistan, 1842.—15. English and Russian relations with Persia, and state of the country to the death of Mahomed Shah, in 1848.—16. General view of the question in 1849 . . . 1—79

CHAPTER II.

OUR POLITICAL RELATIONS WITH PERSIA—*continued.*

PAGE

1. 1848–1852.—State of Persia from the accession of Nassir-ed-dín Shah to the death of the Amír Nizám.—2. Affairs of Herát. Death of Yar Mahomed Khán. Our Convention with Persia regarding Herát, 1853.—3. Persia during the Crimean War, 1854–1856.—4. Herát affairs during the same period. Occupation of Herát by Persia, Oct. 1856.—5. 1856–1858.— Persian War. Treaty of Peshawer, Jan. 1857. Treaty of Paris, March, 1857. Its provisions and their effect.—6. 1858–1863. Teherán Mission transferred to India Office, 1859, and re-transferred to Foreign Office, 1860. The question examined. Our policy in Persia. Affairs of Herát to the death of Dost Mahomed Khán, May, 1863.—7. Disputes between the Persians and Afghans in regard to Seistán.—8. History of the Persian Telegraph. Convention of 1863, &c.—9. Affairs of the Persian Gulf and Bahrein up to 1868.—10. Affairs of Mekrán, and frontier delimitation between Persia and Kelát, 1862–1872.—11. The Seistán arbitration, 1870–1872.—12. Present state of our relations with Persia. The Atrek frontier and proposed expedition against the Turcománs. The Grand Vizier.—13. The Reuter Concession and the Shah's visit to Europe, 1873.—14. Prospects of Persia and policy of England towards her, 1874 . . 80—135

CHAPTER III.

THE RUSSIANS IN CENTRAL ASIA.

(*Reprinted, with Notes, from the "Quarterly Review" for October,* 1865. *No.* 236, *p.* 529.)

1. Apathy of the English public in 1865, in regard to affairs in Central Asia, contrasted with the Russophobia of 1838.—2. Retrospect of Russian policy in Central Asia from the period of the Afghan war. Khivan expedition of 1839–40, and negociations with Bokhara up to 1842.—3. Operations of Russia in the Steppe and on the Jaxartes from 1847 to period of the Crimean war, 1854.—4. Simultaneous advances in the Trans-Ili region to the Eastward.—5. Invasion of Kokand territory in 1863; capture of Turkestan and Chemkend, and Gortchakoff's circular of 1864.—6. Resumption of hostilities. Capture of Tashkand, and creation of Government of Turkestan, 1865.—7. British policy in Central Asia after the Afghan war. Convention with Persia regarding Herát, 1852. Treaty of

PAGE

Paris, 1857; and our general relations with the Afghans.—8. Our unofficial communications with Turkestan from 1842 to 1865.—9. Prospective relations of Russia with Kokand, Bokhara, and Khiva, and their probable effect on British Indian interests.—10. Brief review of the Central-Asian commercial question.—11. Consideration of our future policy . 136—204

CHAPTER IV.

CENTRAL ASIA.

(*Reprinted, with Notes, from the " Quarterly Review" for October*, 1866. *No*. 240, p. 461.)

1. Authorities for Central Asian Geography—German and Russian.—2. English and other travellers in the same region.—3. Apocryphal travels, Col. Gardiner, and Baron George Ludwig von ———.—4. Native explorers.—5. General description of Central Asia.—6. Evidence of its early civilization.—7. Ethnological sketch.—8. Review of the present political condition of its four divisions, S.E. Cashmere and Thibet, N.E. Eastern Turkestan, S.W. Afghanistan, and N.W. Russian Turkestan, with sketch of events there to autumn of 1866. — 9. General political consideratious . . . . 205—262

CHAPTER V.

MEMORANDUM ON THE CENTRAL ASIAN QUESTION, DATED JULY, 1868.

1. Abstract review of Russian progress in Central Asia up to 1868.—2. Relations of Russian military commanders with the Central Government.— 3. Russian view of her present state and prospects in Central Asia, as defined by Grigorief and Romanofski.—4. Probable position of Russia in Central Asia in 1878, if unchecked by England.—5. Effect of that position upon India considered : (*a*) in reference to Russian relations with Cabul ; (*b*) in regard to restlessness of frontier states ; (*c*) in respect to elements of weakness in our own position in India.—6. Arguments for our immediate interference in Afghan politics.—7. More extended view of the Central Asian question in regard to Russia's means in the future of offence against India.—8. Measures required to meet the danger—(*a*) reform of our political relations with Persia ; (*b*) various subsidiary arrangements for strengthening our position on the North-west frontier of India . 263—292

CHAPTER VI.

THE LATER PHASES OF THE CENTRAL ASIA QUESTION.

PAGE

1. Lord Mayo's Afghán policy: *a.* the Amballa conference; *b.* the proposed Neutral zone.—2. Negociations with Russia with regard to the Afghan frontier.—3. The expedition to Khiva, considered politically; its origin and results.—4. The Turcoman question and Merv.—5. A few words on Eastern Turkestán.—6. Present position of Russia in Central Asia.—7. The present relations of England with Afghanistán.—8. Review of the general question and our future policy considered . . . . 293—365

APPENDIX . 366—388

INDEX 389—393

ENGLAND AND RUSSIA IN THE EAST.

CHAPTER I.

OUR POLITICAL RELATIONS WITH PERSIA.*

1. Opening of relations with Persia at the close of the last century.—2. Captain Malcolm's mission and treaty, 1800.—3. War between Russia and Persia, 1802—1806; and opening of relations with France, General Gardanne being appointed minister in 1807.—4. Appointment of Sir Harford Jones by the Crown and of General Malcolm by the Government of India to be Minister in Persia. Malcolm's retirement and Sir H. Jones's treaty, 1807-1811.—5. Our interests in Persia and the policy adopted in support of them.—6. Sir Gore Ouseley's embassy, 1811, and definitive treaty, 1813.—7. Treaty of Teheran, concluded by Messrs. Morier and Ellis, 1814.—8. Summary of our relations with Persia, from 1814 to Russian treaty of Turcoman-chäi in 1828.—9. Modification of the treaty of Teheran, by Sir J. Macdonald, 1829.—10. Origin and explanation of Persian designs upon Herat.—11. State of affairs in Persia, to the death of Futteh Ali Shah in 1834.—12. Our relations with Court of Teheran from accession of Mahomed Shah to the raising of the siege of Herat, June 23, 1838.—13. Suspension of our relations with Persia, and Sir J. McNeill's return to England. Expedition to the Persian Gulf and Afghan war, 1838-1841.—14. Reconciliation with Persia, and retirement from Afghanistan, 1842.—15. English and Russian relations with Persia, and state of the country to the death of Mahomed Shah, in 1848.—16. General view of the question in 1849.

1. PERSIA, which has almost disappeared from the political horizon since the Afghan war, is now again looming in the field of sight. The country is undergoing that shock which it periodically sustains, when the occupancy of the throne is changed; and although, upon the present occasion, neither

---

* Calcutta Review, vol. xii., art. 1: —1. Progress of Russia in the East. 2nd edition. 1838.—2. Quarterly Review, No. cxxvii., art. 7.—3. Foreign Office Correspondence relating to Persia and Affghanistan, presented to both houses of Parliament by Her Majesty's Command. 1839.—4. Records of the Indian Government. 5. The Bombay Times, &c., &c.

does the immediate paroxysm threaten to be internally of a very violent character, nor is it accompanied for the moment with any morbid symptoms from without, still the crisis is not undeserving of our attention.

There is probably no political question, connected with our Indian Empire, which has been treated more frequently, or with greater discrepancy of result, than that which pretends to fix the nature, the limits, and the value of the true interests that we possess in Persia.

Party-writers and economists, historians and pamphleteers, statesmen and journalists, have, at different periods, and under different phases of the subject, examined it with more or less of competency and care; and, if the acts of Government may be taken as an index of the pressure of the times, the effect of these varied agencies upon the public mind must have been to invest our relations with Persia, in popular opinion, with every possible degree of consideration, from that of absolute vitality to one of comparative worthlessness. We commenced with a magnificent embassy, which was followed by complete isolation. We descended in our next essay like Jupiter in an avalanche of gold; but ere long we took advantage of poor Danaë's distress to drive a bargain with her of extraordinary rigour, and even of doubtful honesty. A third time we beheld our Syren transformed into a Hydra, and we plunged into a contest on her account, as momentous as any that figures in the page of Indian History; and yet, although the issue of that war must have increased tenfold our danger —if such danger ever had existed—we have since its conclusion held on our way with an inert complacency, that would hardly have been justified in our palmiest days of security and strength.

"Nil fuit unquam
"Sic impar sibi."

The most remarkable circumstance, however, is, that while we have exhibited this strange inconsistency,—while we have belied, in respect to Persia, the otherwise traditional character of our Eastern policy,—if there has been one branch of our Indian interests, which, from its nature, has been not only less than any other altered, but has been less susceptible of alteration, it has been that which relates to the value (be it for good or ill) of our connection with the Court of Teheran. Oragnic changes are as difficult in nations as they are in individuals. Eastern society above all, immovable alike in its predilections and its prejudices, sustains the action of half a century without any sensible effect; and the picture therefore of Persia, as it appeared to Captain Malcolm on his first visit to the Court of the Shah, conveys, as far as all essentials are concerned, a faithful representation of the country at the present day.* Considered also politically, since Zizianoff crossed the Caucasus, and Lord Lake entered Delhi, the substantive relations of Persia to the European powers (we exclude party intrigues, personal feelings, ephemeral interests, as of no consequence to the general question) can never by possibility have varied. Shut in between her colossal neighbours, the country has been held together by their opposing pressure. She has received influences, but has never imparted them: her condition has been strictly passive, and the tendencies to which she has been exposed have been constant and uniform. If it be wise at the present time to fold our arms in dignified composure, and look on Persia with indifference, then our lavish subsidies have been a folly, and our wars, costly as they have been in blood, in honour, and in treasure, have been a crime. If, on the other hand, our past policy has been sound, then our present supineness may well excite surprise.

Notwithstanding all that has been published on the subject of Persia, we still doubt if the question of her real abstract value, in regard to India, has ever yet been fairly treated. We enter our formal protest against fancy-pieces, party-articles, and against all political papers written for a purpose, whether that

* Malcolm, indeed, ventures to assert, that "the Persians, as far as we have the means of judging, are not at present a very different people from what they were in the time of Darius and of Noosheerwan;" but we cannot concede this dictum in all its latitude. We think it would be difficult to find a greater contrast than that obtained by comparing the autobiographic records of Darius at Bisitun with the Firman issued by Mahommed Shah on his return from the siege of Herat; and, as we judge of Hercules by his foot, so we may surely estimate a nation from the mouth of its ruler.

purpose be detraction or apology. We will go even further, and assert autobiographic history to be in its nature liable to suspicion. The writer, however able and however honest, who undertakes to describe and reason on the political events amongst which he is moving, encounters the same difficulties as a painter, who should seat himself at the library table to sketch the façade of the mansion he inhabits. The "quorum pars magna fui" is a positive impediment. Preconceived impressions, and personal associations, must inevitably disturb the natural current of inquiry, and divert it into stranger channels. Still less, too, are mere programmes to be depended on. Designed to justify some particular line of policy, they explode, if that policy should prove unsuccessful. We do not mean to say that they are useless, or that the utilitarian principle can be applied generally to the science of politics. Doubtless, when an occasion arises, emergent and exceptional, the available lights of the moment must be followed; delay would be fatal. There must be to a certain extent an adventurous movement—a leap in the dark; and posterity can alone benefit by the issue, in obtaining another element for future calculations; but with regard to the "pièces justificatives,"— those specious, often convincing guides—they must still come before the tribunal of experience, and be judged by the result. If their predictions are verified, the arguments on which they rest will remain a proud memorial of human foresight and sagacity. If, on the other hand, they do not stand the test of time, whatever respect may be paid to their ingenuity, they can have no permanent claim on consideration.

These remarks are particularly applicable to the principal "brochures" that have issued from the press on the Persian question. Undoubtedly the two ablest of these papers, which have appeared in modern times, and which, from their opportuneness and ability, have exercised the most influence on the public mind, are those that we have placed at the head of the present article. Sir John McNeill, from whose pen they are well known to have proceeded, was specially fitted to guide public opinion on such a matter, uniting as he did to the most perfect familiarity with his subject, a sound and

accurate judgment, together with the rare advantage of a
freedom both from political bias, and from local prejudice;
yet, after the ample interval of ten years' probation, do his
positions, we ask, sustain their reputation? Can his arguments, flowing as they invariably do, in a clear and continued
series of inductions, or his inferences, legitimate—nay imperative—as they seem, be now quoted as standard authorities? We think not, and for this simple reason, that, if
they prove anything, they prove too much. If "the progress
of Russia in the East" had been, indeed, as constant and
inevitable as the antecedents, which he grouped together, led
him to believe, ten years—and ten such years—could not have
passed over without a much more marked development than
has, in reality, taken place. If it were indispensable in 1838
to establish a strong British influence in Afghanistan, in order
to keep at a distance certain dangers with which India was
threatened, that influence could not have been annihilated as
it was in 1842, without the dangers becoming by this time so
imminent, as to be no longer matters of speculation. Accidental circumstances, we admit, may at any time interpose to
check or divert the natural course of events; but the possibility of those very circumstances—the chapter of accidents
as it is called—should form an item of account in working
out every political problem. This item, indeed, is of the same
value in considerations of policy, as the doctrine of chances in
the calculations of the actuary; and by its omission in argument is as essentially vitiated as by erroneous premises.

We propose then, although at a distance from the scene,
and without such full aids as we could desire, to re-open the
Persian question; and we promise our readers that, if they
should discover no great novelty or merit in our views, they
will, at any rate, obtain a just idea of our general connection
with the country, and will, moreover, find those particular
points, on which opinion is so much divided, treated in a fair
and candid spirit of inquiry.

It was at the close of the last century, under the administration of the Marquis of Wellesley, that the Government of India
first thought of opening political relations with the Court of

Teheran. As we do not profess to be here writing a formal history of the British connection with Persia, whilst at the same time we are loth to leave entirely blank any portion of our outline sketch, we must throw into a mere abstract narrative such information as we possess of our dealings with the Court of Teheran prior to Captain Malcolm's mission. Lord Wellesley's attention had been drawn to the North West frontier of India shortly after his arrival in the country, not merely by the power and avowed hostility of Shah Zeman, and by the notorious fact of an ambassador having travelled from Mysore to the Punjab, but by the discovery that Vizier Ali of Oude had also appealed to the avarice of the Afghan King, by offering a donation of three crores of rupees, in the event of his own restoration to the "musnud" through the Afghan arms, and by proposing in the mean time to assign, for the uses of the Shah, the fifty-five lakhs payable from Oude for the maintenance of the British Contingent.

Mehdi Ali Khan, accordingly, a Persian nobleman naturalized in India, who was then acting as the Company's Resident at Bushire, was instructed "to take measures for inducing the Court of Persia to keep Shah Zeman in perpetual check (so as to preclude him from returning to India), but without any decided act of hostility;" and two or three lakhs of rupees were to be expended annually, at the Khan's discretion, for the purposes above specified,—" the plan of subsidizing the whole army of Persia being (in Lord Wellesley's language) more extensive and expensive than circumstances seemed to require."

Agreeably to these instructions, Mehdi Ali Khan, early in 1798, opened a correspondence with Teheran, for the purpose of persuading the Shah—who, however, needed no persuasion —to send the two refugee princes, Mahmood and Firoz, with a respectable force into Afghanistan.

Some court-intrigue was employed on the occasion, and the expedition actually took place; but there is every reason for believing, that it would have equally taken place without the interference of our agent; for the project was in entire accordance with the temper and policy of the Persian court, and had been moreover actively discussed before the receipt of Mehdi

Ali Khan's communication. This expedition, however, which was badly conceived and worse executed, turned out a complete failure; and so little disposed were we at the time to take credit for having instigated the movement, that it was eight years before the Indian Government could be persuaded to reimburse to the Agent employed at Teheran the paltry sum of 17,000 Rupees, expended on the personal outfit of the princes.

Futteh Ali Shah took the field in person for the first time in 1799, for the avowed purpose of "conquering and reducing the countries of Candahar and Herat," and without any further communication with Mehdi Ali Khan. Letters had been written by that officer to the court of Teheran, which, by the highly-coloured statements which they gave of the atrocities committed by the Afghans on the Sheeahs and Syuds of Lahore, were certainly calculated to excite the sectarian animosity of the Persians;* but it was not in consequence of such letters that the expedition was organized. His Majesty, indeed, received the inflammatory despatches on the borders of Khorassan: and it is evident, therefore, we were indebted for the withdrawal of Shah Zeman from Lahore to Peshawur, which immediately followed his receiving intelligence of the Persian movements, to the ambition of Futteh Ali Shah, rather than to our own diplomacy: and upon this ground we rejected a subsequent claim brought forward by the Persians for indemnification.

The campaign of 1799 was of very short duration, and of no great importance even in its local effects. His Majesty returned to the capital in the autumn, and there received Mehdi

---

* Mehdi Ali Khan was an active and faithful servant of the Company, and not an unskilful negociator; but his florid statements and thoroughly oriental colouring scandalised, on more occasions than one, the British authorities even of that age, when veraciousness was certainly not the distinguishing feature of our political correspondence. He commences the letter in question with a very pretty specimen of his craft. "Lord Mornington," he says, "and Mr. Duncan, and all the Sirdars in the Company's service, are indifferent as to the entering or not of Shah Zeman into Hindustan, as the fame of the European Artillery is well known, a trifling instance of which is that 700 *of their brave troops not long ago defeated three lakhs of Suraj-ed-Dowlah's forces!*"

Ali Khan, who had in the mean while wended his way from Bushire to the capital, to endeavour by personal intercourse with the Shah's Ministers more steadily and effectually to carry out Lord Wellesley's policy. The Agent expended about two and a half lakhs of rupees upon this mission, thus giving the Persians a foretaste of British prodigality: and it is possible— although there is no sufficient evidence of the fact—that it may have been partly owing to his advice and promise of pecuniary aid, that the Shah again marched into Khorassan in the spring of 1800. Mehdi Ali Khan in January of that year returned from Teheran to Bushire, and joined Captain Malcolm very shortly after the first British mission had set foot upon the soil of Persia.

2. The immediate aim of Captain Malcolm's mission, in 1800, was to push forward a Persian army on Herat, as a means of diverting Shah Zeman from his long-threatened descent on Hindustan ; and this was undoubtedly a legitimate object of diplomacy. The invasion of India on the one hand, and the defence of Khorassan on the other, had been the stimulant and opiate which, ever since Shah Zeman's accession to the throne, had alternately inflamed and paralyzed his ambition. The Afghan king had, on two occasions, advanced in person to Lahore, but had been compelled to retrace his steps by troubles in his rear. He was still intent on conquest beyond the Sutlej, when Captain Malcolm quitted India. It is, however, erroneous to suppose that we were indebted to the mission in question for our deliverance from the danger which threatened us.* That the storm was dissipated in the manner suggested by Lord Wellesley before it

---

* For a minute and honest detail of these events, see Elphinstone's Cabul, Vol. II., p. 316. It is of the more importance that historic truth should be vindicated in this matter, as the error that we have noticed originated with Captain Malcolm himself, who in his History of Persia, Vol. II., p. 215, had the assurance to write that his "policy had the temporary success which was desired of diverting the Afghans from their meditated invasion of India." On such authority, Dr. Conder may be pardoned for stating in the Modern Traveller, (Persia, p. 237,) that "the mission fulfilled all its objects. The Shah gladly embraced the opportunity to invade Khorassan ; and his conquest had its anticipated effect of recalling the Afghan chief from his Indian expedition."

reached our frontier, and that the clouds never again collected in dark lowering masses, was creditable to His Lordship's foresight, but was entirely independent of his measures. The second expedition, indeed, of Futteh Ali Shah into Khorassan in 1800, which drew Shah Zeman from Candahar to Herat, took place almost simultaneously with Captain Malcolm's journey from the south of Persia to the Capital. His Majesty received the British mission at Teheran in the autumn of the same year, after his return from Subzewar; and the subsequent proceedings of Shah Mahmood, which disconcerted Shah Zeman's arrangements at Peshawur, and which led, in the sequel, to his dethronement, so far from originating in British instigation, or in Persian support, were in reality indebted for their success to their entire independence of all foreign aid. As the minion of Persia, Shah Mahmood could never have prevailed against his elder brother. As the popular Duráni champion, he was irresistible.

Captain Malcolm appears, however, to have had other instructions than those which related to our relief from the positive danger of Affghan invasion. At this time a Gallophobia reigned rampant in India. Napoleon was the "bête noire" of Lord Wellesley's dreams; and thus, although there seems, in reality, to have been no more reason for suspecting the Directory to have entertained the design of injuring us through Persia, than there was for apprehending danger to British India from the inflated proclamation of a Mauritius Governor, Captain Malcolm was nevertheless empowered to contract engagements with the Shah, in regard to the French nation, of so stringent—nay, of so vindictive—a nature, that they have been characterized by one of our ablest, as well as most impartial, political writers, as "an eternal disgrace to our Indian diplomacy."[*] In those engagements it was provided, that, "should an army of the French nation, actuated by design and deceit, attempt to settle with a view of establishing themselves on any of the Islands or shores of Persia, a conjoint force shall be appointed by the two high contract-

* Sutherland's Sketches, p. 30.

ing parties to act in co-operation, for their expulsion and extirpation, and to destroy and put an end to the foundation of their treason; and if any of the great men of the French nation express a wish or desire to obtain a place of residence, or dwelling, in any of the islands or shores of the kingdom of Persia, that they may raise the standard of abode, or settlement, leave for their residing in such a place shall not be granted." Captain Malcolm further persuaded the Shah to issue a Firman to the provincial Governors, which directed that "you shall expel and extirpate the French, and never allow them to obtain a footing in any place," and added that "you are at full liberty to disgrace and slay the intruders."

Can we be surprised that Monsieur Langlès, writing of these engagements, after the passions of the hour had subsided, termed them "ridiculous and even injurious?"* Is it not, indeed, a significant admission of their inability to stand the test of public opinion at the present day, that the treaty which embodied them was excluded from the State papers presented to the House of Commons, on March 9th, 1839?† We confess that we fully participate in the condemnation which Colonel Sutherland has expressed of them on the score of their morality; but we go even farther, and affirm that they were unnecessary in their nature, unsound in their policy, and pregnant with evil consequences;—unnecessary, inasmuch as they were aimed at an imaginary danger;—unsound in providing for that danger a remedy too potent, or at any rate too violent, to be efficacious;—and of an almost suicidal tendency, in exposing the vulnerability of our Indian Empire, and thus court-

---

* Voyage de Chardin. Tom. X., p. 232. Captain Malcolm coolly replied to the Frenchman's statement that, "*it was exactly opposed to the truth.*"

† It is possible, however, that the exclusion of this document from the Persian State Papers may have been owing to certain doubts being entertained, whether the treaty ever came into operation; for we find Governor Duncan stating in 1806, that "there was an impression on his mind, that the final ratification and interchange of the treaty of 1801 were not to take place till after the arrival of Hadjee Khaleel in Bengal, which never having occurred, the Supreme Government could judge how far it might be allowable to consider it as not now in force." We have never seen the validity of the Malcolm Treaty questioned in any other quarter; but assuredly, if its ratification and interchange never did in reality take place, it was diplomatically allowable to ignore the whole transaction.

ing, instead of averting, attack. It was an unhappy augury for our future intercourse with Persia, that our political relations should have commenced under such auspices. It was ominous of the troubles we should have in the sequel to encounter, that we originated the idea of "the road to the English" lying through the Persian Empire;* and, if we have since had occasion to complain of the insincerity of the Court of Teheran, or of its desire to profit by the jealousy of the European powers, we should do well to remember, that the secret of the value which we placed on the country from its geographical position was first revealed to the wily Persian by ourselves.

But Captain Malcolm's Treaty was not, perhaps, the most objectionable feature of his mission; his prodigality left a more lasting impression, and that impression, in the ratio of its original force and effect, has operated ever since to our prejudice. So lavish was his expenditure, that he was popularly believed to have been granted a premium of 5 per cent. on all the sums he could disburse; while the more intelligent, who rejected an explanation suited rather to the world of romance, could only draw, from his profusion, an exaggerated estimate of the wealth of England, or an inordinate appreciation of the value which we placed upon the Persian alliance. Money, we know, in the moral world, is not unlike opium in the physical. The stomach, once drugged, is insensible to milder stimulants; and thus, ever since we administered the first fatal dose, in order to create an influence, or to persuade the Persians of our really being in earnest in seeking for their friendship, we have had to follow the same pernicious treatment, with a merely temporary effect upon the patient, but to the serious depletion of our Indian store, from which the prescriptions have been drawn.

* This expression has ever since been a bye-word in Persia. Diplomatic etiquette, of course, did not admit of its appearing "totidem verbis" in our treaties with the Shah; but the idea which it embodies forms the very basis of all these treaties; and we hardly understand, therefore, why our nerves should have been so greatly shocked, when Dost Mahommed Khan was reminded by his agent at Teheran, that he held a turnpike lower down "*the road.*"

We cannot close our notice of Captain Malcolm's mission, without alluding to another project which occupied much of his attention, and which, although it found little favour with Lord Wellesley at the time, has since been much canvassed, and sometimes even carried into partial execution. That India was menaced with danger from the European powers, Capt. Malcolm never doubted; and with this position, taken in the abstract, and dependent for its development on time and circumstances, we are hardly disposed to quarrel; but we can only explain it as the effect of that sort of blindness, which, on particular subjects, sometimes distorts the eyes of politicians, otherwise clear-sighted enough, that he should have looked for the approach of the danger *by sea,* and that his line of sight should have been still more strangely diverted, from the Caspian, to the Persian Gulf. Such, however, was the case. He seems to have had a sad misgiving that the French —notwithstanding that they were subjected by his treaty to a perpetual ostracism from the Persian soil—would still establish themselves on the shores of the Gulf, and would thence launch their victorious navies against the coasts of India; and he accordingly proposed seriously, that we should obtain the island of Kishm from the Shah, and should there construct a fort, which, if not "hewn out of a mountain" like Gibraltar, or "cradled in a crater" as at Aden, should at any rate, be so strengthened by all the means and appliances of modern science, as to present a formidable obstacle to any enemy. In a military point of view, this fort was to be a "tête du pont" to the Bombay Harbour. Commercially, it was to revive the extinct glories of Siraf and Ormuz. Politically, it was to give confidence to Asia, while it frowned, like "Castle Dangerous," upon Europe.

It was in vain that Mr. Harford Jones, to whom Capt. Malcolm submitted his lucubrations, objected that France must overrun Syria, Assyria, and Mesopotamia, before she could approach the Persian Gulf; that she must hold those countries as a conqueror, before she could pretend to fit out an expedition against India; that, if she did really contemplate so gigantic an enterprise, she was in a better position for making the attempt from the Red Sea, than if she were in possession of Bushire and Bussorah; inasmuch as the naval resources of Egypt, which she then held, were fully equal to those of Arabia and Persia, while Suez was much nearer than the mouth of the Euphrates to her European base. It was in vain that the fallacy was exposed of ever again forming a great commercial emporium in the Persian Gulf, Vasco de Gama, when he doubled the Cape, having given the death blow to this once famous line of traffic between the East and the West. It was in vain that the resident at Bagdad, with a sagacity that has never been acknowledged, and the full value of which remains yet to be realised, pointed out the true point of danger to our Indian Empire, at Asterabad; "the line of least resistance" lying between the Caspian and the Indus. Captain Malcolm was not to be disabused of his crotchet; he sturdily defended his thesis, and sent in a report of one hundred and eleven paragraphs to Lord Wellesley on the subject, supported by supplementary arguments extending to some fifty paragraphs more. This portentous document, however, happily miscarried: the minutes of the Calcutta Council Chamber stifled the monster in its birth; and, although Malcolm again attempted to vitalize the embryo in 1810, and certain abortive measures, such as the expeditions of 1817 and 1820, and the occupation of Karrack in 1838, may be indirectly traced to the same germ, the only actual embodiment at the present day—and that a mere faint shadow of the original idea—is to be found in our naval station at Bassidore.

3. We must now take a rapid survey of that phase in our Persian policy, which we have before mentioned, as one of complete isolation. For several years succeeding Captain Malcolm's mission, the affairs of Persia excited but little interest in India.* The violent effort we had made in opening

* We must compress into a note the leading features of the Persian question in regard to India during this period. A certain Haji Khalil Khan was dispatched from Persia to India, immediately on Captain Malcolm's retirement, to pay the compliment of a return mission, and to arrange for the ratification and interchange of the treaty. This individual, however, lost his life at Bombay in 1802, in an affray between his servants and the guard of sepoys who were acting as his escort. Much embarrassment ensued; but

an alliance was followed, as usual, by the reaction of languor. The Gallophobia had been lulled for a time by the ill success of the French in Egypt, and the dispersion of Perron's battalions. Danger from beyond the Indus no longer scared us; for Afghanistan was torn asunder by civil war, and Runjeet Singh had founded a kingdom in the Punjab. Although, therefore, we continued to receive intelligence from Teheran by the way both of Bagdad and of Bushire, and although we thus learnt that Persia was sinking gradually before the power of Russia, and that France had offered assistance to the Shah, we made no attempt whatever to preserve the influence that Capt. Malcolm had created, or even to require an observance of his treaty.

Persia in the meantime was suffering grievously. She lost in succession to the indefatigable Zizianoff, Mingrelia and Ganjeh, Shekee, Shirwan, and Karabagh. In 1804, she fought her first pitched battle with a Russian army near Erivan, and, of course, sustained a defeat. When overtures were made by

ultimately, liberal pensions having been provided for the relatives of the deceased, and full explanations having been tendered on the part of the Indian Government by Mr. Manesty, the Company's Resident at Bussorah, who took upon himself in 1804 to proceed to the Persian Court for the purpose, the event was passed over as the inevitable stroke of "fate." We do not believe that any ill-feeling to us was awakened amongst the Persians generally by so untoward an affair: in fact a saying is on record of the minister of Shiraz, that "the English might kill ten ambassadors, if they paid for them at the same rate," in allusion to the princely pensions settled on the family. There was an individual, however, who caused us considerable trouble in the sequel: Mirza Nebi Khan, the brother-in-law of the ambassador, having been named administrator of the estate, conceived the idea of turning the accident to his private account. By enormous bribes to the Persian Court

he obtained the appointment of ambassador for himself, and after much delay came down to India in 1805, not exactly to fill his relative's place, but to exercise the triple functions of minister, merchant, and claimant of blood-money, which he roundly assessed at 20 lakhs of Rupees. It is probable, nay almost certain, that his political mission, which mainly referred to a requisition for aid against Russia, would have failed under any circumstances, for the question was before the Home Government, and in the meantime the Indian authorities were powerless to act; but it is also certain, that his arrogant language, his extraordinary pretensions, and the anomaly of his triple character, contributed in no small degree to bring about the indifferent reception and frigid replies, with which he was greeted by Sir G. Barlow, on his arrival at Calcutta in March 1806. He returned to Persia "re infectâ," and found the French already established there.

France in 1802, proposing the co-operation of a French and Persian army against the Russians in Georgia (all territorial acquisitions to be divided between the contracting parties, and resident French Agents to be established immediately at Teheran and Erivan), they were coldly received.* Mirza Buzurg, indeed, emphatically wrote, that "if Buonaparte in

* These letters were delivered by a certain Shahrokh Khan, who had travelled to Paris on his private affairs, and had met with much attention from the French authorities. They were generally believed at the time to be genuine documents; but circumstances subsequently transpired which led to a suspicion of their having emanated from a certain clique of diplomatic subalterns, who, under the name of "Consular Agents," remained in Syria after the French evacuation of the country, and who continued for many years to pursue a restless course of political adventure, spreading in the sequel a perfect net-work of intrigue over the whole face of Western Asia. These parties, at any rate, led on by those veterans of the Levant, the Outreys, the Rousseaus, Pontecoulant, and the Coranças, were found pushing their "antennæ" into Persia, almost immediately subsequent to the presentation of Shahrokh's letters; and it was in pursuance of their counsels and through their agency, that, in the autumn of 1804, when the Shah was encamped near Erivan, a second communication, formally authenticated, was addressed by the Government of France to the Court of Persia, which claimed, in virtue of a certain treaty concluded with Shah Abbas (a treaty, however, that we do not remember to have seen otherwise noticed in history), a prescriptive right of alliance between the two countries, and which proposed that the Shah and the Emperor should act cordially together against Russia. As France and Russia were at this time ostensibly on terms of friendship, the sincerity of the proposal seems to have been suspected. The Shah, moreover, had already applied to the British Cabinet, through the Resident at Bagdad, for support on the European side; and he was about despatching an ambassador to India to solicit an armed interference in his behalf. The French overtures, therefore, without being offensively or even decidedly rejected, were, for the time being, quietly laid upon the shelf.

In the summer of the following year (1805), war having in the meantime broken out between France and Russia, Colonel Romieu appeared in person at Teheran, accredited under the hand of the Emperor: he was accompanied by a respectable suite, and was the bearer of handsome, if not of splendid, presents: his proposals, too, were sufficiently explicit. If Persia would repudiate the British alliance, which could not avail her against Russia, and would connect herself with France, the Emperor would at once send a Resident Minister to Teheran, would subsidize the Persian troops, and throw an auxiliary army into Georgia. The Shah, who at the first audience of the Colonel had merely vouchsafed three questions: "How are you?" "How is Buonaparte?" "What made you kill your King?" wavered, when he heard of a subsidy and an auxiliary army in Georgia. Would the English fulfil his expectations? Would they abide by the stipulations of the Malcolm Treaty, which was offensive and defensive, the friends of one country being the friends of the other, and the enemies of one

person came to Teheran, he would be debarred admission to the centre of the universe," and, as the ink of the Malcolm

country the enemies of the other? These were the questions which His Majesty again referred to Bagdad, and, pending an answer to which, he was still resolved to avoid committing himself with France. In the meantime Colonel Romieu died at Teheran; and further negociations being deferred until the arrival of a Monr. Rubie, whom it was intended to send out from Paris in an ostensible diplomatic capacity, Sir Harford Jones availed himself of the respite thus afforded, to write soothing and hopeful letters to the Shah, and ultimately proceeded in person to Constantinople, for the double purpose of awakening the King's ambassador to a sense of the critical state of affairs in Persia, and of explaining the anomalous position in which we were placed in regard to that country, by the conflicting interests and the independent engagements of the Home and Indian Governments. In the spring of 1806 the Shah must have received intelligence of the expected result of Mirza Nebi Khan's negociations in India. The Governor-General had left the question of protecting or supporting Persia against Russia for the exclusive consideration of Downing Street; and as his Majesty's ministers had been now for full two years deliberating on the question, without venturing to come even to an approximate solution, the Shah could not help regarding this shifting of responsibility at the last moment from the only quarter whence substantive aid could be afforded, to the same shadowy, silent oracles, as equivalent to a determination to avoid interference. In the first bitterness of disappointment letters were addressed to Napoleon, and confided to Monr. Outrey, a French Dragoman, who had remained at Teheran after Colonel Romieu's decease; but as this gentleman travelled leisurely by the route of Bagdad to Constantinople, he had hardly reached the latter place when he was overtaken by an ambassador appointed by Futteh Ali Shah to repair to the camp of the Emperor. This was the adventurous Mirza Reza, who afterwards concluded the treaty of Fenkestein; and the instructions with which he proceeded on his mission were dexterously conceived and not unskilfully executed. In these instructions, so far from appearing as a suppliant, the Shah adopted the tone of an equal. No undue apprehension was expressed of the power of Russia. On the contrary she was spoken of as an antagonist of ordinary calibre, "equally an enemy of the Kings of Persia and France, and whose destruction accordingly became the duty of the two Kings. France would attack her from that quarter; Persia from this." Then followed a golden pill for the Emperor, "If the French have an intention of invading Khorassan, the King will appoint an army to go down by *the road* of Cabul and Candahar." But the ambassador was thus warned in conclusion,—"If the French require a station or port in the province of Fars for their passage to Hindustan, do not consent; but say that when a respectable confidential person is established at the royal residence for the consummation of friendship between the States, the proposal will be considered."

Nothing could have been more opportune for Napoleon than this communication: he had just fought the doubtful battle of Eylau, and was casting about for new allies against the only power which had yet been able to arrest the march of his legions. A preliminary treaty accordingly was

Treaty was scarcely then dry, this was no very surprising trait of constancy, even for a Persian. By degrees, however, the Minister's coyness wore off. French agents were admitted in 1805 to reside in Persia, and were even treated with distinction; and when the application, addressed from Teheran direct to the Government of India in 1806, seeking for support against Russia, entirely failed—owing amongst other causes to Sir G. Barlow's strict adherence to the principle of non-intervention —the star of France rose rapidly in the ascendant.

It has been asserted, by one who might be supposed to be competent to give an opinion on the question, that the Governor-General's rejection of this application for assistance was a clear "casus fœderis;" * but, in the received language of history, the odium of broken faith rests altogether with the Shah; and Sir John McNeill, indeed, affords an apology, but

formed without delay, and almost at Mirza Reza's dictation, and Mons. Jaubert was at once sent off to Teheran to announce the terms agreed on, and to hold the Shah firm to his new alliance. A few months subsequently, when the convention of Tilsit had entirely altered the relations between Russia, France, and England, General Gardanne was accredited to Persia with instructions very essentially modified from those issued to the Agent who preceded him, and far less satisfactory to the Shah. The treaty of Mirza Reza, who accompanied our General, was barely noticed, or at any rate it was only so far admitted to be in force as it concerned the exclusion of the English from Persia and the hostile designs of the French against British India. The armed opposition to Russia, which had been especially provided for in Mirza Reza's draft, was rendered impossible by the peace of Tilsit; and the Shah, being now committed to the new alliance, was fain to accept of mediation in its stead.

We have been thus particular in describing the origin of the French connexion with Persia, as all the historical notices we have seen upon the subject are deficient either in veracity or fulness: and as Sir John McNeill even, who ought to have known better, has, in his Persian pamphlet (Progress of Russia in the East, pp. 59-62), confounded the different missions in a manner which furnishes a graphic picture, but which is correct neither in outline nor detail.

* "Letter on the present state of British interests and affairs in Persia, 1838, by Harford Jones Brydges," p. 6. Sir H. Jones always maintained the principle, that, as our alliance with Persia was offensive and defensive, the Russian occupation of Mingrelia, Karabagh, &c., was equivalent to an attack on our own dominions, and required to be resented accordingly. It must be remembered, however, that the offensive and defensive article of the Malcolm Treaty referred particularly to the French, and was so understood and admitted both by the English and Persian plenipotentiaries. The validity, moreover, of the treaty in question was, as has been before observed, open to dispute.

no defence, when he says, "that Persia, losing all hope of support from her old ally, had no alternative but to throw herself into the arms of France." Upon whichever party, however, may fall the responsibility of those proceedings which led to the mission of Mirza Reza, the return mission of Mons. Jaubert, and the conclusion of a treaty between France and Persia at Fenkestein in 1807,—no sooner was it known that General Gardanne had been appointed to Teheran, and that French officers might be thus expected ere long to obtain a control over the military resources of the country, than the authorities in Downing Street and Calcutta appear to have awoke almost simultaneously to a sense of danger.

It is currently believed that at the conference at Tilsit, the Eastern question in its full extent was discussed between Alexander and Napoleon, much in the same spirit as the Turkish question had been previously treated by Catherine and the Emperor Joseph. There were formidable impediments, it is true, to a partition of the East between two such powers as France and Russia, not the least of which must have been the difficulty of apportioning the rich prize to be acquired from England; but it may fairly be presumed, that when Napoleon destined the most able and distinguished of his brothers[*] to fill the post of Ambassador at Teheran, he not only really entertained the idea of contesting, with more or less activity, British supremacy in India, but expected the Emperor Alexander to aid in the design. It seemed therefore to be time, when Persia, sulky through disappointment, threatened to place herself a passive instrument in the hands of France, that the British Government should bestir itself; but supposing even this result to have been as imminent as our fears led us to imagine, whether the means employed were the best calculated to avert the danger, is a distinct and much controverted question.

We have said advisedly that Napoleon entertained the idea of contesting our supremacy in the East—such an idea indeed was a necessary element in his design of universal empire—but we are far from intending to commit ourselves to the popular

[*] Lucien Buonaparte. See "Progress of Russia in the East," p. 60.

opinion that India, either then or at any future time, was exposed to the actual danger of an armed European invasion. Among the visions which the Emperor displayed to Alexander at Tilsit, and for which he sacrificed so many substantial interests, we have heard of one proposing the simultaneous march of a French and Russian army, which, combining in the plains of Persia, should operate against our Indian frontier.* It is further known, that Sebastiani endeavoured to obtain permission from the Porte, that the French troops destined for the expedition should pass by Constantinople, and we have little doubt that Gardanne's principal instructions in his Persian Embassy referred to the same subject; but it is also notorious, that in spite of Mirza Reza's engagements, the project from the commencement found no favour with the Persian monarch, and that a very short experience of the Persian character and of the state of the relations of the Court with Russia, sufficed to convince Gardanne, not only of the impossibility of a tripartite alliance, but of the extreme difficulty of persuading the Shah to admit the presence in Persia of an auxiliary army of any European nation whatever. The utmost that the General could have achieved,—if he had fulfilled Napoleon's promise of inducing Russia to relinquish to the Shah all her recent acquisitions in Georgia, and if he had thus obtained a place, dominant and permanent, in the Councils of Teheran,—would have been the direction of a Persian expedition towards the Indus led by European officers; and we may safely venture to predict what would have been the fate of such an army, when brought, after its toilsome march, face to face with the veterans of Deig and of Laswarrie, who then guarded our north-western frontier.

4. Such, however, was not the light in which the Russo-French coalition was viewed at the time. An alarm, exaggerated

* We find the project thus described in an official document of the period, drawn up at Vienna, and circulated "by authority:"—"Buonaparte saisit adroitement l'occasion de la paix de Tilsit pour engager Alexandre d'envoyer une armée le printemps prochain en Perse, qui s'uniriot avec une armée Française qui devait passer par Constantinople et l'Asie Mineure, et de là, traversant la Perse, organiser les troupes que la Cour d'Ispahan devait donner pour sa part, et commencer quelque acte hostile contre les possessions de la Compagnie des Indes."

by the vagueness of the danger, was suddenly called into existence, and measures of defence were taken, which, with the usual untowardness of sudden impulses—an untowardness, indeed, that in regard to Persia seems to operate with a sort of fatality—almost brought the Home and Indian Governments into collision. The British ministry, judging Persia, at war with Russia and courted by France, to come within the immediate range of European diplomacy, appointed Sir Harford Jones, who had lately returned from Bagdad, to be Envoy Extraordinary from the Crown, and sent him out in October, 1807, with a commission which placed him in subordination to the Governor-General, but still granted him full powers to conclude a direct treaty between the Shah of Persia and the King of England: while Lord Minto, either mistrustful of the Agent, or deeming affairs too critical to await his tardy arrival by way of the Cape of Good Hope, and dissatisfied also with the interference of the Crown in arrangements which had hitherto been under the exclusive direction of the Indian Government, and the expenses of which moreover required to be defrayed from the Indian Treasury, nominated his own officer, Brigadier-General Malcolm, to the same duties that had been confided in London to His Majesty's Envoy. We will not follow the details of the unseemly contest that ensued, although an instructive lesson might be drawn from them. We must confine ourselves to results, and to the general questions of policy involved in them. General Malcolm, who was allowed the initiative in this singular diplomatic combat, had no sooner arrived in the Persian Gulf in May, 1808, than, agreeably to his instructions, he opened trenches against the French position at Teheran. But Gardanne was then basking in the full sunshine of Court favour: he had given something, promised much, and led the Shah to hope for more; he was pleading earnestly to Russia for forbearance: his engineers were constructing fortifications: his officers were disciplining the Persian troops: and, although the British Envoy resorted freely to his old strategy of a golden influence, and fairly offered to buy the French out of Persia, he found it impossible to make any way. A discomfiture, so signal and so unexpected, seems to have obscured the General's judgment, as much as it shocked his *amour propre*. Without considering the causes of his failure, or duly weighing its probable effects, or even seizing upon an eligible remedy, he indignantly quitted the shores of Persia, "breathing reproach, defiance, and invasion."

We doubt if General Malcolm was guilty of greater blunders in his dealings with the Peishwa in 1817–18, than he committed in his abortive mission to Persia in 1808. It required no extraordinary penetration, one would think, to have perceived that at the period in question money could possess for Persia but a secondary attraction. Self-preservation was her leading instinct; and whichever power, France or England, could offer her the best chance of protection against her gigantic adversary, Russia, must, of necessity, have had a preference in her Councils. Undoubtedly the "auri sacra fames" was the prevailing vice of Futteh Ali Shah's character, and he had been taught, moreover, to make the jealousy of the European powers subservient to the gratification of his avarice; but what to him was "all the wealth of Ind," if at the same time a Russian army occupied his capital? As the overtures made by Persia to Napoleon were mainly owing to the unwillingness or inability of the Governor-General of India to adopt any measures for placing a check upon Russian aggression, so did Gardanne maintain his ground against English gold by persuading the Shah, that in French mediation lay his only safeguard against absorption by his northern neighbour.

The more extended also the view that may be taken of the Persian question, the less favourable will be the light in which General Malcolm's proceedings must appear. If it be admitted (and there can be few dissentients, we think, at the present day) that a tripartite alliance between Russia, France, and Persia, for purposes hostile to British India, was beyond, and that the march of a Russo-French army to the Indus, in defiance of Persia, or without her assistance, was barely within the range of possibility, the alarm excited by Gardanne's establishment at Teheran must appear quite extravagant. To an ordinary observer it would seem that if the French had really strengthened Persia against further encroachment on the part of Russia, either by treaty, or by placing her in an improved state of military defence, they would have rendered us a service of far more real consequence to our Indian Empire than any dangers arising from their own hostility or intrigues : while, if they failed in that object, which had alone given, and could alone give them, consideration at the Court of the Shah, they were powerless to injure us. But if the rejection by Persia of the British alliance is thus shown under the circumstances to have been not only natural but necessary, and if the consequences of that rejection are also shown to have been altogether misunderstood, what are we to say to General Malcolm's proposed remedy of invasion? It is affirmed, we know, of

"A spaniel, a wife, and a walnut tree,
The more you beat them, the better they be:"

but really we never remember (except perhaps at Navarino) to have heard the proverb applied to international friendships. To have expected to regain the lost affections of the Shah by force of arms seems to have been very like fatuity. To have actually carried that design into execution would have been of positive injury to our ulterior interests. If, indeed, General Malcolm had landed a British force on the shores of the Gulf, and had succeeded, by a diversion in the south of Persia, in driving the French from Teheran, he would have aggravated, instead of alleviating, the only real danger that threatened us. That danger was, as it ever had been, and ever will be, the gradual extension of the Russian power and the Russian territory, and it would have been augmented precisely in the same proportion as Persia was weakened or divided.

The proverbial "Ikbal," however, of the Honorable Company at this time stood us in good stead. Sir Harford Jones, who had been impatiently watching the progress of General Malcolm's negociations, no sooner learnt their unfortunate and even dangerous issue, than he stepped forward with too much perhaps of ostentation, but with undeniable boldness and address, "to throw the Ægis of the British Crown over the imperilled destinies of India." Without entering on the vexed question, whether the affairs of Persia came properly and naturally under the political jurisdiction of Great Britain or of India, we may observe that, as Sir Harford had been placed by the letter of his commission in subordination to the Governor-General of India, and as all arrangements to which he might pledge the Government that he immediately represented must have depended for their execution on the same authority, it evidently required strong and exceptional circumstances to justify his pursuing in any degree an independent course of action. His proceedings, however, were not merely independent,—they were in direct antagonism to the declared policy of his predecessor, which had already received Lord Minto's approval; and it may be suspected therefore that success, even in the general object of his mission, would not have carried him scathless through his perilous adventure, had not the situation appeared to those who were ultimately called on to decide upon his conduct to have been otherwise desperate.

We will now give a brief sketch of his really remarkable career. Arriving at Bushire in October, 1808, he found that General Gardanne had overplayed his game, and that a "reactionary" tendency was setting in against the French. The idea therefore occurred to him to propose England, instead of France, as the power which should protect Persia against the great Northern Leviathan, and time and circumstance both favoured the substitution: for as the French, in their early efforts to undermine British influence at Teheran, had been careful to instil into the minds of the Shah's ministers that the enemy of Russia could be the only natural ally of Persia, and as by force of iteration this doctrine had now come to be received almost as a maxin of international policy; so when Sir Harford revived the argument ("fas est et ab hoste doceri") he obtained a ready—almost an anxious—hearing; and when he further urged its practical application, he had the satisfaction of finding that not only did the precept recoil upon the French, but that the recoil was doubled in effect by experience having proved in the interim the folly of trusting to the feeble powers of mediation and good offices in dealing with such an enemy as the inexorable Czar. So effective indeed was the "coup," that little more remained for diplomatic handling, and that little was accomplished by the Envoy's personal friendship with the Persian ministers, and by the "prestige" which he enjoyed as the direct representative of the British King. He advanced in a sort of ovation to the capital, General Gardanne retiring on his approach, and Monsieur Jouannin, the Secretary, who still clung with a leech-like tenacity to the court, being fairly eclipsed by the rising luminary. A "pourparler" then ensued, not less remarkable for its brevity than for the importance of the matters discussed; and in March, 1809, was concluded the Preliminary Treaty, which, in spite of much Procrustean manipulation sustained during an interval of forty years, continues in force to the present day as the basis of our Persian alliance.

With the tone and spirit of this treaty little fault has been ever found, but its particular engagements, distasteful in many quarters at the time of their conclusion, have provoked criticism ever since. Approbation could never have been withheld when the temperate language of a treaty, which secured the full advantages at which it aimed without a single offensive, or even invidious, allusion to a foreign power, was compared either with those requisitions of 1801, that we have already blazoned in their true Chinese colours, or with certain subsequent stipulations of Mr. Elphinstone's at Cabul, still more preposterous inasmuch as they were founded on a preamble absolutely fictitious;*

* In the 3rd article of Sir H. Jones's treaty, it was expressly provided that "from the date of the preliminary articles (March 12th, 1809) every treaty or agreement which the King of Persia might have made with any one of the powers of Europe became null and void, and that he would not permit any European force whatever to pass through Persia either towards India, or towards the ports of that country."

—Yet three months subsequently (June 17th, 1809) Mr. Elphinstone assumed that "the French and Persians have entered into a confederacy against the state of Cabul," and then went on to engage, that "if the French and Persians, in pursuance of their confederation, should advance towards the King of Cabul's country in a hostile manner," such and such measures should have effect.

but in spite of the contrast thus presented—in spite of the testimony afforded by it to the favourable character of Sir Harford Jones's general diplomacy—when the expulsion of the French from Persia has come to be weighed against the heavy liability of a permanent subsidy, and the inconvenience of being committed indefinitely to a state of quasi-hostility with Russia, a question has arisen whether the Brtish Envoy did not over-estimate the value of the Shah's alliance,—whether in fact he did not make us "pay too dear for our whistle."

Having already recorded our opinions on the real nature and tendency of the French connexion with Persia, we may leave our sentiments to be inferred on the particular question of the penalty thus gratuitously incurred for its disruption; but it is important to observe that a verdict, however unfavourable on the score of expediency, does not by any means reflect on Sir H. Jones's individual judgment or discretion. That Gardanne should be expelled from Persia was a settled thing beforehand, and the agents employed in the transaction had merely therefore to decide whether the end in view was to be attained by force of arms or by persuasion. If by persuasion, it was indispensable to find some means of supporting Persia against Russia; and really under the circumstances we doubt whether any could have been devised less onerous to England, or more likely, on a "primâ facie" view of the case, to advantage the Shah, and to contribute to our own strength, than those which imposed upon the Indian Government the obligation of furnishing a subsidy, with arms, ammunition, officers, and artificers, to be employed against the common enemy. The best reply indeed to the charges which have been brought against Sir Harford Jones—that "he ignominiously purchased the protection of Persia for England;" that, "he saddled the Indian Government with a useless and extravagant debt," &c.,—* is

---

* See Taylor's "History of British India," p. 227. Sir Harford Jones has been mercilessly treated by the majority of writers upon Indian History. A certain doctrine, which he had not only the merit to discover, but the boldness to avow, and the sense to act upon—namely, that the Governor-General was incompetent to conduct political relations on a footing of equality at the court of an independent monarch already closely cou-

to be found in the fact that Lord Minto, who regarded his personal proceedings as actually mutinous, who by anticipation repudiated his possible negociations with the Shah, disavowed his diplomatic character, and ordered him summarily to leave the country, who went the length even of dishonouring the bills drawn by him on the public service—still did not hesitate, when furnished with a draft of the treaty, and while yet in ignorance of the feelings of the Home authorities, to accept all the pecuniary and military engagements which had been contracted in the name of His Britannic Majesty, with the sole proviso that their execution should be entrusted to an officer honoured with His Lordship's confidence, and prepared to uphold the dignity of the Indian Government.

It is needless to pursue this subject further. Sir Harford's importance on the page of Persian political history expires with his treaty. His singular personal fate,—the condemned and persecuted of Calcutta, the approved and honoured of Windsor—may be of interest to our Indian annals, in exemplifying one of the anomalies which impede the working of our Empire in the East; but it is otherwise devoid of consequence. Let it suffice that the preliminary treaty was conveyed to England by the author of "Haji Baba," accompanied by the Persian Ambassador, broadly drawn, we can hardly say caricatured, in that inimitable story; that it was duly ratified and exchanged, and that it came into operation with all convenient dispatch. We must pass over with equal rapidity General Malcolm's resumption of his functions in 1810; for however rich in scientific results may have been the labours of the General and his suite,* and however willingly we may concede

nected with the two chief powers of continental Europe—appeared so monstrous and unintelligible to Indian officials, that unworthy motives were sought for to account for its proposition. Personal vanity and private pique were currently imputed to Sir Harford at the time (we believe unjustly) as having mainly influenced his conduct, and Lord Minto penned some of his most elaborate despatches to prove the injury and inconvenience which would accrue to the national interests from conniving at a crime of *lèse-majesté* against the Governors of India. We could have afforded to laugh at His Lordship's sensibility, had it not cost us, in General Malcolm's supplementary mission, a useless outlay of between fifteen and twenty lakhs of rupees.

* It must be remembered that to

to such results a value superior to the most brilliant diplomatic services, we are fain to confess that, as far as regards the question of our political relations with Persia, we have failed to discover a single vestige of effect, proceeding from so expensive and well-appointed a Mission. A limited supply of military stores, in fulfilment of Sir Harford Jones's promise, and the transfer of a few officers who accompanied the Escort, to the service of the Heir Apparent, then sedulously occupied with the formation of a regular army, give a certain " éclat " to the General's visit, and furnished a not ungraceful epilogue to- the previous drama ; but we cannot persuade ourselves to believe that Lord Minto's object in sending the Mission to Persia was in any way realized. This object, which was nothing less than "to restore and secure the injured credit and insulted dignity of the Indian Government,"* (or, in other words, to teach the Shah that, in all matters which regarded the Persian connexion, the Governor-General was the equal of the King of England) we consider to have been neither practicable nor desirable. We believe, indeed, that if the Shah had been really mystified by General Malcolm's pretensions, and if he had been thus again led to confound vice-regal and imperial responsibility, a confusion which involved a positive error in political ethics, and which was constantly liable to bring on embarrassments of the gravest character, would have required, sooner or later, to have been set right by an explanation still more disparaging to the Indian Government. Fortunately the unambiguous language and the consistent measures adopted by His Majesty's Ministers left no room for misapprehension. While General Malcolm's mission was ignored, or at best regarded as a mere

this Mission we are indebted for Pottinger's "Travels in Beluchistan;" for the journals of Grant and Christie; for Macdonald Kinnier's "Geographical Memoirs ; " for the "Sketches of Persia ; " and for Sir John Malcolm's elaborate History,— a series of works, which not only filled up an important blank in our knowledge of the East, but which materially helped to fix the literary character of the Indian services.

* This is quoted from Lord Minto's despatch to General Malcolm of October 26th, 1809—a despatch of which the strong expressions and uncompromising tone could hardly have been exceeded by Lord Ellenborough in the plenitude of his independence. Sir Harford Jones's appointment from the Crown is termed nothing less than "a solecism in the system of diplomatic delegation."

complimentary pageant, Sir Harford Jones, after the ratification of his Treaty, was confirmed in the post of Resident Minister at Teheran; and on his voluntary retirement in 1811, an officer of even higher rank—of the highest rank in fact in the diplomatic service—was a second time accredited from the Court of Saint James's to watch over our interests in Persia.*

5. At this point of our narrative it is important that we should understand what those interests really were, and how we were disposed to view them. Hitherto we have seen our Persian relations based on two principal objects, the establishment of a counterpoise to the power of the Afghans, and the neutralization of French ambition, both the one and the other of these objects referring immediately to the defence of India. The Russian element has hardly entered into the question. Although in fact it was known that, as early as 1791, the invasion of India by a Russian army marching from Orenburg upon Bokhara and Cabul had been planned by Mons. de St. Genie, and had actually occupied the attention of Catherine;—although the Government were acquainted with various memoirs (among which may be noticed those of Mons. Brutet and Mons. Pavillon, French emigrants of Petersburg and Moscow, and especially a really clever "brochure," drawn up by Le Marquis Beaupoil St. Aulaire, Private Secretary to the Hospodar Ispilanthi,) which had been addressed to Alexander about the period of the peace of Tilsit, and which foreshadowed much of that policy that has since been practically carried out in Central Asia, no one seems, up to the period of Sir Harford Jones's treaty, to have had any clear conception of danger from the vicinage of Russia, or

---

* The opening chapters of Kaye's "Afghan War," published in 1851, contained a masterly review of this portion of our early Indian history, the subject being treated in far greater detail, and with more extensive means of reference than in our own rapid sketch. The conclusions arrived at are, however, very similar, except that Kaye takes perhaps a more favourable view of Malcolm's career in Persia. There can be no doubt indeed but that he made a great impression on the country, which is not yet effaced, and predisposed the Persians in favour of a British alliance. —1873.

any strong desire to keep her at a distance. We had looked on the war in Georgia as a mere local derangement; and the question of supporting Persia in that war had been debated and recommended on the exclusive ground of the superior influence we should thereby secure ourselves at the Court of the Shah. There was a disposition at the outset to estimate Sir Harford Jones's engagements by the same limited standard of value, rather than in reference to their possible efficacy in resisting Russian encroachment. It was not indeed until our officers at the head of the Persian battalions were actually brought into contact with Russian commanders in the field, that we began to notice the formidable power that was growing up in our neighbourhood, and to speculate on its further development. A cursory survey then exhibited to us upon one side the appearance of immense military strength, the lusty energy of awakened civilization, and a certain consistency of movement, which seemed to point to geographical extension as a necessary law of existence. On the other we beheld, or we thought that we beheld, a nation in the last stage of decrepitude, subject to convulsive throes which gave for the moment an unnatural vigour, but bereft of moral confidence, and verging on that state which precedes dissolution. That Russia had been formerly desirous of obtaining a position in Central Asia, which would have brought her into inconvenient proximity with India, was attested by her expedition against Khiva in 1717; by her occupation of Ghilan in 1724, and again in 1796; and by her attempted settlement at Asterabad in 1781. That she was still bent on the same object—substituting, however, for isolated conquest the surer process of gradual territorial absorption—was inferred from the pertinacity with which she had now for twelve years prosecuted a war with Persia, that could not by possibility secure for her any immediate advantage at all commensurate with its expense. Such being her power, and such being her purpose, it was judged that unless we interposed to check her progress, many years could not elapse before, in the natural course of events, Russian troops would garrison cities in Khorassan, within 700 or 800 miles of the Indus; and this prospect, once opened to our view, was sufficient to arrest and fix our attention. The probable consequences of such a dislocation of the map of Asia were differently contemplated by men of different temperaments. Visions of invasion floated before the eyes of the excitable; while practical statesmen were content to weigh the amount of disturbing influence which the neighbourhood of a new mass might be expected to exercise on the still oscillating bodies of the Indian system. This problem was undoubtedly a difficult one to solve, for it depended altogether upon unknown quantities; but it nevertheless furnished the data upon which the expediency was admitted, and the amount was calculated, of the subsidy to be supplied to the Shah. The integrity of Persia was declared to be worth just so much to us as it would cost to counteract the disturbing influence of Russia, if impinging on our frontier; and from ten to fifteen lakhs of Rupees of annual outlay being considered a moderate estimate for the expenses which a mere state of preparation would entail on us, it was determined to apply something like that amount to the formation and support of a Persian army. It must be seen, however, that in thus reducing to a tangible form the value of our interests in Persia, and in proceeding to realize that value, there was a begging of the question upon two points. We jumped, in the first instance, to a conclusion of the imminency of a Russian occupation of Persia, and we arbitrarily assumed in the second that certain means would produce certain ends; that is, that the integrity of the country might be preserved through the instrumentality of a native army. It is now tolerably certain that we were wrong both in the one assumption and in the other. It can be proved, we think, that whatever benefit Persia may have derived, as far as regards the centralization of the power of her monarch, from the introduction into her armies of European discipline, she has been, as a substantive power, progressively weakened by the change, and rendered less capable of sustaining a pressure from without; and it follows therefore that if she had been in danger of absorption by Russia under the old system, she must long ere this have ceased to exist under the new.

It would detain us too long to explain in detail the seeming paradox of discipline engendering weakness. If it be remembered, however, that when the system is affected with chronic paralysis, the attempt is vain to restore any particular member to a healthy action, it will be understood that to a nation devoid of organization in every other department of Government, a regular army was impossible. It thus happened that, notwithstanding the admirable material for soldiery which were offered by the hardy peasantry of Azerbijan and the still hardier mountaineers of Kermanshah—notwithstanding the aptitude of the officers to receive instruction—notwithstanding that a due portion of physical courage appertained generally to the men—the disciplined forces of Persia, considered as an army, and for the purpose of national defence, were from the epoch of their first creation contemptible. Beyond drill and exercise, they never had anything in common with the regular armies of Europe and India. System was entirely wanted, whether in regard to pay, clothing, food, carriage, equipage, commissariat, promotion, or command; and under a lath-and plaster Government like that of Persia, such must have been inevitably the case. At the same time, however, a false confidence arose of a most exaggerated and dangerous character; the resources of the country were lavished on the army to an extent which grievously impoverished it at the time, and which has brought about at the present day a state of affairs that, in any other quarter of the world, would be termed a national bankruptcy; above all, the tribes,—the chivalry of the Empire, the forces with which Nadir over-ran the East from Bagdad to Delhi, and which, ever yielding but ever present, surrounded, under Aga Mahommed Khan, the Russian armies with a desert —were destroyed. Truly then may it be said that in presenting Persia with the boon of a so-called regular army, in order to reclaim her from her unlawful loves with France, we clothed her in the robe of Nessus.

Although it is thus certain that Persia was not saved from the grasp of Russia by any additional strength that we imparted to her, and that in supplying her, accordingly, with a subsidy, our treasures were unprofitably wasted, it is not to be supposed that we were under a delusion, either in judging of her feebleness as a nation, or in assuming an aggressive tendency as an inherent element in her antagonist's policy. Our error lay in giving an undue extension to the operation of that tendency—in over-estimating, in fact, the offensive power of Russia. We were wrong in including the East and West in the same category; in believing that Persia might be annexed with the same facility as Courland and Finland—that she could be suddenly dismembered and occupied like Poland, or cajoled out of her independence like the Crimea—that she might be over-run like Bessarabia, or even subdued like Georgia.

At that time, it is true, the opportunity had not occurred for verifying to its full extent a certain remarkable analogy between the natural and moral laws of the Russian Empire— an analogy which has been casually touched upon in the saying that "her slope is to the East," but which will admit of still happier and more forcible illustration: for it may be added with equal truth that, as her rivers—torrents at the fountain-head—slacken in their onward course, until at length they roll lazily through endless steppes, and stagnate in the Caspian marshes, so do her means and forces, although tending naturally to the East, become attenuated at the extremities of the Empire till their effects are barely sensible.

We had not then seen the striking spectacle of a few isolated mountain bands—powerful because remote—setting for a long series of years her battalions at defiance, nor had we beheld an army of veteran soldiers, like that conducted by Petrowski against Khiva in 1840, annihilated by the mere passive resistance of a distant enemy; but still from the slow progress and inadequate results of the Persian war—the conquests of Russia upon this side the Caucasus in 1813, after twelve years of uninterrupted hostility, being actually of less extent than those achieved by Zuboff in the brief but brilliant campaign of 1796 —we might have fairly suspected either her earnestness, or her ability. To have anticipated, at any rate, for Persia the catastrophe of a sudden extinction, was to violate all probability. To have supposed her even in such danger as to justify any considerable outlay in her defence was to show that we followed the impulse of our fears, rather than the limited,

CH. I.] OUR POLITICAL RELATIONS WITH PERSIA. 33

though perhaps sufficient, lights of our experience. We now resume the thread of our narrative.

6. Sir Gore Ouseley, who reached Teheran as Ambassador Extraordinary from the King of England in the summer of 1811, found Persia still engaged in hostilities with Russia. The officers supplied from India—Christie, Lindsay, and their gallant comrades—had already, under great disadvantages, formed the nucleus of a regular army, which on more than one occasion had beaten the Russians in action: but these successes were transient and illusory. The Persians owed more to the lukewarmness—if not the misconduct—of their enemies, than to their own prowess. In 1812 the reconciliation of England and Russia, which followed on Napoleon's rupture with the Czar, necessitated the withdrawal of the British officers from the battlefield, and the inferiority of the Persian troops became at once apparent. It was evident, that to give the experiment of discipline a fair chance of success, a respite from war was indispensable; and as Russia had occasion for her full resources and undivided attention to shake off the gigantic foe with whom she was now grappling in the death-struggle, the good offices of England, which had been promised to Persia in the preliminary treaty, in the event of our making peace with her antagonist, were accordingly exerted with such effect, that in October, 1813, the treaty of Gulistan was at length signed between the belligerents. This treaty was no doubt sufficiently humiliating to Persia. All the acquisitions of Russia, south of the Caucasus, were confirmed to her. It was further provided, in the same jealous spirit which dictated the secret article of the treaty of Unkiar Skelessi regarding the closing of the Dardanelles against nations at war with Russia —and perhaps also with a view of especially alarming England (for really, as far as Persia was concerned, a power whose maritime inaptitude was proverbial, the condition was not merely superfluous, but absurd)—that "no ships of war, except Russian, should be allowed on the Caspian Sea."* A want of

* A similar condition of exclusion from the Black Sea was imposed, it may be remembered, upon Russia by the allies after the taking of Sebastopol, and was subsequently repudiated by her as an infringement of

D

preciseness also, either culpable or wilful, in the demarcation of the frontier at a most important point, left Russia at liberty, whenever it might suit her convenience, to force on a renewal of hostilities by occupying the disputed territory. We believe, indeed, that the peace of 1813 was regarded neither by the one party nor the other in any other light than as an armistice. Russia had no idea of accepting permanently any frontier short of the Aras (Araxes); but she was unable at the moment to push her conquests. Persia was equally insincere in affecting to have abandoned Karabagh; but she required an interval of repose to recruit her energies, and above all to improve her discipline, and gain some knowledge of European tactics.

Simultaneously with the convention of Gulistan, or immediately following it, Sir Gore Ouseley concluded with Persia, on the basis of Sir Harford Jones's preliminary arrangements, the definitive treaty which he had been especially appointed to negociate; and shortly afterwards he returned with it to England, leaving his secretary, Mr. Morier, in charge of the Mission. This treaty, however, was not accepted in its original form. The British Ministry, with the honest and honourable intention of doing the very best for Persia of which her situation would admit, resolved on more liberal terms of subsidy than those which the Shah's Government had already thankfully accepted; and accordingly, a special Commissioner, Mr. Henry Ellis, was sent out in 1814 to modify Sir Gore Ouseley's stipulations.

7. It is unnecessary that we should examine in detail, and throughout its eleven articles, the treaty of Teheran, which was concluded by Messrs. Morier and Ellis, November 25th, 1814. A brief notice of its more prominent features will suffice for our purpose, and is all, moreover, of which our space admits. In many points of view it was undoubtedly faulty. To have supposed that Persia could interfere to prevent, or even to check, the movements of a Russian army marching upon India by the route of Khiva, or Bokhara, or Kokan; and to have

the law of nations, a precedent being thus afforded of which Persia may avail herself if the "whirligig of time" should ever place her in a position to assert her rights.—1873.

Сн. I.] OUR POLITICAL RELATIONS WITH PERSIA. 35

provided accordingly, betrayed an inexcusable ignorance of political geography.* There was an equal impropriety in engaging that "the limits of the two states of Russia and Persia should be determined according to the admission of Great Britain, Persia, and Russia;" for, if considerations of the public weal, patent and emergent, be alone held to justify under any circumstances the intrusion of mediatory offices, and if an engagement to proffer such offices be thus rarely inserted in treaties between States,—to pledge a third party to accept of them does seem the very acme of diplomatic hardihood. We will say nothing, for the moment, of the subsidy itself; but the 7th article, which-stipulated for the payment of the money in as early instalments as might be convenient, *"since it was the custom in Persia to pay the troops six months in advance,"* might really be very well taken for a burlesque. The obligation, again, which we contracted in the 9th article, to abstain from interference in the event of a possible contest between the Persians and Afghans, is hardly intelligible. Such a proposal could not have proceeded from Great Britain; and, if proceeding from Persia, it indicated that desire of territorial extension which was more fully developed in the sequel, and which, when developed, compelled us upon general grounds to repudiate the treaty altogether.† Lastly, the extradition of refugees, which we also blindly conceded, was a most humiliating (and under the circumstances a most gratuitous) engagement;—an engagement, indeed, so repugnant to Eastern ideas of honour and hospitality, that, although the occasion has frequently arisen for bringing it into operation, we believe that means have been

---

* As the first article provides that Persia shall not allow any European army to proceed towards India, but shall induce the rulers of Kharism (Khiva), Tataristan (Kashgar), Bokhara, and Samarcand to offer all the opposition in their power, a curious complication might have arisen in reference to the recent Russian conquests, if, as has been sometimes supposed, the unrepealed articles of the Treaty of 1814 had been still in force. But it is the fact that the Morier and Ellis Treaty expired "in toto" with our declaration of war against Persia in 1856, though no specific declaration to that effect was entered in the Treaty made at Paris in 1857 on the termination of hostilities.—1873.

† See Lord Palmerston's despatch to Mr. McNeill, dated July 27th, 1838, Correspondence relating to the affairs of Persia and Affghanistan, p. 89.

D 2

sought and found in every instance, if not for rejecting the terms entered in the bond, at any rate for modifying their rigour, and thus saving our credit on one side to expose it on another.

The essential points of the treaty in regard to Persia were the augmentation of the amount of the subsidy, and the definition of the conditions under which the liability of its payment was imposed on us. The annual amount was raised from 160,000 to 200,000 Tomans (or from about 12 to 15 lakhs of Rupees); and, in explanation of that article of the preliminary treaty, which merely declared Persia to be entitled to our assistance in the event of any European forces invading the territories of His Majesty the Shah, our exemption from the pecuniary liability was specifically limited to the possible case " of the war with such European nation being produced by an aggression on the part of Persia."

Undoubtedly, however, the most important feature of the treaty in question was the principle which it involved, that Great Britain had a right to consider any spontaneous act of Russian aggression upon Persia as a demonstration against India. That we should really have propounded so important, and at the same time so questionable, a doctrine may well excite surprise; yet the 6th article will admit, we think, of no other construction; for by that article it was provided, that although Great Britain might be at peace with Russia, if Persia were attacked by the latter power, and if our good offices failed in bringing about an arrangement of differences, then we would continue to pay the subsidy to support the army of the Shah, or, if it were preferred, we would send a force from India to assist in repelling the enemy,—neither the one nor the other of these engagements being compatible with the duties of a neutral State, nor indeed admitting of justification, according to the Law of Nations, on any other grounds than those of *self-defence*, which grounds of course must have pre-supposed the fact of an attack on Persia being an indirect attack upon India. We were in fact by the 6th article of the treaty pledged to a possible war with Russia in defence of Persia, and, what is of more consequence, the pledge remains registered against us to the present day: for when we compounded in 1828 for the expunging of certain articles from the treaty of Teheran, by some inexplicable oversight the 6th article was not included in the obnoxious category; and it still therefore must be considered in force, as far as regards the principle involved in it, and as far as its integrity may be unaffected by our release from the other engagements.*

For a considerable period, subsequent to the treaty of Teheran, our relations with Persia underwent no material change. We were pursuing two objects: one was the improvement of the military resources of the country, to which end we supplied arms, founded a laboratory and arsenal, and furnished officers for the drill and discipline of the army; the other was the creation and retention of such a commanding influence at Court, as should not only guarantee us against the possible intrigues or enmity of a foreign power, but should enable us in some degree to sway the councils of the State. In the former path, our success was hardly equal to our hopes, or even to our expectations. Our officers, it is true, displayed a most creditable zeal, and no little address in contending with the difficulties of their position: and, moreover, the Prince Royal, under whose immediate orders they were acting, seconded their efforts,—not exactly with the same ardour which had inspired him, so long as a regular army added to its substantial advantages the irresistible charm of novelty, but still with sufficient steadiness to have ensured the fashioning, according to the end in view, of any less intractable materials: yet it cannot be denied, that when Persia again came into collision with Russia in 1826, her means and power as a military nation were positively inferior to those which she possessed at the close of her former struggle. During this long interval of thirteen years, she was continually losing ground in that quarter where her real strength lay, while she advanced in a direction where progress was exhaustive, as well as useless. If, however, in the words of Persia's most impartial historian, "the attempt

* It must be remembered that this was written in 1848. The Persian war of 1856, and the Treaty of Paris to which it led in 1857, cancelled all previous arrangements.—1873.

to introduce an effective discipline, and to organize a regular force on European principles was a signal failure;"* and if, in one branch of our policy, we were thus doomed to chew the cud of disappointment, in our other object at any rate we were more than successful. Nothing could have been more satisfactory or more honourable to the parties concerned, than the conduct at this period of our relations with the Court of Teheran.† Still more commendable also was the character of those general measures by which we conquered prejudice, disarmed jealousy, and finally gained a complete ascendency in the public estimation of the nation. To the care, indeed, with which, after the retirement of Mr. Morier, Sir Henry Willock, ably assisted by Sir J. McNeill, then a young officer on the Bombay Medical Establishment, conciliated popular opinion, rather than to the wayward prodigality of Malcolm, or the lawyer-like dexterity of Jones, must be attributed the impressions, which, surviving all party questions—surviving even the shock of wounded pride —enable an Englishman at the present day in any part of Persia, not merely to enjoy personal safety, but to command esteem and respect.

8. We shall not follow in any detail the relations of Russia with Persia during the interval in question. The bearing of the former power throughout was irritating and contemptuous. Unwilling, or unable, to appear as a competitor against England for the favours of the Shah, she rather sought to oppose our influence by acting on the fears of Persia—by exhibiting in fact that disregard for rights and courtesies which could be only supposed to arise from a consciousness of complete superiority. The retention of Talish, the profound indifference with which she received the repeated invitations of

* "Fraser's Persia," p. 301.

† We have not forgotten that a personal misunderstanding between Sir H. Willock and the Shah led to the temporary withdrawal of our Mission from the Court; but the occasion of the rupture was so entirely accidental, and the effects of it were so transient, that it cannot be considered to affect the general character of our relations during the period in question. When our truant Minister, indeed, reported himself at the Foreign Office, Canning is said to have observed "Henry Willock? I know a man of that name at Teheran, but certainly not in London," a remark which sufficiently expressed his opinion of the quarrel, and censured the undue importance that had been attached to it.

Persia to treat for the adjustment of a disputed frontier, and finally the violent occupation of Gokchah, must be imputed as much to a desire to prevent Persia from deriving strength, or even confidence, from British support, as to any real thirst of conquest, or any wish to precipitate hostilities. Russia had doubtless always looked to the absorption of the Persian territory, north of the Arras, as essential to the geographical boundaries of her Empire; and such an absorption could hardly be effected without engaging in a war: yet war was not her principal object. That object was the general depression of Persia, the riveting of chains around her which should annihilate her powers of self-action: and it was valued perhaps less for its immediate results—less even as a movement in advance towards the final act of appropriation—than as a means of exciting the alarm of England, and thus creating a moral leverage against us in Europe. We have not dwelt hitherto upon this occult element of the Russian policy; partly, from a disinclination to ascribe too much astuteness to any plan of attack; partly, from the difficulty of tracing such a plan, where the batteries are masked, the approaches are tortuous, and the sap often shifts its course according to the nature of the ground. During the mission of Prince Menzikoff however to Teheran, in 1826, there was an overt attempt upon his part to commence that system of demonstration which has since so much embarrassed us; and we shall be justified therefore throughout the sequel of our sketch in assuming the probability of there being always two distinct principles of action in the proceedings of Russia against Persia,—the one, real, immediate, and acquisitive; the other, remote, artificial, and working merely by intimidation. If indeed there were any object in the mission in question, it was to give a different direction to the outpourings of the national mind, then in a high state of fermentation; to change the theatre of contemplated war from the North-West to the East: to bring about, through military complications in Khorassan, a state of local politics which should entirely alter the relative positions of Great Britain, Persia, and Russia, and which, whatever might be the result, would advance the interests of the latter power. The project failed for the moment, owing to the sagacity of Futteh Ali Shah, who saw through so transparent a device;* but it has never been forgotten. On several later occasions indeed it has been brought prominently forward, and at the present moment perhaps it as fully occupies the attention of Russia as any direct scheme of territorial aggrandizement.

In glancing at the war, which broke out even before Menzikoff had quitted Persia, and which raged until the spring of 1828, it will be well to consider those points in it only which immediately affected us. To ascribe this war, seriously and in good faith, to the occupation of Gokchah, or to any isolated accident whatever, is to ignore altogether the relative position of the belligerent powers. In real truth it was the mere consummation of a long course of preparation and design. Russia, if not deliberately provoking the contest, had been at any rate for many years previously indifferent to the preservation of peace; while Persia, brooding over her former losses, and smarting under recently accumulated indignities, judged the time to be favourable for resenting them. As, however, the liability of England to assist Persia with a subsidy or an auxiliary army depended upon the first act of aggression, the question of the initiative nearly concerned us; and a discussion therefore immediately arose, as to whether the affair of Gokchah did, or did not, constitute a " casus belli." Persia maintained that she was forced into the war by an aggression on the part of Russia, and accordingly demanded the assistance to which under such circumstances she was entitled by our engagements with her; whilst we replied—with more of casuistry, certainly, than generosity—that " the occupation by Russian troops of a portion of uninhabited ground, which by right belonged to Persia, even if admitted to have been the proximate cause of hostilities, did not constitute the case of aggression contem-

* Menzikoff taunted the Shah with the power and magnificence of his brother potentate in Khorassan, Esau Khan, and observed that it might be necessary for Russia, in a few years more, to open independent relations with him. The Shah's pride was severely wounded, but he had the sense to reply, that he preferred the rivalry of Esau Khan to the enmity of England.

plated in the treaty of Teheran."* We shall not pretend to pronounce "ex cathedrâ" upon a question so very nicely balanced; but, if the case had been argued in court, and if counsel had quoted to a jury, Sir J. McNeill, as a pamphleteer, against Sir J. McNeill, as a Minister,—comparing a passage from "The progress of Russia in the East," which unequivocally stated that "the war originated in the violation of the Persian territory by the Governor-General of Georgia," † with the article of the treaty of Teheran, which provided that we should be excused from payment only "if the war might have been produced by aggression on the part of Persia,"—there can be little doubt, we think, as to how a verdict would have been given. That we did not, indeed, feel that confidence in our immunity at the time, which we have since affected, may be inferred from our anxiety to obtain a release from the subsidy engagements immediately that the war was terminated, as though we still trembled at the risk we had encountered, and indulged a covert hope that to the release once obtained might be conceded a retrospective effect. The actual bargain, however, by which the Shah was persuaded to cancel our engagements, forms, we think, the least creditable feature in the whole "tableau" of our Persian policy. It is this bargain which we have before characterized as one of extraordinary rigour, and even of questionable honesty; and to enable the reader to see if we have judged harshly, we now present him with an outline of the transaction.

9. At the close of the war, when defeat and treachery following closely one upon the other had left Persia, if not so enfeebled, at any rate so disheartened, as to be ready to accept of any terms that might be imposed on her without scrutinizing their claim to moderation, Russia demanded, amongst other conditions of peace, the payment of ten crores ‡ of Tomans (about three and a half millions sterling) as indemnification for the expenses of the campaign. Of this enormous mulct the greater portion was defrayed from the reluctant coffers of the Shah;

* Correspondence relating to the affairs of Persia and Affghanistan, p. 112.
† Page 98.
‡ The crore here mentioned is only 500,000 Tomans.

but for the remainder the Prince Royal was rendered personally responsible, and, as the province of Azerbijan had already borne the chief burthen of the struggle, it may well be understood that neither His Royal Highness's treasury, nor the resources of his government, were in a condition to meet the call. He had recourse to expedients—not of the most dignified character—to obtain even a temporary relief. At his earnest entreaty a small portion of the debt was remitted; a further portion, amounting to a crore, was suffered to lie in suspense: for another crore the rich district of Khoi was handed over to Russia in pledge; and a certain amount of ready money was provided by anticipating the revenues of the province. A considerable sum, however, was still wanting to satisfy the immediate demand, and the prince found himself accordingly compelled to accept of aid tendered by the British minister, however limited in amount, and however severe the terms upon which such aid might be afforded. We are not cognizant of the full details of the transaction which ensued;* but we believe that Sir John Macdonald in the first instance passed a bond to the Prince Royal, pledging himself to furnish a sum of 250,000 Tomans towards the liquidation of the indemnity, provided H. R. H., acting as the plenipotentiary of the Shah, would annul the subsidy engagements of the treaty of Teheran; and that subsequently, when the time for payment arrived, the Envoy declared that he had exceeded his instructions, and that he could only disburse at the moment 200,000 Tomans, in consideration of which assistance a formal act of surrender must be passed to him; but that he would obtain the remaining 50,000 Tomans in the sequel, as a gratuity to Persia from the British crown. Be this, however, as it may, the bond for 250,000 Tomans remained in the hands of the Prince Royal; the act of annulment was passed and ratified on the payment of the reduced amount of 200,000 Tomans; and, when Persia claimed the difference, she was told that "she could not

* There is a singular, and to say the least of it, a most suspicious, want of uniformity in the dating of the documents which refer to this transaction in the published "Treaties." (Indian Papers, No. 2, p. 7.) In one paper, the English date is used; in another, the Mahomedan; and the date of the third is altogether wanting.

establish a right to the greater sum, as she had subsequently agreed to accept, and acknowledged that she had accepted, the less sum as the price of the sacrifice she made."* Now, if nothing positively dishonest can be imputed to us in these proceedings, they must be admitted at any rate to involve as close a practice as was ever followed by a civilized nation. That we had at the outset improvidently contracted the subsidy engagements, and that we were at liberty to seek for a release from them at any time by a fair negociation, may very readily be conceded; but to have obtained that release under circumstances of such extraordinary difficulty for one of the contracting parties was, we submit, to redeem our original error almost at the expense of our good name. With regard to the discrepancy also between the amount tendered in Sir John Macdonald's bond and the sum actually paid, we suspect that Persia has still a valid claim against us for 50,000 Tomans.

The most important consideration however to Persia, resulting from the transaction which we have noticed, was the evidence it afforded of a complete change in our estimate of her alliance. Sir J. McNeill has significantly said, that "the alteration in the treaty was supposed to evince a desire on the part of England to disencumber herself of a falling ally."† Taken in connection indeed with the transfer from the Crown to the Indian Government of the direction of our relations at Teheran, which occurred a short time previously, no other inference could have been drawn from it. We had awoke, it seemed, to a sense of the worthlessness of Persia. Our efforts to make her strong had but contributed to her weakness. We had been building on a quicksand. The country existed only by the sufferance of her northern neighbour; and it was useless therefore to undergo further expense, or to encounter further risk, on her behalf.

But here again we erred upon the side of despondency, as much as we had been formerly too bold and sanguine. Persia

* Correspondence relating to the affairs of Persia and Affghanistan, p. 112.
† "Progress of Russia in the East," p. 135.

was never in that extreme danger of extinction—not when the Russian troops were in full march upon the capital, and when defection spread rapidly among the higher classes,—which in any way called for her abandonment, or even required an essential modification of our relations with the Shah. The prosecution of Paskevitch's march on Teheran, upon which the fate of Persia was supposed to rest, would have been a still more adventurous movement than Diebitch's advance on Adrianople : and if strategists are agreed that the latter movement was altogether false, and must have signally failed, had not Turkey succumbed under the moral pressure, much more certain must it appear—to those who know the contemptible amount of force which was employed on the occasion, and the power of resistance which is offered by the mere principle of vitality in a nation like Persia—that the Russian enterprise in Persia could have led to nothing but disaster and disgrace. We hold it, indeed, to have been morally impossible that Russia, who " during the whole course of the war with Persia had never been able to collect more than 10,000 men in one body, nor to keep together for a month more than half that number,"* should have occupied a territory which contained 10,000,000 inhabitants,† bound together by the common tie of religion, naturally warlike, and detesting the invaders : and, unless the invasion had been followed by military occupation, we conceive that there was no real danger for the country.

10. To proceed, however, with our sketch; no sooner had we abandoned the idea of raising up in Persia an efficient bulwark against Russian encroachments, and had thus limited the functions of our Envoy to observation, or at most to expressions of encouragement and sympathy, than we began to take an augmented interest in the countries intermediate between Persia and India. It cannot be said that we had been indifferent to those countries at former periods. The journeys of Stirling and Arthur Conolly had been undertaken at the instigation

---

* " Progress of Russia in the East," p. 134.
† This was the estimated amount of the population of Persia twenty years ago, but 6,000,000 is the number now more commonly, and apparently with more justice, assigned to the country.—1873.

and under the auspices of the British Mission at Teheran; and it was owing merely to the services of Mr. McNeill being indispensable to the conduct of affairs in Persia, that Sir J. Macdonald was deterred from detaching him on a Mission to the eastward, of an almost identical nature with that subsequently entrusted to Burnes. To the latter officer, however, must our Afghan policy, we think, be properly ascribed. Others recommended the cultivation of a position at Cabul and Candahar, as an equipoise to the pressure of Russia upon Persia—as a means of checking the disposition of the former power to keep up a sustained attitude of attack, while it promised to render the latter more docile to our counsel from our being in a measure independent of her friendship, as well as more confident in herself from our increased facilities of affording her support. But Burnes grappled far more boldly with the question. He would at once have left the Shah to his fate, and have transferred all our solicitude to Dost Mahomed. "Had circumstances," he wrote on returning from his memorable journey, "brought us into an alliance with Cabul instead of Persia, we might have now possessed more trusty and useful allies nearer home than we can boast of in that country; and we should never have incurred a tenth of the expenditure which has been so freely lavished in Persia."

To account for Burnes's prejudice against Persia and his predilection in favour of Cabul, it must be remembered that on his first journey he saw the two countries under very peculiar circumstances. Dost Mahomed at that time was in the plenitude of his power. Uninfected as yet by western propagandism, he was as friendly to the Indian Government as his jealousy of the Sikhs, tempered by a natural circumspection, could render him. His personal character, moreover, stood out in bright relief among the sombre masses of his countrymen. In Persia, on the other hand, the actual state of affairs was gloomy, and the prospect was still more threatening. Groaning under misgovernment, and "broken up into a loose confederation of petty principalities," the country appeared, to those who looked on centralization as the essence of power, and cared not to penetrate a nation's spirit, to be on the point of dissolution. The Court, alarmed, even more than injured, by the relaxation of interest which our altered language and stinted expenditure betrayed, was prepared to conciliate Russia at any sacrifice. The Envoy, who had succeeded Sir John Macdonald at Teheran, was personally obnoxious to the Shah, and had quarrelled with all the Ministers. The Prince Royal too, against the counsel of his father, who was perhaps the steadiest friend to England, as well as the best politician in his empire, had been at length prevailed on to send an army into Khorassan, in order to reduce the refractory local chieftains, and, when Burnes passed through the province, H. R. H. was concerting measures with a Russian agent, Baron Ache, for prosecuting hostilities beyond the frontier. Those hostilities, which it was proposed in the first instance to direct against Khiva, were suspended for the moment, owing to the interference of the only British officer in camp, Captain Shee; but as that officer, with more zeal than prudence, went so far as to pass his bond for a large sum of money in order to dissuade the Prince from the enterprise, and as such a proceeding was, of course, disavowed by the Envoy at Teheran, the circumstance indirectly tended still further to depress our influence. In the following year, 1832, the project of aggression was resumed; but the Afghans were now pointed out as more deserving of punishment than the Uzbegs; and, after some consideration, Herat was at length selected as the destined object of attack. Again, however, did our counsel interpose to prevent the intrusion of the arms of Persia into a territory almost conterminous with India; and again was the interposition successful. On this occasion, too, as Mr. McNeill was the counsellor, it may be presumed that the true aim of the Russian policy was exposed, and that we lost nothing in Abbas Mirza's estimation by warning him of the snare prepared for him.

The Khorassan campaign, of which we are now treating, was the germ from whence sprung our own Afghan war, and it merits, therefore, more than a passing notice. That Russia had instigated the original movement, that she took a marked interest in the progress of the war, that she ever pointed to ulterior conquest, were all matters of notoriety; but the objects which she had in view in thus acting were by no means so patent to observation, nor indeed have they ever perhaps been submitted to a full and fair inquiry. The question has been usually put as follows :—Did Russia propose to push forward Persia as her own pioneer towards India? Or—was the whole scheme a phantasmagoria, designed for the mere purpose of frightening us out of our propriety? Was it a scheme, in short, with no substantial base—no real and tangible outline, and of which it would have been prudent, as well as safe, to have ignored the very existence? Such have been the limits generally assigned to the inquiry: but we have already hinted, and we shall endeavour to prove in the sequel, on what we consider unexceptionable evidence, that there was always a third object, more immediate in its nature, and more certain in its effect, which entered largely into the consideration of Russia. That object was to estrange England from Persia, to create an antagonism of interests between the two countries, and thus force the weaker power into a coalition with herself, —the natural results of such a coalition being that the moral power and influence of the Russian Empire in the East would be greatly strengthened, while there would be entailed on British India either the anxiety and embarrassment of a sense of danger, or the expense of a state of preparation.

It was in the autumn of 1838 that the expedition against Herat, which the remonstrances of Mr. McNeill had caused to be suspended for a full year, was at length put in execution; and unfortunately the command of it was entrusted to the prince who, before another year had expired, was called upon to fill the throne of Persia. We say unfortunately, for to this accident may be proximately traced the events of 1838, and all the evils which followed in their train. That Abbas Mirza was actuated by feelings of hostility to England in sending an army against the capital of Western Afghanistan, no one has ever pretended to assert. That imputation has been reserved for Mahomed Shah: yet if the lust of conquest, and the natural ambition of a military chief, were sufficient to account for the designs of the Prince Royal upon Herat—irrespective of the

advice of Russia—at least the same allowance should be made
for the temptation which must have assailed a leader who,
having been worsted on the first occasion of independent command, found himself shortly afterwards enabled to employ the
resources of an empire to retrieve his failure. We have heard,
indeed, that when the death of Abbas Mirza at Meshed in the
autumn of 1833 compelled his eldest son to raise the siege of
Herat, and return into the Persian territory in order to attend
to the immediate duties of Government, he swore a solemn
oath, after the approved fashion of the knights of old, that he
would sooner or later retrace his steps to the eastward, and
wipe out his disgrace in Afghan blood; and we further know
that the design was ever uppermost in his mind from the
moment that he ascended the throne, and that, however it may
have been matured by Russian counsel, or linked with subsequent considerations of policy, the germ is thus to be sought
in a deep-seated feeling of personal revenge.

11. We now return to the general question. Russia was at
this time singularly placed. Having sown the dragon's teeth
in Khorassan, she was content to await the harvest, without
attempting to force on a crisis, or to disturb in any way the
natural course of events. England, on the other hand (or
rather British India, for the Teheran Mission still continued
under the direction of the Calcutta Council), had been partially
awakened from its lethargy by the recent occurrences in
Khorassan. If no measures of positive and complete relief
were practicable, it was judged, at any rate, that the symptoms
of danger might be alleviated, and that the day of dissolution
for Persia might be postponed. Economists, indeed, suggested
the idea that the expenditure in Persia might be legitimately
carried so far as would equal, but not exceed, the interest upon
the gross outlay which we should be obliged to incur for the
defence of India, in the event of the former country being
swallowed up by Russia; and Lord William Bentinck, although
at that period in the full career of his financial reform, was not
indisposed to undergo some sacrifice, in order to better our
position at the Court of the Shah. A large supply of arms
and accoutrements accordingly was transmitted gratuitously to

Persia in 1832–33; and in the latter year a detachment of officers and sergeants, more complete even than the party which had been furnished from India when we were striving to supplant the French, inasmuch as it provided for the requirements of every branch of the military service, was placed by the Governor-General at the disposal of the Envoy at Teheran for employment with the troops of the Shah.

A certain reaction did assuredly follow on this indication of a renewed solicitude. It was mainly owing to the exertion of British influence that Futteh Ali Shah was persuaded, in the summer of 1834, to appoint Mahomed Mirza, who had just returned from Khorassan, heir-presumptive to the Empire; and a commercial treaty, with the privilege of naming Consuls for the protection of our trade, upon which we set much store, and which we had been long vainly urging on the attention of the Court, might at this time assuredly have been carried, but for a personal misunderstanding between the British Envoy and the Ministers charged with the negociation. In the autumn, indeed, of 1834, when Futteh Ali Shah gave up the ghost at Ispahan, Khorassan had been previously cleared of troops, except in such numbers as were necessary for the internal safety of the province; our officers had been again placed in communication with, if not in command of, the regular army; and, the heir-presumptive being apparently inclined to hold to us, our general position in Persia certainly wore a more favourable aspect than at any period since the Russian war. The accession of Mahomed Shah formed a new epoch in our relations, and deserves to be attentively considered.*

* At the time of Mahomed Shah's accession in 1834, with a view to the consolidation of his power and the discouragement of all pretenders, the British and Russian Governments exchanged some very important notes, expressive of their mutual desire to respect and maintain the integrity of the Persian Empire. It might be a question, perhaps, how far these notes would be diplomatically considered to constitute a valid engagement at the present day—forty years having elapsed since they were passed, and not only a suspension of relations, but the Crimean and Persian wars, which dissolved all previous bonds, having occurred in the interim—but they are nevertheless understood to represent the existing policy of the respective parties, and have been indeed recently referred to as a quasi-guarantee of Persia's continued independence.— 1873.

E

12. Sir John McNeill, in his article in the *Quarterly Review*, has well described the evil auspices under which our intercourse with Mahomed Shah commenced. "The young Shah," he says, "had mounted the throne with the countenance of Russia and the active support of England; but although he was unable to move his army from Tabreez until he received pecuniary aid from the British Mission, and the assistance of British officers to command the troops, and to give the soldiers confidence in the promises which had been held out to them; and although it was known and admitted at the time that the success of the Shah could not have been secured, without hazarding his independence, unless by the opportune and effective assistance he received from England, it unfortunately did so happen that, when he had been firmly seated on the throne, Russian influence was found to have gained an ascendency in his counsels, which, under the circumstances, it would have appeared unreasonable, or almost absurd, to have anticipated."

The sketch, however, is in so far imperfect, that there is no attempt to explain the enigma of this sudden preponderance of Russian influence, and we venture therefore to give its solution. Supposing our views to have been restricted to the continuance of a struggle with Russia for influence at the Persian Court, it was a capital error in our policy ever to have attached ourselves to the Azerbijan party, or to have assisted Abbas Mirza's family in the question of the succession. Whilst Futteh Ali Shah lived, he would never tolerate a permanent Russian Mission at his Court. He resolutely set his face against the establishment of Consuls at the ports on the Caspian Sea, notwithstanding that the treaty of 1828 expressly conceded that point to Russia. He was, in fact, essentially anti-Russian, and, as far as his power and influence extended, he was ever ready to throw his whole weight into the scale against "his cousin, the Emperor." With Abbas Mirza, however, and his family, the case was widely different. Bred up under the shadow of the Northern Upas, they were completely subject to its influence. They had been struck by the eye of the basilisk, and could never possibly regain their confidence.

Mahomed Shah had little love for Russia; he had never forgotten the fatal field of Ganjah, where the fleetness of his groom's horse alone saved him from the grasp of the Cossacks; but he was impressed with a profound conviction of her irresistible power, and he was thus predisposed to yield to any pressure she might exert, however feeble in its nature or injurious in its tendency. The aid which England afforded in seating him on the throne, was ascribed to our fear lest he should immediately sink to the condition of a mere tributary to the Russian Empire, rather than to any rational hope of our supporting him in independence. From the very day, indeed, of Mahomed Shah's accession, all chance of our competing with Russia for influence in the Persian councils was at an end; and the more that power was thrown into the hands of the Azerbijan party, the more difficult did it become that we should ever regain our due position in the country.

Russia in the meantime was fully cognizant of the advantages of her situation. Satisfied that our efforts to consolidate the power of the young monarch must, through whatever channel they were employed, or to whatever point they were directed, terminate to her own advantage, she smiled complacently on our assistance, and was quite content to occupy for a moment, but for the last time, a secondary place in the pageant. It was not even requisite to strike upon the old chord of conquest to the Eastward. So notorious was the young Shah's passion on this subject, that the coronation anthems rang with prophetic pæans of victory over the Uzbegs and Afghans; and His Majesty's speech, delivered from the throne before the foreign Missions on the first occasion of a public *durbar*, dwelt rapturously on the same theme. The constitution of the new Ministry, which, in the place of the old native and independent aristocracy, was composed of parties immediately subject to Russian discipline, either from the accident of birth or from their previous employment and connexions, although contributing largely to our embarrassment, can hardly be cited as a separate element of trouble. This change, indeed, was a necessary consequence of the translation of the Tabriz court to Teheran, and the difficulties, therefore, that arose from it must be added to the catalogue of evils which were entailed on us by the support of the Azerbijan family, and for which we never seem to have contemplated any compensating good, beyond the establishment of a principle of hereditary succession.

Our "home" proceedings now require to be noticed. Mr. McNeill had been sent to England, in the autumn of 1834, to endeavour to arouse the ministry to a sense of the necessity of some more active interference than the mere furnishing of arms and officers from India, in order to preserve the integrity of Persia; and he was so far successful, that, on the occasion of the death of Futteh Ali Shah, the Crown resolved again to place our relations with Teheran under the immediate control of the Foreign Office, and Mr. Ellis was accordingly a second time sent out from London on an embassy of condolence and congratulation to the young monarch. Much more, however, required to be done to fulfil the expectations that had been formed. It was necessary in the first instance that the public mind should be aroused, before Government could be either disposed, or able, to undertake measures involving responsibility, or anything like extraordinary expense; and Mr. McNeill accordingly, assisted by David Urquhart, who had just returned from Turkey, and by Baillie Fraser, who had been travelling on a special mission in Persia, set to work to *write up* the Eastern question.

Press agitation had long been a familiar weapon of attack, and on domestic ground it had been often wielded with almost as much facility as effect; but it was a very different affair when the battle-field was the far East, and when to the impassiveness of languor was added the positive obstruction of ignorance. Perseverance and real talent, however, triumphed at length over all obstacles. The Monthlies poured in a close and galling fire, supported by the light artillery of leaders in the daily journals, and by charges of cavalry in the shape of pamphlets and reports. The heavy Quarterlies, too, brought up their masses to sustain the onset, and the mysterious "Portfolio," which was embodied for this particular campaign, proved in itself a very "Legion" of destructiveness. The public mind of England, that huge burly citadel of selfishness and unbelief, was fairly taken by assault; and when Mr. McNeill came out as minister to Persia in 1836, Urquhart at the same time going to Constantinople as Secretary of Embassy, and Baillie Fraser remaining as Oriental reporter in Downing Street, expectancy was culminating towards some great explosion in the East. We beg those of our readers who have been accustomed to look on the Afghan war as the accident of a moment, a sudden spasm of India in an agony of mortal fear, to attend to these premonitory symptoms, which as surely heralded the movement as the formation of "the League" preceded the repeal of the Corn Laws.

We doubt, however, if our relations with Persia had yet assumed any tangible or definite shape in the deliberations of the British ministry. Mr. McNeill at any rate, on his return to the country with further supplies of arms and further detachments of officers and sergeants, must have still looked to the old object of making use of Persia as a defence for India, and of strengthening her for our own benefit. He was prepared, probably, to advocate a very much more extended and effective system of relief than had yet been resolved on by the ministry. His pamphlet on "The Progress of Russia in the East," which was published just before his departure from England, pointed to the necessity of preserving the integrity of Persia at all risks; although how that object was to be attained —whether by negociation, or money, or military assistance, or a bold defiance of Russia—was purposely left in obscurity. But these visions must have quickly faded, after he was brought in contact with the court. The Shah, he must have seen, no longer needed, nor even wished for, the protection of Great Britain. His Majesty had found a more convenient, if not a more safe, ally in Russia,—an ally who would encourage and promote his conquests, guarantee him against intestine troubles, and shield him, if necessary, against the resentment of England. It does not appear, in the Foreign Office printed correspondence, at what time the scales first fell from our eyes, or how, when the broad truth stared us in the face, that we must henceforward encounter at the Persian Court, not the insidious attack of a power equally suspected by both parties, but the open hostility of a successful rival—we proposed to meet the difficulty. There are certain circumstances which render it probable that then, at the eleventh hour, we did imperfectly shadow forth the only line of policy which, without entailing on us an enormous expense, could have availed us to retrieve our position. The distinguished reception which had been given in England to the refugee Princes of Shiraz, and the handsome pension assigned to them, seemed to point to the eventuality of a restored dynasty under British auspices in the south of Persia. The contumelious dismissal of our civil and military officers from the Royal camp in the summer of 1836 was popularly, though, no doubt, improperly, assigned to the discovery of intrigues tending to the same end; and, as will presently be shown, Russia herself had become alarmed at this possible, and under the circumstances justifiable, resolution of our difficulties. If, however, we ever harboured the idea of extricating ourselves by the semblance, or reality, of such a scheme, the plan must have soon yielded to the more pressing necessities of the time. Witkewitch had already started for Cabul, and the Shah was preparing to besiege Herat.

It enters not into our design to impugn or contradict any part of the evidence which Sir J. McNeill has accumulated in his article in the *Quarterly Review*, tending to prove the complicity of Russia in the proceedings of Persia against Afghanistan, and to show that the ulterior object of Russia in thus acting was hostility against England. We merely reserve two points; first, that the Shah was an unconscious instrument in the hands of Russia, until our opposition to his views kindled discord between us and him; and secondly, that the full scope of the Russian policy (the channel through which the feeling of hostility against us was to work, and its advantages were to be developed) has been either misapprehended or concealed. On the first point it is perhaps unnecessary to enlarge; for, supposing that the Shah can be proved to have acted unconsciously against us, still if his proceedings were injurious, he was as amenable to our resentment as if he had been our wilful enemy. The question is only of interest in proving the complete success of Russia's machinations, which brought England almost into collision with Persia against the wishes of the one party, and without the cognizance of the other. The second point is of greater consequence; for, if the views of Russia were such as we believe them to have been, and if those views were duly communicated at the time to the British Government, it seems the less excusable that we should have taken the bait prepared for us.

We remember to have seen a paper which reached India, long before "the grand army" had crossed the Indus, and which purposed to give the confidential explanations of a high Russian functionary on the policy which his Government had pursued in the affair of Herat. We know not how the paper was obtained, but its verisimilitude guaranteed its authenticity; and, although for obvious reasons it has not been printed in any of the Afghan Blue Books, we venture, after the lapse of ten years, to quote certain parts of it from memory.

"Russia," it was stated, "has played a very successful, as well as a very safe, game in the late proceedings. When she prompted the Shah to undertake the siege of Herat, she was certain of carrying an important point, however the expedition terminated. If Herat fell, which there was every reason to expect, then Candahar and Cabul would certainly have made their submission. Russian influence would thus have been brought to the threshold of India; and England, however much she might desire peace, could not avoid being involved in a difficult and expensive war, in order to avert more serious dangers. If, on the other hand, England interfered to save Herat, she was compromised—not with the mere court of Mahomed Shah, but with Persia as a nation. Russia had contrived to bring all Persia to Herat, and to identify all Persia with the success or failure of the campaign; and she had thus gravelled the old system of partizanship, which would have linked Azerbijan with herself, and the rest of the nation with her rival."

"By interfering to save Herat, and by thus checking for the moment the advance of Russian influence towards India," it was further said, " England has made an enemy of every province whose troops were engaged in the campaign—of Khorassan, Irak, Fars, Mazanderan, and Ghilan. She is now the national enemy, the friend of the Soonees, and the foe to the Sheeah faith; and Russia will not be slow to turn this revulsion of feeling to account." We remember also its being observed that, " Russia feels no anxiety at the interference of England in Afghanistan. The reports of Witkewitch have satisfied her that, owing to the disorganized condition, the turbulent character, and the conflicting interests of the Afghan tribes, Cabul and Candahar can never form a bulwark for India. They are more likely to shatter the fabric to which they are violently attached, and cause it to crumble prematurely into ruin."

It was supposed at the time that, in thus putting the case, Russia was affecting a satisfaction which she did not feel. She had been foiled, it was thought, and it was only natural that she should seek for palliatives to cover her dishonour, and to mitigate the keenness of her sense of disappointment. That we had sustained any real injury in Persia was doubted; and the Afghan war was considered by all, except a hesitating few, to promise the most complete success. But subsequent events verified to a remarkable extent, not only the accuracy of the Russian calculations, but the sincerity with which they were declared.

Upon the actual merits of the Afghan question, we shall not venture far into the arena of discussion; although we might perhaps communicate new facts, as well as new opinions, to the public. The time has not yet come for writing a true and detailed history of the war, either in its origin, its progress, or its close; and we must confine ourselves, therefore, to generalities. The justice of the expedition seems now to be pretty generally abandoned; and the expediency of it, on which ground alone the defenders of the war are obliged to rest their case, is made to depend upon the fact of an imminent danger, threatening the security of British power in the East in 1838, which could be averted, or which at any rate seemed to be evitable, by no other means. Now we will not dispute that, if

Herat had fallen, there would have been a certain amount of positive danger to India. It may be questioned if that danger would have nearly reached the crisis which Lord Wellesley had contemplated with so much serenity in 1799 : but still, as the power of Persia at Cabul and Candahar would undoubtedly have been exerted in a direction contrary to that which our own policy unfortunately took during the subsequent occupation—as she would have brought forward the Sheeah Hazarehs, the Parseewans, and the Kizzilbash, to confirm and strengthen the Baruckzye ascendency, and would thus have escaped the troubles which arose from our pursuing the contrary course of raising into power the turbulent Dooranee aristocracy—it may not be unreasonably supposed, that she would have attained and preserved such a position in the country as would have materially increased that internal agitation of India which had been already called into existence by her mere preliminary measures of attack. To this extent there was, we believe, actual danger to the British power in the East from the aggressive policy in which Persia had allowed herself, through the personal ambition of her monarch, to be inveigled; but at the same time a much stronger exhibition, than we have ever yet seen, of the evils to be apprehended from this increased domestic agitation, would hardly persuade us that a foreign war was necessary to neutralize their effects; still less a war which violated all the acknowledged principles of military and political guidance.

An argument, however, which seems to be fatal to this defence of expediency is, that the war was *not* undertaken to avert the danger that we have spoken of. In our own opinion, the unsuccessful assault of June 23rd, 1838, settled the question of Herat. The siege, we believe, would have been raised even without a demonstration on the part of England in favour of the besieged. It actually *was* raised at any rate before the army of the Indus had begun to assemble, and the fact was communicated to the Governor-General while the troops were still encamped at Ferozpore. Lord Auckland, indeed, did not affect to base the expedition on the facts set forth in his proclamation of October 1st, or on the hostile advance of Persia towards India. He unequivocally stated, that "he would continue to prosecute with vigour the measures which had been announced, with a view to the substitution of a friendly for a hostile power in the Eastern provinces of Afghanistan, and to the establishment of a permanent barrier against schemes of aggression upon our North-West frontier;"—* objects no doubt of a certain abstract value, but hardly more urgently needed in 1838 than in 1798, or than at any intermediate period.

If the Shah raised the siege through the inadequacy of his resources to support the contest, he was a contemptible enemy. The rulers of Candahar and Cabul would scarcely again supplicate, or descend even to propitiation, when their brother chief of Herat had triumphed. Their spirit of independence, and their detestation of a foreign yoke, which had yielded for the moment to the exhibition of superior force, would have revived when the phantom had passed away, and they would have been rendered all the more intractable for the future from shame at their misplaced despondency. If, on the other hand, the siege of Herat were raised, and the designs of Persia on Afghanistan were abandoned, in consequence of our sending a detachment of 500 rank and file with two six-pounders to the island of Karrack, we had, at any rate, a gauge of the power of the nation from which we were apprehending danger. The vulnerable heel was revealed to us; and with this revelation—with the proof of our ability to control the policy of the Court of Teheran by the application of means which could at any time be furnished from the garrison of Bombay—there should have come, we think, a returning sense of confidence, a consciousness that the march of a British army to Cabul could not really be indispensable to the defence of India.

It has been further said that, independently of the advantages which the Affghan war promised to secure for us, the treaty of Lahore bound us to undertake it, and that the safety of Herat did not in any way release us from this engagement; but, in looking over the text of the treaty, we are really at a loss to understand which article can be supposed to involve

* Order by the Right Hon'ble the Governor-General of India. Nov. 8, 1838.

such an obligation. The restoration of Shah Shujah-ul-Mulk to the throne of Cabul was no doubt tacitly assumed as the object of the treaty, and the nature and extent of the assistance to be supplied by Runjeet Singh towards the accomplishment of that object were pretty accurately defined; but whatever may have been the character of the promises and encouragement held out by us to the Shah at Lahore, there was certainly not a syllable entered in the treaty which entailed upon the British Government the liability of furnishing an auxiliary army, or a contingent, or even of affording pecuniary support to the enterprise. "The friends and enemies of each of the three high powers were," it is true, declared "to be the friends and enemies of all;" but a general defensive league of this nature is never held to pledge the contracting parties to mutual support when hostilities may arise from aggressive proceedings on the part of one of them; and to render the condition, therefore, applicable to the case in point, it would be necessary to show, that Shah Shujah's invasion of Afghanistan was not an aggression, or, in other words, to resume the position which we have already stated to have been generally abandoned as desperate, and to maintain that the war was not only expedient but *just*.

So entirely insufficient, indeed, do the ostensible grounds appear, which have been assigned for the prosecution of the Afghan war, after the danger which menaced India from the Russo-Persian movements had been dissipated by the retreat of Mahomed Shah's army from Herat, that, without attaching much importance to the rabid gossiping of Mr. Masson, we still cannot help suspecting, that it was owing in a great measure to the bureaucratic machinery of the Governor-General's camp, that the troops were finally set in motion.

13. We will now consider the effect of our proceedings upon Persia. Herat owed its safety mainly to British interference; more however, we think, to the interest manifested by Mr. McNeill throughout the siege, which inspired the garrison with hope, and to the fortitude and skill of Lieut. Pottinger, which contributed essentially to the military defence of the place, than to our tardy occupation of Karrack. The Shah at

the same time naturally made the most of our demonstration, and professed to have raised the siege, "in sole consideration of the interests of his faith and country;" and the Persians generally, whose vanity as a nation is proverbial, preferred the explanation of being coerced by England to that of being defeated by the Afghans. We had, therefore, appeared in a new character; we had opposed the arms of Persia, and had even threatened her with invasion; and, if the nation had been identified with the court, or even with the army which had besieged Herat, such an attack on the national honour and interests might have been expected to go far to neutralize the effects of all our previous conciliatory policy.

That to a certain extent the Russian prediction of our being compromised with Persia was fulfilled, can hardly be denied; but it is a gross exaggeration to assert, that in general estimation we changed places with Russia, or that we ever sank nearly to her level of unpopularity. There was an element, indeed, working strongly, but silently, in our favour,—the element of nationality, or a distinction of race, of which the full value has only been recently recognized in the science of political government. In the same way that we have lately seen the Scandinavian struggling with the Teuton, the Magyar fighting to the death with the Croat, the Sclavonian rising against the German, so for the last ten years in Persia there has been an antagonism of race, which has been ever deepening in inveteracy, and which will hardly yet pass away without leading to some violent cataclysm. The Toork population, which inhabits the single province of Azerbijan, was never allowed during the reign of Futteh Ali Shah to emerge from that secondary place to which its numbers alone entitled it. Abbas Mirza's army was, it is true, composed of this material; and, in the expeditions of the Prince Royal to Yezd, Kerman, and Khorassan in 1831-33, the Toork power had thus made itself pretty extensively felt throughout the kingdom; but still all offices of trust and emolument were confided to Persians; the executive power in the provinces was wielded through local means; and a native of Azerbijan was hardly to be found in the ministry. On the accession, however, of Mahomed Shah

CH. I.]   OUR POLITICAL RELATIONS WITH PERSIA.   61

the position of the two races was reversed. The Tabriz court was transferred bodily to the capital. Toork governors were sent into all the provinces, and Toork garrisons were detached to support them. The native nobility were ground to the very dust; the native troops were disbanded, or reduced, or neglected. The municipalities were presided over by Toorks: farms, monopolies, all situations, which involved the exercise of power or afforded means for the amassing of wealth, were entrusted to natives of the same race. The consequence was that an antipathy between the Toorks and Persians, which always probably existed, but for which under the old *régime* there was little or no opportunity of display, became suddenly a leading characteristic of the nation. If, therefore, the provinces of southern and central Persia shared in the mortification which was generally felt at the failure of the Herat campaign, they were, at any rate, consoled in some measure by the reflection, that the disgrace principally fell upon their Toork oppressors. The appearance of a British force in the Persian Gulf did not, we think, excite alarm in Shiraz and Ispahan. A fear of conquest, or occupation by a foreign invader, was certainly not the predominant feeling. That feeling was the hope that, through the instrumentality of the British arms, the power of the Toorks might be humbled, and the native race might be admitted at least to an equality of rights and consideration. We have it, indeed, from the best authority, that if the British force had landed on the coast, and had proclaimed any suitable pretender to the throne —one of the old Zend dynasty for instance, supposing that an individual of that family could have been found—the tribe chiefs throughout the southern and central provinces would have risen to aid in the enterprise; their motive being, less that of attachment to the English, or predisposition in favour of the cause which the English supported, than a hatred of the ruling powers, and of the myrmidons by whom they were surrounded. It did not, however, of course, enter into the calculations of Great Britain to incur the risk of precipitating such a crisis. Our object was demonstration, not attack; and in furtherance of that object, it would have required the nicest management to conduct any military movement whatever; for too much diffidence would have hazarded the miscarriage of the enterprise, while too much confidence might have forced us on to a dismemberment of the kingdom, and have thus accelerated that collision with Russia which for thirty years we had been striving to retard.

Fortunately, although the court remained sulky and disposed to listen to any counsel which promised revenge for the affront we were conceived to have put on it, there was no occasion for our exceeding the strict limits of an attitude of observation. Ghorian, a fortress of some strength in the Herat territory, continued to be occupied by Persian troops, notwithstanding that that occupation had all along been declared by the British Government to be equivalent to a hostile demonstration against England. Reparation for the violence which had been offered to the messenger of the British mission, and which had constituted throughout the Herat controversy one of our gravest grounds of complaint, was still refused. Persia had ventured even to impede in some degree the working of our Afghan policy, by opening a friendly communication with Yar Mahomed Khan (" the arch-villain " as he is usually styled in India, but according to Sir J. McNeill " the most remarkable man of his age and country "), for the purpose of sharpening his already awakened jealousy at the magnificent and gratuitous aid which we lavished on Herat: yet, the progress of our arms beyond the Indus was so constant, and the results promised so favourably, that we could afford to disregard such indications of hostility, even had they been more malignantly shaped, and fraught with more immediate injury. Persia being, in fact, for the time innocuous, we were well enough content to await that compliance with our demands which in the natural course of events could not fail sooner or later to take place; the interruption of diplomatic intercourse and the prolonged occupation of Karrack testifying to our offended dignity, while our extreme reserve, in desisting from all intrigue, in rejecting offers of co-operation, in avoiding every measure which might complicate our position, showed that we were not inclined to push the rupture to extremities.

Russia in the meantime was not inactive. The satisfaction with which she had viewed our retirement, and had found Persia left to her exclusive embrace, soon gave way to a feeling of alarm when she learnt of the gigantic preparations which British India was making to appropriate the countries intermediate between Herat and the Indus, and when she further remarked the effervescence in the public mind, and the consequent danger to the Shah, which resulted from our isolated location in the Persian Gulf. After those famous despatches of Count Nesselrode to Pozzo di Borgo, dated respectively October 20th, 1838, and February 21st, 1839, which, however ingeniously imagined and plausibly tricked out, had for their unique objects the moderation of our Afghan scheme, and the withdrawal of our force from Karrack, and which signally failed, not only in attaining those ends, but even in making out a case that should withstand an ordinary scrutiny, Russia began to organize her plans for allaying the commotion which she had, perhaps too precipitately, called into existence, or at any rate for counteracting its effects. As she could make nothing of Persia, divided against itself, and embarked, moreover, in a cause which the Emperor had already declared to be unjustifiable, she turned her attention to Khiva; and hence arose the manifesto of December, 1839, which declared the great object of General Perowski's expedition to be "to strengthen in that part of Asia the lawful influence to which Russia has a right."

No one doubted at the time but that a force, vastly superior both in numbers and artillery to that which Lord Keane led from the Indus in triumph through the defiles of Afghanistan, would be able to cross the open plain of the Desht-i-kipchák, between the Caspian and the Aral. It was in anticipation, indeed, of General Perowski's success, and in deprecation of the advance of our own arms beyond the Hindoo Koosh, which was then in contemplation in order to dislodge Jabbar Khan and Dost Mahomed's family from Khooloom, that Baron Brunnow significantly remarked to Sir John Hobhouse—"If we go on at this rate, Sir John, the Cossack and the Sepoy will soon meet upon the banks of the Oxus,"—and that the President replied, with more spirit, perhaps, than self-conviction—" Very probably, Baron; but, however much I should regret the collision, I should have no fear of the result." Man proposes, however, while a greater than man disposes. The expedition altogether failed, partly, perhaps, from the extraordinary severity of the season, but more essentially from the fact, that Orenburg did not furnish to Russia (any more than did Tiflis in the Persian war) that strategic base for operations beyond the frontier which Ferozpore, faulty, remote, and unprovided as it was, offered to India.

Dispirited by this failure, and by the supposed complete success of our Afghan occupation (for it must be remembered that it was the fashion of the day to paint everything "couleur de rose," and that the few who ventured to tell the truth were mercilessly snubbed), and foreseeing real embarrassment to herself if we should be induced to resort to any active measures for the termination of our quarrel with the Shah, Russia now set to work to bring about that reconciliation between England and Persia which, from the first hour of the rupture, she had professed her desire to accomplish. She believed, or affected to believe, that we were aiding and abetting in certain troubles that broke out in the south of the kingdom. A revolt of the Bakhtiarees was ascribed, absurdly enough, to the presence of an English traveller, Mr. Layard, since so well known as the excavator of ancient Nineveh. The Kerman insurgents, headed by Agha Khan, it was pretended, were supplied with arms and ammunition, with money, and even with artillery, from Bombay. Baron Brunnow, indeed, pleasantly complained that, "at Calcutta they still acted as if Simonich were at Teheran, and Witkewitch at Cabul;" and he further categorically stated, that, in order to put an end to so very unsatisfactory a condition of affairs, the Emperor had called upon the Shah to comply with all the requisitions of England. If the same language had been used by the Russian representative at Teheran in 1838, which was addressed to the Shah in 1840, the British Mission would never have retired from the country. Persia, of course, as soon as she found that all European support was denied to her, Russia seconding the cause of England, and France (which had also in the interim sent a complimentary mission to Teheran) declining to interfere in the controversy, had no alternative but submission. Ghorian was evacuated, yet the party for whose immediate benefit this difficult point was at length carried, had a very short time previously confirmed his claim on our consideration by turning Major Todd out of Herat! Reparation was given for the arrest and ill-treatment of the mission courier. A commercial treaty was guaranteed to us. Sir John McNeill returned once again to Teheran; and the British troops were removed from Karrack.

14. This settlement was opportune. If it had been delayed six months longer, Russia would hardly have proffered the same earnest mediation; nor would the Shah's obstinacy have been so easily overcome. If we had still been in a state of quasi-hostility with Persia at the close of 1841, it would have required something more than a mere moral pressure to right ourselves at Teheran. Even with six months of preparation, Sir J. McNeill must have found it a difficult business to meet the first burst of the Cabul disaster; and the more so as the Persians, with the usual proneness of Orientals to personify all measures of policy, insisted on fixing upon our minister the individual responsibility of their failure at Herat, and he had thus to encounter the irritation and ill-will of almost all classes with whom he was brought in contact at the court. That under such circumstances,—at a season when our Indian Empire had sustained a blow which, in the estimation of those who best knew its strength, shook it almost to its foundations,—and acting at Teheran with one of the ablest and most astute officers who ever represented Russia in the East,*—Sir J. McNeill should have held Persia firm to her engagements; that he should have carried the commercial treaty; and that he should have put our relations with the Shah upon something of their ancient footing, must be regarded as not the least meritorious achievements of his distinguished career. In the spring of 1842, ill-health compelled him to abandon Persia. He had been employed for nearly twenty-four years in that country, and

* Count Medem.

F

during that interval had raised himself by his unaided talent and energy from the humble rank of an assistant-surgeon in the Company's army, to that of a civil Grand Cross of the Bath—a bright example to the Indian services. So high, indeed, was the character he had earned for himself with the ministers of the Crown, that, when he retired from the East, he merely exchanged his diplomatic functions for an office of equal honour, and of more utility, under the Government of his native land.*

15. From 1842, until the recent death of Mahomed Shah, there were few salient points of interest in the politics of Persia. The objects of England were less, it would seem, during that interval, to struggle for influence at Teheran, or to restore strength to Persia, than to keep a watch over the proceedings of Russia; to preserve, as far as might be, the "status quo;" and to prevent at any rate our sustaining injury from sudden impulses, which prudent counsel might avert. Our expenditure was thus reduced within the narrowest possible limits. Interference in the domestic affairs of the country was studiously avoided. When the Shah appealed to us against the imperious bearing of Russia, we assured His Majesty of our sympathy, but never ventured to lead him to hope for our support. On one point only did we transgress the bounds of passive observation. A war was imminent between Persia and the Porte; and as it was evident that such a war, however it might terminate, would essentially weaken one, if not both, of the belligerents, and thus invite aggression, we determined to force our mediation on the pugnacious powers. Relying also on the Emperor's declaration, that the system which the two cabinets had a common interest in pursuing was that of "maintaining the tranquillity of the intermediate countries which separate the possessions of Russia from those of Great Britain," we invited Russia to send a commissioner to the conference of Erzeroom, and to aid us in the work of pacification. The

* Sir John McNeill has been for the last four years one of the "Poor Law Commissioners for Scotland;" and it was partly owing to his admirable management that the famine of 1847, which decimated Ireland, was so little felt in the sister island.

invitation was, of course, acceded to, and the conference accordingly commenced; but in the proceedings of such an anomalous congregation of parties it would have been unreasonable to expect either alacrity or even unanimity. All things, indeed, considered, it is, we think, more surprising that, under the joint mediation of Great Britain and Russia, any agreement whatever should have been concluded between the courts of Constantinople and Teheran, than that negociations, for which five months would have been a very liberal allowance of time, were actually made to extend over as many years.*

At the commencement of our sketch, we have remarked on the little progress that has been made by Russia, since the Afghan occupation, in that path, which the war was specially designed to obstruct, and which the withdrawal of our arms must have left more accessible than ever; and we now propose to consider this subject somewhat more in detail. It would be absurd to suppose that an erroneous view had been taken throughout of the bent of the Russian policy; and yet, if that policy were one of aggression against Persia and of hostility towards England, the question naturally arises how it happened, that the very favourable opportunity for its prosecution, which presented itself on our retirement from Afghanistan, should have been so little cultivated. The reasons, of course, of Russia's comparative inactivity can be mere matters of speculation, but we still give the following explanation with some confidence. The Afghan war, which, in the magnitude of the efforts it called forth, and the success that smiled on its commencement, took Russia somewhat by surprise, and made her almost repent of having provoked the struggle, furnished her in its sequel, not only with cause of congratulation, but with a lesson of much importance, as it might be applied to herself.

* It is a remarkable illustration of the extreme dilatoriness of official proceedings in the East, that the labours of the Turco-Persian Frontier Commission, which commenced in 1840, were only brought to a close by the exchange of the finished maps of the proposed boundary line in 1871; while the execution of the various wards of the Commission in reference to disputed territorial claims has not yet even been taken in hand by the Courts of Constantinople and Teheran. —1873.

If England were unable to maintain herself at Cabul and Candahar, Russia could scarcely expect to fare better at Teheran and Ispahan. All the difficulties that we encountered in Afghanistan would in a much graver form beset a Russian army in its occupation of Persia. The enormous sacrifice, indeed, at which alone a nation, exclusively Mahommedan, could be overrun and held by a Christian power, was exemplified in the case of Algiers; and Russia had neither the same objects nor interests in coveting the realm of the Shah, that impelled France to fasten on her African colony. It is possible, then, that the acquisitive policy of Russia in respect to Persia, and her agitating policy in respect to India, did actually cool, as the result of the Afghan war testified to the transcendent danger of her schemes, and as its corollaries all revealed to her the facility with which England could render abortive any plan of mere intimidation, or meet any system of attack.

The continued rebellion of the Caucasus, the ease with which Sheik Shamil baffled all her efforts to reduce him, rising up like the giant Antæus with renovated strength from every fresh encounter, must have powerfully aided in modifying the character of the Russian policy. We believe, indeed, that if her course had been otherwise uninterruptedly successful,—if Persia had surrendered herself a willing victim into the hands of her enemy, and Great Britain had given up every inch of ground beyond the Sutlej, the resolute resistance of this mountain chief would still have proved the salvation of Asia. We have heard it surmised, that Russia plays with the Caucasus to further her views in other quarters; that she favours the impression of her weakness on an unimportant point, to be enabled to employ her force with more effect where greater interests are at stake; but such is not our belief. We are convinced that for the last fifteen years at least, she has honestly and unremittingly employed her utmost available power to reduce the tribes of the Caucasus; and as Shamil at the present time, independently of his native forces, commands, it is said, the services of 15,000 deserters from the Russian ranks, and can place in battery, at different points, 200 pieces of ordnance, captured from the Russians in the field, or carried off from their entrenchments, we may understand how totally inadequate that power has proved to the emergency,* and how impossible it would have been for Russia, with her communications at the mercy of such an enemy, to push her arms still further to the eastward, or to contemplate territorial extension in that direction. The full value of the mountain war of independence has hardly yet, we think, been appreciated in preserving the balance of power. A moderate support of Shamil might still, perhaps, save the Danubian principalities, and as long as his banner floats from the summits of the Caucasus, so long is Persia safe from the hostile invasion of a Russian army.†

Although, however, the two checks, that we have thus noticed, imposed upon Russia the necessity of abstaining from those active measures which might have been reasonably expected to supervene upon our Afghan reverses, it is not to be supposed that, during the period which has since elapsed, she has exhibited no signs of animation and no tendency to an onward movement. Her conduct, it is true, in Persia has been more guarded than formerly, and more observant, to England in particular, of the amenities which should characterize

---

* A friend has furnished us with the following story, which is currently quoted in Persia, as an example of ready repartee, but which is also not without a certain degree of political significance:— "When the Amir Nizam visited the Emperor of Russia during his Georgian progress in 1837, and introduced the Heir Apparent, then a boy of 7 years of age, His Majesty observed in the course of conversation, 'Who are these Afghans, that they should be allowed to laugh at your beards in this way? Whose dogs are they to stand in the path of Mahomed Shah?' (We quote, of course, the Persian version of the story.) 'Oh!' answered the Amir, 'they are an insignificant set of vagabonds, not worth naming; idle untainted scoundrels, very like those Lesghies and Daghistanis you have in the mountains.' The Emperor looked as black as thunder, but said not a word further on the subject."

† Events have sufficiently verified the correctness of this view, for it was not until after the submission of Shamil in 1859, and the consequent pacification of Circassia, that Russia began to push her way up the Jaxartes. The forecast only failed in anticipating that the first development of the power of Russia, when freed from the Caucasian entanglement, would take place in the direction of Persia; whereas, in reality, her advances have commenced in the far East, and the Persian question is deferred to a later period.—1873.

the intercourse of friendly states; but it has not been less constant in its aim, or less progressive in its action. Her shadow has been gradually darkening over the land. Having coerced into her interests the Prime Minister, a Russian subject by birth, who, by the force of certain rules of the ecstatic school of philosophy to which they both belonged, held the Shah in leading-strings, she pursued, during the closing years of the late monarch's reign, an unobtrusive but an undeviating course of interference, almost of supervision, over the internal affairs of the country. Her protection was granted to all applicants. She recommended candidates for offices, and screened offenders, constituted herself referee in disputed cases, and not unfrequently usurped and exercised the functions of the executive power. Her attention was particularly directed to Azerbijan, and to the countries on the Caspian. She brought the Governor of the former province, the Shah's uterine brother, into direct dependence upon her, supported him against the central Government, and, when his liberty was endangered, granted him an asylum in the Russian Embassy, and ultimately, received and welcomed him as an imperial guest at Tiflis. Upon the shores of the Caspian the extreme jealousy of the littoral tribes compelled her to proceed with greater circumspection. Commencing, however, with a consulate at Resht, and agents at other ports, she obtained in process of time the authorization of the Shah to construct a naval arsenal on the island of Ashoor Ada, for the rendezvous and refitting of her marine.* She then placed a consul in the town of Asterabad, to protect the trade which this establishment had created; and, shortly before the death of the Shah, she is also understood to have proposed to institute another consulate at Meshed, the extension of her commerce being the ostensible, and perhaps really the immediate, object

---

* The Russians are said to have first visited Ashoor Ada in 1838, but it was not till 1842 that Sir J. McNeill drew the attention of the British Government to their irregular occupation of the island. The acquiescence of Persia was obtained on the understanding that the occupation was merely temporary, and was intended to check the incursions of the Turcomans into the territory of Asterabad, and to prevent the extension of piracy —1873.

of her activity; but political influence also, and increased facilities for intrigue will follow, as she must well know, of necessity in the train of that commerce, when it may have once fairly taken root in Khorassan.

Persia herself in the meantime had presented a miserable and melancholy spectacle. She had been undergoing the very extremity of suffering which misgovernment could entail upon a nation. The Prime Minister of Persia, Hajee Mirza Aghassee, had for a period of thirteen years the destinies of the country over which he presided more completely under his guidance than perhaps any absolute autocrat of ancient or of modern times; and lamentably did he abuse the trust reposed in him. Self-sufficient almost to fatuity; utterly ignorant of statesmanship, of finance, or of military science, yet too vain to receive instruction, and too jealous to admit of a coadjutor; brutal in his language; insolent in his demeanour; indolent in his habits; he brought the exchequer to the verge of bankruptcy, and the country to the brink of revolution. Alienating at the outset of his career fully one-half of the revenues of the Empire in extravagant grants to pampered courtlings, personal dependents, upstarts, and empirics, he consumed the remainder in amusing the military mania of the Shah, for whose edification he prepared a park of about 1000 pieces of artillery, and commissioned above half a million of English muskets. At the commencement of 1848, the Government paper—and it must be remembered that the finance of Persia is carried on entirely by a system of assignments—was at ninety per cent. discount. The pay of the army was generally from three to five years in arrears. The cavalry of the tribes was almost annihilated. The intense animosity of the Toorks and Persians had reached a climax which crippled the means of action of the provincial Governors, and threatened to produce complete disorganization. With the exception, indeed, of Azerbijan, in which the whole wealth of the Empire had become pretty well concentrated by the constant return of its inhabitants laden with the spoil of the provinces, Persia generally presented the appearance of a country occupied in force by a foreign enemy. Resistance to the Toorks was hopeless for the moment, but the desire for revenge was only deepened in intensity by the necessity of prolonged endurance.

In his foreign policy we do not think that the Prime Minister wilfully betrayed his country. He never submitted patiently to the tuition of Russia. On more occasions than one he proclaimed concession to have reached its limit, and struggled to break the meshes that were being woven around him. But he was impotent. He had not that confidence in England which might have led him to throw himself upon us for protection, nor had we shown any disposition to volunteer our support, or even to grant it, if it had been solicited. A French alliance had seemed for a time to hold out a prospect of succour from a quarter where no danger was to be apprehended, and had been cultivated, therefore, with more attention than in reality it merited. For a short period, indeed, the Comte de Sartiges held a position at Teheran more favourable, as far as the consideration of the Court was concerned, than that occupied either by the Russian or the British Minister; but a relation of this nature was evidently artificial, and could lead to no permanent result. France had no substantive interests in Persia, for which she could have ventured to put herself in opposition either to Russia or to England; nor, if she had been ever so much disposed in favour of Persian integrity, and had desired to retain the Shah as her own minion, is it very apparent how she could have carried her plans into execution. A categorical reference on this subject was, we believe, made to Louis Philippe before the revolution of February; but that event—the expulsion of a Monarch by his subjects, and the establishment of a republican government, measures utterly repugnant to the oriental idea of the divine right of kings,—scattered, of course, the negociation to the winds; and, until a royal or imperialist dynasty shall be again seated on the throne of France, we venture to predict that French influence will not regain at Teheran that transient lustre which flickered round it in 1847, struck out from the jarring contact of British and Russian interests.

16. On passing events in Persia we must be allowed to express ourselves with some reserve. Mahomed Shah died at

CH. I.] OUR POLITICAL RELATIONS WITH PERSIA. 73

Teheran on September 5th, 1848; and officers of the British and Russian missions immediately rode post to Tabriz to proclaim, and bring to the capital, his eldest son, Nassir-ed-din Mirza, who had been separately and conjointly recognized by the Courts of St. James's and St. Petersburg, as the legitimate successor to the throne. Persia had been so much habituated of late, in all measures of state policy, to receive her impulses from the European powers, that probably under any circumstances the simple declaration of the British and Russian Ministers would have sufficed to settle the immediate question of the succession. In the actual posture of affairs the acquiescence of the nation in that declaration was inevitable; for, of the few competitors who could pretend to exercise any influence on the general body of their countrymen, one, Bahman Mirza, was in honourable exile at Tiflis, and all the others were refugees at Bagdad. In the provinces, also, the peasantry and tribesmen were everywhere too intent upon their local emancipation, to take heed of an abstract matter like that of the succession. It may be said, then, that the Russian and British Missions, and a mere clique of notables,—who had, however, sufficient influence at the capital to cause public property to be respected, and generally to prevent disorder,— effected at the moment a transfer of kingly power, to which, in the best appointed times of former Persian history, the path could have only lain through long avenues of intrigue and blood. The obnoxious Minister was, of course, hurled from power, and only escaped the popular fury by taking sanctuary. The Toork governors generally were expelled from the provinces, and the garrisons either saved themselves by a precipitate retreat, or, where their numbers admitted of defence, shut themselves up in citadels, and awaited attack. The young Shah encountered no opposition whatever on his march from Tabriz to Teheran. He made his public entry into the capital on October 21st: and thus ended the first scene of the drama.

The second scene is not yet played out, or, at any rate, we are not yet acquainted with its result; but as far as it has gone, it is of a much less agreeable character than its predecessor, and it adumbrates progressive trouble. In the disposition of the Shah, so far as his tender age and hitherto obscure career afford materials for inquiry, in the constitution of the court, in the state of parties, in the internal condition of the country, and in its foreign relations, we look in vain for a single element of strength or a single characteristic of permanence. When we say that Nassir-ed-din Shah is a mere youth of eighteen years of age, it may be understood that, for a considerable time, at any rate, he must be a mere cipher in the Government which he is supposed to wield. The future of Persia will depend in a great measure on the training which he may receive during the critical period of the next few years, while his character is being formed for good or for ill; and it is much, therefore, to be lamented that statesmen of the old school, like Mirza Shefi and Mirza Buzurg, who guided the fortunes of the Empire with so much dignity and wisdom in the early days of Futteh Ali Shah, are no longer to be found in Persia, to give their young sovereign the benefit of their counsel and example. With regard to the actual ministry, our only consolation is, that it cannot last, and that any change must be for the better. A fatuous priest has been succeeded by a timid scribe, and the inexperience of the one is scarcely less obstructive to business than were the eccentricities and malignancy of the other. The state of parties is still more pregnant with evil; for, over and above the two great factions, the Toorks and Persians, which have hitherto, in spirit at any rate, divided the kingdom, and which (having whetted their appetite for blood in many an encounter during the recent convulsion in the provinces) may be expected to be henceforward pledged to an internecine struggle, leading too probably to the dismemberment of the empire—there may now be considered to be a third party, which desires nothing more than to promote this struggle, and to profit by the mutual exhaustion of the combatants. We do not think it worth while to particularize petty sections, or mere local divisions—although some of these, such as the tribe party of the Queen Mother, may very possibly play an important part in the future government of the country :—for, if a real crisis were imminent, we conceive that all other feelings would yield to that of a distinction of race, or to the strong impulse of personal ambition.

On the internal condition of Persia, and on the present aspect of its foreign relations, we could say much, if our space permitted; but we have already exceeded the ordinary limits of a political article, and must hasten, therefore, rapidly to a close. In every quarter there is abundant cause for anxiety, and few, very few, faint glimmerings of hope. The rock, upon which the government of the country will first split, will probably be a want of funds to defray the most ordinary and limited expenditure. The treasury has been drained of its last ducat, and we see little chance of its being replenished: for neither will the provinces, after the license of an interregnum, and with the consciousness of recovered strength, be induced to submit to exactions; nor will the Prince Governors, who have been sent to replace the subordinate chiefs employed during the late reign, and who will each endeavour to establish his own independent court, be in any hurry to contribute their quota of revenue for the support of the central government. It will be dangerous, again—at any rate while the "Res dura et regni novitas" hamper the free action of the government—to attempt to resume the grants so extravagantly lavished by Mahomed Shah and his minister upon unworthy objects. Without pretending, indeed, to vaticination, it seems to us that the sustaining or motive power of the government no longer exists, neither can it be renewed; and that, when the original impetus is lost, the wheels of the machine accordingly must cease to work.

The general condition, too, of the provinces is hardly less unfavourable to the consolidation of the young monarch's power, than an empty treasury, and impotent and divided councils. In no quarter, we may safely say, is there any feeling of confidence in the stability of the government. The public mind is still heaving with the agitation of the many local revolutions which followed on the death of the Shah, and extensive *émeutes* have since broken out in Mazenderan, Ispahan, and Kerman, aimed almost undisguisedly against the existing government. Khorassan, however, undoubtedly affords the greatest cause for apprehension. Ever since the Assef-ed-Douleh, the head of the old Persian party, was removed, about two years ago, from the government of the province, very great discontent has prevailed generally throughout that part of the kingdom. An accident, shortly before the death of the Shah, brought this discontent to a head, and raised the population of Meshed in arms against the Toork garrison, which held the citadel. The old Russian colonel who commanded the Toorks* made a brave defence, but was compelled at length to evacuate the place, and to retire with a remnant of his forces, and with the Prince Governor of the province, to the camp of Yar. Mahomed Khan, who had advanced with a considerable army from Herat,—not exactly for the relief of Meshed, but with a view of sweeping the country in the general scramble, and annexing perhaps a portion of the Khorassan territory to his Afghan principality. Yar Mahomed Khan made an attempt to carry Meshed, but failed; the Khorassanis being not less inveterate against the Afghans than against the Toorks, and having now put forward the son of the Assef-ed-Douleh as their *quasi* independent ruler.. It would have been easy, we believe, for the young Shah's government, at this stage of the affair, to have brought about, through British mediation, the ostensible submission of the province. The Khorassanis were resolved to be no longer trampled on by the soldiery of Azerbijan: they had mercilessly massacred the Toorks wherever they had fallen into their hands, and had proclaimed against them a war of extermination; but the Salar, as the Assef-ed-Douleh's son was named, had no pretension to enter the lists as a competitor with Nassir-ed-din Shah for the throne. He boasted, indeed, to have aided the royal cause in forcing the Afghans to retire towards Herat; and the most to which at that time he ever ventured to aspire, was that either his father or himself should govern Khorassan as a fief of the empire—that is, to be placed in fact something on the same footing which

---

* It must not be supposed that this officer belongs to the army of the Czar. He is a Russian refugee, who entered the Persian service some thirty years ago, and is undoubtedly the most efficient military chief at present at the disposal of the Shah.

Ch. L] OUR POLITICAL RELATIONS WITH PERSIA. 77

Mahomed Ali Pasha had been allowed to occupy in his government of Egypt under the Sultan. The ministry of the Shah, however, seems to have shown an invincible repugnance to the inauguration of the new reign by negociation with a party flushed with triumph, and still exhibiting an attitude of defiance.

It was judged indispensable to punish the insurgents before acceding to any terms for a permanent settlement of the province; and reinforcements accordingly were sent to Khorassan to co-operate with the garrison which had evacuated Meshed, but which still held its ground, supported by Yar Mahomed Khan's army, upon the Herat frontier. These reinforcements, consisting exclusively of Azerbijan troops, were beaten off from the first town which they attacked after entering the province; and they have since retired towards Teheran, where efforts are being now made to support them. That the Minister has pledged himself to reduce Khorassan "coûte qu'il coûte," would be of little consequence, if it merely involved the question of his personal fate; but, unfortunately, there are far graver interests concerned in the contest. According to our view, it is impossible that the Toork yoke should be again violently imposed on Khorassan; and the prolongation of the struggle, therefore, in increasing the exasperation of parties, would appear to render only more certain the threatened dismemberment of the kingdom. There is, indeed, an alternative, which has been already freely discussed, and which might be adopted, in order to prevent this disintegration of the empire. An auxiliary Russian army might be disembarked at Asterabad, and pushed on to Meshed, either in avowed support of the royal cause, or preliminary to an arrangement of the same nature as that which made Russia the arbiter of the destinies of the Danubian principalities, and led to her present permanent (?) occupation of Bucharest and Yassy.

It would be premature at present to discuss the eventualities of such a movement. Although, indeed, Russia has seen with great concern the progress of our arms in the Punjab, and would assuredly desire to lessen the effect on Afghanistan of our location at Peshawur and Shikarpur, we doubt exceedingly, after the attentive examination of her career in the East embodied in the foregoing pages, that she would incur the risk at present of military operations in Khorassan. We anticipate that she will continue for some years longer the same course of gradual advance that she has pursued since the Afghan war. The effect of the succession of Nassir-eddin Shah upon the relative positions of Russia and England at Teheran will probably be an exact reproduction of the action and reaction which followed on our united support of Mahomed Shah fourteen years ago. We shall have undergone trouble, responsibility, and perhaps expense, merely to render the Russian predominance more certain. A short blaze of popularity may possibly attend the first indication of our awakened solicitude for Persia; but that we shall fall back into a secondary position, as soon as the season of exertion may be over, and that of fruition may arrive, we hold to be a necessary consequence of the nature of things. As far, indeed, as Russia finds that she can press with safety upon the incapability of a boy king, and the incoherency of a divided government, so far it may be presumed that she will be prepared to push on her approaches. That she will replace her minion Bahman Mirza in the government of Azerbijan may be considered inevitable; that she will strengthen herself at Asterabad, and push her feelers into Khorassan, is equally to be expected: that she will further control the court, and through that control will make herself felt wherever the authority of the court extends, is hardly to be doubted;* but to adopt any more active course of interference, before the outburst of that domestic crisis, which may be imminent, and cannot be very distant, would be to stultify her previous caution, and to plunge herself into needless embarrassments. By what measures on

---

* As we write, we hear of the arrival at Teheran of a splendid Russian Embassy conducted by Lieut.-Gen. Schilling, and charged ostensibly with the empty form of congratulating the new monarch on his accession. We shall be surprised if this embassy does not replace Bahman Mirza in Tabriz, obtain further grants in Asterabad, and perhaps establish a consulate at Meshed.

the part of England the armed intervention of Russia in the north or in the east of Persia, if ever it should take place, would require to be met, would depend, not less upon the European combinations, to which in the meanwhile the election of Louis Napoleon to the Presidency of the French Republic, or other causes, might have led, than upon the state at the time of the finances of India, and upon the degree of fixity and security which might have been obtained for our North-Western Frontier.

BAGHDAD, *April*, 1849.

CHAPTER II.

OUR POLITICAL RELATIONS WITH PERSIA—*continued*.

1. 1848-1852.—State of Persia from the accession of Nassir-ed-dín Shah to the death of the Amír Nizám.—2. Affairs of Herat. Death of Yar Mahomed Khan. Our Convention with Persia regarding Herat, 1853.—3. Persia during the Crimean War, 1854-1856.—4. Herat affairs during the same period. Occupation of Herat by Persia, Oct., 1856.—5. 1856-1858.— Persian War. Treaty of Peshawer, Jan., 1857. Treaty of Paris, March, 1857. Its provisions and their effect.—6. 1858-1863. Teheran Mission transferred to India Office, 1859, and re-transferred to Foreign Office, 1860. The question examined. Our policy in Persia. Affairs of Herat to the death of Dost Mahomed Khan, May, 1863.—7. Disputes between the Persians and Afghans in regard to Seistan.—8. History of the Persian Telegraph. Convention of 1863, &c.—9. Affairs of the Persian Gulf and Bahrein up to 1868. —10. Affairs of Mekran, and frontier delimitation between Persia and Kelat, 1862-1872.—11. The Seistan arbitration, 1870-1872.—12. Present state of our relations with Persia. The Atrek frontier and proposed expedition against the Turcomans. The Grand Vizier.—13. The Reuter Concession and the Shah's visit to Europe, 1873.—14. Prospects of Persia and policy óf England towards her, 1874.

THE interval of nearly a quarter of a century, which has elapsed since the foregoing sketch of our political relations with Persia was published in India, would seem to render it necessary, for the due understanding of the subject, that the narrative should be continued in outline to the present day. I proceed, therefore, to furnish such a supplement, with a brief preliminary explanation on two points. First, in regard to the historical element, as I have been officially connected more or less with the politics of Persia during the whole period under review, and have enjoyed, moreover, unrestricted access to all the public documents concerned, I may claim, I think, a perfect confidence in the accuracy of my record of facts; and secondly, in regard to opinions and inferences, I should wish it to be understood that on all such matters I merely express my personal views, quite independent of the Government policy, to which, indeed, those views will be found to be not

CH. II.] OUR POLITICAL RELATIONS WITH PERSIA. 81

unfrequently opposed; and in order the better to mark this sense of individual responsibility, I propose in the following summary to drop the editorial *we* as unmeaning and inconvenient, and to write throughout in my own name and character.

The first point to which I would draw attention, as confirmatory of the general accuracy of the views contained in the preceding sketch, is that, although twenty-four years have elapsed since it was written, and although events have occurred in the interim—events of such gravity as a suspension of intercourse, and even open war—which usually exercise an important influence on the interests and counsels of nations, still no substantial difference is to be recognized between the political relations of England and Persia as pourtrayed in 1849, and as they exist at the present day. The British and Russian Governments, however cordial in Europe, are constrained, in the present as in the past, to observe to each other in the East an attitude of reserve, if not of mistrust; while Persia, prudently desiring, as she always has desired, to be on friendly terms with both Governments, has acquired the full confidence of neither.

A sort of triangular contest between England, Russia, and Persia is, in fact, the normal condition of Central Asian policy; and in the retrospect which I now propose to take of Persian affairs since the accession of Nassir-ed-dín Shah to the throne of Teheran, the several recent phases of this inevitable complication may be studied with advantage.

During the opening years of the new reign which commenced in 1848, nothing could have been more discouraging than the internal condition of the country. Ruin and revolution, indeed, appeared to be imminent, and were only averted by the high qualities which, contrary to all expectation, showed themselves in the character of the Amír-Nizám, who was now raised to the dignity and power of Prime Minister. This individual, although of plebeian descent, and unfitted therefore to command the respect of the princes and nobles of the Persian Court, had no sooner entered upon office than he gave evidence of very high administrative qualities. Fearless almost to a fault, he grappled with the difficulties of his position in

G

the most determined manner. His first care was finance. By revoking the extravagant grants of his predecessor, regardless of complaint and opposition, and by imposing in some cases additional taxation, he obtained funds for current expenditure, and gradually re-established the revenues of the State on a healthy footing. He then applied himself to political reforms. Resisting all attempts at a compromise, and steadily declining the offer of mediation, he fairly stamped out the rebellion in Khorassan by force of arms, and thereby no doubt greatly strengthened the Shah's authority throughout the Empire; while at the same time he succeeded in suspending for awhile the dangerous antagonism of the Toorks and Persians by a skilful combination of conciliation and firmness. His most difficult achievement, however,—that which required the strongest exercise of will, and which he believed, perhaps with reason, to be of paramount importance to the interests of the Government—lay in his firm but consistent and impartial opposition to European pressure. If he pertinaciously withstood, for instance, the efforts of Russia to replace Bahman Mirza in Azerbijan, he was equally obstinate in refusing to admit the intercession of England in favour of the Assef-ed-Douleh and his family in Khorassan; and so thoroughly, indeed, did he observe this impartiality of political conduct, that when obliged by circumstances to yield in one direction, he at once sought to redress the balance by a corresponding concession in the other. We are thus assured by competent authority* that the Convention of 1851, whereby for the first time our cruisers acquired the right of stopping and searching native vessels in the Persian Gulf suspected of being engaged in the African slave trade, was granted to the British Minister, not in acknowledgment of the justice of our demand, nor even as a personal favour, but simply as a set-off to a somewhat humiliating concession which had been wrung from the Prime Minister by Russia at about the same period, the dismissal of the Prince Governor of Mazenderan having been peremptorily insisted on by the Court of St. Petersburg, in satisfaction for

* See Watson's "Persia," p. 398, quoting Lady Sheil, who was present at Teheran at the time.

his asserted complicity in a recent attack by the Turcomans on the Russian settlement of Ashúr-ada.

There can be no doubt that at this period the interference of the European missions at Teheran in the domestic affairs of the country was carried beyond all reasonable limit. Not only was a constant pressure exerted for political purposes on the chief Ministers of the Court, but a right of asylum to offenders against the State was also far too liberally granted; and in some cases, not merely individuals but large classes of the community were taken bodily under the protection of the foreign Consulates.* The mischievous effects of such a system became soon apparent; for, however desirable it may be in the general interests of humanity to provide a corrective, such as the right of asylum, against the despotic exercise of power in an Oriental state, still it is impossible for an "imperium in imperio" to exist without a serious loss both of character and authority to the native Government; and it is not, therefore, surprising that the Amír-Nizám, as soon as he felt strong enough to assert his rights, addressed himself to the remedy of this abuse as the crying grievance of the Administration. Before any definite change, however, could be affected, his career was brought to an untimely close, and it is curious to observe that he owed his own downfall and death to the very system which he was seeking to suppress. The Shah's jealousy, indeed, of his Minister, which caused his suspension from office, was first seriously aroused by the ill-advised efforts of the Russian Mission to protect him—in opposition to a rival who was regarded as a partizan of England; and the subsequent orders for his death were hastened by the apprehension that instructions might, in the interim, arrive from St. Petersburg, authorizing the Russian Minister's official interference in his favour. The story, however, of the disgrace and death of the Amír-Nizám is one of the saddest that occurs in the whole range of Persian history. Every evil passion, every miserable motive, jealousy, selfishness, perfidy, and hatred,

* The American community of Talríz was thus temporarily placed under the protection of the British Consulate on the departure of the young king for Teheran in 1848.

seem to have combined to cause the death of this really extraordinary person, who was far in advance of his age and country, the only redeeming feature in the tale being the devotion of his royal wife, who watched over the doomed man like his guardian angel, and was only ultimately overreached by the cruellest of frauds.

2. The death of the Amír-Nizám early in the year 1852, shocking as it appeared to the nations of Europe, and arresting as it also did the onward march of progress and improvement in Persia, was still more disastrous in its effects on the external political relations of the country. From this period, indeed, may be dated that resumption of an aggressive tendency to the Eastward, which a few years later culminated in a war with England. Closely following on the change of ministry at Teheran, where Mirza Agha Khan, the so-called English *protégé*, was now installed as *Sadr Azem*, or "Grand Vizier," there occurred a crisis at Herat under circumstances which not unnaturally re-awakened the longing of Persia for territorial extension in that direction, and fairly warranted an expectation of success. Yar Mahomed Khan, who had so long upheld the independence of the Afghan Western Principality, equally against Persia and against the Baruckzyes of Cabul and Candahar, died in the autumn of 1851, and was succeeded by his son, Said Mahomed, a dissolute and imbecile youth, who, meeting with opposition from the Herat chiefs soon after his accession to power, turned for support to Persia, and even proffered his allegiance to the Shah. A difficult question then arose for the consideration of the British Government, committed as it already was in principle by the Afghan War, to the maintenance of the integrity of Herat. My own opinion, which I put on record at the time, and which I still believe to have been sound, was to the following effect: that as there was now no question of Russian instigation or intrigue, nor of hostility to British India, it could not possibly be to our interest to irritate Persia by opposing Said Mahomed's overtures, and insisting on the continued independence of Herat in spite of itself. The ground, indeed, which I took up was even broader, and involved a question of principle that is hardly yet obsolete

for I argued that, looking to the future of Herat and the alternative of its being either in friendly or unfriendly hands, it would be better for us under both contingencies to have to deal with a Persian than with an Afghan power. The friendship of united Persia, I suggested, would more avail us in resisting the advance of Russia than the divided councils of Cabul, Candahar, and Herat; while, on the other hand, if coercive measures were ever requisite to prevent Herat from becoming dangerous to India, it would be a less arduous undertaking to send an expedition to the Persian Gulf, as in 1838, than to march another army above the passes. Had we remained passive at the period in question, there can be no doubt but that the fertile valley of the Heri-rúd, with its formidable fortress, would have been re-annexed to Khorassan without a struggle; for Herat itself was already Persianized to a great extent, and neither Cabul nor Candahar, estranged by half a century of independent rule, would have moved a man to support the family of Yar Mahomed Khan; and regarding the question by the light of subsequent events, and without impugning our present policy, to which we are now irrevocably committed, I am not at all sure that this would not have been the proper solution of the Herat difficulty of 1852. But the responsible officers decided otherwise. Conformably to Foreign Office tradition, as shaped by the Afghan War, the integrity of Herat was to be maintained at all hazards, and a Convention was accordingly imposed upon the Shah in January, 1853,* by which Persia undertook not to send troops to Herat unless the city was menaced from the East, nor indeed to interfere in the internal affairs of the place in any manner whatever, the views of the British Government, as succinctly stated by Colonel Sheil to Said Mahomed Khan, being "a determination that Herat should remain in Afghan hands and in independence."

3. Although the Sadr Azem, who was now in office, submitted to this restriction without any serious resistance, there can be no doubt but that it was most unpalatable to the Shah, and that it predisposed him to be influenced generally by counsels

* The text of this Convention is given in the Appendix.

hostile to England. An indication, indeed, of an altered state of feeling towards us was afforded at this time by the favour with which in the first instance the proposals of Russia were received at Teheran, for Persia's participation in the war against Turkey. England and France had not, it is true, as yet decided to interfere actively in the struggle, but still our views and interests in regard to the pending contest were sufficiently understood; and when Persia accordingly undertook, on the invitation of Russia, to prepare auxiliary armies both at Tabriz and Kermanshah, she was committing herself to a course of quasi-hostility against us. Fortunately the negociations opened in 1853 broke down, owing partly to the opposition of the Sadr Azem, who, when uninfluenced by private considerations, was inclined to England rather than to Russia, and partly to the unseemly impetuosity of the Russian Minister at Teheran, who, in remonstrating with the Grand Vizier against what he conceived to be a breach of faith, was betrayed into an act of direct personal violence; but enough had transpired to show that we were no longer supreme in the councils of the Shah. Considered, indeed, from a Persian point of view, the position of the Shah's Government, when we declared war against Russia in 1854, was most embarrassing. On the one hand there were grievances of long standing against Turkey, principally connected with the frontier, which might be redressed by making common cause with Russia; while the humiliation of England, if she was worsted in the struggle, would also strengthen Persian interests at Herat; but on the other hand, Russia was the normal and hereditary foe of the Persian state, the only power whose aggressive policy really constituted a material danger, and it would be suicidal, therefore, to assist in developing her greatness at the expense of Turkey. There was much vacillation at Teheran, produced, perhaps, as much by our own half-hearted policy as by conflicting views of the true interests of Persia. The Shah's Government naturally expected, if we were in earnest in our desire to cripple Russia's power in Asia, that we should land an efficient British force in Mingrelia, co-operate with Shamil, who was eager for action, raise the discontented population of

Georgia and Armenia, subsidize Persia, and finally turn our Asiatic strength to account by bringing a powerful contingent into the field from India through Baghdad and Kurdistan. Under such circumstances Persia would no doubt have been prepared to cast in her lot with us, and strike a blow for the recovery of Erivan; but when it was seen that Kars was sacrificed without an attempt being made to relieve it, that the threatened invasion of Georgia dwindled to a meaningless demonstration of Turkish troops in the valley of the Ingoor, that India's contribution to the war was the mere loan of a couple of cavalry regiments sent through Egypt to the Crimea, and that Persia was counselled to observe neutrality, instead of being called on to furnish an auxiliary army, there can be no doubt that at Teheran, where the causes which hampered our free action—the jealousies of France and the want of any national enthusiasm in favour of our Turkish ally—were unknown, the effect of the slow progress of the Russian war—confined as it was in the Eastern field of operations to the siege of Sebastopol—was to raise a suspicion either of our sincerity or our power. Our political influence therefore waned in Persia during the years 1854 and 1855, notwithstanding that the identity of the interests of the two countries was never more apparent, and a free scope was thus given to the miserable intrigues which, at the close of the latter year, led to a suspension of diplomatic relations and the retirement of our Minister from the Court.

4. As we had originally quarrelled with Persia in 1838, on the subject of Herat, and had now reopened the old sore, by preventing the acceptance of Said Mahomed's voluntary offer of dependence, so, in the progressive stages of the misunderstanding with us, which may be dated from the Convention of 1853, and which resulted in war, the Teheran Court continued throughout to pay a close attention to the affairs of Afghanistan. Debarred by this Convention from intermeddling in the internal affairs of the Principality, Persia had proposed in the first instance to form a Quadripartite Treaty with Cabul, Candahar, and Herat, for defence, as it was stated, against their common enemies; and, failing in this scheme, through the opposition of

Dost Mahomed Khan, who was now beginning for the first time to realize the advantage of an English alliance, she then sought to bring on a collision between Herat and Candahar, which, according to the first Article of the Convention, would have afforded her a sufficient reason for interference. The attitude, indeed, of the Teheran Court towards the Afghan States during the year 1854 was so threatening, that Dost Mahomed no longer hesitated to throw himself into the arms of England. He made his first overtures for an alliance at the close of 1854, just as Mr. Murray was proceeding to take charge of the Mission at Teheran, and on March 30th, 1855, he concluded a treaty with us at Peshàwer, of perpetual peace and friendship,* by which, after an interval of twelve dreary years, it was hoped that the blunder of the Afghan war would be at length repaired. Simultaneously almost with the conclusion of this treaty, a crisis, involving a change of Government, occurred, both at Herat and at Candahar. In the former city, Said Mahomed Khan, the unworthy son of the Great Vizier, having exhausted the patience of his subjects, was deposed, and a Suddozye prince of good character, Mahomed Yussouf by name, who had been for a long period a refugee at Meshed, and who was everywhere regarded as an instrument in the hands of Persia, was established in his place. To what extent this revolution was really due to the intrigues of Persia, was never officially known. We did not care, without direct proof of the active agency of Persia, to complicate the position at Teheran, where our relations were in the mean time becoming strained, by denouncing the proceedings of Prince Mahomed Yussouf at Herat, as an infringement of the Convention of 1853; but it is certain that in Afghanistan generally the revolution was so understood, the substitution, indeed, of the Meshed refugee for the hereditary ruler of Herat being regarded as equivalent to the transfer of the government of the city to the hands of Persia. So fully impressed with this idea was Dost Mahomed Khan, who was now in alliance with us, and who on the death of his brother, the well-known Sirdar Kohandil Khan, which occurred almost simultaneously with Said Mahomed's de-

* See Appendix No. II.

position, had proceeded to Candahar, in order to re-unite that territory to the crown of Cabul, that he repeatedly applied to us to be employed in vindicating our treaty rights by recovering Herat from the Persians; and when we declined to sanction the movement, regarding it as premature, he proposed, in Afghan interests, to lead an expedition against the western capital on his own account. Events, however, of importance now followed each other in such rapid succession, that this intention fell through. Mr. Murray was compelled, by a long course of studied provocation, to suspend relations with the Persian Court. He accordingly struck his flag at Teheran on December 6th, 1855, and retired to Baghdad; and in the following March the Shah's Government, no longer withheld by considerations of prudence, threw off the mask, and sent an army to Herat, which was at once admitted into the city with the consent of the Suddozye Prince, who thus confirmed his dependency on the Persian Crown. But this first Persian occupation was very brief. An "émeute" occurred after a few weeks, which ended in the Persians being driven out of the city, while Prince Mahomed Yussouf hoisted the English flag, and urged Dost Mahomed, whose alliance with England was now a matter of notoriety, to support him against Persian domination. Immediately following, however, on this application, a second revolution occurred, the Suddozye Prince being deposed, and sent to the Persian camp as a prisoner, while his deputy, Isa Khan, remained in command of the city. A desultory contest now ensued, and was continued for some months, until at length, on October 25th, 1856, Isa Khan, in despair of receiving aid from Dost Mahomed and the English, hauled down the Afghan flag, and surrendered Herat to Persia.

5. This decisive result, whereby the object was accomplished at which Persia had persistently laboured for twenty years, and which we had as persistently opposed, roused the British Government to action. We immediately declared war against Persia, and instigated the Afghans to attack her. It is of interest to observe how our Afghan, and our Persian policy have thus always acted and re-acted on each other. It has

been already shown that the resumption of our relations with the Afghans, which had remained in complete abeyance since 1842, was due to the renewed solicitude of Persia, in the same quarter, Colonel Sheil's Teheran Convention of 1853 having naturally led to the preliminary treaty with Dost Mahomed in 1855; and it is equally certain that our formal engagement with the Ameer of Cabul, concluded at Desháwer on January 27th, 1857,* whereby we contracted an alliance of perpetual peace and friendship with the Afghans, and promised them a subsidy of a lakh of rupees a month, was the legitimate consequence of the declaration of war against Persia, three months previously. If Persia had given us no more serious cause of offence than in writing obnoxious letters to our Minister, or contesting rights of protection which were undefined and almost undefinable, it is probable that we should have judged her to be sufficiently punished by a withdrawal of our countenance and support; but when she proceeded to violate her solemn engagements, and to thrust herself actively into the arena of Afghan politics, we were constrained, not only in vindication of our honour, but in deference to the principles that we had laid down for the protection of our Indian interests, to take up arms against her. There is at the same time no question but that we entered on the Persian War most reluctantly, and with a full appreciation of the political injury it might entail on us—an injury, indeed, which would be likely to become more serious in proportion to our military success. Fortunately the war was of very short duration, and the injury was therefore reduced to a minimum. The expeditionary force from India disembarked at Karrack in the Persian Gulf on December 4th, 1856, and peace was signed at Paris three months later, namely, on the 4th of March, 1857,† though hostilities were locally prolonged for another month, owing to the imperfect means of communication which existed in those days, before the establishment of a telegraph between Constantinople and Bassorah.

During this brief conflict it may also be observed there

* See Appendix No. III. † The text of the Treaty of Paris is given in the Appendix No. IV.

were but three occasions of actual collision between the English and Persian forces, namely, on the landing at Ríshíre, in the action of Khúsháb, and at the capture of Mohamreh, so that the Persians suffered little from military excesses, or any of the usual horrors of a campaign, and the war left behind it but few traces of irritation or ill-will. Persia made no pretension to military equality with England, and was not therefore humiliated by defeat. What she did resent at the time, and what has ever since rankled in the hearts of all patriotic Persians was, that we should have subsidized the Afghans against her. The invasion of her Southern provinces by the troops from India was regarded as the natural consequence of her own occupation of Herat—a mere repetition, indeed, of the proceeding of 1838; but that we should completely reverse the political status which had been established on her Eastern frontier since the Afghan War, and should now supply the Cabul troops, from whose perfidy we had so severely suffered, with arms and money in order to enable them to attack our former friends, disconcerted the Shah's Government exceedingly, and greatly increased its soreness on the subject of Herat—the more so, indeed, as before her rupture with us, Persia had been making strenuous efforts to inveigle Dost Mahomed into an alliance with herself, and had actually brought the frontier districts of Lásh and Farreh into dependence on Teheran, with a view to the further extension of the Shah's political power to Candahar.

This system of subsidizing the Afghans against their neighbours inaugurated, no doubt, a new era in our Central Asian policy, but it hardly possessed—in its origin, at any rate—either the significance or the aggressive character which was attributed to it by the Russians and Persians. Russian official writers have represented the Treaty of Pesháwer as guaranteeing the Ameer in his possessions of Bulkh, Cabul, and Candahar, and inciting him to further conquests, while Persia, conscious that the first subsidy was directed against her occupation of Herat, has taken offence at every subsequent supply of arms and money to the Afghans, seeing in all such efforts upon our part to strengthen her Eastern neighbour, an indication of our mistrust in her own good faith and a desire to control her policy. Perhaps we were in some degree responsible for the exaggerated colouring given by foreign powers to the Treaty of Peshawer, as we had certainly strained the facts of the case in the other direction, by proclaiming in the preamble to the treaty that we merely aimed at protecting the possessions of the Ameer in Bulkh, Cabul, and Candahar, "with which the Shah had manifested an intention to interfere." In reality our main object was then, as it is now and ever has been since Burnes first visited Cabul, to see a strong and friendly Prince ruling over the Afghans, on the north-west frontier of India; but we also looked to the co-operation of the Ameer's forces in turning the Persians out of Herat; and it was thus specially provided that the payment of a lakh of rupees a month was to continue until peace was made between the British and Persian Governments, and no longer. As events turned out, the Afghans gave us no assistance whatever in the Persian War—not from any lukewarmness upon their part, but simply because no assistance was required. Peace was concluded within six weeks of the date of our agreement with Dost Mahomed, and the Persians evacuated Herat in due course under the provisions of the Treaty of Paris. It appears, however, from the official records, that an aggregate sum of £260,000 was disbursed to the Ameer of Cabul during the years 1856-58, the payment of the subsidy, which had commenced in the autumn of 1856, before the formal treaty was concluded at Peshawer, being continued, not only up to the final act of the war—the restoration of Herat to the Afghans, on July 27th, 1857—but for fourteen months longer, or as late as September 30th, 1858. There were, of course, many sufficient reasons for this prolongation of the subsidy beyond its natural limits, of which I may note the following:—1st, we had sent a Mission under Major Lumsden to Candahar, to see that the money advanced for military purposes was properly expended, and so long as our Officers remained in the country it was judged inexpedient to discontinue the allowance to the Ameer. 2ndly. The Indian authorities were much dissatisfied with the form of government established in Herat after the withdrawal of the Persians, and doubted if the continued dependence of the city upon Persia did not violate the conditions of the Treaty of Paris, in which case renewed local interference might be necessary; and 3rdly. During the years 1857-58, we were passing through the most critical phase of our Indian history —the period of the Sepoy mutiny—when it was of the first importance that the Cabul ruler should be on friendly terms with us, and when, indeed, no one less powerful or less loyal than Dost Mahomed Khan could probably have prevented a general Afghan invasion of the Punjab.

The Persian Government is said to have been much surprised at the moderation of the terms which we imposed on her as the price of peace—terms which, in fact, placed her in a better, rather than in a worse, position with regard to us. Ferrukh Khan, the agent who, on Mr. Murray's retirement, had been sent to England to offer explanations and to deprecate our anger, and who might have succeeded in composing the quarrel at the outset, but for the aggravated grievance of the expedition against Herat, was given a " carte blanche " after the occupation of Bushire; and it was expected at Teheran that he would at least have been obliged to cede some portion of territory, and to make other sacrifices before putting an end to hostilities. It has, indeed, been imputed to Lord Clarendon, as an error of policy, by some of our public writers, that as we were completely in the right, and were entitled to compensation for the heavy outlay to which we had been subjected in fitting out the Persian expedition, he did not, on the conclusion of peace, profit by the occasion to have secured us a permanent footing in the Gulf, either at Bushire or Karrack, which might have served as an equipoise to the Russian occupation of Ashoor-ada; but, in my own opinion, he exercised a sound discretion in resisting the temptation to acquire territory in this quarter. A settlement on the coast of Persia would, no doubt, have facilitated trade, and produced other local advantages, but it was not required for the maintenance of our general political influence in the Gulf, and it would have probably occasioned so much irritation to the Shah's Government, as to affect permanently our relations with the country. The only important interests that were held to be at stake at this epoch were those connected with the Afghan frontier, and in that direction, accordingly, we imposed conditions of increased stringency, and even accepted responsibilities which were not only stringent but embarrassing. Not satisfied with renewing the interdict against any interference on the part of Persia with the government or internal affairs of Herat, we further took on ourselves the onerous duty of arbitrating in the event of future differences between the Persians and Afghans, engaging to exert our influence with the latter to prevent umbrage being given by them to the Court of Teheran, and binding the Shah's Government in no instance to take up arms unless our friendly offices had failed to obtain redress. It has always been my opinion, that these terms of settlement were not judicious. They either went too far, or not far enough. If we merely desired to retain the "status quo ante bellum," there was no occasion to commit ourselves to intervention in the Perso-Afghan quarrels. The mere embodiment of the Convention of 1853, in a formal diplomatic treaty, would have answered all our purposes. If, on the other hand, we desired to put a definite end to all connexion between Persia and Herat, we should have provided for the surrender of the city into the hands of the officers of Dost Mahomed Khan, who could alone uphold its independence. As events turned out, we were completely stultified; for when the Persian troops were withdrawn from Herat in July, 1857, under the provisions of the Treaty of Paris, a Baruckzye Sirdar, named Sultan Ahmed Khan, who, having quarrelled with his uncle, Dost Mahomed, had sought the protection of Persia, was sent from Teheran to assume the government of the city; and this chief, succeeding as he did to power at the invitation and under the auspices of the Shah, continued for the next five years to rule almost as a vassal of the Persian Crown. During all this period Persia, in her dealings with Herat, kept herself strictly within the limitations of the Treaty of Paris. She claimed no tribute; she exacted no homage; she did not exercise any real or ostensible authority in the city; but the Afghan chief, under perpetual apprehension of hostilities from the eastward, and disappointed of his hopes of material support from England, made a parade of his dependence upon Teheran, as the best means of maintaining his power. He read the *Khotba*, and coined money in the name of the Shah, thereby officially proclaiming his vassalage; and when he visited Teheran, in obedience to the royal summons, he received robes of honour and other marks of the Shah's favour, as a distinguished servant of the Crown, rather than an independent prince. It was in vain that we remonstrated against so gross a perversion of the relations between Persia and Herat, as defined by treaty, sending a mission from Teheran under Major Taylor, to congratulate the new governor, and to assure him of our moral support. Sultan Ahmed Khan had certainly no affection for Persia, but he was distrustful of us as the close allies of his enemy, Dost Mahomed, and his suspicions of our good faith were further strengthened by some unfortunate intrigues against his power, which were carried on by the native *employés* of the Mission to Herat, without the cognizance of their chief.

6. The interval between the close of the Persian War in 1857, and the death of Dost Mahomed Khan at Herat in 1863, was one of comparative repose in the politics of Central Asia. Although Russia, recovering from the shock of the Crimean War, had already entered on that career of conquest in the valley of the Jaxartes, which has since made her mistress of the Uzbeg Khanates, her successes had not yet excited much attention in India. Nor did the strange spectacle of a Politico-scientific mission conducted by Russian officers, which at this time (in the summer of 1858) appeared at Herat and opened communication with Cabul, attract more than a passing comment from the Calcutta Government, though as Northern India was still heaving with the agitation of the Mutiny, the mission might, if Dost Mahomed Khan had been at all addicted to intrigue, have led to very awkward complications. It seems, indeed, as if the magnitude of the crisis we had just passed through in India had rendered us insensible to minor dangers, and that our usual watchfulness on the North-west frontier had thus for a time forsaken us.

It was during this period of political rest that a change was introduced in the conduct of our relations with Persia, which has since given rise to much acrimonious discussion, and remains an open question to the present day. The change was certainly not intended at the time to indicate a diminution of our interest in Persia. It does not seem even to have been regarded by the British Government as of any political significance at all, but to have been arranged simply as a matter of departmental convenience. Extraneous circumstances, however, gave it an undue importance. There had always been a certain jealousy between the Imperial and the Indian Governments, as to the direction of affairs in Persia. The rival missions of Malcolm and Sir Harford Jones early in the century had brought this disagreement into prominent view; and on several subsequent occasions a shifting of responsibility, backwards and forwards, between London and Calcutta, has shown that the dependency of the Persian Mission on England or India was still undecided. When the Government of India accordingly was transferred, by Act of Parliament in 1859, from the East India Company to the Queen, it seemed a fair occasion for effecting a compromise; and an arrangement therefore was made which placed the Teheran establishment under the charge of the Secretary of State for India, instead of the Secretary of State for Foreign Affairs, so as to concede the point that our Persian interests belonged to Indian rather than to European diplomacy, while at the same time the British representative at Teheran remained under the direct control of the Crown. As a subsidiary measure, Indian officers were appointed to the post of Minister and Secretary of Legation, and an Indian character was generally given to the establishment.

Now there can be no doubt that these measures were all aimed in the right direction. The principle, indeed, that Indian officers were, from their familiarity with Oriental languages and customs, better fitted for political duties in Persia than the home-bred secretaries of the European Legations, had been so universally recognized in former times, that, in the long catalogue of Ministers and Chargés d'Affaires at the Court of Teheran, dating from Malcolm's Mission in 1801 down to the appointment of the Hon. Mr. Murray in 1856, there is no instance to be found (with the solitary exception of Mr. James Morier, the celebrated author of "Hajee Baba") of an officer being placed in charge of our relations with Persia, either temporarily or permanently, who had not enjoyed the advantage of an early training in India. It may also be well understood that the elastic usages of Indian diplomacy—unfettered by strict rule or precedent, and thus permitting a large liberty of action—accord far better than the inexorable traditions of the Foreign Office with the temper and feelings of a Court as irregularly constituted as that of Teheran, where a free interchange of presents, personal tact and address, a nice appreciation of Oriental character, and numberless small matters of language, conduct, and even of dress, unheard of in Europe, are indispensable to the acquisition and retention of influence. But these various considerations were, after all, mere questions of detail. The essential point to be determined in shaping our Persian policy, was whether questions arising between the two Governments were to be viewed from an Eastern or a Western stand-point; whether, in fact, Indian or European interests were to be preferred in the conduct of our relations with the country. If it were once admitted that the geographical position of Persia, in immediate proximity to India, constituted her chief—almost her only—claim on our attention, and that Indian interests must accordingly be the guiding principle of our policy, then it could really signify very little whether the despatches which gave expression to that policy were initiated on one side, or on the other, of the Quadrangle in Downing Street—the so-called rival departments of the State being, it must be remembered, located under the same roof, and in daily harmonious and confidential communication. Such being the real state of the case, divested of all party colouring, it may be doubted, in the first place, if it was worth while in 1859 to disturb the ordinary routine of business, by changing the "personnel" of the Teheran Mission, and placing it in immediate dependence on the Indian Office; but that change having been effected, it was manifestly wrong in the following year to reverse the decision of the Government, and restore the

Mission to the Foreign Office, thereby wounding public sentiment in India, and giving rise to a feeling of antagonism, which has ever since prevailed, to the serious inconvenience of the public service. Since 1860, when Mr. Alison was transferred from the secretaryship of Her Majesty's Embassy at Constantinople to the charge of the Legation at Teheran, the Indian press has discussed the question with a perfect unanimity of feeling, but with an acerbity of expression quite unsuited to the occasion; the most harmless acts of the Persian Government being construed into intentional offences against India, which are only rendered possible because India is unrepresented at the Shah's Court. There is some reason, no doubt, in the complaint of the Viceroy that the substantial interests of India are not unfrequently subordinated to considerations of European diplomacy. There is still more reason in the claim which is put forward that, if India is allowed no voice in the Councils of Teheran, the large subvention, amounting to £12,000 per annum, which is contributed by Indian revenues to the expenses of the Persian Mission, should be abolished or curtailed. This principle, indeed, was distinctly recognised by the Committee of the House of Commons which in 1870 was appointed to inquire into the constitution of the Diplomatic and Consular Services, and which, in regard to Persia, reported as follows :—

"That while they have received conflicting evidence of the highest authority, on either side of the question, your Committee on the whole incline to the opinion that the Persian Mission should be placed under the authority of the Secretary of State for India; but that if the responsible advisers of the Crown decide that such a change is not for the public interest, your Committee recommend that the Members of the Persian Mission generally should be selected by the Secretary of State for Foreign Affairs from Her Majesty's Indian Service, and that the present charge of £12,000 a year on the Indian Revenues for the expense of such Mission should be diminished, so as to throw a larger proportion of the expense upon Imperial revenues."

Although four years have elapsed since this Report was presented to the House of Commons, and although the attention of Parliament has in the interim, on more occasions than one, been drawn to the subject, the suggestions of the Committee have remained as a dead letter to the present day. The Teheran Mission continues to be formed exclusively of gentlemen who belong to Her Majesty's Diplomatic Service and who cannot therefore possess any personal acquaintance with India, while the expenses of the establishment are defrayed almost entirely from Indian revenues, notwithstanding that Persia itself is becoming daily more closely connected with our Indian Empire through the rapid extension of steam and telegraphic communication. It is to be hoped, then, that the question will ere long be again subjected to a very careful scrutiny, and that if it is deemed inexpedient to cancel the present arrangment, which places Persia in official dependence on the Secretary of State for Foreign Affairs and for which perhaps a new and not unimportant plea may be found in the increasing gravity of the Russian question, the recommendations of the Committee, which was presided over by the present Chancellor of the Exchequer, will at any rate be so far accepted as to ensure a certain amount of Indian experience in the "personnel" of the Mission, together with a due regard, in the conduct of our relations with the Court of Teheran, to Indian interests, both financial and political.

To return from this digression, it may now be convenient to consider the local effects in Persia of our thus shifting the responsibility of managing our relations with the Shah from one department of the State to another. As the change in 1859 had been understood at Teheran to indicate a more lively interest on our part in the welfare of Persia, so the return to Foreign Office control in 1860 was interpreted to mean a resumption of the old policy of indifference; and certainly the experience of the next few years immediately following the appointment of Mr. Alison to Teheran, so far from disabusing the Shah of this impression, must have tended rather to confirm it. The distinguishing feature, indeed, of our Persian policy at this period seems to have been a desire to reduce our expenditure to a minimum, and to withdraw as far as possible from all interference with the internal or external affairs of the country. The Shah was prepared, had he met with encouragement from England, to have made a determined stand against further Russian encroachment, and various schemes to this end were discussed by His Majesty's ministers, which however, as they came to nothing, need not be further alluded to. In one instance our excessive caution and perverse economy certainly led to a sacrifice of our true interests. The Shah, dissatisfied with the results of his experiment of employing French and German officers with his troops, and anxious to restore the "prestige" of the Persian army which had sustained a blow from a disastrous encounter with the Turcomans of Merv in the autumn of 1860, would fain have returned to the original system of British instruction and command, under which Persia had first acquired a disciplined force, and which in spite of many drawbacks had on the whole worked well both for British and for Persian interests; but his proposals were never received with much cordiality in Downing Street, and ultimately, on a petty question of account as to the proportion of the officers' allowances to be defrayed respectively by the Indian and Persian treasuries, the whole scheme was wrecked, never perhaps to be revived unless under very much less favourable circumstances.

A further illustration of our determined abstention from interference, which gave considerable offence to Persia—inasmuch as it was held to be inconsistent with our treaty engagements—occurred shortly afterwards on the Afghan frontier, where affairs, which had never settled down since Sultan Ahmed Khan's assumption of the government of Herat, were now rapidly approaching a crisis. The frontier district of Farrah had been recognised as a dependency of Herat, from the time of that state's first becoming independent of Candahar and Cabul, in the old days of the Suddozye monarchy; and it was therefore clearly an act of aggression when in 1856, Dost Mahomed Khan, on the plea of rescuing this outlying district from a malcontent Sirdar of Candahar who was supposed to be in league with the Persians, incorporated it with his own dominions. As soon, indeed, as Sultan Ahmed Khan was confirmed in his own government, he protested against such an alienation of his territory, and although at this early stage of his career he was powerless to act, he kept the recovery of Farrah steadily in view, and ultimately in 1862, took advantage of some local disorders to expel the Cabul garrison, and re-annex the district to Herat. Dost Mahomed Khan instantly took the field against his nephew, and marched in such force to the westward that Persia became seriously alarmed, and made repeated applications to England, both through the Shah's ambassador in London, and through our own minister at Teheran, to avert the troubles which threatened Khorassan from the presence of a large and hostile army of Afghans at Herat. The Shah was naturally disinclined to see the rule at Herat of his voluntary vassal, Sultan Ahmed, exchanged for the vigorous independence of Dost Mahomed Khan ; and he probably therefore magnified the danger of the Cabul advance, in the hope that we should feel ourselves obliged to interfere under the terms of the treaty of Paris ; but Sir John Lawrence had already initiated that policy, which was afterwards characterised as one of "masterly inactivity," and the only response, accordingly, which he returned to the appeal of Persia was to withdraw his agent from the Ameer's camp, whilst in England we cautiously replied that the domestic quarrels of the Afghans could not be held to give any such cause of umbrage to Persia as to call under the treaty for the interposition of our influence or authority. Persia no doubt felt much aggrieved at our thus repudiating responsibility for Dost Mahomed Khan's proceedings, which had already led to the recovery of Farrah and the beleaguerment of Herat; and she would probably have marched an army to the frontier,—which had for some time past been concentrated at Meshed,—in order to protect Khorassan, had not the danger of any further complication been unexpectedly dissipated by the almost simultaneous death of the two Afghan leaders, one immediately before, and the other immediately after the capture of Herat by the Cabul army at the end of May, 1863.

There were not wanting persons at the time who thought

that we committed a grave political error in declining to mediate in 1862-63 between the belligerent forces in Western Afghanistan; and these politicians hold that the subsequent fortunes of Herat have fully confirmed their judgment. No efforts on our part, of course, could have averted the stroke of fate which carried off the redoubtable Dost Mahomed and his nephew within two months of each other in the very crisis of the siege of Herat; but if at an earlier period we had stepped in to arrest the extension of the power of Cabul to the westward, we might have laid the foundation of a strong independent government at the Western Afghan capital, which, remaining under our guarantee in the family of Sultan Ahmed, and supported by us equally against the Eastern Afghans and the Persians, would have constituted a real bulwark of defence to India, instead of offering, as Herat does at present,—owing to the family feuds and intestine troubles which have ever since distracted the province,—the most vulnerable point of attack in the whole line of our north-west frontier, and the one least accessible either to our arms or influence.

7. Another still more notable instance of our do-nothing policy in 1863, which at the time it was difficult to reconcile with the obligations of the Treaty of Paris, and which in its consequences has since involved us in the most serious embarrassment, occurred in connection with the conflicting claims of the Persian and Afghan crowns to the limitary province of Seistan. There is no occasion in this rapid sketch to sift the merits of such claims. It is sufficient to note that, although the Afghan national element had scarcely ever existed in Seistan,— the great majority of the inhabitants being of Persian race and faith, while the remainder were immigrant Belooches,—still the political supremacy of the Afghans, as evidenced by the payment of tribute, had been admitted more or less readily in the province ever since Ahmed Shah established a powerful and independent government in the neighbourhood.

Seistan, in fact, was Persian territory, which had been irregularly attached at different periods to Herat and Candahar, and the recovery of which was always regarded by the Court of Teheran with eager expectancy. At the time of our concluding the Treaty of Paris (March, 1857), the dependency of Seistan was undoubtedly an open question; and as difficulties shortly afterwards supervened between the Persian and Afghan Government, owing to preparations on either side for an invasion of the province, the very case contemplated in the 6th Article of the Treaty seemed to have arisen, in which it became our duty to step forward as mediators, "using our best endeavours to compose such differences in a manner just and honourable to Persia." During the years 1861–63, Persia did indeed repeatedly call on us to interfere under the terms of the Treaty, and endeavour to prevent Afghan aggression on Seistan, to which we merely replied that, as the British Government had never recognised the sovereignty of Persia over the province, they could not oppose the Afghan pretensions; until at length, in November, 1863, being pressed for a definite answer, Lord Russell referred the parties to the arbitrament of the sword, stating that "Her Majesty's Government, being informed that the title to the territory of Seistan is disputed between Persia and Afghanistan, must decline to interfere in the matter, and must leave it to both parties to make good their possession by force of arms."

Surprise has been often expressed by Indian writers at our having thus ignored our duty as mediators under the Treaty of Paris; and it has been further remarked as a serious blot on our home diplomacy that, while we accorded full liberty of action to one of the belligerent parties, we took no steps to notify the arrangement to the other; but in explanation of our apparent inconsistency, it must be remembered that not only had we at this time contracted no treaty obligations towards Cabul, nor obtained any right of interference in its affairs, but that, on the contrary, after the death of Dost Mahomed, in June, 1863, we had studiously held aloof from Afghan politics, neither recognising Shír Ali's right of succession, nor giving him any support whatever in fighting his way to power. To have accepted the office of mediators in regard to Seistan affairs on the requisition of Persia, according to the terms of the Treaty of Paris, would have involved the necessity of upholding Shír Ali's power from the commencement of his career, which was entirely opposed to Sir J. Lawrence's declared policy of "masterly inactivity." But on the other hand it should be noted that if we had thus mediated in Seistan in 1864—as we afterwards mediated in 1872—we should have obtained far better terms for the Afghans, and indirectly for ourselves. Persia, indeed, had not then undertaken any such systematic incorporation of the Seistan territory in her own dominions, as afterwards enabled her to assert a right of possession as far as the left bank of the Helmund, and the Arbitration Commissioners would thus have had a "tabula rasa" for their delimitation of frontier. In respect also to our Afghan relations, so far from regarding the recognition and support of Shír Ali in 1863 as premature and inexpedient, many are inclined to think that it would have been sound policy; inasmuch as it would have saved us from much local trouble and disorder, as well as from certain direct evils, the effects of which are yet apparent in the distrust of us that has ever since, with greater or less activity, rankled in the Ameer's breast, and more especially in the false but dangerous reputation still attaching to Abdur-Rahman Khan from his brief ascendency at Cabul, for which our excessive caution at this period is mainly responsible.

Persia was, no doubt, much disappointed at receiving our final answer declining to put any pressure on the Afghans, and the more so as she was not prepared to accept the alternative of immediate action. Nevertheless, from this time forward, secured against any further remonstrance upon our part, she did steadily pursue her policy of establishing a paramount position in Seistan; until, partly by arms, partly by conciliation, and partly by intrigue, she had brought all the Persian inhabitants of the province completely under her control, and had even tampered to a considerable extent with the Afghan allegiance of the Belooches. At length, in 1870, Shír Ali Khan, being firmly established in power at Cabul, began to look seriously to the vindication of his interests in Seistan; and Lord Clarendon believing from the language held on either side that war was imminent between the Persians and Afghans, proposed that arbitration under the 6th Article of the Treaty of Paris, which ought to have been proposed

CH. II.] OUR POLITICAL RELATIONS WITH PERSIA. 105

seven years before, and which, had it then been carried out, would have probably given half of Seistan Proper to the Afghans.

8. About this period, 1863, the first considerable breach was effected in that crust of exclusiveness which had hitherto isolated Persia from all contact with European civilization, the pioneer of progress in this instance being the electric telegraph, for which Persia was mainly indebted to the enterprise and encouragement of England; though, to say the truth, we are not entitled to any particular credit for conferring the boon upon Persia, since the circumstances which led to the introduction of the telegraph into the country were the result of accident rather than design, and referred, moreover, especially to our own national interests. The history of the affair may be thus briefly described. Turkey, which was far in advance of Persia in the adoption of the useful arts and sciences of Europe, had proposed,—as early as the year 1859-60, and for her own purposes of rapid communication with her outlying dependencies,—to lay down a telegraphic wire from Constantinople, through Asia Minor and Mesopotamia, to Baghdad; provided that we would undertake to continue the line from the latter place to India, so as to give a fair prospect of remunerative return on the initial outlay; and as we were at the time smarting under the disappointment of our first submarine cable in the Red Sea having completely failed, we gladly fell in with a scheme which thus seemed to promise us a continuous telegraphic communication between London and Bombay, at no great expense and with the least possible responsibility. Some years were consumed in the negociations, preliminary surveys, and other measures of preparation, that were required to give effect to our arrangement with the Porte; so that it was not till the year 1863 that our Overland Telegraphic Convention was finally concluded at Constantinople; and, in the meantime, we had come to the conclusion, that however easy it might be to lay down and maintain a submarine cable between our Indian telegraphic terminus at Karrachí, and the head of the Persian Gulf, there would still always be a certain risk and inconvenience in keeping up,—either in our own hands or in those of

the Turks,—the direct line of communication between that point and Baghdad, owing to the pestilential climate of the marshes of the Lower Euphrates, and the lawless habits of the Arab tribes which encamp upon the river's banks. Of so formidable and persistent a character indeed were these evils represented to be, that it was judged indispensable to the successful working of the telegraph between Europe and India to provide an alternative line through Persia, by which the Arab country might, if necessary, be entirely avoided. Hence arose the necessity of opening negociations with the Persian Government, for the construction by our officers of a circuitous line, conducting from the Baghdad frontier, by the populous cities of Kermanshah, Hamadan, Teheran, Ispahan, and Shiraz, to Bushire, on the sea coast. When this scheme was first proposed, it encountered a strenuous resistance on the part of the reactionary party at Court, who denounced it as opposed to the interests of the country, in conceding too much power to a foreign Government; but the terms were, nevertheless, finally accepted by the Shah in 1863, and embodied in a formal Telegraphic Convention, which Convention—having been recently renewed, with some slight modifications rendered necessary by the altered circumstances of the case—is, in fact, in operation at the present day; not, indeed, for the original purpose of supplementing the Turkish line,—which now follows its natural direction from Baghdad to Bussorah, secured by the payment of black-mail from interruption by the Arab chiefs,—but as a main link in the great Indo-European telegraphic system which connects the East and West, through the Persian, Russian, and German Empires. A good deal of jealousy was, as I have said, manifested on the first proposal to surrender into the hands of foreigners a great national industry like the telegraph; but the terms which we offered for the concession were so very advantageous,—being equivalent to the payment of a royalty of over £10,000 a year for the right of transit, together with a free wire for local use, and the ultimate reversion of the entire property,*—that Persian pride was silenced;

* The principle upon which our first Telegraphic Convention with Persia was negociated was simply this, that the line should be constructed by Eng-

and after a short experience, there has been quite a revulsion of popular feeling in favour of the telegraph, which is now appreciated, not merely as a convenience, but almost as a public blessing. There can, indeed, be no doubt, that Persia has derived the greatest benefit from the establishment on her territory of the Indo-European Telegraph, partly from the large expenditure of foreign money connected with the first construction and maintenance of the line, but more essentially, because it has awakened her from the sleep of ages, and brought her into contact with the activity of modern Europe. It is now acknowledged to have been mainly owing to the city of Teheran being placed in direct telegraphic communication with the other capitals of the East and West, that a desire has been created among the Persians for a closer intercourse with Europeans, and that a path has been thus opened for the development of the resources of the country, through the application of European industry, enterprise, and skill.

Nor has England failed to obtain her fair share of the advantages of the undertaking. Economists may think, since the successful laying of the Red Sea Cable, that the possession of an alternative land line is dearly purchased at an annual outlay of about £20,000, at which the expense to us of the Persian line has been approximately assessed; but, on the other hand, there can be no doubt that the free circulation of our officers through the country, in connection with the service of the telegraph, has gone far to restore that influence which the British Government and nation formerly enjoyed in Persia, but which of late we have so much neglected; while at the same time, under the able tuition of such leaders as Patrick Stewart, Sir Fred. Goldsmid, and Major Bateman Champain, a school of young Engineer officers has been formed, who worthily replace the old "British Detachment,"*

land at the expense of Persia to whom we should pay a maximum of 30,000 tomans (about £12,000) a year as the cost of our messages. In the New Convention the yearly amount payable to Persia from revenue is reduced to 12,000 tomans (or about £5,000), while she pays a small contribution to the working expenses. She owes us at present about £50,000 for cost of construction. See Abstract of Conventions in Markham's "Persia," p. 542.

* Four officers, who subsequently rose to high diplomatic office in

and who, being thoroughly familiar with the language and usages of the country, are thus available for those delicate and important political duties which from time to time arise in the East, and for which Indian experience alone is hardly a sufficient qualification.

9. The telegraph, by uniting the Governments of England and Persia in a bond of common interest, helped to mitigate that feeling of soreness on the part of the Shah which had first arisen in the events connected with the war, and had since been kept alive by the indifference we had shown to his applications for assistance and advice. If due and timely advantage had been taken of this improved state of feeling, important results might have ensued, but the Shah was not particularly well served at the period in question. Since the removal, indeed, of the Sadr Azem in 1858, shortly after Mr. Murray's retirement, no individual minister had been allowed on his own responsibility to direct the counsels of the State, nor was there any officer of distinguished ability in power at Teheran. It thus happened that, although in obedience to the impulse given by the successful working of the telegraph, there was certainly a disposition to set other similar enterprises on foot, and various schemes, in which the Shah took a strong personal interest, were thus discussed for attracting British capital to the country, and for establishing under British auspices railways and tramroads, and even a national Bank, still no immediate result was arrived at, nor indeed did the plans of the friends of progress yield any fruit whatever until after a further period of ten years' incubation.

Amongst the schemes which were now considered for strengthening Persia the Shah proposed to purchase two or three steamers, which, being manned by Indian or Arab crews, and being placed under English naval officers, should look after the police of the Gulf in so far, at any rate, as regarded the Persian waters; but His Majesty received no encouragement from us in this respect, as we knew that Persia cherished ambitious

Persia, belonged to this original "British Detachment," namely, Sir Justin Sheil, Colonel Farrant, Major D'Arcy Todd and Sir Henry Rawlinson. See ante, page 49.

designs upon the Island of Bahrein and other independent Arab States, with which we had concluded treaties of friendship; and we foresaw that the presence of a Persian naval force in a sea which was already frequented by the vessels of so many rival powers would be an element of disturbance rather than of order. A misunderstanding, indeed, occurred shortly afterwards between the British and Persian authorities in regard to the possession of the island of Bahrein, which, if there had been any of the Shah's vessels on the spot, might have led to a collision. Persia had, in reality, no right of sovereignty whatever over Bahrein, her last occupation of the island dating from the time of the Suffaveans, but she had nevertheless, with her usual lust for territorial aggrandisement, on several occasions put forward this antiquated pretension: and in 1867 she went so far as to encourage a revolution in the island, adopting one of the claimants to the chiefship as her vassal, and authorising him to hoist the Persian flag in token of his dependency. This intruder, whom we denounced as a pirate, was blockaded in the first instance by our fleet, his correspondence with Persia was intercepted, and he was ultimately driven by force from the island, the supreme authority being restored to his rival, whom we had supported from the commencement. The Persians were naturally mortified at a result which demolished, at one fell swoop, their new-born maritime aspirations, and protested warmly against our high-handed proceedings, complaining especially of our having established a blockade of the island without any warning, of our having intercepted a missive of the Shah's addressed to one whom he considered his subject, and finally, of our having cannonaded a fort over which the Persian flag was flying. Unfortunately, the Imperial and Indian Governments regarded this affair in somewhat different lights. In India it was thought that any concession to Persia would injure our prestige with the Arabs, and lead to serious troubles in the Gulf; whereas the Foreign Office, underrating the local question, and desiring rather to conciliate the Shah, who was said to consider himself personally affronted by the seizure of his letter, would have admitted that the blockade and armed attack had been somewhat precipitate, and have made the " amende " accordingly. Ultimately a sort of compromise was effected between the two departments of the State by our maintaining the absolute independence of Bahrein, whilst at the same time we promised, that in the event of hostile proceedings being again undertaken against the island, due notice of our intentions should be given to Teheran. I am not aware that any inconvenience has resulted, or is likely to result, from this act of diplomatic courtesy to an old ally. Persia is so entirely innocuous as a maritime power that it is impossible for us to feel any jealousy of her, however extravagant her pretensions; and it was manifestly not worth while to continue an irritating correspondence between the two Governments on a mere empty point of honour.

10. Among other beneficial effects of the telegraph may be noticed the employment of our arbitration to adjust territorial differences between the Shah and his Eastern neighbours. In the course of the negociations which our officers were obliged to carry on, both with the Court of Teheran and with the local chiefs—with a view to obtaining a right of way through the districts along the coasts from the Indus to the Persian Gulf —for an aerial wire, to be used as an alternative line to the parallel submarine cable, it had been ascertained that although Persia was admitted to be bounded geographically by the Indian Ocean, still the Shah in practice possessed little authority over the littoral tribes from the island of Kishm to the eastward. Bunder-Abbas, indeed, and the adjacent territory of Mináb, as far as Cape Jask at the entrance of the Gulf; which formed the ancient kingdom of Ormuz, had been leased with very few interruptions for the last fifty years to the Imám of Muscat, while the ports of Gwader and Charbar, the only important settlements along the southern coast beyond the Gulf, were held by independent Arab chiefs who, although located respectively on Belooch and Persian soil, repudiated all connection with either Government.

When the attention of Persia was drawn to so anomalous a condition of affairs in territory which she claimed as her own, and especially when she became alive to the uncertainty of the border line between her territories and those of the

Khan of Kelat, she seems to have required her frontier officers at once to assert and extend their authority. About this time, at any rate, began a sustained series of encroachments on the part of Ibrahim Khan of Bumpoor, which provoked the active opposition of the Khan of Kelat, and which would inevitably have ended in hostilities between the Persians and Belooches, had we not, after some hesitation, intervened to keep the peace. Our remonstrances at Teheran led, in the first instance, to the deputation of officers to examine and report upon the disputed line of frontier; and, ultimately, it was arranged that General Goldsmid, who had served for a long period in Persia, in charge of the Telegraphic Establishment, and had acquired the full confidence of the Government, should mediate between the Persians and Belooches, laying down on the map a line of frontier between their respective territories, such as was admitted at the time in the country and proposing the same for official recognition at Teheran and Kelat. Persia has too often complained on similar occasions that the Indian authorities treat her as their natural enemy and identify their own interests with the parties which she is opposing. Why, she asks, should we support the Belooches against her? Why should we desire to have a barbarous and intensely jealous state—indisposed to commerce and torn by domestic faction—like Kelat, in immediate proximity to our possessions in Scinde, rather than a responsible and friendly Government like Persia? No doubt the Indian authorities act under the instinctive feeling, that in keeping Persia at arms' length and encouraging the growth of intermediate States, they are protecting their frontier in reality against the approaches of Russia, which is the phantom that looms in the distance; but this is an argument that we cannot expect Persia to admit or even to comprehend, and we must be content therefore to remain under the imputation of an unworthy prejudice. In this instance, however, Persia had certainly nothing to complain of. General Goldsmid experienced considerable difficulty in carrying out his mediatory office in Mekran, being impeded both by the jealousy of the border chiefs, and more especially by the guile and perversity of the Persian Commissioner, who was associated with him in his duties; but ultimately he succeeded, with the help of his very efficient Engineer Staff, in laying down as proposed, a provisional frontier line drawn from the sea coast in the Bay of Gwetter as far north as Jalk in 27° 30' north latitude; and that this suggested settlement of territorial claims, which followed as far as practicable the status of occupation or tributary dependency, was not unfavourable to Persia, may be inferred from the fact that, with the exception of one quasi-neutral district the allotment of which was reserved for subsequent adjustment, the Shah at once accepted the distribution proposed in the British programme, which indeed advanced the frontier of Persia two degrees to the eastward, beyond the point that was laid down in the Russian War Office map, published simultaneously with the British survey, as her furthest legitimate limit. The reserved district of Kohek which, although sometimes paying tribute to Kelat, was apparently within the geographical limits of Persia, was also in the sequel virtually abandoned to the Shah, inasmuch as the Kelat frontier line was drawn to the east of it—while the Kerman authorities further proceeded to realize their rights over Charbar which was to the west of the frontier line, by expelling the Arab colony and substituting a Persian garrison, so that real substantial benefits accrued to Persia from our intervention, without any injury being caused, as far as can be seen, to the political interests of India.

11. By an easy transition, mediation in Mekran, on which we entered merely in our capacity of peace-makers, led to an arbitration in Seistan, where interference was more pressingly demanded by our obligations under the Treaty of Paris. The Foreign Office, indeed, had long since become aware that an error had been committed in 1863, in declaring the Shah to be at liberty to make good his claims upon Seistan by force of arms; and when, accordingly, in 1870, a further appeal to us was made to interpose our good offices, in order to prevent actual collision between the Persians and Afghans on the lower Helmund, Lord Clarendon no longer hesitated to accept the responsibility. General Goldsmid was again selected for the arduous task of composing frontier differences, and again he

was subjected in the execution of his duty to every sort of hindrance and annoyance by the intolerable duplicity of his Persian colleague. On this occasion, too, the difficulties of his mission were much aggravated by the conflicting nature of the conditions which were to regulate his decisions, "present possession" being balanced against "ancient right," and a further source of embarrassment being created by the claim which Persia advanced to exclude from arbitration all rights acquired under the operation of Lord Russell's famous letter of 1863. Under such very discouraging circumstances it is greatly to General Goldsmid's credit that he so far succeeded in his mission as to obtain, by a diligent and careful scrutiny of evidence, a reliable account of the gradual extension of the power of Persia over the province, and that he was also enabled, through the active exertions of the same engineer officers, Majors St. John and Lovett, who had so admirably seconded his efforts in Mekran, to bring away with him a good topographical sketch of the disputed territory for discussion and adjudication at Tcheran. It was quite impossible to attempt any local adjustment. The Afghan commissioner, who, in company with General Pollock, joined General Goldsmid in Seistan, was to the full as impracticable on all essential points as his Persian colleague, and as the Indian Government cordially supported Shír Ali Khan in his resistance to any Persian encroachment up the Helmund, while the Shah maintained that it was only in this direction his claims were open to contention—all the territory to the westward being already incorporated with Persia—the prospects of the arbitration looked sufficiently hopeless. When General Goldsmid, indeed, in the autumn of 1872, after a full and fair discussion, delivered his arbitral judgment at Teheran, both parties entered formal protests against the decision. Persia insisted on being allowed to occupy the lands on the left bank of the Helmund, as high up as Rudbár, with a view, firstly, to holding the predatory Belooch tribes in check, who would otherwise have free access to Seistan proper from the desert; and secondly, in order to guard against the abstraction of the river water by canals running to the south, which would starve, if it did not altogether stop, the irrigation of the lower lands con-

I

tiguous to the lake; while on the other hand the Ameer of Cabul complained that all the cultivated land of the province,—the region which would alone repay the cost of administration, and which alone was properly named Seistan,—was removed from his jurisdiction and assigned over to chiefs who kept a considerable force under arms ready at any moment to invade the Afghan territory. General Goldsmid's scheme of partition, which followed the status of recent, if not of actual, possession, was twofold. He assigned to the Afghans in the first place the right bank of the river throughout its course to its embouchure in the northern reedy portion of the lake, thus definitely giving them not only Farrah, Lásh and Jowain, but also Chakánsúr and the lands on the Khásh-rúd, together with several posts quite lately established by the Persians on the Helmund, such as Nad-ali, Keleh-Fath, &c.; and in the second place he confirmed the Afghans in possession of the left bank of the river as far down as the Bend-i-Kohek, where the Helmund turns to the north, and the great irrigating canals come off and carry fertilising streams to the south-west and west; but at this point he drew an arbitrary line to some distant peak in the desert to the south, thus legalising and confirming the hold of Persia over the entire productive plain of Seistan proper, as constituted by the present hydrography of the province. As far as revenue and population were concerned, Persia had no doubt by far the best of the bargain, but the Shah nevertheless resented deeply the curtailment of his jurisdiction up the left bank of the Helmund; and although under great pressure, which, owing to a change of Ministry, we were fortunately able at the moment to exert at Teheran, he did at length formally accept the arbitration, he at the same time reserved his right of appeal to Lord Granville, and during his visit to England he thus made the most strenuous efforts to obtain a modification of the terms of settlement. Any such modification, however, which, in consequence of the deep personal interest manifested by the Shah, who considered his honour pledged to protect the Belooch chiefs residing between Kohek and Rúdbár, we might have been disposed to concede, was rendered absolutely impossible by the critical state of our relations with Shír Ali Khan, who evidently thought that his interests had been sacrificed, and only accepted our terms with the utmost reluctance, notwithstanding that they were accompanied with the offer of a large compensatory money grant, and other conditions of substantial value. Without entering on any elaborate examination of this much-vexed Seistan question, I must now be allowed to make a few general observations on its political bearings. It must be borne in mind, then, that we were ourselves responsible to a great extent for the complications which had supervened since 1863,* and had thus no right to complain if we were forced at last to purchase Shír Ali's acquiescence in our proposed pacification; but in real truth it may be questioned if the Cabul Ameer and the Indian Viceroy have not throughout attached an exaggerated importance to Seistan. Though possessing great natural advantages, the province is in its present aspect a wretchedly unhealthy country, only habitable for a few months in the year, and hardly worth the expense of governing; while in regard to its strategical value, which is the point of view that has been chiefly regarded in India, great misapprehension prevails. So far from Seistan being, as has been so often stated, a convenient base for aggression upon India from the westward, it is in every respect inferior to Herat for that purpose. To the south and south-east it is bounded by an impassable desert; while to the east it possesses one single line of communication along the Helmund, contracted and ill-supplied, and exposed to a flank attack from the northward throughout its whole extent, from Seistan to Candahar. Supposing, indeed, the Afghans to be in strength at Herat, Farrah, and Zamir-Dáwer, it would be quite impossible for a Persian army to march along the Helmund from Seistan to Girishk. The only military value of Seistan consists in its abundant supply of camels for carriage, and these animals are for the most part in the hands of the Belooches, who are Afghan and not Persian dependents, and who might thus be available for our own purposes, though hardly for those of our enemies.

* That is since the date on which Lord Russell had sanctioned an appeal to arms on the part of the Persians and Afghans "to make good their possession" of Seistan.

The object of our recent interference was good, not only in fulfilling a treaty obligation, but in aiming at the prevention of an effusion of blood, and the avoidance of serious frontier complications; and it must be further admitted that General Goldsmid's arbitration was as fair and as practical as was possible under the circumstances. Indeed it would seem that, tied as he was by definite conditions of procedure, no other course was open to him than that which he adopted; but at the same time it is impossible to avoid seeing that there is not one element of permanence in the recorded terms of settlement. The allegiance, for instance, of the Belooches will depend, not on our declared distribution of frontier districts, but on the view taken by the tribes of their own interests; while the proposed line of demarcation between Persian and Afghan territory south of the Helmund, being arbitrary, and, so-to-speak, imaginary, can never be practically observed; and, finally, it must occur to every student of political geography that the refilling of the old or western bed of the Helmund, which the river only left forty years ago,* and to which it may at any moment return, would alter the whole hydrography of the province, and annihilate those distinctive physical features on which the recent arbitration was based.

12. It now remains to consider the general position of affairs at Teheran during the last few years, and the present state of our relations with the government of the Shah. The influence of personal character upon public policy is nowhere more conspicuous than in the East. At Constantinople and Teheran, the gravest European questions have been too often determined, not on a fair consideration of the interests of the country, but rather according to the private predilections of the responsible minister of the day. Our war with Persia, indeed, was notoriously due, in a great measure, to the malevolence of the individual who then exercised the functions of Grand Vizier, and although no minister was appointed to succeed to that position

* Captain Edward Conolly, who visited Seistan on his return from Herat in 1839, has minutely described this change of the course of the Helmund in his "Sketch of the Physical Geography of Seistan." See Journal of Asiatic Society of Bengal. Vol. IX, Part II. p. 715.

of supreme authority, where he might again imperil the national fortunes in pursuit of his own schemes of ambition or revenge, still we have had abundant reason to complain of the bias of the Minister for Foreign Affairs, who, until lately, has been the channel of our official communications with the Shah, and who throughout his long, and not undistinguished, career has done his best on all occasions to disparage England and English interests. It is believed to have been owing to his influence at Court that the advances of Russia in Central Asia, which took a definite form after the Crimean war, and which in reality compromised to a large extent the security of Persia, were nevertheless regarded at Teheran with an indulgent, if not a favourable, eye. This minister, indeed, is said to have congratulated his sovereign on the humiliation by the arms of Russia of Persia's hereditary enemies, the Uzbegs of Khiva and Bokhara, and to have encouraged similar operations against the Turcomans. It was not, at any rate, until the aggressive movements of Russia threatened the tribes upon the immediate frontier of Persia, over whom the Shah claimed to exercise jurisdiction, that any feeling of suspicion or uneasiness was created at Teheran. Then arose a discussion which is of some importance to British interests, and which thus deserves more than a passing notice. When Russia landed her first detachment of troops in 1869, at Krasnovodsk, on the eastern shore of the Caspian, with the avowed object of crossing the desert to Khiva, Persia raised a protest against what she ventured to call a violation of territory, claiming the Bay of Balkán and Island of Cherekan as Persian soil, and she even invited the British government to support her reclamation; but no practical result ensued. Russia merely stated in reply, that as the Shah had no real authority over the Turcomans to the north of the Atrek, he was precluded from interfering with the projected movements, which were, however, directed to the improvement of commerce rather than to territorial conquest, and which, in so far as they repressed brigandage and promoted order on the frontier, would tend to the consolidation of His Majesty's authority. There was no formal convention, either at this time or afterwards, between the two governments on the subject of the frontier; but as Persia omitted to put in a demurrer to the claim, which, in 1869, Russia indirectly advanced to the sea board as far south as the mouth of the Atrek, her right to contest that claim at a future period may be considered to have lapsed. And such, indeed, seems to have been the practical upshot of the discussion, for Russia was no sooner settled at Krasnovodsk, than she began at once to exercise authority over all the country north of the Atrek, and the Governor of Astrabad was notified in due course from Teheran that he was to confine his jurisdiction to the southern bank of the river. It does not appear that Lord Clarendon took any notice of Persia's appeal, in 1869, to support her resistance to the Russian encroachment, notwithstanding that the officer in charge of the Teheran Mission had, with much sagacity, drawn particular attention to the serious interests involved in the question;* pointing out that the passage across the desert from Krasnovodsk to Khiva was, from want of water, quite impracticable, either to troops or caravans, and that if Russia therefore was resolved to penetrate into Central Asia from the Caspian, she would have no alternative but to move down in the first place to the mouth of the Atrek, establishing a post in that vicinity as her starting point, and following up the valley of the river in her subsequent march along the northern border of Khorassan, to the vicinity of Merv, from whence she would command the routes leading respectively to Bokhara and Herat. This forecast was soon afterwards verified in a remarkable manner; one of the first operations of the Russians, after disembarking on the eastern shore of the Caspian, being to found a military post at Chikishlar, near the mouth of the Atrek, from which point, both before and during the Khiva expedition, columns of attack and reconnoissance were repeatedly marched into the interior; while the official maps which were issued to embody the results of the Russian topographical surveys, claimed from this time onward the course of the main stream of the Atrek as the recognised national frontier. Persia, it is true, on more

* See Mr. Ronald Thomson's letter to Lord Clarendon, dated Teheran, November 14, 1869, in the Parliamentary Return : "Correspondence respecting Central Asia." No. II. 1873, page 20.

occasions than one, has repudiated a line of demarcation for which no authority, or semblance of authority, exists, and which, amongst other fatal results, would bring the Russians into the pleasant valley of Monah, in the immediate vicinity of Boojnoord; but it is to be feared that the "Atrek frontier" may, by force of iteration, become, like the cession of Ashoor-ada, an accepted point of history, Persia having no power to right herself, and English interests being hardly engaged at all in the dispute;* inasmuch as the route beyond the frontier claimed by Persia, that is, along "the Attock," or northern skirts of the hills which bound the Atrek valley,—by the line of the Turcoman forts of Kizil-arvat, Kahríz, and Ashkabád,—is actually more convenient for the march of an army from the Caspian to Merv than the parallel line, 30 or 40 miles to the south, which clings to the main stream of the river in Persian territory, and leads through a comparative desert till it reaches the rich Monah valley. But whichever may be the best line of advance from the Caspian, England has always viewed any movements of Russia in this quarter with suspicion. It may have been necessary, she admits, to adopt coercive measures against Bokhara and Khiva, in vindication of commercial or political rights; but she cannot recognise any such necessity for interference with the Turcoman tribes, and least of all with the Tekéhs, who, however ready to resist invasion, or however prone to brigandage on the Persian frontier, are entirely removed at present from all contact with Russian military posts, or with Russian lines of commerce, and afford therefore no legitimate

* It is now reported, as these sheets are passing though the press, that Russia is preparing to claim the sea coast of the Caspian as far south as the mouth of the Kara-Su, in the Bay of Asterabád; and Veniukoff certainly, many years ago, insisted on the right of Russia to this frontier; but Persia will undoubtedly protest against any such encroachment, should it be seriously proposed, as it would be equivalent to the surrender of Asterabád; and we could hardly remain indifferent to so menacing a movement. This reported extension, indeed, of the Russian frontier to the south is the more significant, as it is further stated that the new military Trans-Caspian Government, of which Krasnovodsk is to form the head quarters, is to exercise jurisdiction as far east as Kahríz or Ashkabad, thus intruding into the heart of the Tekéh Turcoman country, and almost necessitating, for the maintenance of order, an advance, at no distant time, to the camping ground of the tribes at Merv.

pretext for hostilities. Russia may, of course, discover such a pretext, by sending an experimental caravan through the country, which would assuredly be attacked and plundered, or by assisting the Khan of Khiva to levy a war contribution on the outlying nomades, which would in all probability be opposed; but the intention to provoke a contest would, under such circumstances, be so obvious, that we should be obliged to look to an ulterior political motive; and such a motive would at once suggest itself, if we considered that the route through the Turcoman country conducted to the important strategical position of Merv, which, being occupied in strength by Russia, would exert a very powerful pressure, not only on Afghanistan, but on India.

It may thus be well understood that the persistent rumours of an intended expedition against the Turcomans of the Attock, which have circulated ever since the conquest of Khiva, and which, although now suspended, on the distinct and pacific assurances of Russia, may at any moment be revived, have attracted considerable attention in England, and the more so as there is reason to believe that Persia, whose interests are seriously compromised by the lawless proceedings of the Tekéh tribes, would be not unwilling to assist in their coercion. That England feels any real alarm on this score, or that she regards the occupation of Merv by the Russians as a vulnerable point in her Indian armour, is hardly a correct statement of the case. What she does foresee is this, that if Russia, not content with her possession of the Khanates, should still further disturb the equilibrium of the East, by absorbing the Turcomans of the Attock and re-establishing a great capital at Merv,* England

* The natural advantages of Merv are so great—situated as it is in an oasis of surpassing fertility, and possessing an unlimited supply of water—that it would necessarily soon attract a large population, if security were only afforded of life and property; while its geographical position at a point where the high road from Khiva to Herat crosses the high road from Persia to Bokhara, gives it a strategical value, superior probably to that of any other city between the Caspian and the Indus, and points it out moreover as the great commercial emporium of the future for all Central Asia. At the time of the invasion of Chenghiz Khan, Merv was the chief city of Khorassan, and was popularly supposed to contain one million of inhabitants. The present town, which is twelve miles to the west of the ancient city, is only occupied by the Turcomans for a few months in the

would in all probability be compelled to meet the requisition for support of her ally, the Ameer of Cabul, by furnishing auxiliary garrisons for Candahar and Herat, a measure that would entail a heavy expenditure on the revenues of India, and would not improbably lead to eventual collision between the two great European powers, both in the East and West.

The possibility of so grave a crisis has undoubtedly occupied the thoughts of our statesmen during recent discussions, deeply affecting, as it does, our Indian interests, and lending exceptional importance to the character of our present relations with Persia. It was in 1871 that an administrative change was effected at Teheran, from which great results were anticipated, though they have hardly yet been realised. His Majesty the Shah, disappointed with the meaningless, and often retrograde, proceedings of a Council of State presided over by a mere departmental minister, and anxious to inaugurate a distinctly progressive policy, resolved once more to appoint a Grand Vizier, or "Sadr Azem," who should be invested with a general control over all branches of the administration; and for this purpose he selected an individual who was probably the most competent, the most enlightened, and the most trustworthy public officer in his dominions. Endowed by nature with an intellect of a very high order, which had received a more careful cultivation than often falls to the lot of an Oriental, and fortified by a large and varied experience, Mirza Hussein Khan entered upon office under peculiarly advantageous circumstances. He had been bred up indeed from infancy in official circles, his father having been a minister of Mahomed Shah's, and he had served his noviciate abroad, partly in Teflis and partly in Bombay, after which he filled for twelve years the responsible post of Persian Minister at Constantinople. On being called by his sovereign in 1871 to the supreme direction of affairs, he did not scruple to avow a belief, from which he has never since swerved, that while it was necessary for the national safety to fulfil with the utmost

year at the period of harvest, and does not contain more than a hundred squalid huts. For a good description of the place in 1840, when it belonged to Khiva, see Abbott's "Journey from Herat to Khiva," Vol. I. Chap. 3.

strictness all treaty obligations towards Russia and to cultivate generally the most friendly relations with that power, still the confidence of Persia should be reserved for England. At the time of his accession to power there were several small matters at issue between the two governments, which occasioned friction, and which might, under less careful manipulation, have been swollen into substantial grievances. The understanding, for instance, which had been arrived at between the Viceroy of India and the Ameer of Cabul at the famous Amballah Conference in 1869, had been magnified, according to popular rumour, into an offensive and defensive alliance which boded ill to peaceful neighbours; and Persia, always jealous and distrustful of our Afghan alliance, was thus disposed, until explanations were given, to take offence at what seemed an attitude of defiance. On her opposite frontier, where chronic disorder prevailed, she also complained of the preference shown by our officers to the Turks when called on to mediate in border quarrels. The special points again, which were reserved in the Mekran and Seistan arbitrations, referring to the dependency of Kohek in the one settlement and the allegiance of the Belooches below Rúdbár in the other, caused perhaps more irritation at Teheran than the general pacification had produced content. Finally, Bahrein was not forgotten, and fresh causes of dispute had arisen, both at Bushire and Charbar. In each and all of these matters the conciliatory influence of the Grand Vizier was exerted with marked, if not immediate, effect; and the improved state of our relations at Teheran thus paved the way to what he intended as the crowning point of his political programme.

13. This programme, which was aimed at the regeneration of Persia, through the identification of her interest with those of Great Britain, embraced two leading features; the one was the Reuter concession; the other was the Shah's visit to England; and each of these subjects it may be now convenient to consider in some detail. It has been already stated that immediately after the construction of the telegraph, various plans were discussed at Teheran for extending the field of enterprise and inviting the participation of European skill and

industry and the employment of European capital. Some of these plans were no doubt sound and honest, but the greater part were put forward by adventurers and speculators, who commanded no confidence, and whose specious offers rather distracted than aided the government. It is asserted, indeed, that it was mainly to escape the risk and turmoil of conflicting schemes and adverse interests, that ultimately, after a very mature consideration, it was determined to confide to the hands of a single company, presided over by Baron Julius de Reuter,* a naturalized British subject, the complete and exclusive control of the whole industrial resources of the empire for a period of 70 years. This gigantic monopoly, at which Europe stood aghast, comprised the following items: the construction of a railway from the Caspian to the Persian Gulf, with any number of subsidiary branches; the laying down of tramways throughout the kingdom; the exclusive working of all the Persian mines, excepting those of gold and silver; the introduction of works of irrigation on whatever scale was deemed expedient; the establishment of a national bank; the issue of a loan of six millions sterling, with a Persian guarantee of 5 per cent. interest, and 2 per cent. sinking fund; together with a right to initiate all remunerative public works, such as lighting with gas, paving and embellishing the capital; making roads, bridges, and embankments; postal and telegraphic extensions; mills, factories, and workshops, &c., and finally a farm of the entire customs of the empire for a period of 25 years. The Grand Vizier, who, with his confidential adviser, Mirza Malcom Khan, now minister in England, was responsible for this extraordinary delegation of Imperial powers to the hands of a private company, no doubt considered that he had sufficiently protected the interest of the Persian Crown, by providing that 20 per cent. of the net profits of the Railway and 15 per cent. of all other net profits should accrue to the government; while in respect to the customs, he had stipulated that the

* This concession, of which an abstract will be found in the Appendix No. V., was granted to Baron Reuter in his individual capacity, but the company he was empowed to form is mentioned in many of the articles as identical with the "Concessionaire."

aggregate proceeds of the present time should be augmented for 5 years by an annual fixed sum of £20,000, and during the remainder of the term by a transfer to the Shah of 60 per cent. of the difference between the present farm and the actual proceeds. He did not apparently regard the concentration of power in the hands of a single individual as objectionable or dangerous, because the concessionary had the right, which he would certainly exercise, of transferring any portion of his privileges with their attendant obligations to other parties, and because the directors and shareholders of the company, or companies, which would thus be formed and their executive officers would be principally of British nationality, which it was the especial desire of the Prime Minister to identify with Persia and Persian interests. There was something grand, something heroic in the idea of sacrificing national pride—almost national independence—to the eventual resuscitation of a fallen country, but the scheme was hardly practical. There can be no doubt that the Grand Vizier was thoroughly honest and in earnest in granting the Reuter concession. He believed that he was advancing the true interests both of Persia and of England, and he expected our countenance and support. What he failed to understand was the enormous political difficulty of realizing so vast a scheme. He miscalculated the serious character of Russia's opposition; he miscalculated the extent of England's indifference, and above all, he failed to appreciate the determined—the almost indignant—resistance of his own countrymen.

While the Reuter concession was still the theme of general wonder and interest, His Majesty the Shah put in execution his long-cherished object of visiting the European capitals. He was accompanied by the Grand Vizier and Mirza Malcom Khan, and by several Princes of the Blood, whom it was judged inconvenient to leave behind at Teheran. There is no reason to doubt the sincerity of the Shah's declaration, repeated on several prominent occasions, that the essential object of his visit to Europe was to cement friendly relations with England, or rather to place those relations on a new footing of complete and mutual confidence; but it may be questioned if his expectations in this respect were realized. In Russia he found intense chagrin—amounting almost to indignation—prevailing in the highest quarters on the subject of the Reuter concession. The ostensible grounds of Russia's dissatisfaction were; firstly, that the negociations for the concession which placed the resources and to a large extent the administration of Persia at the disposal of a rival government —for it was never questioned in Russia but that the British government was privy to the whole arrangement, and intended to profit by it to the utmost—had been conducted in secret, and in a spirit unfriendly to her interests; and secondly, that her trade would be most seriously hampered by being subjected at the various custom-houses on the Persian frontier to the control of British "employés." The merchants, indeed, of Moscow and Astrachan, who drive a large trade with Persia, and compound with the Persian officials on very favourable terms for the free passage of their goods into the country, were seriously alarmed at the prospect of a rigid exaction of custom dues at the ports of entry; but as they could not avow this alarm, nor complain of the correction of an abuse, they shifted their ground to an imaginary grievance on the question of the tariff, and asserted—without any authority whatever—that under the Reuter arrangement an arbitrary power of valuing Russian goods for duty would be in the hands of their commercial rivals! On the part of the Russian government the most serious objection—although it was kept entirely in the background— referred in all probability to the mines of the Elburz, the extraordinary value of which had been long known, and had been discounted by Russia as a reversionary interest of the future. In other respects—so far at any rate as regarded the development of the resources of the country—Russia would have benefited equally with Persia's other neighbours; and indeed in regard to one particular enterprise, which was the leading feature of the concession—the construction of the railway from Resht to Teheran—the advantages, both political and commercial, would for some time to come have accrued to Russia almost exclusively. Under whatever differing shades of feeling, however, Russia may have viewed the principle of the Reuter arrangement, there can be no doubt that she made a most resolute stand against its form and conditions as originally settled; and that when the Shah, accordingly, came to England and found that we were indifferent to the transaction—refusing absolutely to be committed to any guarantee, and hesitating even as to granting a moral support, since we feared that the complications and embarrassment arising from our connection with the scheme, however limited, would outweigh all advantages—the fate of the concession was virtually sealed. It was only indeed under the possible agreement of the European powers to the neutralization of Persia, the Shah's dominions forming a sort of Asiatic Belgium, that the working of the Reuter concession—by means perhaps of a great international company or commission—would have been at all practicable; and although this idea was mooted, and is understood to have received some consideration at Berlin and Vienna, it may be well understood that where the interests of England and Russia were strong, immediate, and conflicting, while the interests of the other powers were feeble and indirect, the prospect of any joint action, or acceptance of mutual responsibility, was altogether visionary. As the ultimate fate of the Reuter concession is not yet decided, I can only briefly notice its later phases. Baron Reuter had taken certain steps to assert his rights before the Shah's departure from Persia. He had sent out engineers, for instance, to make the preliminary studies and surveys, and he had actually laid down a permanent way for the railroad for a few miles at the Resht terminus, so as to escape the risk of forfeiting the caution-money, amounting to £40,000, which had been deposited in the Bank of England, and which was liable to confiscation if the works were not commenced within fifteen months of the date of signing the contract, a term of grace that expired on October 25th, 1873; but beyond these preliminary measures of execution he had made no real progress in bringing his scheme to maturity. Without a guarantee of the British government, or any direct promise of protection, he had found it impossible to place a Persian loan in the London market, or even to form a company in England for working the concession; and he was thus understood to have been in communication with foreign capitalists with a view to a practical transfer of his rights, or to some arrangement for international co-operation, when on the return of the Shah to Persia in the autumn of 1873, the whole contract was summarily annulled by a formal notice in the official Teheran Gazette.

It would be difficult to justify this annulment on legal grounds, if the concession had been a contract between private parties; for the delay in executing the works which was the reason assigned for the proceeding, was mainly owing to the dilatoriness of the Persian authorities in furnishing the required specifications; and moreover the penalty of such delay, in so far as regarded the railway, was declared in the deed to be a forfeiture of the caution-money, not a dissolution of the contract; but the real truth was that the Shah, indisposed to the concession by the pressure exerted against it in Europe, acted under "force majeure" in his final act of authority; for the popular feeling against the surrender of his royal powers into the hands of foreigners which had been fanned and fed, directed and intensified, during His Majesty's absence in Europe, by certain powerful malcontents at court, declared itself so strongly on his return that it could not be prudently resisted. It is indeed a matter of notoriety that the Shah's crown was in jeopardy for some weeks after his return to Persia, an insurrection in the capital being imminent, and the two declared objects of the public rancour being the Grand Vizier and the Reuter concession, on both of which heads His Majesty was compelled to yield, before he could venture to leave his palace and resume his ordinary avocations of pleasure or of business. Under such circumstances of a compulsory abrogation of his rights, it might be assumed that Baron Reuter would be entitled to compensation; but here again the argument arises that the concession itself was against the public polity of Persia, and thus "ipso facto" invalid. How the question may be ultimately settled it is impossible to say. It must needs be in the interests of Persia, that some of the industrial schemes, foreshadowed in the Reuter concession, should be executed, and a fair distribution of such schemes—affording profitable investments of capital with attendant advantages—among the different European nationalities, ought to satisfy all parties, and prevent any further exhibition of jealousy or ill-will. If the construction of railways for instance in the north of Persia may have a special attraction for Russia, England would seem to have a corresponding interest in the railways of the south; and the completion, again, of a longitudinal line through Persia from west to east—that is, from Baghdad to Herat—ought to enlist the common sympathies, and support of all the European powers, as an independent section of the continuous iron road which must before long unite the East and West.

A notice of the Shah's visit to the European capitals may now be resumed. In most of those capitals, in Berlin, Brussels, Paris, and Vienna, amusement mingled with instruction was the chief object in view. It was only in St. Petersburg, London, and Constantinople that politics were at all discussed; and, as might have been expected, amid the turmoil and preoccupation of royal receptions and national festivities, even in these cities no serious results were arrived at. The Shah was anxious that England should, if possible, come to an understanding with Russia as to the maintenance of the integrity of Persia, and he would have desired to see notes exchanged on the subject—not so much, perhaps, in the hope of the question being definitely and permanently settled, as with a view of producing for the time a sense of public security; but it was judged inexpedient, while Russia was yet smarting under the fancied humiliation of the Reuter concession, to address interpellations which, if they had any meaning at such a juncture, would seem to be aimed in the same direction of emancipating Persia from her control. The only result, accordingly, of the Shah's appeal was a reference to the old assurance of a joint support, which had been accorded to Mahomed Shah at the time of his mounting the throne in 1834, and which, having never been withdrawn, might be supposed to apply to his successor at the present day. So antiquated and qualified a recognition of integrity was no doubt far less than had been expected, either by the Shah or his minister. The latter, indeed, with his impulsive temperament and unlimited confidence in the justice of his views, had dreamed of reviving the status of fifty years ago. He is understood to have pointed to the avowed, the traditional policy, of England in the East, to the necessity of providing India with bulwarks against Russian encroachment, which, in former times a mere speculative danger, had now become an urgent and pressing reality. If it were worth while, he argued, to enter on the Cabul and Crimean wars in order to check the development of Russian power in the East, if it were good policy to support the Turks, to subsidise the Afghans, to throw out feelers even as far as Kashgar and Yarkend, why should Persia, the very cornerstone of Indian defence, be neglected and disparaged? It was useless to urge that Persia had been weighed in the balance and been found wanting; that she was false, effete, corrupt in her very core, worthless as an ally, and, in fact, beyond the pale of diplomatic action. The answer would naturally be that she had never yet been fairly tried, that hitherto she had distrusted England as much as Russia, and was now for the first time really in earnest in desiring to combine against the common enemy. As to her vitality, it would be said, no one who knew the country could question it. Although for the moment blighted by misfortune, by mismanagement, by domestic disloyalty, rather than by foreign pressure, yet under the invigorating influence of British aid, of British counsels, and British example, she would rise again stronger than ever, and would play a not unimportant part in the coming destinies of the East. A Persian diplomatist of enthusiastic views, full of faith in the future, and expectant of benefits, could hardly have much in common to discuss with practical English statesmen who had learned their lessons in the past, and rarely committed their country to obligations beyond the necessities of the day; so that it is not surprising if the Grand Vizier of Persia left London without coming to any more clear understanding with Her Majesty's ministers, than that it was generally desirable for the two governments to cultivate mutually the most friendly relations, and to work together for the preservation of the peace of the East. The most valuable result, probably, of the Shah's visit to England, was the impression which he carried

K

away, stamped indelibly on his mind, of the warm and cordial reception that he had met with from all classes of the community, an impression which will assuredly render him in the future more amenable to British counsels, and more disposed to reciprocate our friendly feelings. It is certain also that he saw much to admire in the teeming industry of our great centres of population, in the working of some of our time-honoured institutions, in the abundant evidence of a high civilization, and above all in the perfect order which reigned throughout the land, an order which is almost inexplicable to an Asiatic; but whether the admiration of such striking scenes will lead to any practical result in ameliorating the condition of a country like Persia, where the whole social and moral system is on such an entirely different footing, is, to say the least of it, exceedingly doubtful. We can only hope that the bread having been cast upon the waters will be found after many days.

In passing through Constantinople on his return to Persia the Shah received a further proof of our real interest in his affairs, in the valuable assistance rendered by our Minister to the composition of existing differences with the Porte. These differences referred principally to the exercise of civil and criminal jurisdiction by Persian consular officers over Persian subjects resident in Turkey, and as the subject was approached by the ministers of the two countries from entirely different stand-points—the one claiming by usage and prescription the application to Persian residents in Turkey of the "most-favoured-nation" clause of the European treaties,—so as to secure for Persia the special benefits of the Turkish capitulations with France, England, and Russia,—whilst the other, following the international law of Europe, placed all strangers, including, of course, Persians, on an exact equality in the eye of the law, with native-born subjects,—there did not seem much probability of arriving at a common understanding. Through the joint mediation, however, of the British and Russian representatives at the Porte, a compromise was effected in time to admit of the personal meeting of the two Mahomedan sovereigns—the Sultan, indeed, when the first difficulty was surmounted, receiving his guest with that magnificent hospitality for which he is celebrated;—and though impediments have since arisen to the execution of the terms of settlement which were then agreed to—impediments that have been further complicated by the revival of old frontier feuds and tribal quarrels—still there is no reason to doubt that, if England and Russia continue to act in concert, the Turco-Persian dispute must be accommodated without that appeal to arms which has more than once been imminent.

The Shah hurried his return to Persia in consequence of rumours of intrigue and disaffection, and he had no sooner landed on the shore of Ghilan than the threatened explosion took place. Elements of opposition, discordant in their nature, but each of considerable power, had confederated to force the Grand Vizier from office, and for the first time in the present reign the authority of the sovereign was set at naught. The ostensible ground of complaint against Mirza Hussein Khan, was the grant of the Reuter concession, and to a certain extent no doubt the public irritation against him was really due to this cause, but a glance at the names and characters of the chief conspirators will show that private animosity and political intrigue had at least as much to do with the Grand Vizier's deposition as any real sense of national humiliation. The malcontents, indeed, consisted of the following very dissimilar parties and factions. Firstly, the reigning Sultana, who exercised great personal influence over the Shah, and who was bitterly incensed against the Grand Vizier for being sent back to Persia from Moscow on a point of etiquette, and thus deprived of her visit to the European capitals. Secondly, the fanatical party,—headed by the Ulemá and the Finance Minister,—who repudiated any attempt to Europeanize Persia, and denounced the Grand Vizier on this account as a traitor to his country. Thirdly, the Princes of the Blood, who had accompanied the Shah on his tour, and who had suffered innumerable personal affronts at the hands of the minister, which they were bent on avenging. Fourthly, the Russian party in a body, guided by the Minister for Foreign Affairs, who was, moreover, a personal rival of the Grand

Vizier's; and fifthly, the so-called national party, inspired and led by Ferhád Mirza who had been left by the Shah as Regent at Teheran, and who, although naturally of an enlightened, humane, and thoughtful disposition, and thoroughly loyal to his sovereign, had been nevertheless provoked almost to frenzy by the threatened Reuter monopoly of Persian industry and commerce. Before these antagonists the Grand Vizier fell and for a time even it was doubtful if the tragedy of 1852 might not be repeated; but the danger was only temporary. The Shah managed the crisis with equal prudence and decision. Obliged at first to yield to the popular clamour; he still maintained an attitude of dignity and reserve, and thus soon brought the movement under control, succeeding in the end, not only in asserting his power, but in dealing out a stern retribution to the conspirators. The recalcitrant Princes, indeed, who had headed the confederacy, and thus given it consistency and weight, were deprived of any further power of mischief; while the Foreign Minister, who was not less culpable, was sent into honourable exile at Meshed, where he might cultivate his Russian predilections without any immediate danger to the State; his office, at the same time, which in the present condition of Persia controls undoubtedly the most important department of the government, being conferred upon the ex-Grand Vizier, who has throughout these late troublous proceedings retained the full confidence of his sovereign.

14. Such being the present aspect of affairs, it may be interesting to consider for one moment Persia's political prospects, and especially as regards her relations with England. There can be no doubt that the country is at present in a most depressed condition, probably in a more depressed condition than she has ever before reached at any period of history. A series of natural misfortunes have combined with a long course of misgovernment to produce the most intense and wide-spread destitution. The silk of Ghilan, which was formerly the staple production of the kingdom, has entirely failed of late years, owing to disease among the silkworms, and although there is now a slight improvement in the crops, the export does not reach a fifth part of its former

amount. Scarcity and drought, again, for several years consecutively, culminating in the famine of 1872, have depopulated large districts, converted flourishing villages into a wilderness, and spread the seeds of misery and pestilence broad-cast through the land. In the mean time the circulating medium has so diminished as to check all industrial efforts, and for the moment to annihilate trade. A bankrupt treasury, an unpaid army, corrupt officials, indecisive councils, and a timid executive, these and other chronic evils increase in intensity from day to day, and seem to foreshadow a condition, not merely of political decrepitude, but of what may be almost termed a national atrophy. And yet, notwithstanding this appalling picture, Persia has assuredly a career before her, either for good or for ill. Her geographical position, forming a connecting link between Europe and India, makes her a political necessity of the future, her importance in the eastern scale of nations becoming yearly greater as the powers around her undergo changes of accretion or disintegration. With Turkey crumbling into ruin on one side; with Russia pushing on, not so much perhaps for a steadfast political purpose as under the impulse of irresponsible military ambition; with England stimulating the native mind of India to unnatural activity by an artificial system of education which may well create anxiety; with movement, portentous movement on every side, it is impossible that Persia can remain quiescent. It should be clearly understood that Russia has neither the will nor the power to subjugate Persia. Although the country is very sparsely populated, not containing more than six or seven millions of inhabitants, yet are the Persians so indissolubly bound together by their peculiar heresy, so strongly protected are they by nature, by impregnable mountains, and impassable deserts, that no European power could hold them in permanent subjection, except at a cost altogether incommensurate with the result. Russia could neither spare garrisons for the scores of towns scattered round the central desert, and each, if necessity arose, the focus of insurrection, nor could she penetrate the great chain stretching from Sulimanieh to Kermán, where each separate mountain group would be another Caucasus.

Under great provocation, and almost as a last resource, Russia might appropriate the Caspian shores from Lenkorán to Asterabad, and even occupy the settled districts of Azerbiján, utilizing indeed, the docile and hardy peasantry of that province in consolidating other conquests; but to suppose that she would interfere with the Kurds and Lurs and Bakhtiáries, who have defied all invaders from Alexander to the present day, or attempt to administer a country so utterly unproductive as Central and Southern Persia, would be to suspect her of a want of sagacity of which she has never hitherto shown any trace. What she would naturally desire, and we have especially to guard against, is a domination of the country by means of moral and political pressure, which would enable her to use Persia as a lever against contiguous nationalities, against the Turks on one side, against the Turcomans and Afghans on the other. Persian hostilities against Herat, inspired and guided by Russia, have already on two occasions committed us to the largest measures of retaliation and defence; the same policy, pursued with the same success in regard to Merv and the Turcomans, would possibly lead to another modified Afghan occupation. The question, then, for our consideration is, can such extreme measures be rendered unnecessary by our establishing a strong position for ourselves in Persia? Can we turn the tables upon Russia by converting Persia into a means of defence, rather than of offence, to India? Strategists will point out that any serious Russian advance from the Caspian in the direction of Merv and Herat would be impossible, if the column were threatened on the flank from Persia; and they will further maintain that if we are to defend India from attack, it would be better to fight our intended invader in Persia than upon our own frontier, where any check would raise a host of enemies in our rear. These, however, are mere general military principles, which, although it may be well to remember them, are hardly of immediate application. What we have at present, to look to is the "modus operandi" of turning Persia to account, supposing such a policy to be accepted by the English nation; and here no doubt opinions would differ. The optimists would refer to General Malcolm's mission, when we fairly bought the French out of Persia, and carried the nation by golden storm. Others would advise mere friendly counsel and diplomatic support, a continuance indeed of our present policy, but somewhat strengthened and extended. A mean between the two extremes would probably best meet the necessities of the case. Some activity must be shown, some expense, some responsibility must be incurred, if we are to arrest the downward course of events which are rapidly converting Persia into an outlying Russian dependency. The physical capabilities, as well as the intelligence, of the Persians are far above those of the neighbouring eastern nations, whether Turks, Indians, Uzbegs, or Afghans. In each of these fields then, we might obtain, at no great risk and no great cost, very large results. An experimental contingent force of 10,000 men, raised, armed, fed, paid, clothed, disciplined and commanded by British officers, would not only be a respectable military body, but would elevate the tone of the people and show what they were capable of, if properly handled and encouraged. On the other hand a judicious, but genial support of enterprises, aimed at supplying the wants of the nation, at stimulating their industrial and creative faculties and raising them in the scale of civilization,—not on the selfish and wholesale scheme of the Reuter concession, but with a discriminative regard for native interests and feelings,—would no doubt be well received, and would bear fruit in due season.

At any rate the time is certainly propitious for making a serious effort, owing to the peculiarly favourable disposition of the Shah and his Foreign Minister, and if the country is, as cannot be denied, unnaturally depressed at the present moment, its improvement under our encouraging auspices would be all the more marked and appreciated.

August, 1874.

CHAPTER III.

THE RUSSIANS IN CENTRAL ASIA.

(Reprinted, with Notes, from the "Quarterly Review," for October, 1865. No. 236, p. 529.*)

1. Apathy of the English public in 1865, in regard to affairs in Central Asia, contrasted with the Russophobia of 1838.—2. Retrospect of Russian policy in Central Asia from the period of the Afghan war. Khivan expedition of 1839–40, and negociations with Bokhara up to 1842.—3. Operations of Russia in the Steppe and on the Jaxartes from 1847 to period of the Crimean war, 1854.—4. Simultaneous advances in the Trans-Ili region to the Eastward.—5. Invasion of Kokand territory in 1863; capture of Turkestan and Chemkend, and Gortchakoff's circular of 1864.—6. Resumption of hostilities. Capture of Tashkend, and creation of Government of Turkestan, 1865.—7. British policy in Central Asia after the Afghan war. Convention with Persia regarding Herat, 1852. Treaty of Paris, 1857; and our general relations with the Afghans.—8. Our unofficial communications with Turkestan from 1842 to 1865.—9. Prospective relations of Russia with Kokand, Bokhara, and Khiva, and their probable effect on British Indian interests.—10. Brief review of the Central-Asian commercial question.—11. Consideration of our future policy.

1. To those who remember the Russophobia of 1838-39, the indifference of the English public to the events now passing in Central Asia must appear one of the strangest instances of reaction in Modern History. At the former period there was no special cause of jealousy or ill-will between England and Russia. On the contrary, as far as the state of Europe was concerned, Russia was regarded by us with rather a friendly eye. She was the great conservative power of the West, and might be expected to render important aid to the cause of peace and order, by checking the revolutionary mania of

---

* ART. VIII.—1. A Narrative of the Russian Military Expedition to Khiva under General Perofski in 1839. Translated from the Russian by J. Michell. 1865. (Printed by Government of India at Calcutta, 1867.)
2. The Russians in Central Asia. Translated from the Russian by John and Robert Michell. London, 1865.
3. Invalide Russe. 1865.

France and Germany. In the East, too, it required a very bold effort of imagination to conjure up a sense of impending danger; for at that time Russia was hedged up along her Asiatic frontier by a series of barriers, which promised to prevent—and which, indeed, while they lasted, did actually prevent—any possible extension of her territorial limits towards India. The Caucasus was then unsubdued, and the tribes inhabiting that range found occupation for above one hundred thousand of the soldiers of the Czar. The Caspian was unapproached by rail, and boasted of but two solitary steamers, which timorously trod its waves and peered curiously into the creeks and roadsteads of the Ghilan coast. Ashoor-ada, the island at the entrance of the Bay of Asterabad, which is destined, perhaps, one day in the hands of the great Northern Power to become the Aden of this inland sea,* had been but

---

* (The following notes regarding the Russian proceedings at Ashoor-ada, and in the vicinity, are taken from an official memorandum recently drawn up on the subject. The Russians first set foot on the island of Ashoor-ada, at the mouth of the Bay of Asterabad, in 1837-38. They settled there on the plea of protecting Persian trade against the Turcoman pirates, and the occupation did not attract much notice till 1842, when it was first officially reported to the Foreign Office by Mr. M'Neill. In 1846 extensive buildings were erected in the island, and negociations were opened from thence with the Turcomans. Persia then applied to England to aid in obtaining the withdrawal of the Russians. In 1849 England did appeal to Russia to withdraw, but fruitlessly. In 1854 Persia demanded officially that the island should be evacuated, but was told compliance with such a demand was impossible, though Russia admitted that Ashoor-ada was undoubtedly Persian territory. Efforts were at the same time made by Russia to obtain a fortress on the mainland, which however Persia steadily resisted. In 1856 the position at Ashoor-ada was strengthened, at the same time that a large addition was effected to the Russian naval force on the Caspian. Persistent attempts were made from this time by the Russians from Ashoor-ada to gain over the Turcomans, up to 1865. In 1866 the Shah visited Ashoor-ada, and confirmed the Russians in exercise of a police power over the Turcoman trade. Persia was stated at the same time to have been promised support in her claims on Herat, on condition of raising no opposition to the extension of Russian power on the Caspian, the Oxus, and Jaxartes. Russia also made preparations to garrison the port of Gez on the mainland near Ashoor-ada, as a further check to the Turcomans, but was forestalled in this movement by Persia. In 1868 Russia proposed to move her naval station from Ashoor-ada to the mouth of the Atrek. In 1869 Krasnovodsk was occupied by Russia preparatory to the movement of troops against Khiva. In 1870 Russia assumed that her frontier on

recently detached from Persia, and was still a naked sandbank. Above all, the boundary of Russia, confronting India, was drawn from the Ural River, north of the Caspian, to the old Mongolian capital of Semipolatinsk, or "the Seven Cities," by a cordon of forts and Cossack outposts, called the Orenburg and Siberian lines,* which abutted on the great Kirghiz steppe along its northern skirts, and, to a certain extent, controlled the tribes pasturing in the vicinity, but by no means established the hold of Russia on that pathless, and, for the most part, lifeless waste.

A great Tartar empire which should unite Siberia with the fertile valleys of the Oxus and Jaxartes, had been imagined by the Russian Czars as early as the sixteenth century, and would probably have been realized, either by Peter the Great or Catherine, but for the intervening wilderness of the Kirghiz-Kazzáks. Extending for two thousand miles from west to east, and for one thousand miles from north to south, and impassable, except to a well-appointed caravan, at certain seasons and along particular tracks, this vast steppe seemed to have been

the sea coast extended as far south as the mouth of the Atrek; a claim that was not contested at the time by Persia. In 1871 Russia founded a military post at Chikishlar, near the mouth of the Atrek, and during this year and the next established a control, more or less complete, over the Turcomans from the sea-coast as far east as Ashkabad. In 1873 occurred the great Khiva expedition, one column of attack, which, however, failed in its object, marching from Chikishlar by the Turcoman route. In 1874 the military Trans-Caspian government was formed, subject to the governor-general of the Caucasus, the head-quarters being at Krasnovódsk, and the frontiers extending south as far as the Gurgan, and east as far as Kahriz, half way to Merv. Yemuts and Tekkehs were also enrolled as Russian subjects.—1874.)

* This famous line commences at Guriev, where the Ural River debouches into the Caspian. It follows up the left bank of the river to Orenburg and Orsk, and then crosses by the head streams of the Tobol River to Troitska. From hence it is drawn to Petro-paulovsk on the Ishim, and so on to Omsk on the Irtish; and from Omsk it follows up the left bank of the river to Semipolatinsk and Buktharminsk on the Chinese frontier. The total measurement of the line including sinuosities is 3300 versts or 2200 miles, and the Cossacks employed to guard it number over 20,000 men. It has been often proposed to erect a continuous rampart like the Chinese wall, along the northern part of the line, so as to connect Orsk on the Ural with Omsk on the Irtish; but no great progress has ever been made with the work, and it is now definitively abandoned.

placed by nature as a 'buffer' between the power of civilized Europe, and the weakness and barbarism of Central Asia.

Moreover, at the period in question, our British Indian empire, freed for the moment from internal throes, and warming into active life under the influence of Lord William Bentinck's beneficent administration, was confined within the modest limits of the Sutlej and the north-western desert; so that a broad zone of above twenty degrees of latitude, peopled by strong and independent races, intervened between the most northern districts of India and the most southern settlements of Russia. Yet at such a time, and under circumstances calculated to inspire so just a confidence in our own position, the appearance of a Russian Envoy at Cabul, and the advance of the Shah of Persia against Herat in suspected collusion with Russia, were sufficient to create a panic in India, which shortly led us into a war with the Afghans, the most momentous that has ever occurred in the history of our Indian Empire; both in regard to the immediate sacrifice which it entailed of treasure, life, and honour, and still more in regard to its effect on our "prestige," from which indeed we are still suffering.

Whether the danger apprehended to India at this period was, or was not, imaginary, is a separate question. Those who are best acquainted with the East believe that if Herat had fallen to the Persian army in 1838, and if in pursuance of that victory an alliance, which was actually proposed, had been concluded, under the guarantee of Russia, between the Shah of Persia on the one side, and the Baruckzye rulers of Afghanistan upon the other, the effects of such a combination would have been sensibly felt beyond the Sutlej,—the more sensibly, indeed, that the Calcutta Government had exaggerated the importance of the supposed hostile demonstration against India, and had made its success or failure the gauge, as it were, of British supremacy in the East. Our object, then, in recalling the panic of that fatal period is, not to show that it was wholly unreasonable, but to contrast its excessive violence with the apathy which, under greatly aggravated circumstances, we are now displaying.

At present, whether we regard the geographical extension of

the Russian and Indian boundaries, or the material development of the two Empires, or the political condition of the countries which still separate them, the gravity of the situation is certainly much increased. We have, in the first place, greatly advanced our own frontier. British India has now absorbed both Sinde and the Punjab. Our detachments guard the passes and occupy the valleys which indent the mountain-chain from Peshawer to the Bolan. The shadow of our power still hovers over the more distant points of Candahar and Cabul, Farther eastward, too, Cashmere and Thibet, though nominally independent, are in reality mere outworks of India, and the boundary of our political empire in this direction is the Kara-Koram range. Russia, on the other hand, in the due course of events, and by her own natural growth, has become much more formidable as a prospective limitary power. The Caucasus, after half a century of resistance, has been finally subdued, and although powerful garrisons may yet be required for some time to come for the military occupation of the mountains, still a considerable portion of the one hundred thousand soldiers formerly employed in the field against the Circassians, Chichenses, and Daghestánís must needs have been set at liberty, and thus rendered available for new conquests in Central Asia.* At the same time the material development of Russia towards the East has been enormous. A railway now connects Petersburg with Nijni-Novogorod;† and there are said to be three hundred steamers plying on the Volga between this point and the Caspian. On the Caspian itself the steam-vessels of all classes available for purposes of war number over fifty, and there is besides a small subsidiary flotilla on the Aral, which is being

* (A memorandum drawn up in our War Office, 1873, states as follows: "The war establishment of the army of the Caucasus is 196,414 men (164,038 combatants), 40,897 horses, and 248 guns; of these probably 90,000 or 100,000 could be put in the field immediately."—1874.)

† (Since continued to Saritsin. A line also connects Moscow with Teflis, except for a very short space through the Caucasus, and another line connects Teflis with the Black Sea at Poti, which line is to be continued to Bakú, on the Caspian. A line from Teflis to the Persian frontier is also under construction, and a concession has been further given for a line from Samara, on the Volga, to Orenburg, to be continued in due course to Tashkend.)

steadily increased.* The geographical approximation, however, is, perhaps, the most important feature in this re-cast of the Anglo-Russian position in the East. While England, in taking possession of the line of the Indus from the seaboard to Peshawer, has penetrated on one side nearly one thousand miles into the "Debateable land" of former days, Russia, on the other side, by incorporating the great Kirghiz Steppe into the empire, and substituting the Jaxartes for the Siberian line of forts as her southern frontier, has made a stride of corresponding dimensions to meet us; so that, instead of the two empires being divided by half the continent of Asia, as of old, there is now intervening between their political frontiers a mere narrow strip of territory, a few hundred miles across,† occupied either by tribes torn by internecine war or

* (This rough statement of the naval strength of Russia in the East, was taken from Mr. Long's pamphlet, on "Russia, Central Asia and British India, by a British subject, 1865." The numbers are apparently exaggerated, being greatly in excess of the return given in our War Office report of last year, which states as follows: "On the Caspian, Russia has three launches, of together 180 horse-power and 794 tons; ten steamers, of together 980 horse-power and 3,523 tons; four steam launches and two sailing transports, of together 728 tons. There are three steam-boat companies on the Volga, each with a numerous fleet of fast steamers, besides a number of barges, steam-tugs, &c.; some of these steamers ply on the Caspian, and one of the companies has landing-wharfs, &c., near Ashoor-ada. There are also probably a few traders, sailing vessels, &c. On the Sea of Aral, there are four steamers, of together 170 horse-power and about 650 tons, with one launch of 12 horse-power and 16 tons." As the War Office return is taken from a Russian "Navy List," published before the Khivan expedition, it no doubt understates the present strength of the establishment, but the most liberal allowance for the increase of the last two years, will hardly reach Mr. Long's estimate.—1874.)

† From the most northern point of the Thibet frontiers in the Kara-Koram range to the most southern point of the Russian frontier in the Thian-shan range overlooking the upper valley of the Naryn River, the direct distance across the level plains of Chinese Turkestan cannot be more than 400 miles. If we adhere, however, to our real military frontier, instead of calculating from the point to which our political influence extends, and measure the road distance, the result will be somewhat different. A recent British Envoy, Moola Abdul-Mejid, travelling from Peshawer by Cabul and Badakhshan and across the Pamir Steppe to the Jaxartes, found the entire distance between Peshawer and the town of Kokand to be 1075 miles; and even the direct route by Bajore and Kafferistan to Badakh-shan and Pamir which was also followed by one of the envoys from Kokand, does not diminish the distance by more than 200 miles. (Russia has since extended her territory for a considerable distance south of the

nationalities in the last stage of decrepitude, and traversed by military routes in all directions.

If, then, there was danger to British India from the attitude and possible designs of Russia twenty-eight years ago, that danger must be increased a hundredfold at the present day; yet so far from being now betrayed into any paroxysm of alarm, so far from thinking of intervention in the countries beyond our frontier in order to arrest her progress, her proceedings fail even to excite our curiosity, and we seem, as far as the public is concerned, to await the threatened contact of the two empires with supreme indifference.

In the opening paragraph of this article, so singular a state of quietude on a subject of real national importance has been ascribed to the effects of reaction. No doubt the sense that our alarm formerly betrayed us into errors will account for much of the indisposition now shown even to consider whether there is danger or not, but there are also other influences at work—influences of a loftier and more legitimate character—which have contributed, and still contribute, to the same end. A considerable section of the community—a section numbering in its ranks the principal organs of the Press and the leaders of public opinion, and representing much of the highest intellect and the purest feeling of the age—believes, and proclaims its belief, that the extension of the Russian power in Central Asia is a consummation devoutly to be wished for. To substitute civilization—albeit not of the highest type—for the grovelling superstition, the cruelty, the depravity, the universal misery which now prevail in the Uzbeg and Afghan principalities, appears to this class an object of paramount importance, in regard to the general interests of humanity; of such importance indeed as to override any nice question of right or wrong involved in the substitution of one rule for another, and to throw entirely into the shade any possible injury which our political or commercial interests may

---

Jaxartes, the interval between her extreme limit S.-E. of Samarcand, and our limit N.-W. of Peshawer, as measured on the map, being about 350 British miles.—1874.)

sustain in consequence. Another class of thinkers, who are not prepared to carry their humanitarian feelings to so extreme a length, believe, nevertheless, that the less notice we take of the pending Russian proceedings the better. They remember the axiom uttered by Sir Robert Peel, in the Sinde debate of 1844, that "when civilization and barbarism come into contact, the latter must inevitably give way," and they believe therefore that, as Russia is now fairly in contact with the Uzbegs, the extinction of the separate Governments of Khiva, Bokhara, and Kokand must follow with the unerring certainty of a law of nature. They go further, indeed, and would regard any interference on our part to arrest the movement as positively mischievous; inasmuch as such interference would not only end in a miserable failure, but would recoil upon ourselves, by intensifying the effect of the Russian advance in the countries beyond our frontier, and by more completely unhinging the public mind in India. There are also, perhaps, a few who honestly think that it would be for the advantage of the British rule in India that the country should be conterminous with Russia, and that for two reasons; firstly, because we should then have a reasonable and responsible neighbour with whom to conduct political negociations, instead of hordes of fanatical savages on whom no reliance can be placed; and secondly, because Central Asia, in a settled condition and under a European Government, would naturally be a better customer, both in regard to the export and import trade of India, than the barbarians who now encircle our North-West frontier with transit duties and prohibitive tariffs;* who are

---

* Mr. Davies, in his Indian Report on the Trade of Central Asia, 1862, has certainly given a most formidable list of duties on imports from British territory into Kashmir, the rates of duty on all our staple articles of produce and manufacture varying from 30 to 150 per cent. *ad valorem* (see "Report," p. 32); but it may be doubted if a Russian tariff in the same quarter would be more favourable to us. Mr. Lumley, indeed, in his valuable Report on the Russian trade with Central Asia, says that an attempt is made to exclude superior English cottons from some parts of Russia by a prohibitive tariff of 60, 100, or even 200 per cent. *ad valorem* ("Reports of Her Majesty's Secretaries of Legation," No. v, p. 297); and a similar scale of protective duties applies to all those articles which are likely to compete with the native industry.

too poor to purchase our manufactures, and too indolent to supply our markets with their own produce. But such reasoners leave entirely out of consideration that India is a conquered country, where a certain amount of discontent must be ever smouldering which would be fanned into a chronic conflagration by the contiguity of a rival European power. They forget, too, that although Russia is at present friendly and pacific, occupied with internal reforms and disposed, perhaps, to relax in our favour the stringency of her commercial code, there is no security that such feelings will be of long duration. Let the advocates of Russian neighbourhood consider what would be the effect on the French position in Algeria, if England were to occupy the conterminous territory of Morocco, and they will obtain some notion of our probable political embarrassments when confronted with Russia on the Indus. Such a state of things may possibly be brought about in the fulness of time, and, when it does arrive, will no doubt be met by us with fitting resolution and resource; but every Englishman who has at heart the honour and interests of his country, should pray that the day may yet be far distant.

2. To understand the true bearing of the events now passing on the Jaxartes, and to determine the best mode of meeting, or avoiding, a crisis with which these events may threaten us, it is necessary to take a careful retrospect of Russian and English policy in Central Asia since the period of the Afghan war. This retrospect will not be entered on with any unfriendly feeling to Russia. On the contrary, the views which have actuated Russia in her Asiatic policy, during this period of history, will be given, as far as possible, on the authority of her own officers, and will be compared, in a fair and candid spirit of inquiry, with the views which are believed to have influenced England in the same matters; the object being to show how the two systems of policy have acted and reacted on each other, and thus to arrive at a just appreciation of the difficulties of the present juncture.

There is no need to dwell on the career of the Russian arms in Asia in the early part of the century. It is certain that the absorption of Georgia, the acquisition of the frontier provinces of Turkey and Persia, and the gradual subjugation of the Kirghiz Steppe, although cited by McNeill in his famous pamphlet " On the progress of Russia in the East," as proofs of her insatiate thirst of conquest, were amply paralleled by our own annexations in India during the same period. " The law of Nature " above quoted was, in fact, allowed full scope both in one quarter and the other; the provinces conquered, or annexed, are believed to have benefited by the change; and excepting, therefore, that a certain mutual distrust was created between the two European powers, no great evil arose from their respective territorial extension. It is now declared by Russia that during the ten years antecedent to the Afghan war, while she was suspected of a systematic policy of encroachment towards India, she was in reality exclusively occupied with the consolidation of her hold upon the Kirghiz Steppe, and with measures directed to the development of her commerce in Central Asia. Her proceedings in Persia— where she certainly encouraged, if she did not instigate, the expedition of Mahomed Shah against Herat—merely aimed, as she asserts, at the improvement of her position in that country; and the appearance of her agents at the Uzbeg Courts is explained by the previous activity of English agents in the same direction.

In tracing out, indeed, the origin of those misunderstandings between the two great powers which culminated in the Afghan and Khivan expeditions, allowance must always be made for the fact that they viewed their relative positions in regard to Central Asia from entirely different stand-points. Russia maintained, in the first place, that she had a prescriptive right to the Khanat of Khiva,* which she was justified by the law of nations in seeking to realize whenever an oppor-

* The narrative of the Russian Expedition to Khiva, translated by Mr. Michell, asserts this claim categorically in numerous passages. The following is an example:—" Thus, from the very commencement of the eighteenth century the Khivans had chosen five Khans who were Russian subjects. In 1700 Khan Shah Niáz paid voluntary homage to Russia; in 1703, Khan Aran-Na'amet did the same; from 1741, Abul Khair Khan and his son, Núr Ali, both Russian subjects, ruled over Khiva till 1750; and Khan Kaip, another Russian subject, held the same position from 1770

L

tunity offered. During the 18th century five different rulers of the country had proffered allegiance to the Russian Emperor. The province, indeed, was still viewed as the patrimony *de jure* of the Kirghiz of the Little Horde who had been Russian subjects since 1730, and the present Uzbeg occupants, whose rule only dated from the beginning of the 19th century, were regarded as intruders. The interference, therefore, of any other European power in the affairs of Khiva was almost equivalent, in her estimate, to fomenting rebellion in her own empire; but it was not only on the territorial question that Russia adopted a tone which to us appears extravagant. She also seemed to consider that her geographical position gave her a claim to the monopoly of the trade of Central Asia, and we accordingly find her officers on all occasions resenting the proposed participation of England in that trade as an invasion of Russian rights which was to be opposed at all hazards. The successive travels of Moorcroft and Trebeck, of Arthur Conolly, of Bailie Fraser, of Alexander Burnes, and even of the Missionary Wolff, seem to have excited the gravest suspicions. "The English," it was said in reference to the state of the East in 1835, "have great facilities for strengthening their influence in Central Asia, the principal market for the manufactured goods of Russia, and for doing her serious damage by establishing regular commercial relations with that country. It is only necessary indeed to allow the possibility of the English supplying the Khivans and the Turcomans, the nearest and most hostile neighbours of Russia, as well as the Kirghiz, with arms and ammunition, in order to be convinced of the necessity of counteracting the schemes of England, whose agents do not even try to conceal their hopes, in their published accounts, of becoming masters not only of the trade between the Indus and the Hindú-Kúsh, but likewise of the market of Bokhara, the most important of Central Asia."

to 1780. Hence arises the positive right of Russia to the Khanat of Khiva. Notwithstanding this indisputable claim of Russia to Khiva, the Russian Government only sought one thing; that is, protection for the Russian trade in Central Asia," &c., &c.

Now it is certain that England has always considered, and does still consider, that she is entitled to exercise a fair amount of influence in Central Asia, and to enjoy a fair access to the markets of Bokhara, and the other markets of that region, equally with Russia; but it is also certain that she has never taken any active measures to assert or realize her right, and that the apprehensions of Russia, therefore, on this score, which urged her on to an armed intervention, were altogether unfounded. What England really dreaded thirty years ago, and what she had a perfect right to impede by all the means in her power, was that Russia would gradually absorb,—or would, at any rate, extend her influence, either by treaties or by political pressure, over—the independent countries intermediate between the Caspian and India, and would thus complicate our position in the latter country. We may have been deceived as to the extent, as well as the imminence of the danger, and we undoubtedly adopted very unwise measures for meeting it; but there is no reason to question the correctness of our view in principle, nor is any excuse required for our having inaugurated a policy of resistance which was strictly defensive. If it be borne in mind that the mainsprings of action in the English and Russian movements in Central Asia from this time forward, were a feeling of political jealousy on the one side, and a spirit of commercial rivalry on the other, a light will be thrown on much that would be otherwise unintelligible. When Lord Auckland, for instance, persisted in marching an army across the Indus in 1838, notwithstanding that the object for which the expedition was originally organised, the relief of Herat, had been already accomplished by the retirement of the Shah's forces, under the pressure of our demonstration in the Persian Gulf, it was with the view of preventing the spread of Russian influence towards India. The Proclamation, indeed, of November 8, 1838, stated that the main object of Lord Keane's expedition was "the establishment of a permanent barrier against schemes of aggression upon our north-west frontier," and Lord Auckland had really at the time very plausible grounds for his alarm; for clouds appeared to be gathering on all sides. Persia had been entirely alienated by our interference to save Herat. The Sirdars of Candahar had offered to coalesce with the Shah, if the Russian ambassador at Teheran would guarantee the arrangement. Dost Mahomed, exasperated at his treatment by us, had expelled Burnes from Cabul, and was ready under the inspiration of Vitkevitch, to welcome the agents, or even the arms, of the Emperor. Russia was further known to have been most successful in coercing the recalcitrant Kirghiz. She had fairly broken ground against Khiva by arresting all the Uzbeg merchants resident at Orenburg and Astracan, and her intercourse with Bokhara, ever since the mission of Mons. Demaison, in 1834, and the unaccredited visit of Vitkevitch in 1835,* was understood to be of the most friendly character. What Lord Auckland probably contemplated as the result of

* There seems to have been a strange fatality attending the movements of this unfortunate officer. It can hardly be doubted that he visited Bokhara in 1835, under instructions from the Governor-General of Orenburg, yet his official character was never recognised. In Mr. Michell's published work on the "Russians in Central Asia," p. 436, he is spoken of as "the Russian traveller Vitkevitch, who visited Bokhara in 1835;" and in the other work on Khiva, which is not yet printed, it is stated that "Vitkevitch, when sent in search and for the release of two Russian prisoners reported to be amongst the Kirghiz, wandering on the rivers Irghiz and Turgäi, was driven by a snow-storm to Bokhara, from whence, however, he returned in safety." It certainly must have been a prodigious storm to have driven before it this hardy young Polish officer across the Kara-kum sands; across the Jaxartes; across the still more difficult Kizil-kum desert, a distance of at least 700 or 800 miles from the Irghiz and Turgäi rivers to Bokhara.

The biography of Vitkevitch, given in the note from which this passage is extracted, is full of interest, but we doubt its entire authenticity, particularly in regard to the closing scene of his career. The Russian account says that, "on the return of Vitkevitch to Petersburg, at the end of April, 1839, he was very well received by the Minister for Foreign Affairs, by whom he was immediately recommended for promotion in the Guards, and he was rewarded by an order of Knighthood and a sum in money. About eight days after his arrival at Petersburg, Vitkevitch shot himself, leaving behind him a short note, in which he said he had burnt all his papers before his death. The cause of this suicide remains hidden up to the present time." . . . This may be compared with Kaye's account of the same transaction ("History of the Afghan War," Vol. I. p. 200, foot note), in which it is distinctly stated, and we believe, on the authority of Prince Soltikof, that Vitkevitch blew out his brains and destroyed his papers in consequence of the chilling reception he met with from Count Nesselrode, and the conviction he derived from it, that he was to be disavowed and sacrificed.

this menacing combination, was the immediate establishment of a Russian mission at Cabul, and the opening of friendly relations between the Emperor and Runjeet Singh, and who shall say that the Governor-General was in error in judging that such a demonstration, backed by the whole weight of Mahommedan Persia, required to be arrested by energetic measures of self-defence? That the measures which he did adopt were unsuited to the occasion, and failed as much from their impracticable character as from lamentable faults of execution, is a matter upon which history has already pronounced its verdict, and of which, therefore, it is useless here to reopen the discussion.

Closely following on our own occupation of Afghanistan, occurred the famous expedition of Perofski against Khiva. This expedition had long been contemplated. As a measure of mere frontier police, and irrespective of all considerations of external policy, it was urgently needed. With the exception, indeed, of the claim of prescriptive "suzerainté" over Khiva, dating from the proffered allegiance of the old Kirghiz rulers, there was not a single weak point in the Russian bill of indictment. The Uzbegs of Khiva, either directly or through the Turcomans and Kirghiz who obeyed them, had for years committed every conceivable atrocity against the Russian government. To man-stealing and raids upon the friendly Kirghiz were added the constantly recurring plunder of caravans; attacks upon the Russian outpost; burdens upon trade, which weighed it to the ground; outrages upon Russian subjects who ventured into the country; indignities to the government; and finally a systematic course of agitation in the Steppe, undertaken with a view of inciting the Kirghiz to rebellion. The provocation, indeed, offered by Khiva was not less complete as a "*casus belli*" than the invasion of India by the Sikhs, which led to the battles of Firoz-shahr and Sobraon, and terminated in our own annexation of the Punjab; but curiously enough, blending with these legitimate grounds for hostility, and not improbably of superior weight in determining the precise time of attack, there was the old feeling of commercial rivalry with England. Perofski, it is true, in his proclamation of November 26, 1839, merely stated that one of his objects was "to strengthen in that part of Asia the lawful influence to which Russia has a right, and which alone can ensure the maintenance of peace;" but in the Russian account of the expedition, translated by Mr. Michell, the sore point is laid bare, without any attempt at diplomatic glozing. The object is there stated to be "to establish, not the dominion, but the strong influence of Russia in the neighbouring Khanats, for the reciprocal advantages of trade, and to prevent the influence of the East India Company, so dangerous to Russia, from taking root in Central Asia." In fact, Russia desired to redress the balance which had been so rudely shaken by our advance to Cabul; and what is still more remarkable, as an evidence of her morbid apprehension both of the designs and the power of England, she actually anticipated, by several months, the previously arranged date for the departure of the expedition, dreading lest in the interim English agents should penetrate to Khiva, and, like Eldred Pottinger at Herat, should incite the Uzbegs to a more determined resistance.*

We cannot here afford space to follow out the details of the expedition. The narrative translated by Mr. Michell, and compiled from official sources, is replete with interest, both in a military and political point of view. It is very instructive in the first place to find that a force of 5000 men (3000 infantry and 2000 cavalry), with 22 field guns, and 4 rocket stands, was considered sufficient for the reduction of a country which is said to have a fixed population of about 500,000 souls, and to be supported by an equal number of tributary nomades. And it speaks well again for Russian providence and humanity that upwards of 10,000 camels should have been provided for the carriage of the camp equipage and the ordnance and commissariat stores of this little army, six months' rations for each

* The object is thus stated in the narrative of the expedition to Khiva. "It was, therefore, of the greatest importance to hasten the expedition for the punishment of Khiva, so as to prevent the English from supporting the resistance of this Khanat against Russia, and to anticipate the possibility of any other Central Asiatic rulers being induced to join Khiva by means of threats or promises of reward that might be employed by the English agents." The departure of the expedition was originally fixed for April, 1840, whereas it actually left Orenburg in November, 1839.

man, besides a liberal allowance of warm clothing and comforts, being carried with the force; although the distance to be traversed was only 1000 miles—about the same distance as the interval between Karachí and Cabul—and the march was not calculated to require more than three months, at most, for its performance.

In real truth the expedition, considering the season selected for its march, seems to have been *too* well appointed, and to have broken down in consequence. To have attempted, indeed, to carry with so small a force an unwieldy mass of ten thousand camels across the desolate tract of the Ust-Urt in mid-winter, when the ground was covered with snow, and there was no atom of herbage to be seen for many hundreds of miles, argues the most extraordinary confidence in the power of discipline to overcome difficulties, or the most culpable ignorance of the physical features of the country to be traversed. As is well known, Perofski's force, after advancing into the middle of the desert, became completely crippled, and was obliged to retrace its steps to Orenburg, with the loss of a very considerable portion of its "matériel" and men. The exceptional severity of the season is usually alleged as the cause of this unexpected failure; but it may be doubted if, under the most favourable circumstances of weather and climate, a force composed as Perofski's was could have crossed the steppe from the Emba to the Khivan frontier. On the other hand, an Indian general, of the school of Sir Charles Napier or of Sir Hugh Rose, would probably have found little difficulty in pushing across the waste, with the assistance of the friendly Kirghiz, a succession of flying columns, equipped in the lightest manner consistent with safety, and capable of holding their ground after reaching the cultivated land until a sufficient force had been concentrated for an offensive movement in advance; so that we do not consider the problem of the Russian subjugation of Khiva by a direct movement either from Orenburg or Orsk to be at all solved by Perofski's failure.*

* (The views that are here expressed have received full confirmation from the experience of the recent Russian expedition against Khiva, the column, under General Verefskin, which marched direct from Orenburg,

There are officers still living who were on the point of starting for General Perofski's camp—where, however, they would hardly have been very welcome visitors—when the report of the Russian discomfiture first reached the English headquarters at Cabul; and they well remember that the news was received, not with exultation, but certainly with a feeling of intense relief; for we were then preparing to occupy Syghan, on the Northern slope of the Hindú-Kúsh, and a further advance on Bokhara, for the purpose of dislodging Dost Mahomed and his son Ackbar Khan, was being much canvassed; so that it really seemed, as Baron Brunnow is said to have remarked to the then president of the Board of Control, "that the Sepoy and the Cossack were about to meet on the banks of the Oxus;" and a collision of this nature, although not unpleasing to the army, was viewed by sober diplomatists almost with dismay; since, however it might have terminated, it could not fail to bring on an irretrievable complication of our relations with Central Asia.

So impressed, indeed, were our authorities at this time with a sense of the importance of preserving the independence of the Uzbeg principalities, in order to prevent the contact of Russian and English power, that every effort was made to remove those grievances which had drawn the Russian hostility upon Khiva, and which might at any moment involve Bokhara, and even Kokand, in a similar danger. Stoddart had been originally sent to Bokhara by McNeill on the retirement of the Persian army from Herat in the summer of 1838,

through the Ust-Urt being the only portion of the force, whose operations were thoroughly successful. The following extract from the report of Mr. Schuyler, Secretary to the United States' Legation at St. Petersburg, who, although he did not accompany the expedition, was travelling in Turkestan at the time and obtained full information on all matters of detail, is decisive as to the superior advantages of the Orenburg route over all others for marching troops upon Khiva.

"The Orenburg Expedition, therefore, which had been assented to merely to protect the Steppe against the Turcomans, was the only expedition which found a good road, met with few disasters, beat the enemy, arrived safely and captured the city. Had the action of the authorities at Orenburg been followed at first, no other expedition would have been necessary, and Khiva would have been taken quietly without noise and the consequent diplomatic unpleasantness."—1874.)

upon an errand of this nature. He was to endeavour to persuade the Amír to liberate the Russian prisoners still held in captivity by his subjects, and to abstain from any other provocation, either through unjust exactions upon trade, or through the encouragement heretofore held out to the Turcomans to pursue their kidnapping practices upon the Caspian and along the Orenburg line, by permitting the purchase of Russian slaves in the Bokhara Market. Conolly, who followed in 1840, had general instructions of the same nature in regard to the Khanats of Khiva and Kokand, to which, however, he superadded a certain philanthropic policy of his own; for being naturally of an enthusiastic nature, and having a confidence in the force of a just cause, which the Uzbeg character hardly justified, he seriously proposed to bind the respective Governments of Khiva, Kokand, and Bokhara, by a tripartite obligation to each other, to abandon the slave-trade altogether, and to cultivate friendly relations both with the Russian and the Persian Governments. It was in Khiva, however, that the danger of a renewed Russian intervention appeared especially imminent, since the grievances which had led to the late attack remained unredressed;* and thither accordingly were successively despatched by Major Todd, Envoy at Herat, the British officer nearest to the scene of action, his two assistants, James Abbott and Richmond Shakespeare. James Abbott appears to have exceeded his instructions, which only referred to the liberation of the Russian slaves, and to have given just cause of umbrage to a friendly Power, by proposing, after the fashion of the days of Malcolm and Elphinstone, that Russians should

* (Russia, however, appears to have been so disheartened by the Khiva failure, that she really formed an exaggerated estimate of the difficulty of extending her frontier in this direction. The official narrative at any rate of Perofski's Expedition terminates with these remarkable words: "The cause of the jealousy and mistrust with which the conduct of Russia was received in Europe, proceeded from a complete ignorance of the countries conterminous with Russia on the South-East. A better acquaintance with the regions of Central Asia must long since have shown the world the impracticability of all ideas of conquest in this quarter, even if they ever existed." Subsequent events have shown how entirely the Russian Government mistook or misstated the real bearing of the question.—1874.)

be permanently excluded from the province, an offensive and defensive alliance with England being suggested as a reward for thus breaking with the common enemy. Of course any such extreme measures were repudiated as soon as reported to head-quarters, and the Mission of Richmond Shakespeare was undertaken mainly to repair Abbott's mistake. Shakespeare, however, arriving at Khiva at a very favourable moment, when the Khan had, for the first time, begun to realize the extent of the danger he incurred in continuing to brave the power of Russia, succeeded in bringing about the long-pending restoration of the slaves, and himself escorted the liberated band, numbering four hundred men, from Khiva to Orenburg.* Now it would be difficult to find anything in these proceedings injurious, or even derogatory, to Russia. With the exception, indeed, of Abbott's unauthorised overtures, there was nothing that a friendly Power might not with perfect propriety have undertaken in relation to its Ally; yet Russia took grievous offence at the whole train of negociation. She seemed to consider that the interposition of England in her behalf was almost an insult; that she was humiliated by accepting of any favour at our hands; and she thus refuses to the present day to admit that she was indebted to Shakespeare's intercession for the recovery of her kidnapped subjects.† The extreme

---

* (It is worthy of special remark, that in the official Russian report of Perofski's Expedition translated by Mr. Michell, the name even of Shakespeare is not mentioned, the liberation of the Russian prisoners being ascribed solely to the Khan Hazrat's fears, and Cornet Aïtof being given the exclusive credit of conducting the party to Orenburg. The only published account of Shakespeare's journey is in the June number of Blackwood's Magazine for 1842. —1874.)

† Mr. Kühlewein, who was Secretary to General Ignatief's Mission to Khiva in 1858, thus refers to Perofski's Expedition. "The expedition which numbered 5000 men, had the effect of bringing the Khan to his senses, though temporarily. In the summer of 1840 he released all the Russian prisoners. Shakespeare, an English officer, who had arrived at Khiva from Cabul in 1839, undertook to conduct the prisoners to Russia;" ("Russians in Central Asia," p. 549); and in a still more disparaging spirit, Mr. Michell's second volume says "Both these agents (Abbott and Shakespeare) strove to take an active part in the Russian affairs with Khiva; especially Shakespeare, who wished to take credit for the release of the Russian prisoners. These, however, prior to his arrival at

sensitiveness, indeed, which she has betrayed upon this subject can only be explained by her pretension to exclusive relations with the Uzbeg principalities, both commercial and political; a pretension which of course has never been recognised by England, and which it may yet be of national importance to us distinctly to disavow.

Among the many curious revelations in Mr. Michell's volume on Khiva, there is one of unusual interest at the present time from its bearing on passing events. It is stated to have been determined by the Emperor, in the event of Perofski's complete success, not to bring the country under the direct jurisdiction of Russia, but merely to rule vicariously through a Kirghiz nominee.* There are, it appears, several families among the Kirghiz-Kazzáks of the Little Horde dependent upon Russia which claim to be of the "White bone" as lineal descendants of Jenghiz Khan, and these families,

Khiva, had been collected and registered by the Russian Cornet Altof." Now Shakespeare was doubtless favoured by circumstances, but still it was mainly owing to his individual energy, tempered by discretion, that the Russian prisoners were allowed to leave Khiva; and he is fully entitled therefore to the credit of having effected their liberation.

* It seems that a special commission was appointed to consider and report on an Expedition to Khiva; and that the Emperor on March 24, 1839, approved of the following measures which had been recommended by the committee.

"1. To commence at once the organisation of an expedition against Khiva, and to establish the necessary depôts and stations on the route without delay.

"2. To conceal the real object of the expedition, which should be given out as a scientific expedition to the Aral Sea.

"3. To postpone the departure of the expedition until after the settlement of English matters in Afghanistan, in order that the influence and impression of the Russian proceedings might have more weight in Central Asia; and that England, in consequence of her own conquests, might no longer have any ground for calling on the Russian Government for explanations. On no account, however, to delay the expedition later than the spring of 1840.

"4. In the event of the expedition terminating successfully, to replace the Khan of Khiva by a trustworthy Kazzák Sultan; to establish order and security as far as possible; to release all the prisoners and to give full freedom to the Russian trade.

"5 To assign 425,000 silver rubles and 12,000 gold ducats for the expenses of the expedition."

It is further curious to compare the estimated expenses of the Russian expedition, which are here given at about 70,000*l.*, with the actual expenses of our own Afghan expedition, amounting from first to last to about 15,000,000*l.* sterling.

which had supplied Governors to the Khivan territory in the last century, still retain a powerful hold on the respect and veneration of the Nomades. If one of these Sultans, then, combining the requirement of undoubted fidelity to the Emperor with an hereditary claim on the affections of the Khivans, had been raised to the "White felt" ("Vambéry's Travels," p. 387), it would have been a wise, and probably a successful, solution of the difficulty; inasmuch as it would have secured to Russia the full advantage of political supremacy without the expense or the danger of a permanent military occupation. And arguing from the known to the unknown, it may thus fairly be inferred that, should the Russian arms in Central Asia attain that dominant position which is promised by their hitherto unchecked career, there is reserved for all the three Uzbeg States an intermediate stage of tributary dependence upon Russia under Kirghiz rulers, before their final incorporation in the Empire.*

There can be no doubt that these demonstrations and counter-demonstrations of the great European Governments powerfully affected the Uzbegs. Bokhara had ever been less inimical to Russia than the sister States of Khiva and Kokand. While she continued, indeed, to overtax Russian trade, and even held Russian subjects in slavery, she still kept up an appearance of friendliness, and despatched frequent Envoys to St. Petersburg. It thus happened that, in compliance with an urgent appeal from the Amír, who was seriously alarmed at the position of the English in Cabul, a singularly well-appointed Russian Mission found itself at Bokhara in 1842. The real object of this Mission—which was presided over by Colonel Butenef, and which numbered among its members Mons. Nic.

---

* (During the nine years which have elapsed since this forecast of Russian policy was sketched, all its anticipations have been realized, except in one particular. Russia *has* obtained a dominant position in all the Khanates, and *has* reduced them to a state of tributary dependence, but she has found it more convenient to govern through the instrumentality of the native chiefs than to introduce foreign rulers from the Kirghiz tribes. At the same time this condition of affairs is avowedly provisional, and will terminate when the war party at St. Petersburg is strong enough to carry out its programme of annexation —1874.)

de Khannikof, who was even then an accomplished Orientalist, together with Lehmann the naturalist,[*] and special officers for the contemplated mining and exploring operations,—was to repair the damage caused by Perofski's failure. Bokhara, in fact, was to be made, through political influence, to subserve —though, perhaps, in a minor degree—the same purpose in regard to Russia, as Afghanistan had been made to subserve in regard to British India, by military power; and it is not improbable, if all had gone on smoothly at Cabul, that Butenef might have succeeded in his object. But storms were now gathering around that city, and the effect at Bokhara was to involve English and Russians in a common disgrace. No sooner, indeed, was the news of the murder of Burnes and Macnaghten and the insurrection at Cabul known at Bokhara, than Stoddart, and Conolly, who had recently joined him, were consigned to a rigorous imprisonment, from which, after months of suffering, they were led forth to public execution; while, the necessity of Russian mediation or support having passed away with the danger of an English invasion, Butenef was in the mean time dismissed with studied disrespect, and the various proposed arrangements which were "to strengthen Russian influence and to develope Russian trade in this part of Asia," were one and all scattered to the winds.

One of the most remarkable portions of Mr. Michell's miscellaneous volume is the 11th chapter, containing M. Zalesoff's account of the diplomatic relations between Russia and Bokhara from 1836 to 1843. The narrative of Colonel Butenef's mission, in 1841, is of especial interest, for it not only places us, as it were, behind the Russian scenes during the most eventful phases of our own Afghan occupation, but it also presents us with a report by an eye-witness of many details relating to the captivity of Stoddart—that most mo-

[*] (Khannikof and Lehmann both published papers, giving the scientific results of their Bokharian experiences at St. Petersburg in 1851, but a popular work of the former author had appeared previously, and was afterwards published in London in an English version by the Baron de Bodé, under the title of "Bokhára: its Ameer and its People. 1845."—1874.)

lancholy episode of a period fraught with error and misfortune —which were before but imperfectly known to any of us, and which are now for the first time rendered accessible to the ordinary English reader. That the Russian Government had throughout exerted itself to the utmost to obtain Stoddart's release has been frequently stated on the best authority, and that Col. Butenef would, on his arrival at Bokhara, carry out his renewed instructions on this head with loyalty and firmness, was no more, perhaps, than might be expected; but the terms in which the Russian envoy notified his success to his colleague at Khiva are entirely new to us, and deserve to be specially recorded, because they convey a spontaneous and most favourable tribute to the personal qualities of the British officer, a tribute indeed all the more striking, that the two agents, representing adverse systems of policy, must necessarily have regarded each other with feelings of official mistrust. "Lieut.-Colonel Stoddart," says the Russian envoy, in his Report to Nikiforof, at Khiva, "a very clever, well-educated, and agreeable man, has, to my great pleasure, been removed this day to the house we occupy;" and in this house, as the honoured guest of the Russian mission, did Colonel Stoddart dwell for a period of two months, during which time he was at any moment at liberty to have taken his departure to Orenburg.* Lord Clanricarde, indeed, our Ambassador at

---

* Mr. Kaye, whose chapter on the Bokhara tragedy is one of the most thrilling portions of his classic work on the Afghan war, was evidently not aware of this intimacy between the Russian and English envoys. The only evidence, indeed, which he could obtain on the subject was the statement of a servant that "There was an ambassador at this time from the Russian Government at Bokhara, who came twice to see the English gentlemen who also visited him." ("Afghan War," Vol. II. p. 506). We may also notice a discrepancy between the dates given by the two authorities for the commencement of Stoddart and Conolly's captivity, which is, to say the least of it, embarrassing. Kaye, calculating from Conolly's letter of March, 11, 1842, which is stated to be the 83rd day of the captivity, shows that the two officers must have been thrown into prison about the 17th of December; whereas Butenef would antedate the event by at least a month; but in truth the Russian dates are not only irreconcilable with the English dates, but with each other; for Butenef reports in one letter that "Conolly was arrested on his arrival at Bokhara in October," whilst in other Reports he says that the Amír only returned from Kokand

St. Petersburg, had urged him to adopt this mode of escape from the country; but a nice—most persons will say an exaggerated—feeling of honour forbad him to acquiesce. It was inconsistent, he thought, with the dignity of England, and consequently with his own duty as a British officer, that he should owe his liberation to the intercession of a foreign Government. He preferred to wait until the British Government could interfere directly in his behalf; but that opportunity never occurred. In the middle of November, as already stated, he was, on receipt of the Cabul news, a second time thrown into prison, and although the sojourn of the Russians at Bokhara was prolonged till the following April, they never again could obtain access to the English prisoners, nor exert any influence on their fate. During the latter part of their stay, indeed, they were even apprehensive of sharing Colonel Stoddart's captivity.

For several years subsequent to the Afghan war there was a lull in Central Asia. Nikiforof had visited Khiva at the same time that Butenef had been despatched to Bokhara, and they had both sought to place the Uzbeg States under treaty obligations to Russia; but the moment was not propitious. A year later, that is in 1842,—while " the avenging army " was doing its work at Cabul, Colonel Danilevski made another attempt; and on this occasion he succeeded in concluding, for the first time, a direct treaty between Russia and Khiva. The precise terms of the Danilevski treaty are nowhere given, but it is understood to have provided for the due protection of the Russian trade; for an entire cessation of slave dealing, and for restraining the Turcomans, Kara-Kalpáks, and Southern Kirghiz, from all inroads on the Russian territory or molestation of Russian subjects; and it is only fair to say that until Russia, five years later, proceeded to establish a military station on the Sir-Daria, or Jaxartes, and thus undertook to exercise a control over tribes, hitherto dependent

on November 7; and that he then promised the Russian envoy, before the arrest of the British officers, that they should accompany him back to Russia. These perhaps are small points, but they are important as tests of trustworthiness.

upon Khiva, the Uzbegs of the Oxus observed with sufficient fidelity the stipulations that had been imposed on them. During this same period, too, commenced that internecine conflict between Kokand and Bokhara, which, up to the present time, has raged with varying intensity, and in more ways than one has facilitated the Russian advance.

8. We have now arrived at a point in the recent history of Central Asia, where a more careful record must be observed of facts, and a more careful consideration must be given, both to motives and results, than have been attempted in the earlier stages of the inquiry. It was in 1847, contemporaneously with our final conquest of the Punjab, that the curtain rose on the aggressive Russian drama in Central Asia, which is not yet played out. Russia had enjoyed the nominal dependency of the Kirghiz-Kazzáks of the Little Horde, who inhabited the western division of the Great Steppe, since 1730; but except in the immediate vicinity of the Orenburg line she had little real control over the tribes. In 1847-48, however, she erected three important fortresses in the very heart of the Steppe; the Karabutak and Ural forts on the Irghiz river, intermediate between Orsk and the Aral Sea, and the Orenburg Fort on the Turgäi river, where the great caravan route from the Jaxartes bifurcates to Orsk and to Troitska. These important works, the only permanent constructions which had been hitherto attempted south of the line—excepting the Mangishlak Fort, on the Caspian, and the Emba and Ak-Bulak entrenchments thrown out as supports to the expedition against Khiva, and afterwards abandoned—enabled Russia for the first time to dominate the western portion of the Steppe, and to command the great routes of communication with Central Asia; but the Steppe forts were after all a mere means to an end; they formed the connecting link between the old frontier of the empire and the long-coveted line of the Jaxartes, and simultaneously therefore with their erection arose the fortification of Raimsk, near the embouchure of the river, subsequently called Aralsk, or "the fort

of the Aral," and now bearing the official designation of Fort No. 1.*

In the manifesto which Russia has lately presented to the various Courts of Europe in explanation of her Central-Asian policy, she has traced with some ingenuity the successive steps by which a civilized Government, in contact with nomadic tribes, may be compelled to advance in the mere interests of order, and without any aggressive tendency whatever. She undertakes to show that the territory inhabited by a migratory population is an impossible frontier for a fixed Government; that there is no resource, indeed, but to push on, until a point is reached where the limitary nations are sufficiently advanced in social organization to admit of definite relations being established with them. The argument seems to be made for the occasion, rather than to be of general application, and is, besides, strained to an extreme point to furnish the required ground of justification. It is quite conceivable that the occupation of the valley of the Jaxartes may have been judged by the Emperor Nicholas to be indispensable to the due development of Russian power in Central Asia, and indeed it is well known that this has been the traditional creed of the empire since the days of Ivan Vasilevitch; but it is impossible to admit that the southern skirt of the Great Steppe is in reality a more defensible barrier against aggression than the northern skirt; and it is really pushing the prerogative of civilization to an absurd extent to pretend that it was necessary for the legitimate exercise of trade, or in the general interests of humanity, to assume the goverment of 2,500,000† independent Kirghiz.

---

* (Fort No. 1 does not occupy the exact position of the original fortified work of Aralsk, but is in the immediate vicinity.—1874.)

† Humboldt in his "Asie Centrale," tom. ii. p. 129, note 2, has collected and compared all the most reliable evidence with regard to the strength of the Kirghiz population, and the result of his calculation is a total of 2,400,000 for the aggregate of the tribes in 1843. In this estimate, however, he includes the Kara-Kirghiz, or Buruts, whom he persists in regarding as a portion of the Great Horde, though the Russians have conclusively shown that no such connexion exists. In collating the English and Russian accounts of Turkestan it must be borne in mind that we apply the name of Kazzák alone to the Kirghiz of the three hordes, called by the Russians Kirghiz-Kaisak; and that when we speak of the Kirghiz we

M

At any rate the recent British annexations in India, which are alluded to in the manifesto as parallel cases, repose avowedly on very different grounds, the Punjab having been forfeited in retribution for the invasion of our territory by the Sikhs, and the treachery of the Amírs having, as it was always maintained, led to their expulsion from Sinde.

Before tracing the Russian progress up the course of the Jaxartes it may be as well to glance at the previous condition of this country. At the end of the last century the Kara-Kalpáks (or "black bonnets"), then a very powerful tribe, who had proffered their allegiance to Russia at an earlier period (1723), and had furnished a ruler to Khiva, Khan Kaip, a Sultan of the "white bone," in 1770, pitched their tents on both sides of the lower portion of the river, and were regarded as masters of the region. The Kirghiz of the Little Horde, who were Russian subjects in name, though certainly not at that time in reality, gradually dispossessed the Kara-Kalpáks, and these Kirghiz were in their turn subjugated by the Uzbegs of Kokand, who, between the years 1817 and 1847, erected a series of forts along the river from Turkestan as low down as the 64th degree of longitude, from whence they levied black mail on passing caravans, and exacted tribute from all the nomads in the vicinity. The Khivans, too, who had always claimed a right of sovereignty over the country adjoining the Aral and intermediate between the mouths of the Jaxartes and

mean the Buruts, or Kara-Kirghiz, usually named by the Russians Diko-kameni. It is worth observing, too, that the Kipcháks, who, according to Vambéry, confirmed as he is by the reports of the recent English envoys, form the most influential section of the Kokand community, are hardly mentioned by the Russians as an independent body; in fact, Valikhanoff asserts ("Russians in Central Asia," p. 103) that the Kipcháks, together with the Naimans and Kitáis, have to a great extent become incorporated with the Kara-Kirghiz, or Buruts. See also p. 89 for the common origin of the Kipcháks and Kirghiz. (The War Office Confidential Report of 1873 has the following passage on the Russian subjugation of the Kirghiz tribes. "In a work of much research on the subject by L. Oliphant, he states as the result of his investigations, that the Little and Middle Hordes gave in their allegiance in 1730-40; that the Middle Horde revolted at the beginning of the reign of Catherine about 1760-70; and again submitted towards the end of her reign, about 1790; and that the Great Horde was first subjugated during the reign of that Empress."—1874.)

the Oxus, established, in 1846, a strong position on the Kuvan-Daria, one of the chief southern arms of the Delta of the Jaxartes, which took the name of "the Fort of Khoja-Niáz," from its first Governor, and which besides commanding the two routes through the Kizil-kum (or "red sand") desert, leading respectively from the Russian frontier to Khiva and Bokhara, also effectually controlled the Kirghiz in their migrations to the south of the river. When the Russians, therefore, by direction of General Obruchev, Governor-General of Orenburg, first planted their foot on the Jaxartes, both the Khivans and the Kokandis at once took the alarm and commenced a series of desultory hostilities, sometimes against the Russian detachments traversing the Steppe from Orenburg and Orsk, sometimes against the Kirghiz who assisted their advance. In fact, from this time, Danilevski's treaty of 1842 must be considered to have been virtually abrogated, the Khivans on the Kokand frontier resorting to every sort of opposition short of an open declaration of war.

In the meantime the Russian progress was necessarily slow. Notwithstanding the support afforded to troops crossing the Steppe from the Orenburg line, by the Ural Fort upon the Irghiz, there was still a tract of considerable difficulty to the southward of that point, and skirting the north-eastern shores of the Aral, across which all the Russian convoys and detachments must necessarily pass in their onward march to the Jaxartes. This tract has been hitherto but very imperfectly understood. By some it has been supposed to be almost impassable: by others it has been deemed so easy as to be called "the highway to India." In reality the road across it is in no way comparable, either in length or in difficulty, to the desert portion of any of the other Steppe routes, leading to Khiva westward of the Aral, or more to the eastward to Fort Perofski or Tashkend. The Kara-kum, or "black sands," which enclose the Aral to the north-east, are not traversed on this line from north to south, but are merely skirted on their western border, and the worst part of the road,—the only really bad part indeed—is its lower portion which crosses the saline Steppe from the extreme corner of the Aral to the bed of the Jaxartes. The utmost extent, moreover, of this difficult portion, bordering the Kara-kum Desert, is under two hundred miles; and even here, according to the Russian description of the route, translated by Mr. Michell, "wells exist at every stage in sufficient numbers for the supply of considerable caravans."* While therefore, owing to the limited supply of water and to a general scarcity of forage along the entire route, it may be held to be impassable to any large number of troops marching in a united body, there would not seem to be any serious hindrance to the passage of detachmemts of moderate strength; and in fact it is along this track, which is everywhere practicable to wheeled carriages, that have passed, not only the troops, supplies, artillery, ammunition, and stores belonging to the Russian field-force and garrisons now serving on the Jaxartes, but also the boilers, iron plates, machinery, and heavy armament of the steamers and vessels of war that were put together at Fort Aralsk.

Simultaneously with the erection of the fortress of Aralsk the Russians prepared to launch a small flotilla which might occupy the sea of Aral and facilitate the further ascent of the Jaxartes. Three small vessels, accordingly, which were built at Orenburg and afterwards taken to pieces and transported overland to the Jaxartes, first carried the Russian flag upon this inland sea in 1847-48. They were followed in due course by two iron steamers, which, being constructed originally in Sweden, were then passed on in pieces *viâ* Petersburg to Samara, on the Wolga, and ultimately to Aralsk, where they were put together and launched in 1852; the total cost of the two vessels, including their conveyance to the Jaxartes and the salaries of the artisans employed in constructing them, amounting to no more than 7400*l*. Having thus prepared a secondary base of some strength on the Sea of Aral, Russia proceeded to put in execution her great scheme of occupying

* "Russians in Central Asia," p. 130. In tracing the routes and marches described in Mr. Michell's work, great care must be taken to distinguish between the Ural Fort or Uralsk, on the Irghiz, and the Aral Fort or Aralsk near the mouth of the Jaxartes; for, throughout the work in question, the orthography of Aralsk is employed for both positions indifferently. See particularly pp. 340, 370, and 391,

the lower portion of the valley of the Jaxartes, her avowed object being to establish, in the first place, a line of fortresses along the river as far as the point where the Kara-táú range sinks into the desert, and from thence to supply other links, either along the old frontier of the Chú or by the more southern line of the Talas, which should connect the Jaxartes chain with the eastern settlements about the Issi-kúl. In this arrangement she professed to recognise no territorial encroachment, as her own Kirghiz already camped on the right bank of the Jaxartes, and the Chú had been adopted long previously as the southern frontier of the Steppe; but, nevertheless, there is no doubt that the Uzbegs of Kokand, who were then in possession of the great river, considered the Russian approach as a direct invasion, while the despair of the Khivans on the southern bank found vent in their piteous exclamations that "if the Russians were to drink the waters of the Sir-Daria with them they could no longer exist."

The principal fort on the Jaxartes, which had been constructed by the Kokandis in 1817, and had ever since dominated the river, was named Ak-Mesjed (or the "White Mosque").* It was situated at the distance of about three hundred miles from the mouth of the river, and in Uzbeg estimation was a place of very considerable strength. The first offensive movement of the Russians was a reconnaissance in strength against this place, an expedition being organised for the purpose, the details of which are calculated to impress the military reader with a very high opinion of Russian daring. That a small detachment, indeed, of four hundred men, with two field-pieces, should have been sent forth into an unknown country, and have been directed to penetrate to a distance of

* In the Russian maps and geographical papers this place is usually called Ak-Meshed, which is nonsense. *Meshed* signifies "the place of martyrdom," being the locative noun of the root *shahad*, to witness, and the name thus very properly applied to places like Nejjef, the scene of the martyrdom of Ali, Meshed in Khorassan, where the Imam Raza was martyred, &c.; but *Mesjed* (from whence the corrupted form of Mosque) simply means "the place of worship," being the locative noun of the root "*sajad*," "to bow down," or "make obeisance," and is thus of much more general application.

220 miles from their base, with no support in the interval, and liable to be attacked at any point of the march by overwhelming numbers of the enemy, would have been considered an act of foolhardiness, had not the expedition been crowned with signal success. The detachment being unprovided with heavy guns, or scaling ladders, was unable indeed to capture the inner citadel of Ak-Mesjed, which was defended by stout mud walls, twenty feet high; but it made a complete reconaissance of the locality, destroyed and burnt all the outer works and buildings, and, on its return-march, demolished three auxiliary forts which the Kokandis held lower down the river. The temper of the enemy having been thus tried, and found to be far from formidable, in the summer of the next year, 1853, a second expeditionary column, amounting to 1500 men, with ten pieces of artillery and three mortars,—being part of a much larger force which had been sent from Orenburg, especially for the reduction of the Jaxartes valley,—marched again from Aralsk up the river, supported on this occasion by the steamer "Perofski." When the column reached Ak-Mesjed, the place was found to have been so much strengthened since the reconnaissance of the previous year, as to be only assailable by regular approaches. The first battery was accordingly erected on July 5th, and, after three weeks labour, a covered sap having been run across the ditch, and a breach effected by springing a mine, the place was stormed and taken by assault on the 27th of the month;—230 bodies of the Kokandis, which were counted in the ditch and about the breach, testifying to the obstinacy of the defence.* At the same time that Ak-Mesjed was captured, a small detachment from the Russian column took and destroyed the fort of Julek, one hundred versts higher up the river; and this was the extreme point of the Russian advance for the next eight fol-

---

* (The first expedition against Ak-Mesjed in July 1852, was commanded by Col. Blaremberg. The second expedition, which took place a year later (July 1853), was led by Perofski in person, who imposed his own name on the fort after its capture. Yacûb Khan, the present Amír of Kashgar is understood to have belonged to the Ak-Mesjed garrison, when the place was stormed by the Russians, and to have escaped with difficulty from their hands.—1874.)

lowing years. The object of the Russians, indeed, seems to have now been to consolidate their position, which at first was far from secure, instead of attempting further conquests. For some months after the loss of Ak-Mesjed, repeated efforts were made by the Kokandis to recover the place; and on one occasion (December 14, 1853), a pitched battle was fought under the walls of the fort, in which the Kokandis were said to have lost two thousand men. The Khivans also,—without avowedly breaking with the Russian authorities,—from the fort of Khoja-Niáz, which flanked the Russian line, were continually threatening the detached forts between Aralsk and Ak-Mesjed, until at length General Perofski (in 1857) deemed it necessary to send a detachment to destroy the fort. Even the Bokharians, although at war with Kokand, showed great dissatisfaction at the Russian advance. But the most serious impediment to further progress, which assailed Russia at this time, was the unsettled state of the Steppe. A Kirghiz leader of the name of Izzet Kutebar, an hereditary robber, threw the whole country into disorder from the Orenburg line to the Aral; and, for five years, from 1853 to 1858, set at defiance all the Russian efforts to capture or expel him. During this interval, too, the exhaustive effects of the Crimean war were felt, even at such a remote point as the Jaxartes, and Russia was only too well satisfied to hold her ground, without provoking the further active hostilities of the Uzbegs. Instead of extending her line of forts, therefore, she merely gave them a fresh distribution with a view to their better mutual support. Fort Aralsk was thus transferred to a more convenient position, at the point where the Cazala branch of the Delta left the main river, and was officially named, Fort No. 1, retaining, however, in the country its more correct geographical title of Cazala, under which name it will now be found at the passage over the Jaxartes, in all the itineraries leading from Orenburg, either to Khiva or Bokhara.* A second fort, called No. 2 (originally Fort Karmakchi), connected Cazala with Ak-Mesjed, which, under the Russian rule, took the name of Fort Perofski in honour of the

---

* See for instance the pamphlet published last year by the Italian silk merchants, relating their captivity at Bokhara. Pp. 4 and 5.

Governor-General of Orenburg, who in 1853 led the famous expedition against it.* Above Fort Perofski, also, another position was established as late as 1861, at the old Kokandi settlement of Julek; and it is these four fortifications only, which form at the present day the Russian line of posts along the desert portion of the Jaxartes valley. It must be remembered, indeed, that the physical features of this river are somewhat remarkable. Watering with its numerous affluents in the upper part of its basin one of the most fertile and delightful countries in the world, and fringed throughout its course with the richest cultivation, it debouches below the town of Turkestan upon a saline steppe, and its character becomes entirely altered. Where the banks are high, a thin belt of jungle alone separates the river from the desert; where they are low, inundations, forming reedy lagoons and impassable morasses, spread for hundreds of miles over the face of the plain; in the intermediate portions alone, where the banks admit the river over the adjacent lands at the time of flood, but cut off the supply of water at other seasons, is there at present much cultivation or pasturage. In such positions the lands are said to be still exceedingly fertile, the irrigating waters overlaying the surface with a rich alluvial loam, which, in combination with the saline soil, is found to be peculiarly favourable to agriculture. Whether Russian engineering science, by a skilful management of the waters of the river, will be able to conquer the general sterility of the adjoining steppe to any appreciable extent remains to be seen; but it is certain that in all history the lower basin of the river has been regarded as an irreclaimable desert, the town of Otrar, the scene of the great Timour's death, and situated a short distance from Turkestan, at the confluence of the Arys with the Jaxartes, being the last inhabited place in the descent of the river towards the Aral.†

---

* (A third fort, called No. 3, had also been established at Komish-Kurghan, between Ak-Mesjed and No. 2, but was abandoned in 1855.— 1874.)

† Admiral Boutakoff of the Russian Navy, already well known to geographers for his admirable survey of the Sea of Aral in 1849-50, recently submitted to the Société Impériale Géographique de Russie (December 2, 1864) a most interesting report of his ascent of the river Jaxartes, for a distance of 1505 versts, above 1000 miles,

The Emperor Baber, indeed, who, as the king of the country and a man of singular intelligence, ought to have been well acquainted with its geography, states positively that "the river is wholly swallowed up in the sandy desert below Turkestan, and disappears."

4. We must now briefly trace the march of events to the eastward. It was not merely in the country of the little Horde that Russian power had been making its way since Perofski's expedition of 1889. Similar success had attended the efforts made from the Siberian line to bring under control the Kirghiz of the Middle Horde in the northern division of the Steppe, and of the Great Horde, around Lake Balkash. The Russian occupation, however, of Zungaria or the Trans-Ili region, as it is usually called by them, to the south-east of Lake Balkash, is of quite recent date. Fort Vernoé, on the site of the old Mongolian city of Almaty, was founded in 1854, and the extension of the line to the westward, by Kastek and Tokmak to the Uzbeg fort of Pishpek, was only gradually effected between that time and 1862. Vernoé is one of those military-agricultural colonies which Russia provides for her veteran soldiers, and which, wherever they can be planted, under favourable circumstances of soil and climate, give so much solidity to the frontier. Between four and five thousand colonists were here congregated at the outset, and their numbers have since much increased, as the two great commercial routes from Kokand to Kulja, west and east—and from Kashgar to Semipolatinsk, south and north cross each other at this point and thus attract traders to the spot. In the vicinity of Fort Vernoé and Lake Issi-kul, which is immediately to the south,*

from its embouchure to the vicinity of Tashkend. He was unable to ascend higher on account of the exhaustion of his fuel, but understood that the river continued navigable for several hundred miles further on. Admiral Boutakoff's tracing of the river, verified throughout by astronomical observation, is being now published at St. Petersburg.

* Lake Issi-kûl (or "the warm lake") has attracted much interest in modern times, from the singular fact that in the famous Catalan Map of 1374, which gives the caravan route pursued by the Genoese traders from the northern shore of the Caspian to China, an Armenian monastery is noticed to the north of the lake, apparently in the position of Almaty (the modern Fort Vernoé), which is said to contain the body of St. Mat·

the Russians first came in contact with the Kara-Kirghiz or Buruts (usually named by the Russians Dikokameni) ; but neither from this tribe, whose wanderings extend from Fort Vernoé over the whole Kokand territory of Badakhshan, nor from the Kirghiz of the Great Horde, who, throughout the south-eastern part of the steppe, are a good deal mixed up with the Buruts, was any serious opposition experienced in the establishment of the authority of Russia in this remote and almost unknown region. Her officers, combining the zeal of explorers with the national passion for fresh acquisition, surveyed and mapped, and took possession,* until the frontier of the empire attained in one direction the crest of the Tian-

thew. Modern criticism is not disposed, in default of other evidence, to recognise this isolated settlement of Armenian monks at a distance of nearly 3000 miles from Echmiadzin, but no other reasonable explanation has been offered of the old Spanish notice. We would suggest, however, that the monastery alluded to was Buddhist and Thibetan, similar to, or perhaps identical with, that visited by Semenoff in 1857 at Alma-Arassan, near the southern shore of the lake, where he found "inscriptions in Thibetan characters still in excellent preservation." (See "Journal of the Royal Geographical Society," vol. xxxi. p. 362.) (It is not impossible that the story of St. Matthew brought back by the Genoese traders to Europe, may have originated in the name of Almaty, which however in reality is derived from "*alma,*" an apple."—1874.)

* A series of very excellent papers on the geography of this part of Asia, by Semenoff, Golubef, Abramof, and Veniukof, have been translated from the Russian by J. Michell, Esq., and published in the 31st and 32nd volumes of the Royal Geographical Society's Journal; and others of still greater interest remain untranslated. The travels, indeed, of Wilyaminow-Sermow (written by Michell as Veliaminof-Zernof), who appears, from the extracts in Mr. Lumley's Trade Report, to have visited most of the cities of Kokand; and the routes by which Valikhanoff—the Russianised Kirghiz whose adventures form the most curious portion of Mr. Michell's volume—passed to and fro, between the Thian-shan Mountains and Kashgar, would be of surpassing interest at present to the English reader. It is to be hoped, also, that we shall be favoured with an English version of Boutakoff's survey and map of the Jaxartes. (As the papers of Wilyaminow-Sermow, which were published at St. Petersburg in 1859, have been superseded in interest by the later publications of Fedchenko, Schuyler and other travellers who have visited Kokand under more favourable circumstances, so on the Kashgar frontier the scientific reports of Osten-Saken and Colonel Gordon have ably supplemented the easier and lighter narratives of Reinthal and Valikhanoff. Boutakoff's survey of the Jaxartes continues however to be the best, and almost the only authority on the subject.—1874.)

shan or "Celestial Mountains" overlooking Chinese Turkestan, and abutted in another upon the line of forts with which the Kokandis had tesselated their north-east border.

5. According to the original programme which Russia had put forth, the work of reconstruction was now complete without any further dislocation of territory. As her position had been consolidated to the East by the settlement of Kopal, Fort Vernoé, and Kastek, between the Chinese border and the Kokandi outpost of Tokmak on the Chú; and as a chain of forts had been also constructed to the west, along the Jaxartes from the Aral to Julek, it merely remained to establish a cordon of outposts along the valley of the Chú, which should connect these two flanking portions of the frontier together, in order to possess the great desideratum of a continuous military line to the south of the Steppe, in substitution of the old Siberian line to the north. It was hardly to be expected, however, that Russia would remain content with the arid and inhospitable line of the Chú, when, at a short distance to the south beyond the Talas, which runs parallel to the Chú, and along the northern slopes of the Kara-táú and Boroldäi ranges, a chain of forts were ready to her hand, which the Kokandis had constructed to protect their own frontiers from invasion from the Steppe, and to curb the predatory Kirghiz. These fortresses, indeed, bearing the name of Suzak, Cholak-Kurgan, Avliata,* Merké, and Pishpek, were so conveniently situated for the Russian purpose as almost to invite attack. Although nearly isolated from support, in no case did they surrender without a struggle. At Pishpek, indeed, in October, 1862, and at Avliata early in 1864, the garrisons offered a most determined resistance; but eventually they one and all succumbed to the Russian power. Even this advanced position, however, did not now satisfy the Russian requirements. The line within the Talas was still too near the desert. It failed also to

* This name is usually written in the maps Avlié-Ata, but in the Russian official papers it appears as a single word, Avliata. It is supposed to mark the site of Taraz or Talas, which was the most westerly point laid down by the missionaries Arochi, Espigny, and Hallerstein, in their astronomical survey of Turkestan, conducted under the orders of the Chinese Emperor in 1759.

furnish the troops with sufficient supplies, and, above all, it did not circumscribe the unruly Kirghiz tribes who had sought refuge in the fastnesses of the Kara-táú and Boroldäi mountains. The Russians, therefore, seem to have now laid aside all further scruple; and having already cleared away in 1860-61 the two intermediate outposts of Yañi-Kurgan and Dín-Kurgan, which the Kokandis had erected beyond the last Russian settlement of Julek, to cover the approach to the town of Turkestan, they boldly continued their advance up the valley of the great river, so as to include within their frontier the ranges north of Kokand, and intervening between that fertile region and the desert. The bulwark of Kokand, on this side, was the town of Hazret-i-Turkestan, so called from the tomb of a famous saint, otherwise known as Khoja Ahmed;[*] and this place surrendered to the Russians early in 1864.[†] The Kokandis then fell back on their next defensible position, Chemkend, a city about 100 versts in the rear,[‡] which they proceeded to fortify to the best of their ability, and from whence they directed a series of attacks on the Russian outposts, intended to impede their further advance. In repelling such attacks, the Russians assert that they were led on to the town of Chemkend itself, the capture of which in the month of October closed the campaign, and placed them in command of one of the richest districts of the provinces, a district, indeed, which the "Invalide Russe" describes from the official reports as "le grenier de toute la contrée entre le Tchou et le Syr-Daria."

[*] The Russians usually name this place *Asret* for Hazret; but Hazret or Hazret Sultan is merely a title of honour which was borne by the famous Saint, Khoja Ahmed, who was buried at Turkestan. Turkestan is constantly mentioned in the memoirs of Baber, as the chief place of a district of the same name beyond Ferghaneh and on the confines of the desert; but the name is not old, and is not found in the Arabic geographers.

[†] (It would appear from the Russian published accounts, that the expedition of Tchernaiyef from Fort Vernoé against Avliata, and the expedition of Verefkin from Fort Perofski against Turkestan were simultaneous, and formed parts of the same general plan of operations, the two columns subsequently combining in the attack on Chemkend.—1874.)

[‡] Chemkend is also a new name, the town having apparently risen into note since the day of Baber. The chief place of this very fertile district was anciently Seiram, which is now stated to be a mere village.

So grave a violation as this invasion of Kokand and capture of its chief cities involved of the principles on which Russia had hitherto professed to be acting, and which merely regarded the strategic requirements of her southern frontier, could not fail to attract the serious consideration of England, interested —and very properly so—as we always had been in the preservation of the independence of the Uzbeg states. The circular letter, already alluded to, which was in November last addressed to the "Legations and Embassies of the Russian Emperor in Foreign Countries," and which professed to place before Europe in its true light the Asiatic Policy of Russia,— this letter, although somewhat grandiloquently expressed, was nevertheless to a certain extent reassuring; for it explained how the late territorial acquisitions had been brought about "by imperious necessity," and in opposition to the wish of the Emperor; and it further asserted, with categorical precision, that the expansion of the Empire in Central Asia had now reached its limit. The only unsatisfactory part of the explanation was the doubt which it seemed to imply, whether, in spite of the best intentions on the part of the Russian Government, the peace of the East was not liable to be compromised at any moment by the indiscreet or over-zealous conduct of a military commander.

There will probably be abundant opportunity in the sequel for testing the value of Prince Gortchakoff's Circular; indeed the prosecution of the Kokand campaign during the present year has already furnished an instructive commentary, having completely stultified the Russian assurance of a finality of conquest. The peroration of Prince Gortchakoff's Circular, however, is so important, and is so likely to become the subject of future reference, that we make no excuse for quoting it in extenso:—

"En effet, la ligne primitive de nos frontières le long de la Syr-Daria jusqu'au fort Pérovsky d'un côté, et de l'autre jusqu'au Lac Issyk-Koul, avait l'inconvénient d'être presque à la limite du désert. Elle était interrompue sur un immense espace entre les deux points extrêmes; elle n'offrait pas assez de ressources à nos troupes, et laissait en dehors des tribus sans cohésion avec lesquelles nulle stabilité n'était possible."

"Malgré notre répugnance à donner à nos frontières une plus grande étendue, ces motifs ont été assez puissants pour déterminer le Gouvernement Impérial à établir la continuité de cette ligne entre le Lac Issyk-Koul et la Syr-Daria, en fortifiant la ville de Tchemkend, récemment occupée par nous.

"En adoptant cette ligne nous obtenons un double résultat; d'un côté, la contrée qu'elle embrasse est fertile, boisée, arrosée par de si nombreux cours d'eau; elle est habitée en partie par des tribus Kirghises, qui ont déjà reconnu notre domination; elle offre donc des éléments favorables à la colonisation et à l'approvisionnement de nos garnisons. De l'autre, elle nous donne pour voisins immédiats les populations fixes, agricoles, et commerçantes du Kokand.

"Nous nous trouvons en face d'un milieu social plus solide, plus compacte, moins mobile, mieux organisé; et cette considération marque avec une précision géographique la limite où l'intérêt et la raison nous prescrivent d'arriver et nous commandent de nous arrêter, parce que, d'une part, toute extension ultérieure de notre domination rencontrant désormais, non plus des milieux inconstants comme les tribus nomades, mais des Etats plus régulièrement constitués, exigerait des efforts considérables, et nous entraînerait, d'annexion en annexion, dans des complications infinies; et que, d'autre part, ayant désormais pour voisins de pareils Etats, malgré leur civilisation arriérée et l'instabilité de leur condition politique, nous pouvons néanmoins assurer que des relations régulières pourront un jour se substituer, pour l'avantage commun, aux désordres permanents qui ont paralysé jusqu'ici l'essor de ces contrées.

"Tels sont, Monsieur, les intérêts qui servent de mobile à la politique de notre auguste maître dans l'Asie Centrale, tel est le but final que les ordres de Sa Majesté Impériale ont tracé à l'action de son Cabinet."*

6. Now the ink was hardly dry with which this Manifesto was written when hostilities had been resumed on the Jaxartes with greater bitterness than ever. According to Russian accounts the Kokandis were again the aggressors, and it is possible that, exasperated by the loss of Turkestan and

* (As there is no conceivable reason why Prince Gortchakoff should have advisedly put forth a mendacious manifesto, to be contradicted immediately afterwards by the inexorable logic of facts, we can only believe him to have been guilty of an entire want of political foresight in supposing that he could thus control the course of events, and impose an arbitrary limit to the extension of Russian power by a mere expression of the will of the Emperor. In reality when Russia had once crossed the Steppe there could be no substantial or permanent check to her expansion, until she was arrested by the barrier of British-Indian influence, "neutral zones" or intermediate independent states being mere temporary expedients to lessen the friction of impact.—1874.)

Chemkend, they were determined to keep the Russian lines in a constant state of alarm. Skirmishes seem to have been incessant, and one very serious affair occurred near the close of the year, in which a " Sotnia " of Cossacks, which threw itself, at Ikhaneh, in the way of an Uzbeg army marching from Tashkend upon Turkestan, was almost annihilated. With the new year was promulgated an Imperial decree, constituting " the Province of Turkestan " which was to be subordinate, according to the official statement, both in civil and military government, to Orenburg, but which in reality seems to have exercised, ever since, that autonomy which belongs of necessity to an exposed frontier territory. Turkestan comprised the whole country stretching west and east from the Aral to Lake Issi-kul and north and south from the Chú to the Sir-Daria; but it seems to be still a matter of doubt whether the name was given with a view to its general geographical propriety, the province in question forming one of a group with Uzbeg Turkestan and Chinese Turkestan, or whether, as in the time of Baber, the chief place in the district, Hazret-i-Turkestan, was allowed to impose its name on the surrounding region.* General Krishanovski of Orenburg was nominally at the head of the civil administration of this territory, but General Tchernaieff, who continued comm toand the army, was virtually the governor. In April last, the Bokharians, having again invaded Kokand, and possessed themselves of Khojend, according to the normal routine of their

---

* The 'Journal de St. Pétersbourg' of Feb. 26, 1865, in replying to the criticism of the 'Morning Post' on the creation of this new Government of Turkestan, has the followiog passage :
—" C'est à cette même insuffisance de notions géographiques qu'il faut sans doute attribuer les communications du 'Morning Post' sur la nouvelle dénomination du *province de Turkestan* que le Gouvernement Russe vient de donner à la région des Steppes Kirghises ayant pour chef lieu et point central la ville de Tourkestan ou de Hasrett, région qui fait depuis longtemps partie de l'Empire. Pour ne pas voir dans une simple mesure administrative qui s'explique d'elle-même, un motif d'alarme ou d'appréhension, i suffirait de jeter un coup d'œil sur la earte de l'Asie Centrale. On y verrait que le nom de Turkestan est donné d'une part à la contrée qui s'étend des rives méridionales de la mer Caspienne au frontières de la Chine, et de l'autre à cette partie de l'Empire Chinois luimême qui se trouve enclavée entre le Thibet et les Montagnes Célestes."

campaigns, Tchernaieff marched out of Chemkend, as is alleged, "to observe the Bokharian proceedings." He had a preliminary skirmish with the Kokandis at Niáz Beg, on the river Chirchik, upon the 27th of April, and fought a pitched battle with them on May 9th, in the immediate vicinity of Tashkend, the Kokandi leader, Alim Kúl, who was Regent of the State during the minority of the Khan, Sultan Sahib, falling in the fight with three hundred of his followers. It would have been only natural that the Russians, after this signal victory, should have marched at once to the assault of Tashkend ;* and indeed why they remained for another five weeks, hesitating to pluck the pear which was ready to fall into their hands, can only be a matter of conjecture. According to their own reports, they expected that the inhabitants of Tashkend, a commercial race who ardently desired, as it is said, to come under Russian protection, would themselves rise and expel the Kokandi garrison; and it was only when they found this to be impracticable, and that in default of Russian assistance the Tashkendis were prepared to call in the aid of the Bokharians from Khojend, that Tchernaieff decided to avoid this threatened complication by leading the Russians to the assault. The place was accordingly stormed on the night of June 15th, 1865, and from that hour the fate of Kokand may be considered to have been sealed; for although it has been stated that the conquest of Tashkend is exceptional, and, being directed to a temporary political purpose, will not be persevered in beyond the period required for the rectification of the military frontier, and for assuring the future independence of the city as a free emporium for the trade of Central Asia, there is in reality, as far as can be seen, no possible reason for the abandonment of Tashkend, that would not equally apply to Turkestan and Chemkend. The loss of Tashkend is in fact a death-blow to the independence of Kokand. It places the commerce of the country, on which its prosperity depends, entirely at the com-

* Tashkend is the ancient *Shash*, a place of great celebrity from the very earliest times. For a good account of its modern state see Vambéry's Travels, p. 384; and Lumley's Report on the Russian Trade with Central Asia, p. 283.

CH. III.] THE RUSSIANS IN CENTRAL ASIA. 177

mand of Russia, since all the great lines of communication from the north concentrate at this place, and the only question therefore for the consideration of the Emperor's Government would now seem to be, whether the new province of Turkestan should be made to comprise at once the whole Khanat of Kokand, or whether it may not be more prudent to employ a friendly Kirghiz Sultan*—and there are many such who have · strong family claims on the allegiance of the Kokandis—in the administration of the country, until Russia may be prepared to enter on the direct government of this noble principality, which stretches north and south from the Kirghiz Steppe to the mountains of Badakhshan,† and west and east from the Aral Sea to the Chinese border at Kashgar.‡ Before we pro-

---

* (Kokand has in fact been administered for the last nine years by an Uzbeg Chief, named Khodáyár Khan, who was first placed in power by his son-in-law, the Ameer of Bokhara, but who has ever since conducted himself with · the strictest loyalty in his relations with Russia. He represents the Kirghiz faction in Kokand as opposed to the Kipcháks, and is understood to be now in danger of losing his crown, through the preponderance of the latter tribes.— 1874.)

† (The Southern frontier of Kokand is not very clearly defined. The Murghábi river, however, a branch of which flows from Karakul, is the boundary in the Pàmir Steppe between Kokand and Wakhan; and further west, Shignan and Darwaz, belonging respectively to Badakhshan and Bokhara, enclose the Kokandian district of Kara-tegin to the south.— 1874.)

‡ There is one other point in Central Asia to which Russia has been directing her attention with some earnestness, and upon which, therefore, it behoves us to bestow a passing notice. We allude to the city of Kashgar, the northern capital of Chinese Turkestan. Russia acquired a right, by the late Treaty of Pekin, to establish a factory and nominate a Consul at Kashgar, but she has not yet attempted to realize that right. Her persistent declaration, however, throughout the Turkestan discussions, that Kashgar is the aim and limit of her commercial policy in Central Asia, betrays her real anxiety on the subject; and such anxiety—as in the case of Tashkend—but too often foreshadows military occupation. Now Kashgar, with some rare intervals of independence, has been for the last century in the position of a conquered state, held in subjection by the presence o a foreign garrison ; and notwithstanding, therefore, the great size of the city—containing 16,000 houses—and notwithstanding the fanatical disposition of its Mahomedan inhabitants, the transition from Chinese to Russian rule would not be likely to be of a very violent character. Nor, we presume, would there be much difficulty in establishing a direct military communication between Kashgar and the new Russian settlements on the Upper Naryn (Kurtka, Truz, &c.), and through them with. Fort Vernoé and the districts beyond the Thian-Shan

N

ceed, however, to show the probable course which the Russian policy will take in the new field now opening out to her ambition, it is important to review the position of England in regard to Central Asia, and especially in regard to Afghanistan,—the portion of Central Asia which most concerns us—during the period of this great development of Russian power to the North.

7. It was not so much our retirement from Afghanistan, in 1842, as the circumstances under which that retirement was affected that disparaged our position in Central Asia. Had we remained in the country for another year after the recovery of the prisoners; and had we then withdrawn in an orderly and honourable manner, and in pursuance of an arrangement with the parties into whose hands we had committed the Government of the country, the effects of our previous disasters would have been mitigated, if not entirely removed; but retiring as we did, without any understanding with the Doorání chiefs, and pursued by an implacable foe down to the

range. Again, it is probable that Kashgar in the hands of Russia would become a great emporium of trade, being centrically situated, with China to the east, India to the south, Turkestan to the west, and Siberia to the north; and it is further certain that the presence of the Russians, if securely seated in this Tartar capital at the distance of 300 miles from our political frontier, would be sensibly felt in India. But on the other hand, Kashgar, owing to the sterility of the adjoining territory, could never become a nucleus of extensive colonization like the rich districts on the Jaxartes; and so long, therefore, as the Russians remained quiescent, and merely occupied with commerce, the advanced geographical position would be of little real moment, the impassive and prayer-grinding Thibetans, indeed, serving the purpose of a "buffer" far more effectually than the restless and impressible Afghans, who cover the more westerly portion of our northern frontier. (Since this was written Kashgar has occupied a large share of public attention, owing to the adventurous journeys of Messrs. Shaw and Hayward, and the subsequent missions of Mr. Forsyth. The position is one at present of considerable complexity, Russia and England having both concluded treaties with the Amír, Yacúb Khan, and having established commercial relations with the country, while China, which is bent on reasserting her supremacy, is said to have massed a very large body of troops on the Eastern frontier with a view to immediate invasion. If the Amír should be really in danger, it would seem that his European allies must interfere to protect him, though it would no doubt be very inconvenient to us to afford material aid, while the presence also of a Russian auxiliary force at Yarkend would cause excitement both in Cabul and Cashmere, and lead, perhaps, to serious results.—1874.)

last pass debouching on the plains, the previous ill effects on our reputation were no doubt enhanced; the general impression, indeed, being, both in India and Central Asia, that we were fairly driven from the mountains. It is not unusual, even, to find a belief amongst our own officers, that in retiring from Afghanistan we yielded to superior strength; whereas in reality the country was more completely in our power at the moment of our retreat than it had been at any previous period of the occupation. If we except, indeed, the fatal winter of 1841-42, when by the strangest concatenation of accidents our forces at Cabul had become completely demoralised, there never was an occasion on which the Afghans could stand for an hour against either British soldiers or Indian Sepoys. No officer, we are confident, who served through the Afghan war, would hesitate with a well-appointed brigade of British troops to meet in the field the whole assembled forces of Cabul and Candahar combined; and even in mountain warfare, where the Afghan marksman with his "jezäil" had formerly an undoubted superiority over "old Brown Bess," the substitution of the Enfield rifle has now redeemed our only weakness. We make these observations, not by way of encouraging the idea of our again ascending the passes; for it is hardly possible at present that such a movement—at any rate in the direction of Cabul —could be of political advantage, but in order rather to correct the erroneous impression which is generally entertained of the military strength of Afghanistan, and which, so long as it exists, must vitiate any estimate of the difficulties of a Russian advance.

For many years after the Afghan war we studiously avoided all intercourse with the country. Cabul, Candahar, and Herat had resumed their old position of independent governments, and Persia was too much occupied with domestic affairs to attempt any interference to the eastward. It was not indeed until the death of Yar Mahomad Khan, the too famous vizier of Shah Kamran, in 1852, that we were again brought, even indirectly, into connexion with the Afghans. At that time, Persia, reviving her old project of Eastern aggrandisement, would have sent an army against Herat, which, distracted as the city then was, would almost certainly have achieved its conquest; but we interfered to arrest the march of the troops, and, under the pressure of a threatened suspension of diplomatic relations, compelled the Shah into a convention, which debarred him from any future attack upon the Afghan territory. This convention was much canvassed at the time, as it was foreseen that it might commit us to hostilities with Persia at an inconvenient moment; but the importance of rescuing Herat from the risk of dependence on Persia, through which the place might possibly be transferred to Russia (in exchange, for instance, as it was at one time proposed, for Erivan), was judged to be paramount; and this doctrine of the necessary maintenance of the independence of Herat, as against these two powers, has remained a standard article of our political faith ever since.

In due course of time the contemplated contingency came to pass. The troubles at Herat continuing, and the Khorassan frontier being much disturbed in consequence, Persia again sought to bring this outlying Afghan state under her rule; and as the British Minister, at this particular juncture, had already broken off relations with the Court of Teheran on other grounds, there was no further check on her proceedings. In the spring of 1856, accordingly, the Shah's troops for the first time occupied Herat; and as this was done in defiance of England, and in violation of the convention of 1852, it was at once accepted as a "casus belli," and resented on our part by a declaration of war.* The war, however, was neither very long nor very bloody. Persia had no political purpose to subserve, either on her own account or on that of Russia, in retaining possession of Herat. Her military ambition had been satisfied

* There were other causes of offence, it is true, connected with the notorious Mirza Háshem, and with personal affronts offered to the British Minister, which fully justified the suspension of diplomatic intercourse, and which were duly considered at the conclusion of peace; but they certainly were not of such importance as to require the despatch of an expeditionary force from India, and the capture of the chief places on the sea-board of Persia, for the vindication of the national honour. We say advisedly, then, that the Persian war was undertaken for the recovery of Herat, and was directed against Russian rather than Persian aggression.

by the conquest of the place ; and she did not scruple, accordingly, to purchase peace by its abandonment, after a year's occupation. But in settling the conditions of the treaty concluded at Paris in 1857, our traditional dread of Russian encroachment towards India again showed itself by special provisions about Herat. · Persia was required to bind herself to exercise no interference whatever in the affairs of that state. If she was attacked or threatened in that quarter, she was not even to send troops to the frontier until our good offices had been tried and had failed to preserve peace ; and immediately after invasion had been repelled she was to withdraw within her own limits. It was preposterous to suppose that these precautions, which saddled us with a sort of responsibility for the police of the Afghan frontier, could have been adopted merely to prevent aggression on the part of an effete government like that of the Shah. Although Persia was alone named in the treaty, the phantom that loomed behind was Russia, then just beginning to rally after the exhaustion of the Crimean war, and showing, perhaps, her first tendency to retaliate by the increased activity of her movements in Central Asia. There is no reason to imagine that Russia has been actuated by any direct feelings of hostility to England in her recent aggressions on the Jaxartes. She certainly has not contemplated anything like an invasion of India ;* but it would be to convict her of the strangest

---

* The question of the invasion of India has been purposely omitted from these pages, lest it should distract attention from the immediate subject of inquiry. On two occasions, however, since the commencement of the century, British India has been thus threatened. The project of a joint invasion by a French and Russian army is well known to have been submitted by Napoleon to Alexander at Tilsit, in 1807, when it was hoped that Persia, under the inspiration of Lucien's counsels, who was to be sent on a special mission to the Shah, would have also joined in the scheme. But a similar proposal of · an earlier date is not so well known, and has, in fact, as we think, been first brought to notice in this country in Mr. Michell's work. "While yet First Consul," it is said, in Mr. Michell's Khiva volume, "Napoleon I., in 1800 proposed to the Emperor Paul the plan of a combined French and Russian campaign to India; and as at that time a rupture had broken out between England and Russia, the despatch of Don Cossacks to India was agreed on ; and the Cossack Hetman, or commander-in-chief, Count Orloff-Denisof, received orders to march on India with all the Don regiments. The rescript of the Emperor Paul I. relating to

political blindness to imagine her ignorant of what is patent to all the rest of the world, that if England has any vulnerable heel it is in the East; that, in fact, the stronger may be the position of Russia in Central Asia, the higher will be the tone she can command in discussing with us any question of European policy.

So indisputable is this view of the Anglo-Russian relations in the East that surprise has often been expressed at our unaccountable forbearance during the Crimean war. If we had taken advantage, it is said, of Russia's crippled condition in 1855 to throw a strong body of British troops into Georgia, supporting them with the auxiliary resources of Persia, and perhaps also with an expeditionary column from India, there can be no doubt but that we could have driven all the Russian garrisons beyond the Caucasus ; and as Shamil was then unsubdued, and the mountaineers were in a position which admitted of their being organised for permanent defence, the growth of Russia in this part of the East might have been retarded, perhaps, for a generation ; while a little encouragement to the Uxbegs and Turcomans would have cleared off the intruders from the Jaxartes and the eastern shores of the Caspian, and have relegated them to the north of the Kirghiz

---

this is inserted in the appendix of General Miliutin's work on Suwarrow's campaigns in 1779, published at St. Petersburg in 1853." An invasion on this colossal scale would have been quite impossible at the commencement of the century. Even at the present day, with all the appliances of modern art, it would be barely within the reach of possibility. The utmost that Russia proposes at present is thus stated by Mr. Michell: "With respect to a military expedition to India, the Amú-Daria (or Oxus) may be used for despatching a small force to its upper course ; not with an idea of conquest, but for making a demonstration with the object of alarming the enemy and diverting his attention from other points." ("Russians in Central Asia," p. 404.) (A memorandum, it appears, of some importance, "on the Invasion of India," was presented to the Emperor Nicholas, by General Duhamel, at the time of the Crimean war. (See *Times* of January 29, 1873.) The success of the scheme was made to depend mainly on the co-operation, or at any rate the connivance of Persia, and it is probable that the Court of Teheran was sounded on the subject in the negotiations of 1853, to which allusion has already been made at page 86 of this work; but the Persian Minister who was then in power was not favourable to Russian aggrandisement, and if appealed to would certainly have discouraged the project.—1874.)

Steppe. Schemes of this nature were, it is well known, before the Government, and, if the war had been continued, might, perhaps, have been put in execution; but there were counterbalancing considerations of great weight, which prevented their adoption at the time, and which it may not be amiss to glance at, as they partially affect the present question at issue.

In the first place the Government of the Emperor Napoleon was notoriously sensitive in regard to the Eastern phase of the war, the popular notion in France being that the quarrel with Russia was an Asiatic quarrel which exclusively concerned the English, who made use of their French allies very much as the monkey made use of the cat's paw in the fable. We could thus never reckon on French co-operation in an invasion of Georgia, and had we undertaken the task single-handed it might seriously have imperilled the alliance. In the next place we should have incurred a fearful responsibility had we compromised the Georgians and Persians with Russia; for, although we might have insisted on an amnesty-clause at the conclusion of peace, nations so accessible to attack would assuredly have sooner or later paid to Russia the penalty of their resistance, without the possibility of our rendering them any efficient aid. And, thirdly, we had every reason to wish to avoid a contest with Russia in the far East; the ground was too dangerous for both of us to be tried except in the last extremity, as it might have led to endless complications and to the gravest consequences. It was, in fact, the localisation of our last contest with Russia that deprived the war of all its worst features. Had it spread over the East from the Black Sea to Lake Issi-Kúl, its reverberations would be echoing up to this day.

Whether it was prudent, as a precaution against the possible approach of Russia to Herat, to burden ourselves with a liability at any moment to attack Persia in the event of her marching to the Eastward may well be doubted. Still more open to objection would seem to have been a barren stipulation in the Paris treaty against the Shah's interference with the Government of Herat, which, being unaccompanied by any safeguard against the voluntary dependence of the Afghan Governor upon Persia, turned out in practice to be wholly inoperative, and in fact led to nothing but our own stultification. Sultan Ahmed Khan, a nephew of the Amír Dost Mahomed, who was a refugee at Teheran at the time of the conclusion of the Treaty of Paris, and was really the most eligible candidate for the vacant chiefship, was sent by the Shah to assume the reins of government on the withdrawal of the Persian garrison from Herat; and in this position he remained for the next five years in undisguised dependence upon Persia, striking money in the name of the Shah, receiving "Khelats" (or robes of honour), arms and pieces of artillery from Teheran, repairing to Court even to render personal homage, exhibiting in fact every token of direct vassalage, although the British Government and the Shah, in deference to their mutual obligations, continued ostensibly to proclaim his independence. During this transition period, when Herat was thus oscillating between Afghan and Persian nationality, there was some more indirect skirmishing between the two European powers on the Afghan battle-field. A deputation of British officers from the Teheran mission sought, in the first place, to render Sultan Ahmed Khan virtually, as well as nominally, independent by the moral support of England's recognition and sympathy; but this did not satisfy the Afghan chief, and the mission therefore may be said to have failed. The Indian Government, indeed, could render no effective aid to Herat without compromising its relations with Dost Mahomed Khan, of Cabul, who regarded his nephew with intense jealousy; while Sultan Ahmed, in default of such aid, was compelled to rely on Persia to shield him from his all-powerful uncle. But if our own policy thus miscarried, the Russian counter-demonstration was hardly more successful. The mission under M. Khannikof, which visited Herat in 1858, may take credit for having confirmed the dependency of Sultan Ahmed upon Persia: but if M. Khannikof proposed, through that dependency, to strengthen Russian influence in Western Afghanistan, or to pave the way to the realisation of the long-cherished scheme of establishing in the city of Herat a permanent factory with exclusive privileges, he must have been grievously disappointed; for

Persia herself disapproved of being thus enveloped by Russian *antennæ* to the east as well as to the west; and Sultan Ahmed, with the remembrance of the old Cabul catastrophe ever before him, when his uncle had been driven into exile for having given countenance to the interloper Vitkevitch, had no inclination, as he said, to provoke a similar fate. Khannikof, it is understood, was prepared to have sent officers from Herat both to Candahar and Cabul, had he met with any encouragement; but we had fortunately at this time preoccupied the ground.* The importance, indeed, of securing the neutrality, if not the active friendliness, of Dost Mahomed Khan during the critical periods of the Persian war and the Indian mutinies, had for once induced us to step aside from our policy of nonintervention in Afghan affairs. In 1857, fifteen years after our withdrawal from Cabul, we again sent a friendly mission to the country under Major Lumsden; and although our officers were not allowed on this occasion, from prudential considerations, to proceed further than Candahar, we succeeded in purchasing the Amír's good-will at a lakh of rupees (10,000*l*.) per mensem for so long as his services might be of use to us. The morality of this bargain may appear questionable, and the price exorbitant to English politicians, but when work is to be done subsidies are still the rule in the East, and experience has ever shown that true economy consists in paying well, or not at all. †

Revolutions, however, were now imminent in Afghanistan, which had been long foreseen, and the expectation of which had been the main cause of our having so long abstained from any close, or permanent, engagements with the rulers of the country.

The Candahar chiefs at the commencement of the Herat

---

* (The writer had the advantage of repeated confidential conversations with Sultan Ahmed Khan, during this chief's visit to Teheran in the spring of 1860, and was fully informed by him as to Monsr. Khannikof's proceedings at Herat. There was nothing, he is bound to say, in the report that indicated a hostile feeling to England, though Russian interests were of course mainly consulted in the Russian Agent's proposals.—1874.)

† (For further details as to the Cabul subsidy, see ante, p. 92.— 1874.)

troubles, and before the Persian occupation of the city, had invaded the territory with a view to its entire conquest; but their forces proving inadequate to this end, they had contented themselves with taking possession of the outlying district of Farreh and its dependencies, which they attached to their own province. When Dost Mahomed accordingly, some years later, overran the Western Afghan province on the death of Kohandil Khan, the head of the Candahar family, the Herat district of Farreh fell naturally into his hands as a part of the conquered territory. But Sultan Ahmed had never relinquished his claim to this district as an integral portion of the old kingdom of Herat, and in attempting, therefore, as he did, to recover it on the first favourable occasion, he can hardly be said to have initiated the fatal contest with his uncle. During the continuance of this contest (1862-63) we were placed in a position of some embarrassment. Persia complained that we had instigated—or at any rate that we had not discouraged—the advance of Dost Mahomed on Herat, which was fraught with danger to the Khorassan frontier, and was opposed to the spirit, if not to the letter, of the Treaty of Paris. Dost Mahomed, on the other hand, disregarded our counsels and even our protest, which were carried to the length of withdrawing our agent from the Afghan camp; and showed an inveteracy against his nephew, aggravated probably by the latter's Persian predilections, which was hardly natural to his character. As far as our own interests, too, were concerned, it was desirable, on the one hand, that we should be rescued from the undignified position we had occupied, whilst Herat remained a virtual dependency of Persia in defiance of the Treaty of Paris; and, on the other, we were not anxious—as we never have been, and probably never shall be—to see Afghanistan consolidated under a single chief.* In this

* (The question of a united or disunited Afghanistan is one upon which there has always been a great diversity of opinion among Anglo-Indian politicians. If the ruler of Cabul could be thoroughly depended on, no doubt it would be to our advantage to extend and consolidate his power in every possible way; but what security can we possibly have for Afghan fidelity beyond the passing interests of the hour? My own view, therefore, rather inclines to the policy of detaching Herat and Candahar from

dilemma we remained as nearly passive as possible, and the "dénouément" was brought about in the summer of 1863—without any participation in it upon our part—by a triple and almost simultaneous catastrophe, the death of Sultan Ahmed by apoplexy, the fall of Herat to the Cabul army, and the crowning misfortune of the death of Dost Mahomed himself. Since that period Afghanistan has been torn with convulsions, and we have resisted all appeals to favour one pretender or another. Shír Ali Khan, who was designated as heir-apparent by the old Amír before his death, still holds his ground in Cabul, though his position has been successively assailed by his two brothers, Mahomed Afzal and Mahomed Azím, who formerly ruled beyond the Hindú-Kúsh, and has been further shaken by the recent defection of another brother, Mahomed Amín, at Candahar. What may be the precise position of affairs at the present moment it is impossible to say, since revolution and counter-revolution follow each other with the rapidity of the shifting scenes of a pantomime. A battle was fought at Candahar during the summer, in which the son of Shír Ali Khan, who led the Cabul forces, engaged in a hand-to-hand combat with his rebellious uncle, and the two warriors, like Paladins of old, fell dead upon the field. The action, however, seems to have been indecisive, and it may be presumed, therefore, that Candahar is still struggling for independence under a brother or nephew of the slaughtered chief; but if Candahar is thus broken off from Cabul, it will be morally impossible that Shír Ali Khan can retain an efficient hold upon Herat. Up to the date of the last accounts the young Sirdar, Mahomed Yacúb, who had been left by his father Shír Ali at Herat when the latter hastened to Cabul to seize the "musnud" on the Amír Dost Mahomed's death, was still in power, and seemed to show some capacity for government; but in the present distracted state of Afghanistan, and considering that the Persian element has now overpowered and almost displaced the Afghan in the population of Herat, it seems

Cabul, and of confining our attention to the Western Afghan states, which indeed are alone of importance to us, in providing for the security of our Indian frontier from attack.—1874.)

only natural to expect that the influence of the Shah will gradually resume its sway, and that our treaty obligations with Persia will thus again force us to intermingle in the fray. So long, indeed, as the Treaty of Paris remains in force on the one side, while on the other we have no co-ordinate treaty with the Afghans enabling us to control or guide their policy, we must remain in a false position, liable at any moment to be circumvented by intrigue, or to be outraged by a violation of engagement.

8. With Turkestan we have had no regular diplomatic communication since the period of Thomson's return from Khiva in 1842; but complimentary correspondence has been nevertheless almost uninterruptedly maintained between the Teheran mission and the Khan Hazret of Khiva, either by direct messenger or through the British Agent at Meshed, ever since the time of the Afghan war; and even from Bokhara we have been supplied with intelligence of passing events, though we have never had an accredited agent at the Court. In respect to Kokand, too, from the date of the capture of Ak-Mesjed by the Russians the appeals to India by the Uzbeg rulers for mediation or assistance have been incessant. In 1854 a special envoy came from the Jaxartes across the table-land of Pamir to Badakhshan, and thence, as the Cabul road was closed, by the difficult and almost unknown route through Kaferistan and the Upper Kuner and Bajour valleys to Peshawer. The next communication with Kokand took place in 1858, through the agent Mahomed Amín, who was despatched by the Indian Government to ascertain the fate of Adolphe Schlagentweit; but this agent travelled to the Jaxartes by way of Thibet, Yarkend, and Kashgar, and returned along the high road through Bokhara and Cabul; so that the narrative of his journey, which has been printed for the Records of the Political Department in India, differs but very little from the original itinerary of Mír Izzet Ollah in 1812, which first made us acquainted with the physical geography of Chinese and Uzbeg Turkestan.* In 1860 a second envoy of the name of

---

* Mír Izzet Ollah's journal has been repeatedly published. It was first brought to the notice of geographers in 1816, by Lieutenant Waddington,

Khodai Nazar appeared at Peshawer with renewed supplications for British aid to stop the advancing Russians, who were then first threatening Turkestan; and the return mission under Moola Abdul Mejid, which carried back a letter and presents from the Governor-General to Mulla Khan, the reigning Prince of Kokand, if barren of political results, rendered at any rate important service to geography. The detailed itineraries, indeed, which Abdul Mejid has supplied of his journey from Badakhshan across the Pamir Steppe to Kokand, and of his return to the same point by Kara-tegín, Derwáz, and Koláb, fill up a blank in the map of Asia,* which has often been deplored, and which could have been remedied in no other way. The loss of Turkestan and Chemkend wrung forth a third and still more bitter cry of distress, which was borne to India by the Uzbeg Ambassador who appeared in Sir John Lawrence's Lahore Durbar of last winter, and who recounted

of the Bombay Engineers, who mainly relied on its authority for the construction of his map of Ferghâneh, to illustrate Leyden's "Memoirs of Baber." The journal was then published *in extenso* in the "Calcutta Quarterly Magazine" for 1825; and later Professor Wilson republished it, in an enlarged form, with copious notes, in the Royal Asiatic Society's Journal for 1843, p. 283. It affords a very favourable specimen of what an intelligent native of India may accomplish in the way of extending our geographical knowledge of countries into which a European cannot penetrate except at great personal risk. (The Government of India has recently (1872) published in Calcutta a new translation of Mír Izzet Ollah's travels by Captain Henderson, in apparent ignorance that any previous version had appeared in print. It may be added that the first complete translation of the MS. in a European language was given in 1824 by Klaproth in the "Magasin Asiatique," tome ii. p. 1.—1874.)

* We would recommend to the special consideration of the Royal Geographical Society Major James's "Report," No. 83, of October 19, 1861, which extends to fifty paragraphs, and gives a most interesting detail of Moola Abdul Mejid's outward and return journey through the regions between the Upper Oxus and Kokand, which regions in the best and latest published map, that of Stanford, accompanying Mr. Michell's volume, are marked as "unexplored." (The most important portions of this "Report" have been since published in the "proceedings" of the Royal Geographical Society, vol. x. p. 149; and convey the only information yet available of the track across the Pamír plateau from South to North. The high road, however, from West to East has been repeatedly followed and described of late years by Md. Amín, Major Montgomerie's Mirza, Feiz Bakhsh, Ibrahim Khán, and finally by Col. Gordon's party, whose survey of the route on two lines leaves nothing to be desired.—1874.)

his country's wrongs to the assembled nobles of the north-west frontier. It was proposed, we believe, by the Government of the Punjab that certain English officers should accompany this Ambassador on his return to Kokand, not in any official character, but merely as travellers visiting the dominions of a friendly power and desirous of information as to passing events; but in the present state of the Anglo-Russian negociations respecting Central Asia, there were obvious objections to such a course, which would have been aggravated by the subsequent capture of Tashkend; and we are glad, therefore, that Sir John Lawrence, on mature consideration, put his veto on the expedition.* We have alluded to these repeated journeyings between Peshawer and Kokand of late years, not so much for their intrinsic interest—though no doubt they have a very high interest in the additions which they have furnished to our geographical knowledge—as in order to show on the one hand the feeling which animates the Uzbeg Princes, and which leads them to look to British India as their natural protector, and to explain on the other the manner in which the conquests of the Russians on the Jaxartes have come to exercise a disturbing influence over the native mind in the north of India, that justifies, if it does not demand, our protest against further encroachment.

9. Our retrospect is now complete. We have traced, in more or less detail, the progress of Russia from her first pioneering movement in the Steppe to her final capture of Tashkend, and we have compared the synchronous action of England in Turkestan, in Afghanistan, and in Persia. It remains to consider what is the most probable issue to passing events, and what line of policy it will best suit the interests of England to adopt.

* We cannot mention the name of this distinguished officer without paying a passing tribute of respect to the solid judgment, the untiring energy, and the high moral conscientiousness which have ever characterised his public administration. The country is, we think, to be congratulated that in the recent juncture there is at the head of our Indian empire a man who is so thoroughly conversant with its external as well as its internal relations, and who is thus so capable of appreciating and meeting any dangers that may arise from the growth of Russian power in Central Asia.

We have no intention of impugning the good faith of the Russian Government in its recent proceedings. It may be assumed that Prince Gortchakoff's manifesto of last November did really express the Emperor's views as to the danger and inexpediency of any further extension at present of the Russian frontier in Central Asia; but experience has proved, as indeed might have been perceived pretty clearly before, that Russia cannot stop midway in the career on which she has now entered. If she merely desires a continuous military line for her southern frontier, she must abandon Turkestan and Chemkend, as well as the more advanced position of Tashkend, and fall back on the forts beyond the mountains. If, on the other hand, she determines to sever Tashkend from Kokand, either holding it as her own frontier city, or maintaining it as a free town for the general resort of traders, she will encounter the very same—so-called aggressive—provocations which compelled her to advance beyond her former line. Khojend and Kokand itself will be a standing menace against Tashkend, precisely as Tashkend was against Chemkend, and still earlier Chemkend was against Turkestan. Indeed, the further she advances the more imperative will it become for her to take complete possession of the country, since the governmental power, which is nominally vested in the boy, Sultan Sahib, will be usurped in the different districts by Kara-Kirghiz and Kipchák chieftains, and universal anarchy will be the result.* A further element of strife is also being now introduced upon the scene, which will assuredly acquire grave dimensions as the drama advances towards a climax, and by which, in fact, public interest will probably in future be pretty well engrossed. This element of danger is the position of Russia relatively to Khiva, and especially to Bokhara.

*(The transition period, as it avowedly is, of Kokand semi-independence, has lasted much longer than was expected, Khodáyár Khan the Chief having ruled, during the last nine years, with exemplary skill and prudence, while Russia, notwithstanding much provocation, has resolutely held aloof. It is understood, however, that revolution is now imminent, and that strong pressure will be exerted to compel the direct interference of the Russian Government. To carry out the military occupation of Kokand, 10,000 men would probably be required to be added to the army of Turkestan.—1874.)

In tracing the advance of Russia along the Jaxartes towards Kokand, we have only incidentally alluded to the condition of the two other Uzbeg States ; nor, indeed, was a more detailed notice required ; for, with the exception of General Ignatief's mission in 1858, which at length effected the release of the Russian prisoners at Bokhara, and confirmed the salutary terror with which the uniform success of the Russian arms on the Jaxartes had inspired the Khivans, there was no political intercourse between Orenburg and the southern Uzbeg States for a period of upwards of twenty years. During this long interval most of the grievances of which Russia had formerly complained had been redressed. Her subjects were no longer kidnapped, nor were her caravans plundered, except within the range of the Jaxartes hostilities. Bokhara, indeed, had profited so much by the sustained Russian pressure upon Kokand, that she was inclined to overlook the ultimate danger to herself, and Khiva was only too glad to see the military strength before which she formerly quailed diverted to another quarter. The time of trial appears, however, to be now approaching for both of these states. As regards Khiva, indeed, the Aral flotilla is considered to have taken possession of the mouth of the Oxus; and on several occasions the Russian steamers have certainly ascended, without questioning, as far as Kungrad, though no permanent settlement has, we believe, been yet formed upon either bank of the river. What this will probably lead to we shall presently see by a quotation from the last Russian work on the subject.

But the more immediate question concerns Bokhara. Here the Russian and Uzbeg forces are at present actually in face of each other, and a collision may at any moment occur between the advanced pickets thrown out respectively from Khojend and Tashkend. It is further evident that Russia regards the Bokharians with suspicion and dislike, since she has been content to incur the obloquy of Europe in the matter of the capture of Tashkend, in order to anticipate their nearer approach to her frontier; but with all this we venture a prediction that she will not, under present circumstances, hazard an open rupture. Her tenure of Kokand will, for a long time, be too precarious to admit of her having another enemy upon her hands. Willyamminof-Sermof, the only Russian officer who has described the country from personal observation, estimates the population of Tashkend at 50,000, and of Kokand at 60,000 souls, and Khojend, Andiján, Nemengán, Oosh, and Ura-tepeh, are of hardly inferior consequence. What number of troops, then, if military occupation were alone attempted, would be required to furnish garrisons for all these numerous towns, and to keep up an efficient line of communication with Fort Perofski and the Aral? It seems to us that the "manifest destiny" marked out for Russia in the present aspect of the East, is to colonize Turkestán thoroughly before she moves another step in advance. The genius of the nation has already displayed itself in this direction, Amuria and Zungaria having been reclaimed from barbarism through the means of military-agricultural settlements. The basin of the Jaxartes, too, presents greater facilities for successful colonization than any other portion of Central Asia. The fertility of the soil is proverbial, and there is every variety of climate, from the perennial snows of the Belúr-Tágh to an almost tropical heat in the valley of the river; so that not only may the staple articles of corn, cotton, silk, madder, and tobacco be produced to an unlimited extent, but in certain situations it may also be found possible to cultivate the sugar-cane, and perhaps even opium and indigo. The rivers, likewise, are auriferous, and mines of silver, lead, copper, and iron are known to exist in the hills on both sides of the Jaxartes; while a still more valuable product is the coal which has been found in large quantities both in the Kara-taú and Ala-taú ranges, and which may be expected before long to supersede the anthracite of the Don throughout South-Eastern Russia.*

---

* This account of the cereal and mineral wealth of Kokand is principally taken from Mr. Lumley's report, p. 281, seq. For a notice of the coal discovered in the Kara-taú and Ala-taú ranges, see "Russians in Central Asia," p. 481. Compare also the following passage in "Leyden's Baber." Introduction, p. xl. "Abulfeda ('Chorasm. Descrip.,' p. 38) mentions, that in the mountains of Ferghána (Kokand) they have black stones which burn like charcoal, and when kindled, afford a very intense heat. The fact of the existence of coal in the Ala-tàgh

It is not, indeed, too much to expect that when security has been established in Turkestán, when the wandering Kirghiz have been induced to exchange a pastoral for an agricultural life, when Russian colonies are scattered over the country, and European energy and intelligence have been directed to the due development of its resources, this province will resume the title which it enjoyed in ancient times of "the garden of the East." What England, then, has to apprehend from the progress of affairs in Central Asia, is not the immediate, or even proximate, invasion of our Indian empire, which is a notion peculiar to the panic-mongers of London and Calcutta, and which we should have thought hardly required the serious refutation that was given to it in the Anniversary Address—admirable in all other respects—delivered by the accomplished President, Sir Roderick Murchison, at a recent meeting of the Royal Geographical Society of London.* What we really

range, and to the east of it, is confirmed by recent travellers. It is found in great plenty, and forms the ordinary fuel of the natives." Mr. Bogoslovski, also, who visited Samarcand in 1842, in company with Khanikoff and Lehmann, found coal formations in the upper valley of the Zar-afshán river; and coal of an inferior quality is likewise known to exist in the Mangishlak Peninsula on the Caspian. "Russians in Central Asia," pp. 326 and 444. The Don anthracite formerly used by the steamers on the Jaxartes, owing to the enormous expense of carriage cost 12l. per ton. (We have no very recent statistics regarding the production of coal in Turkestán, but in 1868 there were three principal mines at work, one near Chemkend in the hands of the Government, which produced about 5000 tons annually, and two others near Tashkend and Khojend in private hands, which were still richer. Coal is now said to be sold at Khojend at the rate of ten shillings per ton.—1874.)

* Sir Roderick Murchison's address appears to have given immense satisfaction in Russia, where it was made the subject of a leading article in the "Journal de St. Petersburg" of June 19, 1865. It is unfortunate, however, that the journalist, who probably drew his inspiration from Prince Gortchakoff's Bureau, should have quoted from the original draft of the address, since this draft contained a paragraph on the new frontier at Issi-Kúl, taken from a Russian source, but so strangely incorrect that it was expunged from the later copy prepared for incorporation with the Journal. The Rev. Mr. Long, also, who has recently published an elaborate defence of Russian policy in the East, under the title of "Russia, Central Asia, and British India, by a British Subject," has been misled by Sir Roderick's authority, and has drawn special attention to this rejected paragraph, as a proof of Russia's moderation, by quoting it at full length and in Italics! p. 20. The additional note "on the boundaries of

have to apprehend is, that an Asiatic Russia will arise to the north of the Hindú-Kúsh, possessing within itself a germ of vitality and vigour that will enable it to replenish rather than exhaust the parent stem, and will render it, in due course of time, a formidable rival to our Indian Empire. What we may not unreasonably expect is, that under the condition of Russian colonization, the principle of development may be reasserted, which seems to be peculiar to this favoured region of Turkestán, and of which the world has already seen such memorable instances in the career of Jenghiz Khán, of Timour, and of Baber, each of whom, it should be noted, nursed their nascent fortunes in the valley of the Jaxartes before pushing on to foreign conquest and dominion.* But the growth of such a Satrapy, acquiring the strength and consistency of an empire, will be a work of time—a work, perhaps, of ages; and the "chapter of accidents" may at any moment intervene to deliver us from the threatened incubus.

The Bokharians, we must remember, are an enemy of a very different calibre from the Kokandis, and their conquest will not, we think, be lightly undertaken by Russia. In actual population there may not be much disproportion between the two states; but in strength they differ widely. The oligarchical constitution, indeed, of the Kokandi Government, where the Khán is in most cases a mere puppet in the hands of the Kara-Kirghiz or Kipchák chiefs, prevents anything like a combined resistance, and thus renders the country an easy

Russia and Northern Turkestán," appended to Sir R. Murchison's address in its corrected form, is all that could be desired; clear, accurate, and giving full credit to Russia for the great services she has rendered to geographical science.

* (It must be confessed that the experience of the last ten years does not encourage a belief in the speedy realization of this picture. The colonization of Turkestán has proceeded at a very slow rate, and to a very limited extent. Russian institutions do not take root in the country, and there is no approach to amalgamation between the native inhabitants and their conquerors. Tashkend and Samarcand are still, indeed, to all intents and purposes military cantonments in a foreign country, and the expected influence of European civilization has not yet begun to develop itself. According to Mr. Schuyler's report, also, the export trade of Turkestán remains almost stationary, while the import trade, contrary to all expectation, has actually diminished.—1874.)

o 2

prey to an invader; whereas at Bokhara, on the other hand, there is the most complete autocracy, and the Amír can direct the whole resources of the country for the purpose either of offence or defence. The standing army, moreover, of Bokhara is said by Vambéry to consist of 40,000 men, who have been well seasoned by continued conflict; and the Turcomans beyond the Oxus could certainly furnish an auxiliary force of equal strength composed of the best horsemen in Asia.* According to our view, then, until Kokand is finally settled, there will be no attempt to coerce the Bokharians, further than by commercial pressure; such as has been this year inaugurated on the Orenburg frontier, where the merchants of Bokhara have been interdicted from appearing at the fair of Nijni-Novgorod to purchase their usual supplies of merchandise and arms; and, even when Russian Turkestán is fully prepared to receive the accretion of other portions of Uzbeg territory, the work of amalgamation will be very gradual, and will probably be consummated through the intermediate stage of a protectorate. If we proceed, then, to quote from Mr. Michell's book the views which are entertained by sanguine politicians at St. Petersburg respecting the future now opening out in Central Asia, to the ambition and the greatness of Russia, it is not that we participate in those views or consider them at present other than premature, if not chimerical; but that we think it only due to the public in England, and especially in India, that they should know what is fermenting in the minds of our northern neighbours, in order to form their own opinions of the practicability and probable results of such a policy—

"Judging, therefore," says a Russian author, "by historical precedents, one cannot but foresee that the occupation of the mouth of the Amú-Daria (the Oxus) will necessarily be followed by the appropriation of the whole river. The Russian Government may not have this in view, and

---

* (Bokhara and Khiva have both shown themselves utterly unable to cope with Russia in the field, whatever may be the disparity of the numbers engaged, but they have still been allowed to retain a qualified indepen- dence, because the permanent occupation of their territories by Russian garrisons would entail an expenditure altogether incommensurate with any possible political advantage.—1874.)

will in all likelihood oppose the encroachment; but nevertheless, sooner or later, it will come to pass of itself. Officially, the boundary of Russia will remain unchanged; practically, however, Russian emigrants will ascend the river higher and higher by degrees; they will at first open intercourse with Khiva, the nearest khanat, and eventually make their way to Bokhara. Examples of this are afforded by the Amúr and Syr-Daria (the Jaxartes)."

The history is then given of the occupation of the Amúr from its embouchure to its source; after which we have—

"The same order of events is observed on the Syr-Daria, of which the lower course alone is held by Russia; yet this river must now be considered more Russian than Kokanian, more especially as the necessity of possessing it for the whole extent of its course is year after year more urgently and clearly felt. . . . . . . Since the days of Peter the Great, Russia has diligently advanced, and at great sacrifice, through the Steppes that barred her progress. She has passed them and reached the basins of two large rivers—two important water-ways—whose sources flow through fertile and densely populated countries. She is fully justified in seeking to be rewarded here for her labours and losses, extending over a hundred years, and in endeavouring to secure her frontiers by pushing them forward to that snow-capped summit of the Himalayas, the natural conterminous boundary of England and Russia.

"From this stand-point Russia can calmly look on the consolidation and development of British power in India." *

10. Now it is evident from these and similar passages interspersed among the historical and geographical detail of Mr. Michell's valuable compilation, as well as from the series of elaborate letters published last year by Major-General Fadeieff in the "Gazette de Moscow," that there is a very general feeling in Russia in favour of extending the frontier at once to the Hindú-Kúsh, which of course involves the complete absorption of the independent Uzbeg States. And this extension, be it remembered, is recommended, not by the facilities it will afford for promoting a trade with India, but

---

* "Russians in Central Asia," p. 400, seq. It is not clear from what Russian source the end of the 10th chapter of Mr. Michell's work is taken, but it is the portion of the volume which we least like; the worst in point of style and the most extravagant in tone. It bears a marked contrast, indeed, to Chapter xii., which is also anonymous, but which is clearly expressed, puts forth moderate views, and is full of the most valuable information.

in the more questionable hope of forestalling the English in possession of the markets which will thus be opened up to Russian enterprise. "These markets," it is said, "are situated on the upper course of the Amú-Daria (or Oxus), whose mouth is in the possession of Russia; and Russia cannot, and must not, relinquish them in favour of England, because she is connected with them by a natural waterway." The commercial argument, indeed, which some among us are wont to use in favour of Russian extension, operates, as we think, exactly in the contrary direction. The trade of Russia, indeed, with Central Asia is mainly a trade in cotton, and it is difficult to see how the improvement of that traffic, which is her avowed object, can possibly benefit Manchester.

Russia now exports annually to the Uzbeg States goods to the value of about 300,000*l*., and receives annually from those states about double the amount in raw produce and manufactures; Bokhara counting for about two-thirds, both of the export and import trade; and the remaining third being divided between Khiva and Kokand. Of the export trade nearly one half consists of inferior cotton goods, a cheap but showy article being manufactured in the governments of Moscow, Vladimir, Kaluga, and Kostrema expressly for the Central Asiatic market; while of the import trade cotton forms at least three-quarters, the larger moiety being the raw staple and yarn for which since the American Civil War there has been a great demand in Russia, while the smaller moiety is a stout and warm but plain fabric, the produce of Uzbeg looms, which is greatly preferred by the Kirghiz, Cossacks, and Bashkirs to the cheaper prints and calicoes of Russian manufacture. But Russia now finds that, as the price of labour has sensibly increased, owing to the emancipation of the serfs, she cannot hope in future to supply the cotton goods required for the Central Asiatic market at anything like their former prices; and she sees, therefore, that unless she can devise some method of meeting this difficulty, she will run the risk of being undersold by the English manufacturers, who are striving to push their goods up the Afghán passes and across the Hindú-Kúsh to the valley of the Oxus. As far as the cost of transport is concerned there cannot be much difference between the route from Moscow to Bokhara, and the route to the same place from Karachí. The carriage of goods along the former line has been calculated at 18*l*. 10*s*. per ton; and any sensible reduction of this charge would therefore place the Russian goods in the Bokhara market at a corresponding advantage over the English. The great aim accordingly of Russia seems to be "to establish spinning and weaving manufactories at a short distance from the Bokharian frontier;" probably at Tashkend itself; from which she would not only continue to supply the cheap and bright-coloured goods suited to the local market, but which would also enable her, by the diminished cost of the raw material, to compete with the Uzbeg manufacturer in the supply of the superior article affected by her own Mussulman subjects in the Steppe; and " if at the same time she could establish a Russian factory at or near Bokhara itself, where the native growers might be instructed in the best method of cultivating the cotton plant, while the factory-owner would also exercise the function of a broker in condemning all cotton unfit for manufacture in Russia," she seems to think that she might convert Central Asia into an almost exclusively cotton-producing country, reserving to herself all the profits of manufacture and subsequent traffic. It will be seen from this detail that Russia is now endeavouring to do for Central Asia, very much what the native mill-owners are attempting for Western India; but with this difference, that the Russian manufacturers in Turkestán would have a beneficial premium of 18*l*. 10*s*. per ton upon their goods, instead of the mere saving of 2*l*. or 3*l*. per ton freight from Liverpool to Bombay.*

* This view of the Russian cotton-trade with Bokhara has been chiefly taken from Mr. Lumley's very excellent Report. It is ungracious, perhaps, to find any fault with a paper drawn up with such remarkable ability, and embodying information not easily accessible to the English reader; but we cannot help wishing that some of the young gentlemen in Downing Street, fresh from the honours of competitive examination, had been allowed to test the accuracy of the numbers before the Report in question was submitted to Parliament; in which case we should hardly have had two errors in the simple sum of adding up three sets of figures, in order to find the aggregate of the imports of Central Asia for the decennial

We have not yet spoken of the prohibitive tariff which Russia still keeps up with regard to the woollen and cotton goods of England; but it is our firm belief that the more her hold upon the Uzbeg States may be extended and confirmed the greater will be the difficulties thrown in the way of a trade with India. With the exception, indeed, of articles of tropical produce, such as indigo, opium, spices, coffee, and perhaps sugar, it is not likely that any Indian articles will be allowed to penetrate into Russian Turkestán, and we should fear even that the export of horses, silk, wool, and dried fruits, which are the principal articles that we now receive from that country, would be in a great measure diverted to the north.*

11. It now remains to consider the duty of England in the present crisis. We think enough has been said to show that

---

period from 1850 to 1859 inclusive. The line in the report is as follows:—

Bokhara.   Khiva.   Kokand.   Total.
£1,607,937 + 375,789 + 18,731 = 1,902,447 - properly 2,002,457.

See Reports of H.M.'s Secretaries of Embassy and Legation, No. 5, p. 314.

We fear that Mr. Davies was too sanguine in his view of the British trade with Central Asia as compared with the Russian trade. He says, p. 21, "English cotton piece goods have to a great extent displaced those forwarded through Russia in the Bokhara and neighbouring markets," but Vambéry in 1863 still found the Russians in almost complete possession of the Bokhara market, and Mr. Lumley dwells throughout his report on the difficulty which English manufacturers have found in opposing the low-class goods of Russia. As the balance of trade, however, with Russia is 100 per cent. in favour of Central Asia, there must be, as Mr. Lumley remarks, "a considerable surplus balance of roubles for investment in the much prized, though as yet too inaccessible, fabrics and cutlery of England;" and if our manufacturers, therefore, will consult the peculiar tastes of the Central Asiatics, and the cost of transport through Afghanistán can be somewhat diminished, there will still be some chance of our competing successfully with Russia in the Bokhara market, *so long as the country remains independent.*

* (In her treaties with all the Uzbeg Khanates, Russia has adopted the very moderate rate of 2½ per cent. *ad valorem*, which is the regular Mohamedan assessment, for the import duty on all native goods entering Russian Turkestán; but she has not yet published any special Tariff for the produce and manufactures of England or India, and the European rates must be considered, therefore, to be applicable. Practically it is understood that the introduction of all Indian goods is discouraged, and that in regard to Himalayan or Assam tea, which alone would pay the cost of transport, it is declared contraband, the object being to protect the direct tea-trade between Russia and China. —1874.)

Russia has no right—except the right of the strongest—to impose her rule upon the Uzbeg States, and also that her nearer approach to India, however likely, is not desirable in the interests of either one country or the other. As far as can be judged from the tone and comments of the Indian press, there would seem to be coming on—even while Russia is still at so great a distance—that same disturbed and dangerous state of native feeling which was observable at the time of the first Persian siege of Herát, and which has been so well described by Kaye in his history of the Afghán war.

"Even in our own provinces," he remarks, in narrating the events of 1837, "these rumours of mighty movements in the countries of the North-West disquieted the native mind; there was an uneasy, restless feeling among all classes, scarcely amounting to actual disaffection, and perhaps best to be described as a state of ignorant expectancy—a looking outward in the belief of some coming change, the nature of which no one clearly understood."*

It has been suggested, in order to calm this troubled feel-

* "History of the Afghán War," vol. i. p. 290. We have no wish to discuss dangers which may not after all be realized, but it must be obvious that the nearer the Russians approach to India, the greater will be their disturbing influence, and the more difficult it will be to maintain order in the frontier districts. If, indeed, an army of 70,000 Europeans is required for the garrison of India under present circumstances, an augmentation of 50,000 would not be an extravagant estimate for our enhanced necessities when confronted with Russia on the Indus; and considering the strain put on our home resources to meet the present demand, where, let it be asked, is such an additional force to come from? There is one more point connected with this subject which seems deserving of notice, because great stress has been often laid on it, and because it seems likely to mislead the public. We mean the peaceful and enlightened character of the Emperor Alexander II., which is held to divest the Russian neighbourhood to India of all danger and to render it rather a source of strength and profit. When the Italian Parliament was exulting a few years back in having secured the good will of the Emperor Napoleon at the trifling cost of Nice and Savoy, Cialdini reminded it that the Emperor was not immortal, and that under his successors Italy might rue the day when she had consigned the keys of the country into the hands of its traditional enemy. Even so would we remind our readers that the Emperor Alexander is not immortal, that the traditional policy of Russia, as consecrated in the testament of Peter the Great, is hostile to the British power in the East; and that if we acquiesce in placing her in command of the Indian Caucasus, it may be a not less fatal error than Italy's surrender into the hands of France of the Passes of the Alps.

ing—which is already making itself distinctly felt, and which may be expected to increase if left to the mere natural course of events—that the British Government should now form some engagement with Russia; either with regard to absolute immobility within present limits, or with regard to certain prospective limits to be mutually agreed upon and notified beforehand, so as to obviate any further doubt or misconception of design; and if it were possible to forecast the map of Central Asia, as a skilful player prepares for "le grand coup" at whist, this latter alternative would probably be the most successful—as it would certainly be the most humane—way of solving the difficulty. But with the abnormal elements of calculation furnished by Kirghiz and Uzbeg and Afghán nationalities, it seems hopeless to look for stability in any such arrangement of future relations. And with respect to the other plan, of a mutual guarantee against any further advance, the objections to it are of so obvious a nature as hardly to require to be recapitulated. Russia, in the first place, has already pledged herself to observe a certain definite frontier in the manifesto so often alluded to; and we should derive, therefore, little additional security from the formality of a reciprocal engagement. In the second place, it must be remembered that a convention, on the basis of the *uti possidetis*, would be manifestly unfair to England. We do not stand at all in the same position in regard to Russia as Russia occupies in regard to us. Our annexation of Bhootán, for instance, or the substitution of the direct for the indirect dependence of Cashmere could not possibly affect public opinion in Russia, or give the Russian Government any ground for interpellation; whereas the conquest of Khiva or Bokhara would doubtless very sensibly affect us in India by creating a vague impression in the native mind that our Asiatic supremacy was about to be challenged. And thirdly, it appears to us that it would be a suicidal policy on the part of England to place in the hands of Russia such an instrument of possible mischief as the right of interference in the rectification of our north-west frontier which she would derive from any mutual agreement to remain within our present limits. It would be, in fact, to invite rather than to stave off the threatened evil; to call up to the hall-door the wolf that is now merely prowling in the back-yard. On these united considerations, greatly as we desire to see a friendly intelligence prevailing between Russia and Great Britain, we sincerely trust we shall not be committed to any mutual engagement against an extension of frontier. If Russia is bent (as she probably is) on further encroachment, we must accept the position, but above all things, let us preserve an uncontrolled liberty of action, and be guided alone in our future relations with Central Asia by the exigency of the occasion, and an enlightened view of the real welfare of our Indian empire.

The great danger seems to be that, as Russia was led, in 1854, by an erroneous estimate of the state of public feeling in England, which was judged to be essentially anti-warlike, to commit herself to a policy at Constantinople that ultimately led to war, so she may be deceived at present by the apparent apathy of the public on the one side and by the encouragement held out by the press upon the other, into a persuasion that the country at large can really look upon her advance towards the Hindú-Kúsh with approbation, or even with indifference. Were she assured of impunity in this respect, the difficulties of the enterprise would be more than half overcome; but if, on the contrary, it is made plain to her that every step that she advances is watched by England, as it certainly must be when our attention is once awakened, with a vigilant and scrutinizing eye; and that in a case of this sort, where the vital interests of our Indian empire are at stake, the general feeling of the country will give a cordial support to whatever Government may be in power, we cannot believe that she will press forward in a policy which must certainly cast on her the odium of bad faith, and may lead to still more serious consequences.

So long as Khiva and Bokhara preserve their independence, there may not be occasion for any more active interference upon our part than a constant reference to Prince Gortchakoff's circular, and a continued protest against the promotion and decoration of contumacious commanders, who—in defiance of orders, as it is said, and to the manifest risk of the peaceful relations of the country—press forward from one conquest to another; but if to the final subjugation of Kokand is added an attempt to subvert the independence of the other Uzbeg States—if Russia should take possession of the Oxus, as she has already taken possession of the Jaxartes, then, as her outposts will be in contact with the Afghán outposts along the whole line of the mountains from Mymenah to Badakhshán, it will become a question for serious consideration, whether, leaving Cabul and Ghazni, the scene of our old disasters, to struggle on in isolated anarchy, it may not be incumbent on us to secure a strong flanking position by the reoccupation of the open country of Shaul, of Candahar, and even of Herát. There is a strong impression abroad, amongst those best acquainted with the subject, that ultimately—not perhaps in this generation, but whenever Russian Turkestán shall include the basin of the Oxus, and a Russian Governor-General shall be enthroned at Bokhara—it will be necessary, for the due protection of the Punjáb and the north-west provinces of India, that we should erect and hold first-class fortresses in advance of our present territorial border and on the most accessible line of attack; and it is thus satisfactory to find that the positions of Herát and Candahar, which precisely meet the military requirements of such an occasion, have been already pointed out by one of our most cautious diplomatists as the true political frontiers of India; * while it has been also shown that these districts may be administered with comparative ease, since the Doorání population—the only element of danger in Afghán government—is here outnumbered and neutralized by docile Hazárehs and pliant Parsíváns, who gratefully remember our former beneficent rule, and would gladly welcome its return. It is to be hoped that we shall not prematurely take alarm. At present there is no pressing danger, no cause for unusual precautions; but the time may come when it will be our duty to remember that outworks are as necessary to the defence of empires as of fortresses, and that in this view Herát and Candahar are the Malakhoff and Mamelon of our position in the East.

* See an excellent paper by Sir Justin Sheil in the Appendix to Lady Sheil's "Life in Persia."

CHAPTER IV.

CENTRAL ASIA.

(Reprinted, with Notes, from the " Quarterly Review," for Oct. 1866, No. 240, p. 461.*)

1. Authorities for Central Asian geography—German and Russian.—2. English and other travellers in the same region.—3. Apocryphal travels, Colonel Gardiner, and Baron George Ludvig von ————. —4. Native explorers. —5. General description of Central Asia.—6. Evidence of its early civilization.—7. Ethnological sketch.—8. Review of the present political condition of its four divisions, S. E. Cashmere and Thibet, N. E. Eastern Turkestán, S. W. Afghanistán, and N. W. Russian Turkestán, with sketch of events there to autumn of 1866.—9. General political considerations.

1. CENTRAL ASIA is a conventional rather than a strictly geographical title. The name is not confined to that particular portion of Asia which is centrically situated in respect to latitude and longitude. It is rather used as a convenient and general designation for the whole interior of the continent, and is thus made to cover a greater or less extent of territory, according as the writers who employ it refer to the ethnology, or the physical geography, or the political distribution of the countries, which are contained within its limits.

In the present sketch, which proposes to consider our sources of information with regard to these countries, as well as their actual condition and prospects, Central Asia must be understood to mean the regions which intervene between the Russian empire to the North and the British-Indian empire to

---

* ART. VI.—1. "Mémoire sur la partie Méridionale de l'Asie Centrale." Par Nicolas de Khanikoff. Paris, 1862.
2. "Mémoire sur l'Ethnographie de la Perse." Par Nicolas de Khanikoff. Paris, 1866.
3. "Journal of the Imperial Russian Geographical Society, St. Petersburg."
4. "Proceedings of the Royal Geographical Society of London." Vol. X. No. IV. London, 1866.
5. "Le Livre de Marco Polo." Par M. G. Panthier. Paris, 1865.
6. "Invalide Russe." 1866.

the south, including, perhaps, a portion of the Persian province of Khorassán to the west, and Chinese Turkestán to the east. When Alexander von Humboldt, a quarter of a century ago, compiled his celebrated work on the "Orography and Comparative Climatology of Central Asia," though the materials at his disposal for gaining a general acquaintance with those subjects were most abundant, yet he often found himself at fault in searching for precise and trustworthy details. He himself had proceeded no further than Lake Zaisan, at the foot of the southern slopes of the Altäi ; and the Ili River, which disembogues into the Balkash Lake, at a short distance to the southwest, was the extreme limit of Russian scientific exploration.

At that time no traveller from the north had invaded the solitudes of the Thian-Shan since the Jesuit commission of the preceding century,* nor had any adventurous Englishman penetrated as yet to the icy summits of the Kara-Koram and Kuen-Luen. Since then, however, vast additions have been made to our accurate knowledge of these regions. Not only have the theodolite and barometer been extensively used along both the mountain-chains, which bound the plateau of Chinese Turkestán to the north and south ; but hardy travellers, passing in

* The Chinese Emperor Tsian-lun (or Khian-loung, according to Klaproth) appointed a commission, consisting of a German Jesuit, Hallerstein, with two assistants, Felix d' Arocha and Espinha, to accompany the expedition which he sent against the Eleuths of Zungaria in 1755, for the purpose of determining the astronomical position of all the principal sites in Central Asia ; and the results of their observations were subsequently embodied in an official map published at Pekin. This map was translated by Klaproth, from a comparison of several copies, and published by him at Berlin in 1833 ; and it has served as the basis of all our Central Asiatic geography until modern times. The Russians, indeed, who through M. Zakharof, Consul at Kulja, have recently acquired a more authentic register of the Jesuit observations, still maintain their rigid accuracy ; but our Indian Trigonometrical Survey, which has been now pushed into Tartary, does not bear out this favourable verdict to the same extent—Mr. Johnson's plane-table survey, for instance, giving 79° 25' for the approximate longitude of Khoten, while the Jesuit register has 80° 21'. The Jesuit survey extended westward as far as Sarík-kúl or Tash-kurghán, and northward to the valley of the Talas. No account of the journeyings or personal adventures of these remarkable explorers is believed to be extant, but the Jesuit College published at the time, from their Reports, a very interesting record of the military and political events of the expedition.—(See "Lettres Édifiantes," tom. xxvii.)

disguise through the length and breadth of the land, have visited all the principal cities of Central Asia, have mixed familiarly with the tribesmen and villagers, and—except in regard to some particular localities which still stand out in isolated inaccessibility—have made us almost as well acquainted with the manners and customs, the dialects, the religions and the ethnic relations of the races intervening, between Russia and India, between Persia and China, as with the inhabitants of any other part of the East. To describe in any detail the sources from which such information has been derived, would be neither very easy, nor very interesting. A brief abstract of authorities must suffice, explanations only being added, where the travels are but little known to the public, or where their authenticity is questioned.

With the ancient and mediæval travels in Central Asia, we do not propose at present to meddle. In the "Erdkunde von Asien" of Carl Ritter, and the "Asie Centrale" of Alexander von Humboldt will be found a *résumé* of all our early, as distinguished from our recent, Asiatic knowledge. Profiting by the labours of Abel Remusat, Klaproth, Julien, and Landresse, the two great geographers of Berlin were able to collate the authority of Chinese Encyclopedias and Buddhist travels, with the hearsay evidence of the Greeks and the more circumstantial accounts of the contemporary Arabs. With the aid of other translations, they drew much valuable testimony from Turkish and Mongolian histories; they further traced the routes of the envoys and traders from Europe, who visited the territories of the great "Cham of Tartary," in the middle ages; they examined Missionary journals, and sifted Caravan itineraries, and finally summarized all available reports both of Russian and of English agents; thereby bringing into one focus rays of information from a hundred different quarters, and furnishing for the first time an intelligible scheme of Central Asiatic geography. The subject, as it appears to us, has not since received the consideration which it merits; no attempt having been made to keep the public acquainted with our improved geographical knowledge, notwithstanding that exploration has been carried on ever since, continuously, and with marked success. In this field of honourable emulation Russia is entitled to a very prominent place. As her arms have advanced upon the one side from the Ili River and Lake Balkash to the Issi-Kúl Lake and the great Thian-Shan Range, and upon the other from the Aral Sea for twelve hundred miles along the course of the Jaxartes, to Turkestán, Chemkend, Tashkend, and now to Khojend itself, so have the scientific officers, who accompany or precede her army, continued to lay before the world the results of their professional labours. The Journal of the Imperial Geographical Society of St. Petersburg has been enriched for many years past with a series of papers by Semenoff, Golubieff, Veniukoff, Boutakoff, and others, describing the progress of discovery in Zungaria and Russian Turkestán; and many of these excellent Memoirs—which, among other valuable results, connect all the recent acquisitions of Russia as far south as the Thian-Shan Range with the great Siberian survey, and further determine for the first time, on certain data, a series of astronomical positions along a belt of 30° of longitude from the Aral Sea to the Chinese frontier—have been transferred to the pages of our own "Geographical Journal" in London. But these are not the only contributions of Russia to our recent knowledge of Central Asia. A more hazardous, and, in some respects, a more interesting, journey was performed in 1859 by Captain Valikhanoff, the son of a Kirghiz Sultan, who, having entered the military service of Russia and received a professional education, was thus enabled to combine the accomplishments of a European traveller with the free movements of a native of the country. In company with a caravan of traders he crossed the Thian-Shan by the Záúkú defile, and passed the winter in Kashgar and the neighbourhood, collecting much solid information regarding the geography, the ethnology, the natural productions, and the modern history of Chinese Turkestán, which has been recently made accessible to the English public in the Messrs. Michells' work on "The Russians in Central Asia."

Mons. Nicolas de Khanikoff is a Russian traveller of a still higher class. His first introduction to Central Asiatic life was in the suite of Colonel Buteneff, when that distinguished officer was sent to Bokhárá on a diplomatic mission during the English occupation of Afghanistán. On this occasion he visited Samarcand, and collected copious topographical details of the city and its neighbourhood (which he afterwards embodied in a statistical account of the Khanat of Bokhárá), thereby establishing his claim to be the first European, since the days of Clavijo (in A.D. 1404), who has given us from his personal observation a plan and description of that famous capital of the empire of Timour. After many years of laborious service in Persia, where he relieved the toils of office by an earnest study of Oriental literature and antiquities, Khanikoff was recently employed, in 1858–59, in conducting a scientific expedition through Eastern Persia, which he somewhat fancifully calls 'the southern part of Central Asia,' and he has since published two separate volumes giving the geographical and ethnological results of his travels. Both of these works are valuable. The one contains a very careful record of the scientific observations of Khanikoff and his companions, including some most important rectifications of the map of Persia, and an admirable general description of the province of Khorassán ; in the other we have an ingenious, if not entirely convincing, argument, drawn from a large field of induction, as to the original seats of the Iranian race, together with a good review of the general ethnic relations of the present inhabitants of Persia. Mons. Khanikoff occupies such an eminent place among the Orientalists of the present day, that no apology can be needed for including his two volumes amongst those placed at the head of the present article.*

* (During the eight years which have elapsed since this was written the progress of Russian Geographical research throughout the northern portion of Central Asia has been continuous ; and the results obtained are far too extensive and important to admit of being compressed into the limits of a note. It must suffice then to mention the names of the following distinguished explorers, and the regions in which they have travelled. For the geography of the Steppe between the Caspian and the Aral we are principally indebted to the discoveries of Scobolef, Stebnitzky, and Glukhofsky ; Kuhn and Krause having also sent in valuable reports. Stoletof is our great authority for the Oxus. Struvé's astronomical observations in the Bokhárá territory leave nothing to be desired. The lamented

P

2. Let us now glance at the progress of English discovery in Central Asia in recent times. Our greatest activity was naturally displayed in connexion with the Afghán war, as the period of Russia's greatest activity has coincided with her conquest of Turkestán. In extending the limits, indeed, of Asiatic empire, war and science march hand in hand, and the difficulties and dangers of the one—and would we could also say the triumphs and rewards—are not less conspicuous than those of the other.

In reviewing our own fortunes during the period in question, it would really seem as if a fatality had attended us, so few—so very few—of the English officers who advanced the cause of geography in Central Asia having lived to wear the laurels which they had earned. Stoddart, who was the first to cross the mountains from Herát to Bokhárá, and Arthur Conolly, who travelled by an entirely new route from Cabul direct to Merv and so on to Khiva, Kokand, and ultimately to Bokhárá, both perished miserably at the latter place in 1841. D'Arcy Todd, a traveller of some note himself, and to whom we are indebted for the adventurous journeys of James Abbott and Richmond Shakespeare from Herát to Khiva and Orenberg, was killed at the battle of Firoz-shahar. Edward Conolly, the first explorer of Seistán, was shot from the walls of an obscure fort in the Kohistán of Cabul; and Dr. Lord, the companion of Wood in the valley of the Oxus, was killed in the same district and nearly at the same time. Dr. Forbes, a most promising young traveller, was also murdered in Seistán, in 1841; and Lieut. Pattinson, the only officer who ever explored the valley of the Helmend from Zamín-Dawer to the vicinity of the Lake,* was butchered by the mutinous *Ján-báz*

Fedchenko explored Kokand and Kara-tegin. Osten-Saken conducted a survey which penetrated some distance within the Kashgar boundary. Captain Reinthal and Baron Kaulbars visited Kashgar itself. Further to the east Kulja has been incorporated n the Empire and Mongolia has been thoroughly examined by Fritsche, by Paderin, and especially by Prjevalsky —whose travels are about to be published in London in an English version, simultaneously with their appearance at St. Petersburg.—1874.)

* (This was true in 1866, but Sir R. Pollock and Dr. Bellew have since followed in Pattinson's footsteps along the Helmend from Girishk to Seistán on their recent deputation from India to join Sir Fred. Goldsmid in the latter

at Candahar, soon after the outbreak at Cabul. Col. Sanders, of the Bengal Engineers, who compiled from his own observations an excellent map of the country between Candahar and the Hazáreh Mountains to the north-west, also fell a few years later at Maharajpoor; Eldred Pottinger, who on two occasions crossed the mountains direct between Cabul and Herát, survived the Cabul massacre and the dangers of an Afghan captivity, merely to die of fever at Hongkong; and the list may be closed by a name—still more illustrious in the annals of geographical science—that of Alexander Burnes himself, who, as it is well known, was the first victim of the Cabul insurrection. Through the labours of these men and of their worthy coadjutors—the officers of the Quartermaster-General's Department—Afghanistán Proper may be said to have been very extensively, if not thoroughly, explored between the years 1838 and 1843. The great map, indeed, which was compiled by Mr. John Walker, Hydrographer to the Indian Office, at the close of the first expedition, and which was subsequently enlarged and amended as further information was acquired, will ever remain a noble monument of the collective science and industry of the Indian Army. It furnishes an accurate outline, and in many quarters a very comprehensive detail, of the country extending from the Lake of Seistán on the west to the frontiers of Cashmere on the east, and north and south between the Oxus and the Indus, and is altogether a most valuable contribution to our knowledge of the East. Since the period of the Afghán war, discovery has somewhat languished; yet there are still a few recent journeys which must not be overlooked. A French officer, General Ferrier, in attempting to push his way from Persia to the Punjáb, performed some very remarkable marches over new ground in 1844-45, exploring an unvisited part of the Seistán frontier in one direction, and crossing the great Paropamisan range from the vicinity of Balkh to Herát in another.* Still more recently

province. The chapters indeed, descriptive of the Helmend and Seistán are not the least interesting portion of Dr. Bellew's new work, "From the Indus to the Tigus."—1874.)

* Some doubt has been expressed with regard to the genuineness of this latter portion of General Ferrier's travels, because, in addition to certain discrepancies of distance, it also con-

the mission of Major Lumsden to Candahar has made us acquainted with the ranges beyond the Indus which buttress the Afghan plateau to the south-east, and through which no European had before penetrated; while at the same time our own line of frontier, conterminous with the mountains, from Scinde to Pesháwer, has undergone the closest investigation, as evidenced in the exhaustive Report of Mr. Temple, and in Major Walker's admirable map. Putting aside for the present all discussion of the elevated region between Pesháwer and the sources of the Oxus, which nevertheless contains matter of considerable interest, we pass on to the scene of England's greatest geographical triumph. Cashmere and Thibet, which even as late as the time of Humboldt were to a certain extent enveloped in mystery, are now as well known as the provinces of India Proper. Something had been done in the way of description and geographical outline by the preliminary labours of Moorcroft and Trebeck, of Jacquemont, Vigne and Hugel, and still later by the more scientific inquiries of Cunningham and Henry Strachey, but all this sinks into insignificance when compared with the grand achievements of Captain Montgomerie and Godwin Austen. The Great Trigonometrical Survey of India, having, under the direction of these officers, passed the Himálayas, and swept over the

tains an account of a colony of Pagans amongst the Hazáreh mountains, at whose hands the General asserts himself to have received that unreserved hospitality of bed and board which so vehemently scandalises Mahomedans, and which is by them referred exclusively to the Siyah-push Kaffirs; but the fastnesses of the Deh Zangi and Deh Kundi uplands have really been so little visited by European, or even by any reliable native travellers, that we are not in a position to pronounce authoritatively on the manners and customs of the inhabitants; and since every other portion of the General's narrative can be fully verified, it is hardly fair to discredit his Hazáreh journey and adventures merely on the ground of their apparent improbability. General Ferrier has the further merit of having performed his journeys in the avowed character of a European officer, a character which involved no little risk so soon after the termination of the Afghan war, and among a people who at that time classed all nationalities, English, French, and Russian, in the one hated category of 'Feringi' and Infidel. Colonel Pelly has since, in the year 1860, ridden the whole way from Teherán *viâ* Herát and Candahar, to India, dressed in the uniform of a British officer, and he encountered no serious danger except among the lawless frontier tribes in the vicinity of Farrah.

Cashmere valley, has, during the last few years, fairly grappled with the Trans-Indus region. It has worked its way from station to station at elevations sometimes over 20,000 feet. It has mapped the entire range of the Kara-Koram and Kuen-Luen, and, amongst its latest successes, has pushed out a supplementary reconnaissance both to Yarkend and Khoten in the great plain of Chinese Tartary beyond the mountains. That a survey of this extensive and exhaustive nature should have been carried on by British officers in a country under foreign rule, and at a distance of 500 miles from the British frontier, is not less creditable, we think, to their diplomatic skill than it is to their hardihood and professional zeal. We may fearlessly, indeed, compare the beautiful maps of Cashmere and Ladakh that have been recently published by Captain Montgomerie with the best productions of Russian geographers, and rest assured that the present Staff of the Indian Trigonometrical Survey are worthy successors of Lambton, of Everest, and of Waugh.

Whether the Kara-Koram and Kuen-Luen are the southern and northern crests of the great range which bounds the high table-land of Thibet, according to the mountain system of Humboldt, or whether the names do not rather apply to two culminating ridges which are western and eastern portions of the same range, as the Messrs. Schlagentweit first asserted, and as the observations of Mr. Johnson, in his journeys between Leh and Khoten, would seem to show, is of no very great geographical consequence. It is certain, at any rate, that the south-western or Kara-Koram ridge, the pass over which, forming the main road between Thibet and Yarkend, rises 18,341 feet above the level of the sea, is the true watershed between India and Central Asia, the Indus absorbing all the streams which flow from the southern slope of the range, while the northern rivers, which form the Kará-Kásh and which were followed by the Schlagentweits and by Johnson, force their way through, or round, the outer barrier of the Kuen-Luen, and wend north-eastward to the Gobi or sandy desert.

There is something which appears powerfully to strike the

imagination when the explorer of Central Asia ascends the last step of the ranges which bound the great plain of Tartary to the north and south, and gazes over the magnificent landscape at his feet. It is thus interesting to compare the report of Semenoff, from the top of the Záúku Pass, with the report of Johnson overlooking Khoten, the two travellers confronting each other as it were on the extreme limits of the Russian and British-Indian empires :—

"At last," says the Russian traveller, "we attained the object of our journey, and found ourselves on the summit of the mountain-pass, when a landscape of unexpected beauty spread out before us. We now gazed on a vast plain, which, extending in every direction from us, formed a kind of broad longitudinal valley between the foremost and the main ranges of the Thian Shan. . . . There I found myself in the very heart of Asia, rather nearer to Cashmere than to Semipolatinsk, to Delhi than to Orsk, to the Indian than to the Northern Ocean, and midway between the Pacific and the Euxine. . . . I very much wished to descend the southern slope of the Thian-Shan, but was obliged to abandon the project, fearing to jeopardize the safety of the party, and incur the moral responsibility of any disaster."

"I ascended," says Mr. Johnson, in his Report, "three peaks of the Kuen-Luen range, which had been previously fixed by the trigonometrical operations of the Survey. The contrast between the view to the north and that to the south was very striking : on the one side there was little but plain ; on the other, mountains and deep valleys. I might almost have fancied myself on one of the southern ranges of the Himálayas, with the plains of India to the south, and great mountain ranges to the north. . . . From these peaks, however, I could not get a view of any of the important towns of Khoten, which I was so anxious to see ; and I should have been obliged to have been satisfied with the extent of exploration which I had already accomplished, had not an opening presented itself for me to proceed to Khoten under the protection of the Khan of that country. . . . The whole country of Khoten, north of the Kuen-Luen range, is an immense plain, sloping gently down to Aksú, which place is fifteen long marches north of Ilchi.*

---

* It is to be hoped that this report of Mr. Johnson's, which is addressed to Col. J. T. Walker, Superintendent of the Great Trigonometrical Survey of India, under date April 22, 1866, and which is full of interest, will soon be made public. According to statements in the Indian newspapers, Mr. Johnson's conduct in extending his journey to Khoten, and being thus drawn into political communication with the rulers of Chinese Turkestán, has been disapproved by the Government of India ; but it is impossible, we think, that Sir John Lawrence should withhold his admiration at Mr. Johnson's intrepidity in venturing into such a country, and his skill in

As it is across these plains of Chinese Tartary that the most direct route lies between Russia and India, and as it is in this quarter that the first contact between the two empires may be expected to take place, some further notice of recent travels in Tartary may not be uninteresting.

Towards the close of the last century (A.D. 1786) a Russian sergeant of the name of Ephraimoff published an account of his travels in Central Asia, which may be regarded as something of a curiosity in literature. He had been carried off as a prisoner by the Kirghiz from the Siberian line and taken to Bokhárá, where he languished in captivity for many years. Ultimately, however, he escaped, and made his way to India by the route of Kashgar, Yarkend, Ladakh, and Cashmere, reaching Calcutta in due course, from whence he was conveyed to St. Petersburg. His personal adventures are of some interest, and a vocabulary which he gives of the Bokhárá dialect of that time, and which is almost entirely Persian, may deserve the attention of philologists; but he was a man of no education, and his geographical illustrations are thus almost confined to the dry detail of an itinerary.

It is believed that many Russian agents were employed in Central Asia at the commencement of the present century in connexion with the contemplated march of the Don regiments under Count Orloff-Denisoff upon India, but their reports have never yet been made public. The same reticence, how-

---

effecting a retreat from it. Mr. Johnson met with an Indian native officer at Khoten in command of the Khan's regular infantry, who, although now professing Mahomedanism, and calling himself Mahomed Ali, appeared to have been originally a Hindoo. It is said in the Indian papers that Mr. Johnson suspected this individual to be the notorious Nana Sahib, while the Calcutta editors suggest the Prince Firoz Shah, as a more likely identification; but in reality there seems to be no ground for believing the officer in question to be a personage of any such distinction. He is more probably a refugee from the old Bengal army, one of those many native officers who, after the mutiny, fled to the northward, where they are now to be found acting as instructors or commanders at all the Afghán, and Uzbeg, and Turkestán courts. (Mr. Johnson having since left the Indian service, has been appointed by the Maharaja of Cashmere his Commissioner at Ladakh, and in that capacity did excellent service in facilitating the passage of Sir Douglas Forsyth's party through Thibet on their recent journey to Yarkend and Kashgar.—1874.)

ever, has not been observed with regard to the reports of the merchants, who from this period seem to have prosecuted a tolerably active traffic between Russia and India across the plains of Tartary.

A Georgian trader, in the first place, of the name of Raphael Danibeg, published in 1815, at St. Petersburg, an account of his return journey from India to Semipolatinsk. Another traveller of the name of Agha Mehdi—who, being a Cabul Jew by birth, professed Mahommedanism or Christianity according to circumstances, and who seems, under the guise of a merchant, to have been employed by the Russian Government between 1810 and 1822 on various delicate negociations with the independent chiefs on the north-west frontier of India —embodied his geographical experiences of Central Asia in a memoir which is often quoted by the Russian authorities, and which, though as yet unpublished, must be still in the archives of St. Petersburg;* and a third report by a Bokhárá trader of the route from Semipolatinsk to Cashmere is given by Professor Senkowski in the appendix to Meyendorff's Bokhárá. In all these notices we find that the caravan route passed from Cashmere through Ladakh to the Kara-Koram range; that it then crossed the plains of Tartary by Yarkend and Aksú to Turfán at the foot of the Thian-Shan; and finally ascended the mountains by the famous Muzart defile (or "Pass of Glaciers," as it is usually called), and so on by Kulja to Semipolatinsk. A more direct line—and one which, from the report of Mr. Johnson, would, we should think, become the high road of traffic in future years—conducts from Aksú along the river to Khoten, and thence ascending the mountains either by the Sanjú or the Yangi Devan pass debouches upon Leh. The passes of the Kuen-Luen on this track are not more difficult than the Kara-Koram defile, while the road distance from Khoten to Leh is very considerably less than

* Mr. Moorcroft happened to be at Ladakh in 1822 at the time of Agha Mehdi's death, in the Kara-Koram mountains, on his third mission from Russia; and he had thus an opportunity of inspecting the letters, addressed by Count Nesselrode, on the part of the Emperor Alexander, to Ranjit Singh and the Raja of Thibet. See "Moorcroft's Travels," vol. i. p. 383; and for further notices of Agha Mehdi, see "Meyendorf's Bokhara," p. 340.

that to the same place from Yarkend; and Leh, moreover, is much more conveniently situated than Cashmere for communication with Northern India. If it be true, indeed, according to the information supplied to Mr. Johnson at Khoten, that by proceeding seventy or eighty miles to the south-east, the Kuen-Luen mountains may be turned, and wheeled carriages can thus pass along an elevated table-land by Rodokh and Gardukh to the immediate back of the Himálaya range, we may expect in due time that the great Hindustan road will be prolonged from the Niti Pass so as to open out upon these uplands, a direct line of traffic being thus secured with Tartary, which shall be independent of the difficulties both political and geographical, that are attached to the old route by Cashmere and Ladakh.*

There are still a few more authorities to be mentioned. Dr. Thomas Thomson, the associate of Cunningham and Henry

* This route, to which Mr. Johnson has recently drawn attention, was known, however, to Moorcroft, and is also mentioned by Cunningham and H. Strachey. There has always been a report in the country that there was a royal made road from the Niti Pass by Gardukh and Rodokh to Khoten, and Moorcroft in one of his journeys actually lighted upon a portion of this road towards its southern extremity, which he describes as "in some parts substantially paved with pebbles, and in others formed out of the levelled rock." It was no doubt a work of the Delhi emperors, executed for the purpose of facilitating commercial intercourse between India and China; but the old road seems to have passed to the west of the Kuen-Luen, instead of to the east of that range, as recommended by Johnson, for the Sarikia, which Moorcroft mentions as the northern terminus of the route between Khoten and Yarkend, can be no other than the Surikia of Johnson, which is a name for the valley of the Kara-kash river.—(See "Moorcroft's Travels," vol. i. p. 373; Cunningham's "Ladakh," p. 147; and "Journal of Royal Geog. Society of London," vol. xxiii. p. 5.) (Further enquiry has not confirmed the favourable view which was at first taken of this eastern route for commercial purposes. Mr. Shaw, while residing at Ladakh, obtained from natives of the country an itinerary of the route from Rodokh to Kiria, east of Khoten, which he published in the Geographical Proceedings, vol. xvi., No. iii. The topographical description is confused, as native accounts usually are, but the general result at which we arrive is that, although there are no stupendous passes to be surmounted, like those of the Kara-Koram and Kuen-Luen, still the route does pass over a culminating ridge of very considerable elevation and then descends along a rough ravine for some 200 miles, till it debouches on the plains of Turkestán, the track lying throughout across a desolate waste, entirely devoid of inhabitants or supplies, or even of fuel or forage.—1874.)

Strachey in the Ladakh Boundary Commission in 1847, was the first Englishman who fairly crested the Kara-Koram range and determined the true geographical position of the defile, a service for which the Royal Geographical Society, with a somewhat tardy recognition of merit, has this year presented him with its Founder's Medal. The next travellers who followed in the same direction were the brothers Schlagentweit. Adolphe, the youngest, not only crossed the mountains, but penetrated to Yarkend and Kashgar, where he was murdered by a sanguinary fanatic, Walí Khán, who happened at the moment to be in power, and may thus be classed among those martyrs to science whose early fate we have already deplored; but the two other brothers, Herman and Robert, are hardly entitled to the pre-eminent position which they claim as geographical discoverers. It is true that they ascended the Kara-Koram pass and made a détour beyond the range in the direction of Khoten, which occupied them for twenty-six days and extended to about three hundred miles, but they seem to have been as unsuccessful both in observing and recording their observations, as they were bold in assigning positions on insufficient evidence; the consequence of this empirical system of survey being that they dislocated the entire map of Tartary by placing everything between the Kara-Koram and the Thian-Shan from 1° to 3° to the westward of its true emplacement.*

* The Schlagentweits head their chapter on the passes into Tartary with this proud declaration:—"We are fortunate enough to have been the first Europeans that ever crossed the chains of the Kara-Koram and of the Kuen-Luen" (see "India and High Asia," vol. i. p. 25); and it was to commemorate so glorious an achievement that the Emperor of Russia conferred on the brothers the honorary title of Sakunlunski. In reality, however, the Russian Ephraimoff and the Georgian Raphael Danibeg had crossed the mountains from Yarkend to Thibet long before the Schlagentweits; and Dr. Thomson's ascent of the Kara-Koram, which was rarely mentioned beyond the immediate circle of his friends, was hardly a less creditable performance than the boasted exploit of the Germans. Mons. Golubief severely handled the Schlagentweits in an article in the "Russian Geographical Journal," Part IV., 1861; and his criticism was endorsed by Mons. Semenoff, the President of the Section of Physical Geography. This article was reproduced in an English translation in the last number of the "Bengal Asiatic Journal," Part II., No. 1, p. 46; and Sir Andrew Waugh, at the recent meeting of the British Association, showed, from a comparison of the Schlagentweit figures with those of Captain Montgomerie and Mr.

In the interior of the country the principal European travels to be cited are, firstly, the invaluable record by Lieut. Wood of his journey from Cabul to the sources of the Oxus; and, secondly, the recent work of M. Vambéry which has been already reviewed in this journal, and which describes the wanderings of the Hungarian dervish—carrying, as the Orientals would say, "his life in his hand"—from Asterabad, at the south-east corner of the Caspian, through the Turcoman desert to Khiva, and so on to the mouth of the Oxus; from that point to Bokhárá and Samarcand, and back again across the mountains to Herát.

There was not much, perhaps, of actual discovery in Vambéry's explorations, since Arthur Conolly, in 1829, had preceded him on the line from Asterabad to Khiva as far as the Balkan hills; and Muravieff, ten years previously, had landed in the Bay of Balkán, and travelled across the desert from that point direct to Khiva, almost on the same track as the Hungarian dervish; but his personal experiences nevertheless are full of interest, and especially with reference to his successful personation of a travelling mendicant. In this character, indeed, he baffled all attempts to penetrate his disguise; and only once, as we have heard him relate, was he in any danger of detection, when a curious fellow-worshipper at noonday prayer remarked that he must be a nondescript sort of Mahomedan after all, since the hairs on his arms were laid across, instead of up or down: the explanation of this singular criticism being, that as the Soonees and Shíahs in their ablutions wash their arms respectively from the elbow to the wrist, and from the wrist to the elbow, so may the members of the two opposing sects be recognised by the direction in which the hairs of the arm are laid, such direction following, of course, the daily manipulation. We have nothing to say to the moral question involved in this personation of the Mahomedan character. We are merely now alluding to the difficulty of sus-

Johnson, that the error of the Germans, in regard to the longitude both of Cashgar and Yarkend, was more than 3°; and that even in regard to Khoten, which they claim to have fixed, they were in error to the extent of 37' of longitude.

taining such a disguise for any long continuance. Burckhardt, the most accomplished European Arab who ever trod the desert, was often embarrassed by remarks on his arched instep, differing so much from the flat foot of the unfettered Bedouin, and he once narrowly escaped detection because he happened to take a draught of water after, instead of before, his coffee. Forster, again, was recognised as an Englishman in Cashmere from his "head being flattened at the top, instead of being conical like a Mussulman's;" and we have often witnessed the agony which Europeans endure in endeavouring to sit for a few hours together on their heels, or to ride in a native saddle with their knees bent to a right angle. The crucial test under which Arthur Conolly succumbed was of another character. Professing to be a Mahomedan merchant, he betrayed himself by his readiness to purchase articles of the Turcomans at the price demanded, instead of haggling for an hour ere the bargain was completed.*

* (As the British Government has been politically quiescent in the East during the last lustre, while Russia has been continually extending her frontier, there has been much less geographical activity in the southern division of Central Asia than in the northern. Still there are certain names of British officers which deserve to be recorded in bringing up the sketch of Central Asian exploration to the present day. Sir Fred. Goldsmid, for instance, has done excellent service to geography by filling in the map of Persia through the surveys of the provinces of Mekrán and Seistán, conducted by his assistants, Majors St. John and Lovett of the Engineers, in the recent settlement of the frontiers between Persia on the one side and Belúchistán and Afghanistán on the other. Col. Valentine Baker and Lieut. Gill have also surveyed the course of the Atreck to its source, and Capt. Napier is now continuing the examination of the Turcomán and Afghán frontier. Our most important explorations have been, however, in Thibet and Turkestán, where Messrs. Shaw and Hayward, some years back, and more recently Sir Douglas Forsyth and Colonel Gordon, have thoroughly examined the country between Cashmere and the Russian frontier beyond Kashgar, including a portion of the Pamír and the hill country of Gilgít and Yassín. The journey also of Mr. Ney Elias from the great wall of China through Mongolia to Western Siberia, for which he received the gold medal of the London Geographical Society in 1873, may well compare for interest and importance with M. Prjevalsky's remarkable visit to the Koko-nor; and finally may be noticed the mission which has recently been sent under Colonel Brown from India through Burmah to Talifú in Yunnán, for the purpose of opening up an old trade route to Western China, and thus letting in light upon one of the least-known portions of the whole mysterious region of Central Asia.—1874.)

3. Other travels in the East, which have been recently communicated to the world, would be of the utmost interest if they could be relied on as authentic and sober recitals; but at present a grave shadow of suspicion hovers over them. There have always been European adventurers in Central Asia, sometimes established in the cities as military instructors or jewellers, sometimes wandering about the country in search of mines and metals. Herát, Cabul, and Bokhárá, have rarely been without such visitors, and it is a free-lance traveller of this class whom we are now about to introduce. A Mr. Gardiner, who was the son of a medical officer in the Mexican service, and who had been educated at the Jesuit College of Clongoose, in Ireland, found himself, at the close of some very strange adventures, at Herát in the beginning of 1830. He seems to have been of an essentially erratic disposition, for although his ostensible object at this period was to take service in the Punjab, he passed several years in perambulating, or circumambulating, the intermediate countries before he finally reached his destination. An abstract of a portion of his travels was published in 1853 in the "Journal of the Asiatic Society" at Calcutta, and as this abstract professes to describe a route passing from Herát to Bokhárá, from thence to Kundúz, and through Badakshán to Yarkend, Ladakh, and Cashmere, and beyond that point among the mountains to Kafferistán on the Cabul frontier, it ought to be full of interest and value; but unfortunately the names, distances, and bearings are so distorted and mutilated, and the descriptions of antiquities and natural phenomena are further so monstrously exaggerated, that the narrative reads like a romance rather than as a journal of actual adventure. Mr. Gardiner, however, who is still living, and who holds, indeed, a Colonel's command under the existing Seikh Government in Cashmere, is understood, now that age has somewhat tempered the exuberance of his fancy, to have re-written his travels, including his description of Kafferistán, the original notes of which were supposed to have been lost in the pillage of Sir A. Burnes' house at Cabul; and if, as is said to be likely, Mr. Cooper, our Commissioner at Lahore, whose name is a sufficient guarantee for careful and

conscientious editing, can spare time from his official duties to prepare the MSS. for the press, the public may expect to be soon gratified with the appearance, in a readable shape, of this unique record of Central Asiatic discovery.* We say unique, notwithstanding that a German work, which we have reserved for the last on our list, claims to have reference to the same mysterious country of Kafferistán, as we have the most serious misgivings with regard to the genuineness of this latter record.

A question of literary authenticity is always provocative of curiosity, but in the present case it is also of real importance to the science of geography. "If the manuscript," it was recently stated to a meeting at Burlington House, "were genuine, it was one of the most valuable contributions to our knowledge of Central Asia that had ever been given to the world; on the other hand, if it were not genuine, it was one of the most successful forgeries that had ever been attempted in the history of literature." The subject, indeed, is one of so much interest, and the evidence for and against the German is so nearly balanced, that we shall merely state the heads of the story, and leave our readers to draw their own conclusions; or if we hazard a solution, it must be understood to be a mere suggestion unsupported by authority. It appears, then, that a few years ago Monsieur Veniukoff, an officer especially interested in geographical exploration in Central Asia, to which, indeed, he had been himself an active contributor, discovered in the archives of the Topographical Department of St. Petersburg, an anonymous MS., purporting to be the journal of a German traveller, who had passed from Cashmere to the

* (It is understood that Mr. Cooper had already printed about a hundred pages of Col. Gardiner's Journal when death put an end to his labours in 1871; and no competent editor has been since found to continue the work; nor, indeed, is it known what has become of the MSS. A very excellent epitome of Colonel Gardiner's life and travels was published by Sir Henry Durand in the "Friend of India," for September 1870; but it may be questioned if the original journals, drawn up apparently from memory aided by a few desultory notes, are worth publication. Colonel Gardiner is still living in Cashmere, and has been employed during the present year by the Amír of Kashgar as a sort of agent in purchasing arms and other articles of European manufacture.—1874.)

Kirghiz Steppe in the early part of the present century, and had executed a quasi-scientific survey, verified by astronomical observation, of all the regions he had visited. This MS. was duly brought under the notice of the Geographical Society of St. Petersburg, and copious extracts from it were published, with annotations, by M. Veniukoff, in the Russian "Geographical Journal." No one in Russia presumed to contest the genuineness of a document thus authoritatively brought forward. It was received with acclamation by the Imperial Academy, and the alterations which it introduced into the geography of Central Asia were at once transferred to the Government maps, and thus obtained circulation throughout Europe. When the Russian papers, however, were translated and came under the cognisance of savans in London, who had made a special study of the geography of Central Asia, doubts were immediately expressed as to the genuineness of the narrative. Inconsistencies—nay impossibilities—were pointed out of a most damnatory character. Proofs of authenticity were asked for, and a controversy arose between Russian and English geographers, which is still being carried on without much chance of a satisfactory issue.

The MS. professed to have been written in 1806 by a German nobleman, who had been employed by the East India Company towards the close of the last century to purchase horses in Central Asia for the Indian Cavalry. He had started, it was said, from Cashmere, accompanied by Lieutenant Harvey and forty sepoys, had traversed the mountains between Little Thibet and the Upper Oxus, debouching finally upon Kashgar; from that point he had returned to Badakhshán and had passed several months in the neighbouring districts, after which he had struck across the Pamír Uplands to Kokand, and had sought to return to Europe by traversing the Kirghiz Steppes. Arrested, however, in his progress northward and plundered by the Kirghiz, he was compelled to fall back on Bokhárá and Samarcand, from whence he regained India by the high road of Kashgar, Yarkend, and Ladakh. A series of maps, forty in number, accompanied the Journal, and personal adventure, historical relation, geographical and statistical details, and a general description of the countries traversed, varied by notices of their inhabitants, climate, and products, were blended together in a sufficiently interesting, though inartistic manner, in this singular narrative. It was further stated in the memoir that over 1100 horses had been purchased by the German agent, 132 in the mountains near the source of the Oxus, which had been sent back to India at once under charge of Lieutenant Harvey, and 980 more from the tribesmen near Kashgar, which had also been duly forwarded to their destination. These horses, however, having been plundered by the Mahrattas in Northern India, the German, on his return to India, was unable to obtain reimbursement for his outlay from the Calcutta authorities. Thereupon arose an angry correspondence, at the close of which the agent, having cleared his honour but smarting under a sense of injustice, betook himself to St. Petersburg and placed his maps and journals at the disposal of the Russian government. An explanation was further tendered by the Russian officials that it was in consequence of this betrayal of trust, as it might be deemed, that the name of the traveller had been suppressed, and that the MS., after being allowed to remain for nearly sixty years in obscurity, had only been brought out when it might be hoped that all traces had been lost which could lead to the identification of the writer.*

Now, however legitimate would have been an introduction of this nature to a sensational novel, or however circumstantial and consistent the story may have seemed to the Russian

* Mons. Veniukoff gives the following title to the MS. in the Russian archives: "Travels through Upper Asia, from Kashgar, Tashbalyk, Bolor, Badakshan, Vakhan, Kokan, Turkestan, to the Kirghiz Steppe, and back to Cashmere, through Samarkand and Yarkend;" but this title in reality can only refer to the second portion of the travels, as it omits all mention of the journey from Cashmere to Cashgar, which is, nevertheless—or ought to be — the most interesting part of the narrative. Mons. Veniukoff's further description of the MS. is remarkable. "The travels," he says, "form a magnificent manuscript work in the German language, accompanied by forty sketch maps of the country traversed. The text has also been translated into French in a separate manuscript, and the maps worked into one itinerary in an admirable style. The Christian name of this traveller, George Ludwig von ———, appears over the preface ; but the surname has been erased."

academicians, jubilant with the honour of their great discovery —for if the travels were genuine they were of the utmost importance to geographical science—it did not by any means satisfy the more calm and rigid scrutiny of the English critics. Objections were taken on two grounds; firstly, that the framework and incidents of the pretended journey were impossible; and secondly, that the so-called geographical results, as far as they could be tested on the Indian side, were altogether false. Inquiries set on foot both in India and in London showed that no trace existed in the records of the East India Company of any such arrangement as that described by the pseudo-agent, either with himself or with any one else. There was no Lieutenant Harvey in the India Army list at the close of the last century; nor any cavalry force that could have required recruiting. Cashmere was then held by the hostile Afgháns, amongst whom it would have been madness for a couple of officers with a party of forty Sepoys to have attempted to penetrate. Forster, indeed, the only European who had visited the valley under Afghán occupation, was indebted for his safety to disguise. The story of the horses, moreover, was manifestly fabulous. The only animals obtainable in the region indicated would have been Uzbeg ponies, utterly unfit for cavalry purposes, and when obtained at the sources of the Oxus, to have conveyed them in safety to India under the escort of a lieutenant and seven Sepoys, would have been little less than a miracle. Then in regard to geographical results, the German pretended to have passed from Cashmere to Kashgar with camels and foot soldiers in twenty-five days, whereas three months would have been a more reasonable allowance for the journey. He crossed the Indus according to his own statement on the third march, from Srinagar, with his whole caravan, the distance being in reality nearly 200 miles, and occupying usually a period of twenty days. He passed too, as he asserted, in this interval an active volcano; no such physical feature existing in the valley. To trace his exact footsteps was obviously impossible, as there was not a single name of a town, or mountain, or river, excepting the Indus itself, on the entire route from Cashmere to Kashgar that admitted of identification; but it was known from the actual explorations of Messrs. Winterbottom and Vans Agnew beyond the Indus in 1848, as well as from the information collected by Captain Montgomerie of the march of the Seikh force in 1860, that there was in reality but one available road through the mountains in this direction*—namely, that which left the Indus at Bonji, ascended the Gilgít River by Gilgít and Shirni to Yassín, crossed by a difficult defile to Mastúj in the Upper Chitrál valley, then passed over the great range to Badakhshán, descended upon the Oxus, and followed up a branch of that river to the plateau of Pamír which it traversed till it reached Kashgar; and this route, although not unfrequently followed by lightly-equipped travellers, was in many parts of it impracticable even to loaded mules, whilst the German pretended to have carried his camels with him throughout his journey, and did not, except on one occasion, speak of any extraordinary difficulties in the transit. Another fatal discrepancy which attracted notice was, that the inhabitants of the whole country between the Indus and the Oxus were described as Pagans, all speaking dialects of one language called the Bili, whereas in reality the Pagans, or Siyah-púsh Kaffirs, were known to be confined to the western corner of this tract, and would hardly have been met with upon our traveller's line at all; and in the second place, whilst no such language as the Bili had ever been heard of before, the dialects which would have been encountered on the transit from Cashmere to the

* (There are in reality three passes, all more or less easy, which cross the great range into Wakhán near the point where the Chitrál and Gilgít valleys converge. The most westernly is Birogil, and leads from the head of the Chitrál valley down upon Serhad Wakhán, the summit of the pass, which is quite open, being hardly 1000 feet above the level of the Oxus. The next is the Darkút pass, where poor Hayward was murdered in 1870. It is the most difficult of the three, and conducts from Yassín down on Wakhán. The most easternly is the Ishkaman pass, which is easy and open like the Birogil, and is of the most importance to India of any of these passages across the Hindú-kúsh, inasmuch as it leads direct to Gaokash, the frontier Cashmere post in the Gilgít territory. All these passes were recently examined by Capt. Biddulph on the return journey of Colonel Gordon's party from Panja to Tashkurghán, and the information thus acquired is regarded as one of the most important results of Sir Douglas Forsyth's mission.—1874.)

Oxus (such as the Balti, the Dardu, the Cashcári, the Kaffir, and the Badakhshi), were essentially dissimilar to each other, and could not possibly have been all understood by one so-called Bili interpreter.

In regard to the second portion of this pretended journey from Kashgar by Badakhshán to Kokand, on the authority of which extensive modifications had been introduced into our standard maps, we may quote the following *résumé* from Sir Henry Rawlinson's address on the subject to the Royal Geographical Society, at their meeting on the 26th of March of the present year :—

"The ascent of the Yaman-yar river, from Kashgar to the Lake of Kará-kúl ('the Dragon Lake' of the Chinese), seemed to be genuine, but the description of the town and river of Bolor were probably fictitious. The positions, moreover, of Badakhshán ('Fyzábád' of Wood) and Vokhán were reversed, the latter being far to the east of the former, instead of to the west, as the 'Travels' and longitudes would seem to indicate. Again, that there was ever a Chinese garrison in Badakhshán, as stated by the German, is opposed to our historical knowledge; and Malik Shah Buzurg resided at Fyzábád, and not at Vokhán. In continuation, the extent of the Pamír Steppes seemed to be much too contracted, and the positions of Tanglak and Terek-chai were transferred from the north to the south of the plateau ; and it was further suspicious that in pursuing the valley of the Jaxartes to Kokand, there was no mention of Oosh, or Marghilán, or any of the other large towns of the district."

The only rejoinder that has been hitherto made to this exposition of errors and impossibilities is something to the following effect. As far as the Russian surveys have extended along the valley of the Jaxartes, the correctness of the German maps has been abundantly verified, testifying beyond all possibility of dispute to their having been executed from actual observation, since at the commencement of the present century—indeed up to times comparatively modern—the whole country of Kokand was almost a "terra incognita." The same inference may be drawn from the German's description of Samarcand, which Mons. Khaníkoff, who himself visited the city in 1841, declares to be rigidly accurate, though no other modern notice of the place is extant. The Russians again appear to underrate our Indian knowledge of the country between Cashmere and Kashgar, and to think that the alleged ocular observation of the German may be after all as trustworthy as the hearsay evidence of Elphinstone and Raverty, or of Moorcroft, Vigne, and Cunningham. At any rate they appeal to the singular coincidence between the testimony of the German writer and all subsequent information as to the products of the country and the remarkable manners and customs of the inhabitants, and they ask from what source such knowledge could have been acquired in 1806, if not from personal experience. Such arguments assuredly—if the date of 1806, which is endorsed at present on the Petersburg MS., be admitted to be genuine—do appear to be of the utmost cogency;* and a not less strong collateral proof of authenticity is to be found in the admitted fact that, although the names assigned to the various localities are not be recognised in modern geography, still most—or many—of these names are philologically correct; Thibetan affixes, for example, being found on the Upper Indus, true Kaffir names in the mountains, Persian vocables in Badakhshán, a thoroughly Turkish nomenclature in Kashgar and Kokand, and even a *bonâ fide* Calmuck title referring to a Zungarian chief. †

Now in view of such a singular conflict of evidence, if we were called upon to pronounce judicially on the question of the authenticity of these remarkable travels, we should, we think, reject unhesitatingly the whole framework of the story, while

* (The date of 1806 has since been proved to be fictitious, the simulated antiquity of the MSS. being, in fact, an essential part of the original imposture. The travels were probably compiled about the year 1816; at any rate after the publication of the first edition of Elphinstone's Cabul in 1815, from which work indeed the information regarding the Kaffirs must have been taken.—1874.)

† The following examples may be quoted of linguistic accuracy in the geographical nomenclature of the travels:—*Lumba*, which is "a mountain ravine" in Balti, occurs in the names of the villages, supposed to be on the frontiers of Baltistan. *Imbra-Embra* (said to mean "the seat of God") is the name of a peak in the Kafferistan mountains, and *Imra* is really the Kaffir name for God. In Badakhshán there is the Persian name of *Shah-rúd*, or "royal river," and there are also numerous *derehs* or passes. Of true Turkish vocables about Cashgar we have *kara-baliq*, "black-fish;" *kara-agatch*, "black-wood;" *kara-kul*, "black-lake;" *ak-su*, "white-river;" *Tamgha*, "a seal;" *Ulus*, "a camp;" *kishlaq*, "a winter pasture," &c.; and *Zeisan* is also correctly quoted as a Calmuck or Mongolian title.

we should admit to a certain extent the genuineness of the materials. We should disclaim all belief in the individuality of the German traveller, or in any of his pretended adventures, but we should think it not unlikely that the travels had been compiled and the maps executed from the information and experience of parties who had actually visited Central Asia at the close of the past or beginning of the present century, and had heard accounts of the routes and localities described; such accounts, however, being but imperfectly remembered, and being moreover in many cases so confounded in the report as to be hardly recognisable. With regard indeed to the opening chapters of the Journal, which from their obvious inapplicability to the line of country by Gilgít and Yassín, are sufficient to discredit the entire narrative, we have a suspicion that the route which it was intended to delineate was that conducting to the plateau of High Asia from Peshawer and not from Cashmere. The geographical nomenclature was probably fictitious from the outset; and it would be useless therefore to compare the itinerary with the map; but the general features of the Bajour and Cashcár valleys—as far as we are acquainted with them—would seem to correspond to some extent with the pseudo-traveller's description, and the transfer of the line of route moreover from the north-eastern to the south-western quarter of the mountain range would serve to explain those notices of true Kaffir characteristics, for which, if the MS. be really of the date assigned to it—and for this the Russian Government is said to hold itself responsible—it would be otherwise impossible to account. We allude especially to the description of the auriferous streams, the vineyards and wine-bibbing propensities of the inhabitants, their arms, costume, and general appearance, their excessive jealousy of Mahommedans, their singular customs in entertaining guests, their sacrifices and Pagan habits, and even the words which are reported of their language,* together with other traits of verisimilitude,

* For instance, *Immir-umma* is given as the name of the spot where the Kaffirs offer sacrifice; and this is the exact title applied by Elphinstone to the Kaffir temples. It means "the place of God." See Elphinstone's "Cabul," vol. ii. p. 379.

which at the commencement of the present century certainly could not have been learnt from any published authority. In the same manner it may be conjectured that the information regarding Badakhshán, Vakhán, Bolor,* and Pamír, which is involved in inextricable confusion, was obtained second-hand at Kashgar, while the alleged accuracy of the details relating to the valley of the Jaxartes and Samarcand must be held to prove the actual presence of the agents in those localities. Who the agents may have been, or what was their object in weaving into a pretended personal narrative reports which in their plain unadorned official form would have been equally valuable to the Russian Government, it is of course impossible to ascertain. We have heard it surmised that the anonymous composition may have been a 'jeu d'esprit' of the celebrated Klaproth, founded partly on the vast stores of information regarding Central Asia which he had accumulated from Chinese, Mongolian, Arabic and mediæval authorities, and partly on the modern and unpublished reports of the Jewish agent, Agha Mehdi, Dr. Honigberger,† and others; and cer-

---

* The notice of a large town entitled Bolor, and situated upon a river of the same name to the west of the Pamír plateau and north of Badakhshán, is entirely fabulous; and certainly suggests a modern date for the compilation, since Klaproth, misunderstanding his Chinese authorities, has fallen into precisely the same geographical error in his memoir in the "Magasin Asiatique" for 1821. The name of Bolor or Belur was unknown to the old Mahomedan geographers, and is very rarely used even by modern Arabic or Persian writers. It owes its chief celebrity to the notices of Marco Polo and of the Chinese, and, as far as these authorities are concerned, agrees sufficiently well with the explanation first suggested, we believe, by Cunningham (see "Ladakh," p. 45), that it is nothing more than a corruption of the vernacular title of *Palolo*, by which Baltistan is known to the Dards. In this view Belur will apply to the whole country stretching from Ladakh to Pamír, including not only the modern Baltistan, but also Hunza-Nager, Gilgít, and Yassín. Bournouf's derivation of *Belur* from the Sanscrit *Vidur*, which is a name for the lapis-lazuli, though approved by Von Humboldt, has really nothing to recommend it but its ingenuity. The resemblance, indeed, of Bolor to the Persian word Bilúr, used for "crystal," is probably a mere accident. (Col. Yule has since written an exhaustive note on Bolor showing that the name applied in its greatest extent to the whole mountain region bounded by Peshawer, Cabúl, Badakhshán, Ladakh, and Cashmere. "Journal of R. Geograph. Soc.," vol. xlii. p. 473. At present it is used by the Kirghiz to denote Chitrál, and by the Dards to denote Balti or Little Thibet.— 1874.)

† Dr. Honigberger was a medical man in the Sheikh service who tra-

tainly if any one, who had not personally visited Turkestán, were capable of the mystification, he was the man; * but here again the date of 1806, attached to the MS. and registered, as it is said, in the official archives of Russia, would seem to be fatally opposed to such an explanation, since Klaproth at that early period was only just commencing those Oriental studies for which he was afterwards so famous. We shall be glad, then, if the pending controversy between the English and Russian geographers leads to any definite result; not only in the interests of science, but with a view to the extrication of all unprejudiced inquirers from a state of most disagreeable suspense.†

4. Our present sketch would be imperfect if we did not

velled from the Punjâb by Cabul, Bokhârâ, and Kokand, and thence through Russia to Europe, shortly before the period of the Afghán war. Dr. Honigberger is still, we believe, residing in Cashmere, but we are not aware whether any detailed account of his travels has been ever published.

* Suspicion has probably fallen on Klaproth because he is known at different periods of his life to have been engaged in the preparation of reports on Central Asia of a secret and confidential nature. One of these reports, indeed, "On the Geographical and Political Condition of the Countries intervening between Russia and India," is said to have been purchased by our Government at the time of the Afghan war for the enormous sum of one thousand guineas, and to be still reposing in the archives of our Foreign Office, enriched with marginal notes in the handwriting of the late Lord Palmerston. If this be true, we would recommend the indefatigable President of our Royal Geographical Society to undertake the disinterment of the Report, not only in the interests of science, but with a view to its possible bearing on the

vexed question of the authorship of the anonymous Russo-German manuscript. (This manuscript has been since examined and found to exhibit certain proof of having been forged by Klaproth. It was purchased while Mr. Canning was at the Foreign Office, and must have been read by Lord Palmerston, as there are a few unimportant marginal notes in his handwriting.— 1874.)

(† In the "Proceedings" of the Royal Geographical Society (Vol. x., Nos. 4 and 6; and Vol. xiii., No. 1), and in the Society's Journal, Vol. xlii., p. 484, will be found a summary of the evidence which has satisfied British geographers that the Central Asian travels of the early part of the century, adopted by the Russians as genuine documents, are in reality a pure invention, assignable to the perverse and perhaps interested ingenuity of Klaproth. This celebrated Orientalist seems to have deliberately forged three independent geographical works; 1, the so-called travels of an anonymous German baron in 'the British service, from Cashmere to Kokand, which he sold to the Russian Government; 2, the confidential Report of a Russian Surveying Expedition stated

acknowledge the obligations which Indian and Central Asian geography lies under to its native auxiliaries.* That Russia has largely profited by this source of supply has been already mentioned in our notice of Agha Mehdí, and the traders between Semipolatinsk and Cashmere; and the reports of English agents from the same countries have been not less valuable or extensive. Meer Izzet Ollah, indeed, who was Moorcroft's factotum in his early wanderings, was the first to make us acquainted with the high road from Ladakh by Yarkend and Kashgar to Kokand and Bokhárá; and the same route was followed forty years later by another native agent, Khwajeh Ahmed Shah, who was sent from India in 1852 in search of Lieutenant Wyburd. Other travellers have since verified the accounts of the native explorers along different portions of the route, but no one else has traversed the entire

to have been sent by the Emperor Paul from Semipolatinsk to the Indian frontier in 1801—1802, which he sold to our Foreign Office for 1000 guineas as stated in the preceding note; and 3, the translation of a pretended Chinese Itinerary which he also deposited in the Russian archives, to serve as corroborative evidence of the genuineness of the other travels. As geographical romances after the manner of De Foe, these works possess a certain merit, but they are of no political value whatever; and they even involve serious errors of location owing to a mistaken projection in the original Chinese map, which was used by Klaproth, as first discovered and verified by Col. Yule. See "Geographical Journal," vol. xlii., article xix. It deserves further to be noticed that, notwithstanding the complete exposure of the Klaproth fraud in England, the Russian geographers appear to be still unconvinced, reference being often made to the German baron in the late M. Fedchenko's notes, as a genuine authority, and the oracles Veniukoff and Khanikoff remaining "dumb."—1874.)

* (The names of several other native explorers deserve to be recorded as having rendered important service to geography, in the interval between 1866 and 1874. Major Montgomerie's "Pundits" are especially to be commended for their survey of the Brahmaputra river above Lassa and their daring visit to the Thouk Jalong gold fields. Not less remarkable journeys were made by other agents trained by the same officer; by "the Mirza," in 1868-69; and by the Havildar in 1870. See "Geographical Journal," vol. xli. p. 132; and vol. xlii. p. 180. Colonel Yule has further done justice to the valuable Reports on Central Asian geography, furnished by Pundit Manphúl, and by Feiz Bakhsh. See "Geographical Journal," vol. xlii., p. 438; while Ibrahim Khán, who has been extensively employed by Sir Douglas Forsyth on political duty in the Oxus valley, also promises to become a most efficient auxiliary in exploring unknown and inaccessible countries.—1874.)

line from point to point, nor is there any account of the route in English to be consulted by the student of geography but the above-mentioned itineraries, first published in Calcutta periodicals. It must also be remembered that Captain Raverty was indebted to native travellers for all the geographical details contained in his excellent papers on Swát, on Kafferistán, on Chitrál or Cashcár, and on Panj-korah, which have severally appeared in the Calcutta Asiatic Journals, and which afford us the only exact information that we as yet possess regarding what may some day become the high road of commerce between the Punjab and Tartary. This route was first investigated by Lieutenant Macartney, and is twice alluded to in Elphinstone's work on Cabul.* Edward Conolly attempted to explore it in 1840, but was driven from the mountains by the Bajouries, especially jealous at that time of an intrusion upon their fastnesses; nor indeed has any single European that we are aware of, except Mr. Gardiner, succeeded up to the present time in disarming suspicion, and obtaining access to this interesting region. The route in question, according to Raverty's information, follows up the Penj-korah branch of the Landaí river to Dír, the capital of the district (other authorities would conduct it up the Bajour river which lies in a parallel valley); it then crosses the Las-púr range to Drush in Lower Cashcár, and from thence follows up the Cashcár or Chitrál valley to Mastúj, where the road bifurcates, one branch continuing up the valley to the tableland of Pamír and descending on Yarkend, while the other, which has been already alluded to, crosses the great range to Badakhshán and the valley of the Oxus. Raverty says of this line of route:

"The road is somewhat difficult between Panj-korah and Drush" (perhaps the line by the Bajour valley may be easier), "but beyond it is very good, and the country is like a vast plain, gradually sloping upwards towards the high table-land of Pamír to the north-east; . . . consequently there would be no difficulty for the passage of light artillery.'†

And a friend of Colonel Gardiner's, quoting his authority, uses almost the same language.

* See Elphinstone's "Cabul," pp. 26 and 389.
† "Journal of the Asiatic Society of Bengal," No. 294, No. II., 1864, p. 130.

"The best road," he says, "to the north from Pesháwer is by the Swát valley. It is a caravan road as far as Anveh (or Mastúj?).* Colonel Gardiner travelled over this route, and describes the dividing range between the Anveh territory and the Badakhshán valley as very gradual and easy of ascent, and declares that guns could be taken over without dismounting them. There is no traffic by this route at present, owing to the war in Gilgít, but Colonel Gardiner always declared—and from all I have heard in the country I am quite ready to endorse his opinion—that the true road from Northern India to Yarkend, as well as the valley of the Oxus, was viâ the Swát and Chitrál valleys."

Again, in Major James's celebrated Report on the Kokand embassy in 1861, he particularises this route by the Bajour and Upper Kunér valleys, as the most direct, though, perhaps, the most difficult, of the various lines connecting Pesháwer with Tartary; and he observes that it was actually followed by the envoy who came from Kokand in 1854. May it not then be fairly surmised that the compiler of the Russo-German MS., inquiring at Kashgar or Kokand for the nearest route from India, may have been informed of this line leading *direct* from the Indus to Pamír, a line which would have really led for a great part of its course through outlying tribes of the Siyah-Púsh Kaffirs, and would, moreover, have been practicable for camels; and that in adopting at some later period the description he had received, he may have given rise to our present mystification, partly by his ingeniously attempted restoration of the names which he had forgotten, and partly by his having erroneously taken Cashmere instead of Pesháwer for the starting-point? †

---

* Anveh is only mentioned in one passage of the published Journal of Mr. Gardiner, p. 19; but it is probable that it was more fully described in the account of his journey through Kafferistán, which was lent to Sir A. Burnes, and was supposed to have been lost in the plunder of the Resident's house at Cabul.

(† A good deal of information has been accumulated of late years with regard to this route from Major Montgomerie's Havildar and from other sources, the result of which is confirmatory of its suitability to the purposes of commerce in so far as regards its physical character. It is indeed well watered and supplied throughout, and with the exception of the Lahori pass, conducting from the Panj-kora to the Chitrál valley, the entire route from Peshawer to Wakhán is easy and open, and for the greater part practicable to wheeled carriages; but, on the other hand, the valleys of the affluents of the Cabul river, through which the

And now having alluded to Major James's Kokand Report, which was first, we think, brought to the notice of the public in the Quarterly Review article for October, 1865, on "The Russians in Central Asia," we must congratulate the native agent Moola Abdul Mejíd, whose march from Cabul to Kokand is there reported, on his having been presented at the Anniversary Meeting of the Royal Geographical Society of London for 1866, with a gold watch, in recognition of the great service he had rendered to geography by his adventurous journey across the Pamír Steppes. A not less distinguished service, and one which we venture to think is also entitled to honorary reward, has been since rendered by the native assistant of Captain Montgomerie, who, by his reconnaissance of Yarkend, has brought that city into immediate connexion with the great trigonometrical survey of India, and has thus for the first time in the present century determined a fixed geographical position on the southern border of the great plain of Tartary.*

5. The preliminary branch of the subject being now exhausted, we may pass on to a brief general description of Central Asia and its inhabitants. The whole country between India and Tartary may be considered, then, as one broad

route passes, are inhabited by the wildest and most intractable of all the robber tribes of Afghanistan. If the three limitary governments were to direct a combined movement in force from Peshawer, Cashmere, and Cabul against the mountaineers, it is possible that they might be brought into subjection and compelled to give hostages for their future good conduct, but it would be a difficult and most expensive undertaking, and even if successful, the political advantage would be doubtful. At present the valleys of Swát and Chitrál, although in close proximity to our frontier, are probably the most inaccessible districts to Europeans in all Central Asia ; and yet it is along this very line that the advocates of the Lesseps Central Asian Railway would propose to lay down

their iron road, with no more misgivings apparently as to its practicability than if they were operating in the civilized regions of the West. See "Oriental" for April of this year. —1874.)

* Captain Montgomerie communicated this interesting journey of his assistant, Mahomed-el-Hamíd, from the Kara-Koram to Yarkend, to the Royal Geographical Society of London at the meeting of May 14th, 1866, and showed from the road-book, which seemed to have been very accurately kept, that the true position of that city was in lat. 38° 19′ 46″, and long. 77° 30′. In the Jesuit Register the numbers are, lat. 38° 19′, long. 76° 3′, while the Schlagentweits give lat. 38° 10′, long. 74° 10′.

mountain range, the Himálayas forming the southern crest, and the Kuen-luen the northern; while the interior is sometimes cheered with lovely valleys like Cashmere, but is more usually broken into rocky ravines, through which the affluents of the Indus force their way towards the plains; or else stretches away in those vast treeless uplands which are one of the chief characteristics of the range through its whole extent. The direction of this range is from east to west, trending to the northward; while the parallel chain which bounds Siberia to the south, and the outer crest of which is the Thian-Shan, trends somewhat to the south; so that at a short distance to the west of Yarkend and Kashgar, the great interior depression of Chinese Tartary terminates, and the bounding ranges coalesce in the elevated table-land of Pamír. According to Humboldt's system, which is still adopted generally as the groundwork of our maps of Asia, the northern and southern ranges were united to the west of Kashgar by a transverse ridge, which he names the Belút-Tágh, or "Cloud Mountains;" but recent observation assures us that there is no such separate connecting chain. The ascent from Yarkend and Kashgar westward to the table-land of Pamír is gradual and almost imperceptible; and when that lofty position is gained, where the average elevation is probably as much as 15,000 feet above the level of the sea, a vast plateau is seen —seamed with rocky ridges running generally from east to west—which stretches from the valley of the Jaxartes in one direction, across the head-streams of the Oxus to the top of the Cashcár or Chitrál valley in another.

From this great plateau, which may be 700 or 800 miles in extent, and which is throughout studded with lakes, descend four great river systems. Firstly, through a long valley between the culminating ridge and outer range of the Thian-Shan comes down the Narym, which is the main stream of the Jaxartes. This outer range being the connecting link between the Thian-Shan and Pamír, the river which flows in a luxuriant valley at its foot drains all the northern edge of the plateau.*

(* Recent discovery has modified in some degree, though not essentially, this general sketch of the orography of the Pamír. According to the ob-

The Oxus again taking its rise in a Pamír lake, which is at least 300 miles to the south of the Jaxartes, and of which the true name is the Sárík-kúl, or "Yellow Lake," is fed on its right bank by a multitude of smaller streams, which run west and south from the Pamír uplands, breaking up the face of that region into a series of rugged valleys, such as Hissar, Ramíd, Derwaz, Shignán, and many others, which, although amply described in the Arab geographies, and in the "Memoirs of Baber," are hardly known in modern times, except from the confused accounts of Mr. Gardiner and the occasional notices of native agents. The western face of the Pamír, as it may be called, between the Jaxartes and the Oxus, is far more precipitous than the eastern. Numerous lofty and difficult ridges run out in this direction as far as Samarcand and Karshí, and the streams which drain off from the uplands between these ridges, and which form the Zar-afshán and Karshí rivers, belong of course to the water system of the Oxus, though the streams are at present entirely consumed in irrigation before they reach the great river, and, in fact, constitute that perennial supply of water which has given its worldwide reputation for fertility to the plains about Bokhárá and Samarcand. The third water-system is that of the Indus. From the south-eastern extremity of Pamír, where the tableland is lost in the rocky summits of the Múz-tágh, a number of streams drain off to the southward, forming two subsidiary Indus systems. A culminating ridge which runs out from the southeast corner of Pamír, and which the geographers usually call Pusht-i-khar (or "the back of the Ass "),* is the true watershed

servations of Fedchenko, the continuation of the Thian-Shan is not the outer range which immediately bounds the valley of the Jaxartes to the south, but the next range which bounds the Alaí plain to the south, and subsequently divides the river system of Samarcand from that of Hissár. Although, however, this range appears from its height to be the culminating ridge of the chain, it does not form the watershed between the Oxus and Jaxartes;

for the Surkháb river, which rises in the Alaí plain north of the ridge, instead of turning northward to the Jaxartes, forces its way south through the mountains, and ultimately debouches in the Oxus.—1874.)

(* The name of *Pusht-i-khar* was first introduced into geography by Macartney, and has ever since retained its place unchallenged in our maps; but it is entirely unknown at present in the country, and indeed there is no between Thibet and Cabul, the streams flowing to the south-west being separated by the shoulder which joins the Hindú-kúsh, from the streams descending through Vakhán and Badakhshán to the Oxus, and forming the Cabul river, which falls into the Indus at Attock; while those which flow to the south-east, and which are divided by the Múz-tágh range from Tartary, descend through a series of rocky valleys and precipitous gorges into the Upper Indus in Little Thibet. The eastern face of Pamír, again, which, as we have before observed, slopes off very gradually into the plains of Tartary, supplies a fourth water-system, being drained by a series of small streams, which, passing by Yarkend and Kashgar, are ultimately lost in the sandy desert, or in some cases reach the central lake of Lob-núr. If there is any geographical foundation, then, for the fanciful scheme of Buddhist cosmogony which describes the four great rivers of the world—the Ganges, the Indus, the Oxus, and the Jaxartes—as issuing from a single, central lake, the allusion must necessarily be to this lake country of Pamír; but in that case Lob-núr must have been supposed to communicate with Gangotri, or the Pamír must have been considered to include within its limits all the Thibetan uplands.*

Although the water-systems of Central Asia may be thus satisfactorily traced, it is hardly possible to lay down a corre-

culminating peak in this part of the range which could have been thus specially named. The most probable explanation of the title is that it is equivalent to the common Persian name of *Pusht-i-koh*, "back of the hill," which is applied to the inner or hinder side of a range (*khar* being a corruption of *ghar*, Sans. *giri*); and in the same way the title of *Pir khar*, also used by Macartney, which applies to the outer or front side of the range (See Davies's Report, Appendix IV. B., p. xxii., i.) may be for *Písh-khar* or *Písh-koh*, which is the co-relative of the other.—1874.)

(* See Remusat's " Foě-kouě-ki," p. 36. In the Brahminical Cosmogony, which is given in the 6th canto of the "Mahabharata," Mount Meru —explained by Wilson as "the Highland of Tartary"—takes the place of the Central Lake of the Buddhists; and the Bhadrasoma, which Humboldt, strangely enough, identifies with the Irtish, is substituted for the Sintou or Indus. See Humboldt's "Asie Centrale," tom. i. p. 4. The name of Meru, however, is connected by Bournouf with *Mír*, "a lake," so as to signify "the lake country;" and the same scholar suggests that Pamír may be a contraction of *Upa-Meru*, "above Meru," or in fact "the Lake Uplands." It is impossible to avoid comparing the myth above noticed with the Mosaical account of the rivers of Paradise; and it is fur-

sponding scheme of orography, since the concentration of the two great parallel chains in the Plateau of Pamír renders it most difficult to discriminate their respective prolongations. Perhaps, however, the most natural system is that which regards the chains to the north of the Jaxartes, the Ala-Táú, the Boruldäí, and the Kara-táú, not as mere spurs of the Western Altai, but as the prolongation of the terminating ridge of the Thian-Shan itself. The outer range, again, of this great chain, which forms the southern boundary of the upper Narym valley, and which is broken by the Terek pass, through which lies the high road from Kashgar to Kokand, may be recognised, it is thought, in the outer crest of the Pamír (or Aläí Plateau, as it is locally called), along its northern border, and may thus be traced as the left-hand barrier of the Jaxartes valley as far westward as Khojend, where it begins to lessen in height until it is lost in the desert north of Bokhárá.* Further south, Afghanistán must be looked upon as a continuation of Thibet, the southern or Himálayan crest running between Cashmere and the head waters of the Swát, Penj-korah, Bajour, and Chitrál valleys, till it just touches the Pamír nucleus at Pusht-i-khar, at its extreme southern corner, and then turning south-west by the Sufid-Koh of Jellalabad to the great Soleimán range; and so on by the Bolán and Gandáva passes to the chain which borders the Indian Ocean and the Persian Gulf; while the northern crest, which under the names of Kuen-luen, Kara-koram, and Múz-tágh, runs into Pamír, is prolonged to the west above Badakhshán, and forms the watershed between

ther curious to observe how the same tradition repeated itself in modern geography, the maps of Jeyháni, for instance, representing the four rivers of Afghanistán, the Murgháb, the Heri-rúd, the Helmend, and the river of Balkh, as issuing from a Central Lake in the Hazáreh mountains, though in reality the sources of these rivers are many hundreds of miles asunder. (Further research has suggested that Pamír (or Famír as the name is always written by the Arabs) is a mere contraction of Fán-mír, "the Lake country of the *Fání*," Φαῦνοι of Strabo) as explained in Geographical Journal, vol. xlii. p. 489, foot-note.— 1874.)

(* See the note to page 236, which, on the authority of the late M. Fedchenko, defines the culminating ridge, which is the true continuation of the back-bone of the Thian-Shan, to be the rocky range running to the south and not to the north of the Aläí, and continued at a high elevation as far as Shehr-i-sebz.— 1874.)

the Oxus and the Cabul river, continues under the names of Koh-i-Bábá, Hindú-kúsh, &c., to the north of Cabul, and finally traversing Khorassán at a much diminished altitude, reappears in the Elburz, to the south of the Caspian.

The elevated space between these ranges, which gradually opens out from the apex at Pusht-i-khar till it meets and dies away in the Persian desert, exhibits many of the characteristics of Thibet. The great Hazáreh plateau between Bamián and Herát is thus very like the uplands around the Pangong lake, and the Cabul valley may be compared, not unworthily, with that of Cashmere. As the ground, however, gradually sinks to the level of the Seistán lake and the sandy waste of Belúchistán, the resemblance is no longer perceptible.

If we look at the character of the physical geography of Central Asia, we observe everywhere a conflict, as it were, of the forces of nature, which may well remind us of the struggle between the principles of good and evil that was the dominant creed of the old inhabitants of the country. The desolation of the desert is brought face to face with the beneficent influence of the mountain ranges. Where the streams bring down the mountain detritus and deposit a thin coating of soil, the sandy waste withdraws for a space before advancing cultivation; but it reasserts its supremacy immediately the influence of irrigation is no longer felt. This contrast is especially remarkable in Chinese Turkestán, where the general character of the country is one of complete sterility, the river courses in the interior being merely fringed with a narrow strip of verdure, and the agricultural population being thus almost confined to the slopes of the mountain sides, where alone is water to be found for the purposes of husbandry. The upper valleys, it is true, of the Oxus and Jaxartes are so enclosed on both sides by mountains, and so entirely filled up with a rich alluvium, that in these favoured localities the usual characteristics of the country disappear; but no sooner have the rivers fairly debouched from the spurs of the Pamír plateau than they enter upon arid and saline steppes, and thus continue for hundreds of miles, unblessing and unblest, until on approaching the Aral the sluggish streams scatter themselves over the Delta in a network of canals, both natural and artificial, and again furnish the means of subsistence to a teeming population.

On the western face of the Afghan uplands there are precisely the same physical features. The Murgh-áb, the Tejen, and the Heri-rúd are all lost in sandy deserts. The Farreh-rúd, the Khásh-rúd, and the Helmend passing from the mountains through a sterile waste to the lake of Seistán, are the counterpart of the river system of Chinese Tartary struggling on from the surrounding ranges to the central reservoir of the Lob-núr. The Arghendáb and the Ternek are consumed in irrigation before they reach the Helmend, precisely as are the rivers of Balkh and Sir-púl on the left bank of the Oxus, and the Karshí and Zer-afshán on its right or northern bank. Throughout the whole region, indeed, of Central Asia there is a triple division of territory, which naturally produces a triple division of population. Firstly, there is the mountain region with its invigorating climate, its vast upland downs well suited for summer pasturage, and its rocky ravines carrying foaming torrents to the plains. Here dwell a hardy peasantry, descendants in some cases of the primitive inhabitants, but more often intermingled with offshoots of the many migratory races who have since swept through the country. At the foot of the mountains again are tracts of surpassing fertility, rich well-watered plains, where the great mass of the population congregate in towns and villages and pursue the peaceful arts of life, the miscellaneous character of the inhabitants of these marts of commerce and industry being unequalled perhaps in any other part of the East.* And thirdly, beyond the cultivated plains stretches

* The following list, which is given in the anonymous Russo-German travels, of the component parts of the population of Kashgar—though the numbers, if referring to individuals rather than to families, are far too limited, and though the pretended Armenian element is probably an invention of the author—would seem to be otherwise relatively correct, and may be taken as a fair sample of the mixture of races in a Central Asiatic town :—

Turks of Kashgar	7,690
Bokhárians, speaking Persian	1,960
Kalmucks (Mongolians)	850
Kirghiz and Búrúts	1,230
Ouigours, from Tourfan	680
Manchus	640
Chinese, merchants & tradesmen	1,470
Armenians	325
Indians and foreigners	250
Total	15,095

R

out in every direction the pathless desert, which has been tenanted by pastoral nomades ever since the earth was peopled. Here rapine and disorder seem to have their natural home, and here, at the present day, to the ordinary excesses of brigandage is superadded the detested occupation of man-stealing.

6. Those who have been accustomed to regard Central Asia solely under its present condition of political and social degradation, may find it difficult to realise the idea that it was ever the seat of arts and industry, or had made any great advance in civilization, yet such was undoubtedly the case. We are not able, it is true, as in the case of Egypt, or Babylonia, or Assyria, to appeal to contemporary monuments in support of a Central Asiatic development at a period of any remote antiquity, but the evidence to this effect, derived from a large field of induction, is not less significant and sure. In the first place, the belief in a very early empire in Central Asia, coeval with the institution of the Assyrian monarchy, was common among the Greeks long anterior to Alexander's expedition to the East, and could only have been derived from the traditions current at the court of the Achæmenian kings. This belief again is connected through the names of Oxyartes and Zoroaster with the Iranian division of the Arian race, and receives confirmation from the earliest memorials of that people. Without seeking, indeed, to penetrate the myth of Iran-víj, the legendary birthplace of the so-called Persian race, there can be no reasonable doubt that the enumeration of the other fifteen localities successively created by Ormuzd, which is given in the opening chapters of the "Vendidad," indicates the progress of Iranian colonization during the earliest phases of the national existence; and it is thus of much ethnological importance to find that the empire commenced with Sogdiana, Merv, and Bactria; that in its subsequent development it included the modern provinces of Khorassán, Afghanistán, and Kharism,* and finally at its period of greatest extension stretched from

---

* It is singular that neither Mons. Khanikoff himself, nor any of the modern commentators on the Vendidad whom he enumerates—Spiegel, Bréal, Haug, and Justi—should have recognised Kharism among the sixteen localities created by Ormuzd. There can be no doubt, however, but

Seistán on the south to the Jaxartes on the north, and from the Indus on the east, till it touched the extreme limit of the Median frontier to the west. It was formerly argued from this classification of the Iranian settlements that the antiquity of the legend must be enormous, since neither the Medes nor Persians, whose cognate nationality is unquestioned, and who are historically mentioned as early as 2000 B.C., were included in the series; but modern criticism prefers to explain their omission from the list by supposing that there were in reality two distinct systems of civilization among the Iranian division of the Arian race, synchronous in their action, though geographically and politically divided. Of these the Eastern system described in the "Vendidad" may have had its primæval seats upon the Oxus, and have been identified with the dualism of the Zend Avesta; while the other—or Western—system may have been more immediately connected with Magism, and have belonged to western Persia, being, perhaps, locally centralised in northern-Media, but with ramifications extending into Armenia and Asia Minor. The Persians, indeed, when they are first met with in the Assyrian inscriptions of the ninth century B.C., are not settled in the south, but appear as a cognate race with the Medes in the modern province of Azerbijan; and that offshoots of this race must even at that early time have been pushed far on towards the west is proved by the names of Kustaspa, king of Comagene, and Aspabara of Armenia, who are mentioned amongst the adversaries of Tiglath Pileser and of Sargon. In this western, or Magian, division of the Iranians were included no doubt both the Medes and Persians; their language was probably that with which we are acquainted from the tri-lingual inscriptions of Persia, and it may be conjectured from many circumstances connected with the history of Darius Hystaspes that it was in

that the eighth name, which immediately precedes *Vehrcan*, or Hyrcania (modern Gurgan), and which is read as *Urvan*, represents the well-known title of *Urganj*, the old capital of Kharism, the Zend *v* being regularly replaced by the Persian *g*, and the terminal *j* being dialectic, as in the names of the Kharismian months, which, according to Abu Rihán, are optionally written with or without a final *j*.

his reign, and in connection with the overthrow of the Magian usurpation that the dualism of Oromasdes and Arimanes was first introduced from the far East, in supersession of the old national faith.*

It is with the Eastern Iranians, however, that we are principally concerned, as the founders of Central Asian civilization. This people, on the authority of the Vendidad, may be supposed to have achieved their first stage of development in Sughd. Their language was probably Zend, as distinguished from the Achæmenian Persian, and somewhat more removed than that dialect from the mother-tongue of the Arians of the South. To them must be referred the old Greek traditions of the Bactrian Zoroaster, and the entire framework of Persian historical romance, culminating in the famous Epic of Firdousi. A more important evidence, however, of the very high state of power and civilization to which they attained is to be found in the information regarding them preserved by the celebrated Abu Rihán, himself a native of the country, and the only early Arab writer who investigated the antiquities of the East in a true spirit of historical criticism.† This writer supplies us with an extensive specimen of the old dialects of Sughd and Kharism. He gives us in those dialects the names of the twelve months, the names of the thirty days of the month, and of the five Epagominæ, together with the names of the signs of the zodiac, of the seven planets, and, lastly, of the mansions of the moon. A portion of this nomenclature is original, and offers a most curious subject for investigation; but the majority of the names can be compared, as was to be expected, with the Zend correspondents, and, indeed, are much nearer to the primitive forms than are the better known Parsee equivalents. According to Abu Rihán, again, the solar calendar of Kharism was the most perfect scheme for measuring time with which he

---

* This subject is ably and exhaustively treated in Rawlinson's "Herodotus," vol. i. p. 426.

† We quote from a most excellent work of Abu Rihán's on general chronology, which has not, we think, received the attention that it merits at the hands of European scholars, though there is a copy of the MS. at Paris, which was formerly much referred to by Quatremère, under the title of "Athar-el-Bakíeh."

was acquainted; and it was maintained by the astronomers of that country, that both the solar and the lunar zodiacs had originated with them, the divisions of the signs in their system being far more regular than those adopted by the Greeks or Arabs; and the very name, moreover, by which an astronomer was designated in the language of Kharism being taken from the asterism of the eighth mansion of the moon.* All this information is exceedingly curious in its bearing upon the controversy which has so long raged in the scientific world, as to the superior antiquity of the lunar zodiac used respectively by the Indians and Chinese, leading as it does to a suspicion that neither the one nor the other of these systems may have been original, but that their similarity may be explained by their derivation from a common centre in Bactria, where astronomy was first cultivated by the Eastern Iranians. An argument of some weight, indeed, in favour of this derivation is furnished by another statement of Abu Rihán's, which asserts that the Kharismians dated originally from an epoch anterior by 980 years to the era of the Seleucidæ, a date which agrees pretty accurately with the period assigned by our best scholars to the invention of the Jyotisha or Indian calendar.† Abu Rihán further speaks of the Kharismian writing and records, which were carefully investigated by Koteibah Ibn Moslem when he conquered the country, and strengthens the authority of these

* This term is *Akhír vinak*, "the observer of *Akhír*," which is the name of the 8th mansion.

† The date of 980 years before the era of the Seleucidæ is equal to B.C. 1304. Now, the date derivable from the Jyotisha observation of the Colures has been variously calculated by different Sanscrit scholars; the earliest date being that determined by Davis and Colebrooke in the last century, namely B.C. 1391, and the most recent being that lately adopted by Archdeacon Pratt and approved by Professor Max Müller, namely B.C. 1181. Professor Whitney, it is true, does not agree with either of these results, and thinks, indeed, that the data for calculation are so faulty and uncertain that a margin of several centuries should be allowed for possible error; but Sir E. Colebrooke, on the other hand, in replying to his criticism, has shown that a mean calculation of the two Equinoctial stars Revatí (or ξ Piscium) and Chitrá (or Spica) will bring us to the end of the thirteenth century B.C.; which is almost identical with the Kharismian date of B.C. 1304. This date, too, is almost certainly an astronomical rather than a political era, and was connected with the institution of the lunar zodiac, which, like the original Indian zodiac, commenced with the asterism of the Pleiades.

native documents, by showing that a single family named the Shahíyeh, and supposed to be derived from Cyrus, had reigned in Kharism—with the exception of a Turkish or Scythian interregnum of 92 years—from the Achæmenian period down to the time of the Mahommedan invasion.*

We have specially alluded to this evidence † of early Arian civilization in Central Asia, furnished by a writer of Abu Rihán's authority, as we believe it to be entirely new to Oriental students; but there are many other notices of a corroborative character, which have been often quoted. Justin's notice, for instance, of the thousand-citied Bactria which revolted under Theodotus, indicates a very high state of prosperity and power. Balkh and Kharism, again, furnish all the most favourite illustrations for the old Persian romance. The temple of Núbehár, at the former place, in which the Barmecide family, previous to their emigration to Baghdad, were

---

* As an example of the accuracy of the chronology of the Kharismians, Abu Rihán further quotes from their annals the date of the building of the famous castle of 'Ir, near the city of Kharism, in A.S. 616 (=A.D. 292) —a date which afterwards became a national era—and adds that this place continued to be the royal residence till it was destroyed by inundations of the Oxus in A.S. 1305 (A.D. 981). We have never seen in any other Arabic author an account of this castle, which is compared by Abu Rihán with the celebrated Ghamdán of Yemen; nor, indeed, do we think that the antiquities of Kharism are elsewhere at all noticed. (There can be no reasonable doubt—although the dates do not exactly correspond, owing probably to the gradual demolition of the place—that the destruction of the castle of 'Ir described by Abu Rihán is the same event as the destruction of the castle of Kát, which took place in the interval between the visits of the Geographers El Istakhrí and Ibn Houkal (A.D. 951—970) to the country of Kharism, as explained by the present writer, in the "Edinburgh Review," No. 275, p. 8, foot note; but it must still be a question if the 'Ir of Abu Rihán be a Hebrew equivalent of Kát, or Medíneh, (the city *par excellence*), or an error of the copyist for *Fíl*, which was the original name of the Kharismian capital.—1874.)

† (The attention of Orientalists having been drawn by this notice to the extraordinary value of Abu Rihán's work on Chronology, it was determined to employ the remaining assets of the Oriental Translation Fund in obtaining a scholarly version in English of the Manuscript in possession of the present writer, which was copied from a very ancient exemplar in the Library of the Royal Mosque at Teheran. The services of Dr. Sachau of Vienna were accordingly put in requisition, and he has now been employed for some years on the translation, having already published two preliminary brochures on different interesting portions of the work.—1874.)

servitors, was one of the most famous shrines of the Buddhist faith throughout the East; and the original fire of King Jem, the Eponym of the Iranian race, was supposed to have survived unextinguished on an altar in Kharism until the introduction of Islam. Of course fable was abundantly mingled with truth in these glimpses of old-world history. The pretended expedition of the Himyarite king, who founded Samarcand, from the south of Arabia, cannot, for instance, command a moment's attention; but there was certainly an ancient tablet, in an unknown tongue, over one of the gates of the city, which was supposed to commemorate this expedition; for Jeyhani, the Samanide vizier, distinctly says that he saw it in about A.D. 920, and that it was destroyed during a popular *émeute* whilst he was resident in the city. Whether this inscription was in Zend, or in Greek, or in Bactrian Pali, can be now of course a mere matter of conjecture, but the mention of such a tablet may well excite our curiosity.

7. The Iranian people who were thus settled between the Oxus and the Jaxartes, as early as the time of the Judges of Israel, still hold their ground in the country, notwithstanding the continuous flood of foreign races which has ever since swept over the region, surging up from those prolific slopes of the Altai that have been called the "officina gentium." Under the names of Tát, Tájik, Sert, Galsha, and Parsiwán, a primitive and not impure Iranian population is to be found in almost every district from the Indus to the Jaxartes, subject to the dominant Afghans to the south, and Uzbegs to the north. The same nationality prevails throughout the valleys of the upper Oxus in a quasi-independent position; and these mountaineers, who, in their modern name of Vakháni, retain the old ethnic title which originated the 'Οξος of the Greeks, are perhaps the best representatives extant of the primæval race.* To the east of the Pamír the Iranian element is now almost, if not totally obliterated, though Khoten itself was essentially

* This primitive title we suppose to have been *Vakh*, or *Vakhsh*, but its signification is unknown. It gave rise, however, not only to the 'Οξος of the Greeks, but to the title of *Vah*-rúd, by which the Oxus is known in the Bundehesh, and among the old Zoroastrians generally, and also to the modern names of *Vakham*, *Vakhsh-ab*, *Vash-jird*, &c.

an Arian settlement, and many of the names of places in the vicinity still retain their Arian etymology.* M. Khanikoff has drawn particular attention to the Jemshídís of Herát, and the Seistánees, as approaching nearest to the true Iranian type, founding his argument, not merely on the physical characteristics of these people, but on their language and traditions; but in reality the Seistánees are beyond all question a mixed race; and it may even be suspected that they derive their peculiar physiology from their Scythian rather than from their Arian descent.†

It would be a curious subject of inquiry to trace the successive stages of transformation through which the population of Central Asia has passed, in exchanging its primitive homogeneous character for the kaleidoscope variety which now distinguishes it; but to render such a sketch at all intelligible, it would be necessary to enter on ethnographical details hardly suited to the pages of a non-scientific Journal; and so many links, moreover, are still wanting in the chain that, after all, we should probably fail in making out a satisfactory tradition. It must suffice, then, to explain that for about 1000 years, from B.C. 700 to A.D. 300, a succession of Scythian tribes, belonging apparently to the same family as the Uralian tribes of Russia, and the Fins, Lapps, and Hungarians of Europe, burst in from the Jaxartes, and swept over all the western portion of the Continent of Asia, extending to India in one direction and to Syria and Asia Minor in another. No doubt this vast Scythian immigration and long-continued occupancy, must at the time have left its impress, more or less strongly marked, on all the countries intermediate between the Jaxartes and the Euphrates; but that impress has been gradually effaced by the scour of a later and still larger influx of tribes of another family, so that at the present day there is no distinct

* For full details regarding the early Buddhist history of Khoten, and the evidence that the name itself is a mere corruption of the Sanscrit title Kou-stana, "mamelle de la terre," see Abel Remusat's "Histoire de la Ville de Khoten." Paris, 1820.

† (The writer has since published a paper in the "Geograph. Journ.," vol. 42, art. 12, "Notes on Seistân," in which the ethnic relations of the Seistânís are examined more in detail —1874.)

trace of the old Scythian nationality to be found in Western Asia, except perhaps among the Brahúi division of the Beluches of South-Eastern Persia.

The Turkish immigration which followed the Scythian, and the evidences of which are still in full activity throughout Central and Western Asia, must be also very cursorily treated, notwithstanding that it involves questions of the utmost ethnographical interest. From the fourth century to the tenth there seems to have been a continuous stream of Turkish tribes pouring in from the Altäï, and not only overwhelming the contiguous countries, but in some cases, as for instance, under Attila, pushing on to the very centre of Europe; and after this systematic colonization had ceased, the expeditions of Chenghiz Khan and Timour, leaving extensive military settlements along the various lines of march which the armies followed, gave a still deeper colouring to the Turkish complexion of Western Asia. We see the result of this great ethnic revolution at the present day in the substitution of a Turkish for the old Greco-Barbaric population of Asia Minor, in the introduction of an extensive Turkish element among the Semitic races of Syria and Mesopotamia, and in the displacement also of a very large portion of the Arian population of Persia. Further eastwards, too, as we have already stated, the Turcománs, the Uzbegs, and the Kirghiz, hold the entire country up to the frontiers of Mongolia. The origin of these tribes, which are of a very early Turkish parentage, is involved in deep obscurity, and even their recent history is not free from doubt.

The only one which, from its present important position in Central Asia, it seems incumbent on us to notice in any detail is the Kirghiz, and this notice should be of the more interest as the present condition of the Kirghiz exemplifies in a striking manner the process by which the great nomadic nationalities of the East are formed, not by the real development of their own numbers, but by the absorption into their body of the heterogeneous fragments that are floating around them. We see, indeed, examples of this irregular formation going on before our eyes in different parts of the East at the present day, and we need not wonder therefore at the difficulty we experience in identifying the lost tribes of history, or in tracing the origin of those which have taken their places. The Mongolian race, for instance, after the death of Chenghiz Khan, must have been spread in considerable numbers over the whole East from the wall of China almost to the Mediterranean, yet at the present day, with the exception of the Russian Calmucks and a petty clan in the mountains of Ghúr, south of Herát, there is not a single tribe speaking Mongolian or retaining the name of Mongol, beyond the frontier of Mongolia proper.* The Afgháns, again, in the time of Mahmoud of Ghazni were a single small clan in the mountains of the Suliemán range. They have since absorbed all the tribes from the frontiers of Cashmere to Herát, and have imposed their language indiscriminately on the whole population, Indian as well as Turkish, excepting a few small and inaccessible clans, such as the Pasháí, Paránchí, Berekí, &c., and excepting also the great Turkish race of Hazárehs and Eymáks, which inhabit the Paropamisan range from Cabul to Herát, and which must have taken up the Persian, the language of the country of their adoption, before the Afghán influence became excessive. Mons. Khanikoff, as an illustration of this self-creating principle among the minor tribes of the East, has drawn attention to the case of the Shahsewans of Persia, who are at present one of the most numerous and powerful of the nomadic bodies of that country, but who are notoriously a recent agglomeration of detached parties from other clans, clinging to a common centre for support; and he might also have referred to the Arab tribe of Muntéfik, which has been formed within the last hundred years of refugees and offshoots from a multitude of neighbouring clans bordering the valley of the Euphrates, and which now numbers over forty thousand families and dominates all Lower Chaldea. The Kirghiz, as a tribe, are no doubt of considerable antiquity, for the name occurs in the account of

* It is singular, too, that so very few Mongolian geographical names have been retained to the westward of the Oxus. The only such names, indeed, which occur to us at present are *Olán-Robát*, "the red caravanserai," which marks the site of the ancient city of Arachosia; and *Kizil-ussun*, "the red river," forming the south-eastern frontier of Azerbijan.

the mission of Zemarchus in the sixth century, and the Chinese annals have also preserved notices of the same people under the names of Hakasis and Khilikizi from that period to comparatively modern times ;* but they were originally limited in numbers, and settled in a remote corner of Southern Siberia upon the banks of the Yeniséi river, from, whence they only emigrated, or were removed, in the seventeenth century to the shores of the Balkash and Issi-kúl Lakes. In their new abodes they have thriven beyond all precedent. Having amalgamated with the Kaisaks and Burúts, and having no doubt absorbed a host of smaller tribes, the *débris* of the old Ghúz, Cománs, and Kipcháks, they have gone on increasing until at the present day they number nearly three million souls, and constitute almost the exclusive population of the Steppe from the Ural river on the west to the Mongolian frontier on the east, and north and south from the Siberian line to the plateau of Pamír.†

8. We propose to terminate our sketch with a brief review of the political condition of Central Asia at the present time, following the order of the four sections into which, roughly speaking, the country may be considered to be divided. The south-east section, according to this distinction, would extend from the Himálaya to the Kuen-luen, and would include the Hill States, Cashmere, and Thibet. This country is both geographically and politically a mere outwork of India. The various states of which it is composed paid tribute to the Moghul Emperors of Delhi; and must again in due course, naturally and necessarily, come under British jurisdiction. Cashmere, indeed, rescued from the Afgháns by Runjeet Singh, may be considered a direct dependency of the Punjáb; and Little Thibet has already, on two occasions, both through

---

* In Mr. Gardiner's travels, wherever Kirghiz are mentioned, they are spoken of as Akas, or Hakas; but we are unable to say whether this is to be considered a mere mispronunciation of the name, or whether the old Chinese appellation is still used as a vernacular ethnic title.

† (All who are interested in this subject, are strongly recommended to consult the papers of Mr. Howarth on "The Western drifting of the Nomades," where they will find an immense amount of information and as little generalization as could be wished. —1874.)

Moorcroft and Dr. Henderson, proffered its allegiance to the British Crown as a means of escape from Seikh domination. Politically perhaps we should derive no strength from this extension of our frontier four hundred miles beyond the plains of the Punjáb, but the possession of Cashmere and of the two natural adits to Central Asia before alluded to, one by the Bajour and Chitrál Valleys to the Pamír Plateau, and the other by the Niti Pass and Rodokh to Khoten, would commercially be of vast importance; and in view, moreover, of the undoubted tendency of Russia to encroach in this direction, it would be well, we think, to preoccupy the ground against the possible exertion of a foreign influence, adverse to our interests, within the boundary of the Kara-koram and Kuen-luen.*

The second or north-east section of Central Asia is Chinese Turkestan. This country has long been called Alti-shahar or Alti-chakan, "the six cities," from the six towns in which are concentrated by far the greater portion of its population and wealth. Until quite recently these towns of Kashgar, Yengi-shahar, Yarkend, Khoten or Ilchi, Aksú, and Ush-Turfán,† were garrisoned by Chinese soldiers, the region

---

* (Since this was written, serious and sustained efforts have been made by the British Indian Government to open up commercial relations with Turkestán—not indeed along the lines above indicated, for they are as yet politically impracticable, but by the high road conducting from Leh to Yarkend. Missions have been exchanged, treaties have been made, depôts of supplies have been formed, and escort and carriage have been provided; but still, notwithstanding all these extraneous aids, the natural difficulties of the country appear to be insurmountable, and trade languishes accordingly. Unless, indeed, under some extraordinary conditions of supply and demand, it seems impossible to push a successful trade through a country like Thibet, where the ordinary track lies at an elevation of 15,000 feet above the level of the sea,—intersected, however, by ridges rising as high as 18,000 or 19,000 feet, —and where there are no inhabitants, no food, no fuel, and no forage over a space almost equal to a month's journey of a caravan. At the same time, the political value of Thibet is no doubt enhanced by the nearer approach of Russia to India, though rather as a "buffer" than as an outwork to be occupied by either one party or the other.—1874.)

† The towns constituting this group of the "six cities" do not appear to have been always the same, for the authorities followed by Prichard substitute for Yengi-sheher and Ush-Turfán, the Great and Little Kulja, on the river Ili. These two latter towns, however, do not belong to Chinese Turkestán at all, but to Zun

having been conquered by the Chinese from the Eleuths of Zungaria in 1755, and in spite of frequent insurrections on the part of the Mahommedan inhabitants, headed by their hereditary religious leaders who have ever been most influential, having been since held by military force as a subjugated territory. The great mass of the inhabitants are Turks, descendants of the old Ouigours, and they have long been in active communication with the Uzbegs and Kirghiz of the towns on the Upper Jaxartes, especially with those of Andiján. With the assistance of these allies the standard of revolt was again raised against the Chinese by the people of Kashgar and Yarkend in the beginning of last year, and it is understood at the present time that not a single Chinese soldier is to be found in the province. The natives appear, however, to have only exchanged one master for another; for the Kokand troops, reinforced by multitudes who are retiring eastward in dismay at the advance of the Russians up the Jaxartes, are now said to be in possession of the greater part of the towns and territory both of Kashgar and Yarkend; and quite recently the ruler of Khoten fought a pitched battle with those Uzbeg invaders from Yarkend in defence of his little principality. There can be no doubt that the people of the Six Cities are thoroughly disconcerted at the menacing attitude of the Russians both on their north and north-western frontier; and that they are most solicitous of British protection and support. Earnest applications for aid have been indeed addressed to us both from Yarkend and Khoten; and although, of course, under existing circumstances, it would be preposterous to think of direct interference in the affairs of states removed five hundred miles from our frontiers, yet the time may come

garia, and hardly fall, therefore, within the limits of the present sketch. Still it may be noted that the great Kulja on the Ili, after a twelvemonth's fighting, has also been lately conquered from the Chinese by the Turks of Kashgar, led by the son of the famous Khoja Jehangír; and that the Russian factory which was established in the city under the provisions of the Treaty of Pekin, and which was presided over by the great Chinese scholar Mons. Zakharoff, has been burnt down and entirely destroyed in the course of the contest. The Russians enjoy a similar treaty-right with respect to establishing a factory at Kashgar, but since the expulsion of the Chinese, such a right has become a dead letter.

when, as the inheritors of the present territorial limits of Cashmere and its dependencies, it may consist both with our interests and our convenience to extend a helping hand to the fluttered communities immediately beyond our mountain barrier.*

The western half of Central Asia may be considered, like the eastern, to be divided into two sections, the Uzbeg portion to the north and the Afghán to the south, and it is with these divisions of the country that British interests are more immediately concerned. In regard, then, to the south-western section, extending from the British Indian frontier to the Oxus, the general position has not materially altered since the sketch of Afghán politics was drawn up, which was published in the Quarterly Review a twelvemonth ago.

There has been another revolution, it is true, at Cabul, and Shír Alí Khán, who was designated by Dost Mahomed as his successor, and whose claim to the "Musnud" was coldly recognised by us, has been forcibly expelled from power. By the last accounts he still maintained a precarious footing at Candahar, and his son conducted nominally the government of Herát. It was believed by some that they were both prepared to withdraw into Persia on the first application of any real pressure from Cabul; by others it was expected that Shír Alí would still regain his position at the capital. But although

* (Shortly after this sketch was penned, in 1866, the leader of the Andiján party, Yacúb Beg by name, who first appeared on the scene as the General of Buzurg Khán, the hereditary chief of Kashgar, assumed the government of the country, and by a wise and energetic rule soon succeeded in establishing an absolute authority throughout the region, such as was never enjoyed by the Chinese in their palmiest days. It is to this chief, who has now received the title of *Amír* from the Sultan, as Caliph of the Faithful, that all the recent missions from India and Russia have been accredited, and it is no exaggeration to say that he is at present the most powerful Mahomedan potentate throughout Central Asia. At the same time it is not to be denied that he has a stormy and doubtful future before him. He is viewed with intense jealousy both by Russia and by China, and he has no hereditary hold on the affections of his subjects. He is upheld indeed merely by the force of his personal character, and has done nothing whatever as yet to found or consolidate a dynasty. Mr. Shaw's "Travels in High Tartary" has done much to familiarise the British public with Kashgar and Yarkend, and the account which Sir Douglas Forsyth is now preparing of his recent mission will complete the picture.—1874.)

the occupancy of the throne of Cabul has thus been changed we have adhered as rigidly as ever to our policy of nonintervention, and are still content simply to watch the progress of events. A state, indeed, of vigilant though inactive observation has been Sir John Lawrence's avowed and wellconsidered policy throughout the Afghán troubles, and certainly up to the present time there has been no reason to question its wisdom.* The Russian press at the same time has not given us much credit for our forbearance. On the contrary, it has not hesitated to ascribe this recent Afghán revolution to British encouragement and design. As Abdur-Rahman Khán had been for some time a refugee at Bokhárá, where he had married the daughter of the Amír, and as it was with the aid of a considerable Uzbeg contingent that in the course of last winter he succeeded—in concert with his uncle Azím Khán—in driving Shír Alí from Cabul, and transferring power to his father, Afzal Khán, who as the senior surviving member of Dost Mahomed's family is now the acknowledged ruler of the country, it seemed only natural to the political quidnuncs of St. Petersburg to recognise in this *dénouement* the result of an elaborate scheme concerted by England for the purpose of uniting Cabul and Bokhárá in a strong and confederate opposition to Russia. That a certain identity of interest has been established between the Afgháns and Uzbegs

---

* (As recent Afghán politics will be fully discussed in the succeeding chapters of this work, it seems unnecessary to continue the historical summary in this place, further than by stating that Afzal Khán having died at Cabul in 1867, while still in possession of the supreme power, was succeeded by his brother, Azím, who, again, in the following year, 1868, was finally driven out by Shír Alí, and died on his subsequent march to Teheran. Shír Alí leaving his son Yacúb Khán in the government of Herát, which had throughout remained in his hands, then established himself at Cabul, where he has ever since remained. In 1869 he visited Lord Mayo at Amballa, and made his first treaty with the British Indian Government. In the following year, 1870, Yacúb Khán broke into rebellion at Herát, but submitted, and was restored to favour in 1871. In November, 1873, Shír Alí nominated his youngest son Abdullah Ján to be his successor; and ever since that event has been engaged in a renewed difference with Yacúb Khán at Herát, which difference, though it has not yet led to open warfare, has seriously disorganised the country and strained its friendly relations with the British Government.—1874.)

through the family alliance contracted by Abdur-Rahman, and in consequence of the accession of that chief and his father, Afzal Khán, to the supreme power at Cabul, is not to be denied; and that the attitude of sustained hostility and intimidation which Russia preserves against Bokhárá will have the natural effect of drawing closer those bonds of amity and leading the Afgháns and Uzbegs to rely on each other for support, is also highly probable; but we are quite certain that any such result will be entirely independent of the counsel or instigation—or we might almost say of the approval—of the British Indian Government. Afzal Khán and Abdur-Rahman are understood, indeed, to have manifested unfriendly feelings to the English throughout the recent troubles at Cabul, owing to our previous cordial relations with their rival Shír Alí, and the Bokhárá tragedy of 1841 is still too strong in the recollection of Englishmen to admit of a finger being raised by us in favour of the present Amír, who is the son of our old enemy, Nasr-Ollah Khán, even though our political interests were seriously imperilled by the overthrow of Uzbeg independence.

It remains that we should glance at the course of recent events in the north-western section of Central Asia, the country which contains the three Uzbeg Principalities and their dependencies; and for this purpose we have only to condense the information given in the Russian Official Reports. It appears, then, that a contingent of Bokhárá troops had already joined the garrison of Tashkend when the Russians assaulted the place on June 25, 1865, and that the Amír's flag taken on the occasion was suspended among the other Uzbeg trophies in the Cathedral of Orenburg. War may be therefore considered to have broken out between Russia and Bokhárá from the above date, though for some time later no further overt acts of hostility were had recourse to. The Amír, who had obtained possession of the person of the boy-chief Mír-Said, and had thus transferred to himself all supposed rights of sovereignty over the province, occupied Khojend and Kokand in the course of the summer, and summoned the Russians even to evacuate Tashkend, but did not venture on any advance into the country beyond the Jaxartes.

An angry correspondence ensued, at the conclusion of which General Tchernaieff took the strange resolve to send a party of four Russian officers to the city of Bokhárá, for the purpose, it is said, of coming to an amicable arrangement with the Amír, and with "a view of counteracting the intrigues of certain European emissaries who had visited Bokhárá to submit proposals to the Amír most prejudicial to the interests of Russia."* These officers were, of course, "more Usbeco," placed in confinement soon after their arrival. Thereupon Tchernaieff protested, and ultimately on the 30th of January 1866, crossed the Jaxartes from Tashkend with fourteen companies of infantry, six squadrons of Cossacks, and sixteen pieces of artillery, with the avowed purpose of marching on Bokhárá and compelling the Amír to release his officers. Such a force, however, was manifestly inadequate to any serious attack on the power of the Amír, and the march therefore must be supposed to have been merely intended as a demonstration, though the Russian press certainly endeavoured at this period to prepare the public for the possible news of the capture of Bokhárá, and the Russian Government, whilst disclaiming any views of permanent conquest, did not disavow the advance. Be this as it may, the expedition turned out a complete failure. Tchernaieff, after crossing the desert to Jizakh within twenty-five miles of Samarcand, found himself unable to proceed further. Whilst on this expedition he also heard of the arrival at Tashkend of General Romanofski, who had been sent from St. Petersburg to supersede him, and he accordingly beat a retreat to the river, which he reached with-

* For this serious charge, which is copied textually from the official Report in the "Invalide Russe," of June 27, 1866, and which can of course only be understood as applying to England, we believe there is not the slightest foundation. No communication, either by agent or by letter, has passed as yet between the Governor-General of India and the Amír of Bokhárá; and we are at a loss to understand whether General Tchernaieff was deceived in the matter, or whether the charge was put forward as an excuse for the mission of Colonel Struvé and his colleagues, in case inquiries should be made as to its aim and object.

out incurring any serious loss. The effect of this abortive demonstration was naturally to embolden the Bokhárians to assume the offensive, and we find, accordingly, that from this time collisions were frequent on the right bank of the river between the Russian and Uzbeg outposts. A considerable skirmish occurred at Mirza Robat, near Chinaz, on the Syr-Daria, upon April 5, and a more serious affair took place a month later in the immediate vicinity of Tashkend, which is dignified by the title of "the Battle of Irjar." As the Amír commanded in person upon this occasion, and his force is stated at 21 pieces of artillery, 5000 regular infantry, and 35,000 auxiliary Kirghiz, against 14 companies of infantry, 5 squadrons of Cossacks, and 20 guns on the side of the Russians, there would really seem to have been the elements of a serious engagement; but that the actual fighting must have been of the most meagre description is proved by the Russian return of *twelve wounded* as their total loss. If these figures are to be relied on, and if the estimate be also true of 1000 dead left by the Uzbegs on the field of battle, it must have been a massacre rather than a fight. Indeed, there would seem to have been a panic flight in consequence of the destructiveness of the Russian artillery fire; the whole of the camp equipage and baggage of the Uzbegs were left on the ground, and the Amír carried back with him to Samarcand but 2000 horsemen and two guns.

After this signal success General Romanofski seems to have hesitated whether he would at once follow up the flying Uzbegs, and profiting by the panic, occupy the great capitals of Samarcand and Bokhárá, thus committing the Russian Government, perhaps prematurely, to the conquest and permanent annexation of the whole Khanat of Bokhárá; or whether in accordance with the more cautious plan of operations, which had regulated all the previous Russian proceedings in Turkestán, he would be content to secure that single step in advance which was the natural and legitimate fruit of the recent victory. He preferred the latter course, and proceeded accordingly with due deliberation to take possession of the strong fortress of Náú at the extreme angle of the river where it bends from a westernly to a northernly course, and where the road also from Kokand and Khojend strikes off to Bokhárá. This fortress, considered of great strategic importance, was surrendered without striking a blow, and the Russians then pursued their march upon Khojend, which they reached on the 17th of May. Khojend, after Kokand and Tashkend, is the most considerable place in Turkestán. It was found to be surrounded by a double line of very high and thick walls, of which the circuit was about seven miles; but the garrison and artillery defences were not in any proportion to this extent; there were indeed but thirteen guns of small calibre mounted on the walls, and as the Bokhárian garrison had been withdrawn after the Amír's defeat and had not yet been replaced by troops from Kokand, the townspeople prepared to man the defences as they best might. A week was consumed in reconnaissance and skirmishing, and in discussing proposals of capitulation, which however fell through, and at the expiration of that time, on May 21st, the Russians took the place by escalade. The resistance seems to have been considerable, for 2500 dead bodies are said to have been counted about the point where the assault took place, and the Russians confess on their own side to a loss of 138 in killed and wounded. What may be the effect of this very brilliant success in Central Asia generally we are not prepared to say, but it is rumoured that the Amír is now really humbled, and will be glad to submit to any conditions that may be imposed on him, as the price of preserving his independence.* There is no doubt much truth in the following remark, which we extract from the official report in the "Invalide Russe:"—"Quant à la conquête de la Bouk-

* The last intelligence received from the seat of war reports that the Russian officers had been released from confinement immediately after the capture of Khojend, and had returned to head-quarters unscathed. Peace is also said to have been concluded between Russia and Bokhárá; the most important concession which has been wrung from the Uzbegs being a free right of navigating the Oxus, and of establishing posts upon the banks of the river. The reported occupation of Samarcand and evacuation of Tashkend are so entirely at variance with each other that they are probably both untrue. Russian garrisons will, we are satisfied, continue to be maintained both at Tashkend and at Khojend; but any further active measures are alone to be looked for at present upon the Oxus.

harie, séparée de nos possessions par la steppe, dépourvue d'eau de Kizil-kum, quelque facile qu'elle pût être dans l'état actuel des affaires dans l'Asie Centrale, non seulement elle ne saurait être le but de nos opérations, mais encore elle serait positivement inutile ;" but the situation will be essentially altered, as far as communications are concerned, when Khiva has been already annexed, and when Russian colonies and garrisons are scattered along the entire line of the Jaxartes. Then and not till then do we expect a serious attack upon Bokhárá. In the meantime the capital city of Kokand will assuredly soon follow the fate of Khojend, being either peaceably surrendered by Bokhárá as the price of her own immunity from attack, or being captured by another brilliant passage of arms, in retaliation for alleged encroachments on the recently-acquired Russian territory of Khojend.*

9. Our view of the Russo-Indian question, as presented to the public in the "Quarterly Review" for October, 1865, is in no way altered by the occurrences of the last year. Although a war with Bokhárá has occurred sooner than we expected, its consequences have not been of any great political moment. Many a long year must yet elapse before the Russian Empire by a gradual accretion of territory can become conterminous with British India ; and in the mean time it should be our earnest endeavour so to set our house in order as to meet the crisis when it does come, without flinching or misgiving. We must expect before long to see a Russian embassy permanently established in Bokhárá. We must expect to hear of Russian agents at Cabul, at Candahar, and at Herát. We must expect to find amongst our northern feudatories an augmented restlessness and impatience of control, the natural effect of the intrusion of a rival European power into the circle of our

---

* When the Amír of Bokhárá occupied Kokand in the autumn of last year, he restored his father-in-law, Khodáyár Khán, the champion of the Kirghiz faction, as opposed to the Kipcháks, to power; and it is understood to be a part of the recent arrangement between the Amír and the Russian Government, that this chief, who belongs to the royal family, and has on previous occasions occupied the "musnud," should continue to administer the capital and its adjoining territory, "pending good behaviour, and almost as a Russian feudatory.

Indian relations. We must expect to find our commerce with Central Asia impeded by the restrictions and protective duties of our Russian competitors; but we certainly need not apprehend any actual, or immediate danger, from the military or political pressure of our rival.* If we could, indeed, make the people of India feel that their interests were identical with our own, and that an invader from the north would be a scourge rather than a deliverance to the country, then we might safely hold out the hand to Russia and welcome her to the Indus; but under present circumstances, and pending the establishment of such a state of mutual confidence between the Government of India and its subjects, let us not sacrifice substantial interests to a mere sentimental feeling of philanthropy. Let Russia pursue her policy of aggrandise-

* (The successive stages of Russian aggrandisement in Central Asia have not followed the precise course, which is here indicated, but the general scope and direction of her policy have turned out very much as anticipated. Instead of advancing on Kokand after the capture of Khojend, in the summer of 1866, Romanofski pursued the Bokhárá troops and captured Urateppeh and Jizakh. Time was then taken to consolidate Turkestán into a provincial government, independent of Orenburg, Kokand being permitted to remain in friendly vassalage. In 1868, Bokhárá being still recalcitrant, Samarcand was occupied by General Kauffman, and the frontier was pushed on towards Bokhárá, the Amír being reduced to a state of complete dependence upon Russia. The only considerable extension of Russian power since that period has arisen from the Khivan expedition of 1873, which not only broke up the power of the Khán Hazrat, and rendered him for the future a mere cypher in the politics of Central Asia, but secured to Russia a large extent of territory on the Lower Oxus, and above all left her free to deal with the Turcomán tribes of the desert as her interests might dictate. There are several territorial arrangements now imminent which will exercise an important influence on the future of Russia in Central Asia. She may be compelled to interfere in Kokand, where a powerful insurrection has broken out against the chief. She may be compelled to advance on Merv from her Caspian base in order to control the Tekkeh Turcománs, who threaten her communications and impede her commerce. She may be compelled even to occupy Khiva and Bokhárá in supersession of the native rulers, who are powerless to maintain order and give her a constant occasion for interference. Having once embarked, indeed, on her career of conquest, by crossing the Steppe to the Jaxartes valley, she may be forced to advance, step by step, whether she desires it or not, until she finds herself arrested by the resistance of the British Indian Empire and its dependencies. This contact may be the work of time, but sooner or later it is inevitable, and it is as well, therefore, to familiarise ourselves with the idea at once, and to prepare for it accordingly.—1874.)

ment—or, as her admirers term it, of civilization and commercial activity—in Central Asia. She will meet with some successes and some reverses. Let us have neither part nor parcel in her proceedings, but reserve an entire liberty of action in reference to our future conduct. England has already gone through the first or aggressive phrase in her Eastern policy. She is now strictly conservative, and intent on the improvement of what she already possesses; but we think we may say that she is also fully alive to the gravity of the Eastern question in all its bearings, and that she would not hesitate again to take up arms, if her rights or interests were seriously menaced, either in Turkey, or in Egypt, or in Central Asia.

CHAPTER V.

MEMORANDUM ON THE CENTRAL ASIA QUESTION, DATED JULY, 1868.*

1. Abstract review of Russian progress in Central Asia up to 1868.—2. Relations of Russian military commanders with the Central Government.—3. Russian view of her present state and prospects in Central Asia, as defined by Grigorief and Romanofski.—4. Probable position of Russia in Central Asia in 1878 if unchecked by England.—5. Effect of that position upon India considered: (a) in reference to Russian relations with Cabul; (b) in regard to restlessness of frontier states; (c) in respect to elements of weakness in our own position in India.—6. Arguments for our immediate interference in Afghán politics.—7. More extended view of the Central Asian question, in regard to Russia's means in the future of offence against India.—8. Measures required to meet the danger—(a), reform of our political relations with Persia; (b), various subsidiary arrangements for strengthening our position on the North-west frontier of India.

1. WHEN Russia began to recover from the torpor and exhaustion consequent on the Crimean war, her first care was to repair and strengthen her position in Asia. She had suffered a grievous blow in Europe, but she had escaped a still greater calamity in Asia, where, if a British force had been employed instead of a Turkish, and means had been

* (As this memorandum has all the appearance of an official document, it may be as well briefly to explain its true history. Towards the end of June, 1868, I had given notice of motion to draw the attention of the House of Commons to the state of affairs in Central Asia, and was second on the list for a Friday evening, which in those days was given up to private business. First on the list, however, was Mr. Fawcett with a motion for inquiry into the state of the Irish University, and as this was a subject equally distasteful to both parties, no House could be made to open the debate. It was late in the season and the chance of getting another place on the Friday evening list was small; so, as I had already made considerable preparations for the speech which never came off, it was suggested that I should embody my notes in a memorandum to be submitted to those in whose hands the conduct of our Eastern policy was placed, and to whom the arguments, even if delivered in the House, would have been in reality addressed. This was accordingly done; the memorandum, which was a mere amplified form of the unspoken speech, was drawn up and submitted to the Secretary of State for India, by whom it was sent officially to Calcutta for the consideration of the authorities; and arriving as it did at a critical moment, when the question of a change in our Afghán

taken to utilise the co-operation of the Circassian, she might have lost all her Trans-Caucasian provinces.* To obviate the possible recurrence of such a danger required her immediate attention; and as the Treaty of Paris had left the Circassians exposed to the full burst of her hostility, 150,000 soldiers were accordingly soon arrayed in line against them. In 1859, Gounib, the stronghold of the mountaineers, was stormed, and Shamil was taken prisoner. Success followed on success till the disheartened Circassians, preferring expatriation to submission, abandoned their native mountains and sought a refuge in the Turkish territory. The importance of this extinction of Circassian nationality was certainly not recognised at the time; it has hardly perhaps been recognised at the present day; yet it was the turning-point of Russian Empire in the East. So long as the mountaineers resisted, they formed an effective barrier to the tide of onward conquest. When they were once swept away, there was no military or physical obstacle to the continuous march of Russia from the Araxes to the Indus.

The termination of the Circassian difficulty was immediately followed by renewed activity to the eastward. Whether, when Russia began to feel her way across the Steppe, in 1847-48, and to erect fortresses on the Irghiz and Turgäi rivers, she was merely obeying a natural law of increase, or whether she was deliberately resuming an old traditional scheme of terri-

relations was actually under discussion, it may have had some weight in influencing the decision of the Government. At any rate, although in the voluminous minutes which were written upon the memorandum exception was taken in some instances to matters of fact and the remedial measures suggested were not universally approved, still there was a complete identity of opinion in favour of the leading feature of the proposed new scheme of Afghán policy—namely, the substitution of friendly interference for the "masterly inaction" of the preceding period.—1874.)

* (Several detailed plans to this effect were submitted to Lord Clarendon in 1855, and there is good reason to believe that the matter would have been taken into the serious consideration of the Government, but for the jealousy of the French, who could not be persuaded to look with favour, or even with patience, on an Asiatic campaign where, as they affirmed, the "hard knocks" would fall to the lot of France, while the benefits accrued exclusively to England.—1874)

torial conquest, is really a matter of very little moment. One thing at any rate is manifest, and must always have been manifest to so astute a power, that her advance from Orenburg to the Jaxartes, the transfer of her frontier from the northern to the southern limit of the Steppe, was a certain prelude to bitter and interminable war. As long as the Kirghiz Steppe, which is a zone of almost uninhabited desert stretching 2000 miles from west to east, and nearly 1000 miles from north to south, intervened as a "buffer" between the military colonies of the Orenburg and Siberian lines, and the swarming centres of Mohamedan population beyond the Aral, so long peace was possible in Central Asia; but when once the "Debatable ground" was passed, and Russian garrisons jostled against Uzbeg posts upon the Jaxartes, there was no longer a possibility of quietude or amicable relations. No sooner was one portion of Uzbeg territory annexed than the Russian outposts came in collision with the tribes beyond. One extension begot another with the unerring certainty of a law of nature. Between 1853 and 1863, notwithstanding the interruption of the Crimean war, Russia gradually worked her way from the Sea of Aral through the Saline marshes of the lower Jaxartes to the confines of the fine alluvial valley above the desert; but she did not during these years attempt the actual invasion of the Kokand territory. It was only at the latter period, when her hands were freed by the pacification of the Caucasus, that she entered on a death struggle with the Uzbegs. Advancing into the rich and populous districts, shut in between the river and the northern mountains, she took in rapid succession the great cities of Turkistán, Chemkend, Tashkend, and Khojend, not perhaps in accordance with any definite plan of aggrandisement, but rather, as she herself asserted, from the actual necessity of the case. An attempt, indeed, was made, and apparently in good faith, after the occupation of Chemkend, to arrest the tide of conquest. Negociations were set on foot for a delimitation of frontier, and a manifesto was published by Prince Gortchakoff, in November, 1864, proclaiming that the late territorial acquisitions had been brought about by "imperious necessity," and against the wish of the Government, and asserting with categorical precision that the expansion of the empire had now reached its limit. But, as has been well said, the ink was hardly dry with which this Manifesto was written * before its pacific promises were completely stultified. Hostilities indeed were resumed upon the Jaxartes early in 1865, and they have been continued ever since with little intermission, and, as might have been expected, to the uniform advantage of Russia. Various pretexts have been alleged for so flagrant a departure from Prince Gortchakoff's Manifesto. In the first instance the Bokhárians, with whose outposts the Russians came in contact after the capture of Chemkend, are said to have challenged the invaders and to have forced on a battle, in conjunction with the Kokandis, in the vicinity of Tashkend, which led to the capture of that city. The detention of certain Russian officers † in Bokhárá, where they had been sent ostensibly to negociate, brought on a renewal of hostilities in 1866. In this campaign, conducted by General Romanofski, the town of Khojend was taken,‡ and the power of Kokand was completely crushed, a portion of the territory being incorporated in the new Russian province of Turkestán, while the remainder was left to be administered by a native chief (Khudayár Khan) pending good behaviour, and almost as a Russian feudatory. The next step in advance was the direct invasion of the Bokhárá territory in 1867, General Romanofski's avowed object being to establish a "tête-de-pont" beyond the desert country skirting the Jaxartes, which should immediately threaten Samarcand and Bokhárá, and should thus, as it was asserted, protect the frontier. But if Romanofski's aim had been to exasperate rather than to conciliate, he could not have devised a more

* See *ante*, p. 174.
† (Among these officers were Councillor Struvé, son of the famous astronomer, and Captain Gloukhovsky, now employed in the survey of the old bed of the Oxus. They were released after the capture of Khojend. —1874.)
‡ (The town of Khojend had long been in dispute between Bokhárá and Kokand. At the time of Romanofski's advance, it was held by a Bokhárá garrison, but these troops withdrew on the advance of the Russians, and the defence was then continued by the townspeople, avowedly as subjects of Kokand.—1874.)

effective expedient than this establishment of a fortified post at Jizakh, almost within hail of Samarcand, bearding the Amír, as it were, in the high place of his power, encouraging the malcontents throughout the province, and holding out a standing menace of invasion. That the Uzbeg chief, indeed, under such circumstances should act in good faith, and execute the treaty of peace which was offered for his acceptance, was an unreasonable expectation. He believed himself to be marked out for destruction, and naturally, therefore, in default of better means of defence, resorted to intrigue and duplicity in order to prolong his existence. Russia may have had very good grounds, both strategically and politically, for provoking the recent contest. No military commander, indeed, could allow a force of 40,000 men to be concentrated within an easy distance of his position without taking measures for opposing it, and General Kauffman no doubt, when the crisis arrived, acted judiciously in assuming the offensive instead of waiting to be attacked; but to attribute the war, as has been done in the Russian official papers, to the bad faith of the Amír, is simply to confound cause and effect.*

2. Another point of some importance to the true appreciation of the Central Asia question is the relation which exists between the local commanders and the central government at St. Petersburg. Russia has always attributed to her military chiefs a degree of power in influencing the national policy which in this country we find it difficult to realise. She used to explain the slow progress that was made in subjugating the Caucasus by pointing to the self-interest of the army which forbade the premature closing of so fertile a source of promotion and honours. The same antagonism of feeling between the civil and military authorities is said to have existed in Turkestán from the first outbreak of hostilities.

* (The Russian explanation of the "casus belli" was to the following effect, that General Kauffman having been obliged during the negociations with Bokhárá to occupy Ukhum, an advanced position on the northern slope of the Nurata Mountains, in order to disperse the brigands of the neighbourhood, the Amír broke off peaceful relations, and at once assembled 40,000 men at Samarcand with a view of attacking the Russian post at Jizakh.—1874.)

General Tchernaief, the captor of Tashkend, was recalled from his command, avowedly in consequence of the aggressive character of his policy, and a few years later his successor, Romanofski, was deprived of all military rank for the similar offence of having invaded the Bokhárá territory against orders. General Kauffman, too, is likely to be publicly rebuked for his recent brilliant success. But are these marks of the Emperor's displeasure real, or are they intended merely to satisfy the clamours of a peace party in Russia, and to anticipate foreign complaint? It is well known that Tchernaief, notwithstanding his apparent disgrace, received a diamond-hilted sword from the Emperor as the conqueror of Tashkend, and Romanofski is understood to be about to be restored to his full rank and honours. General Kauffman also is pretty sure to be rewarded for his military achievements at the same time that he is reprimanded for his undue political activity,* the result of this double action being that while Russia maintains—or at any rate claims to maintain—her character for moderate and unselfish views; and while she also respects the feelings of those politicians who honestly believe her territorial extension to be a source of weakness rather than of strength, her progress, nevertheless, is as constant and uniform as if she were really the grasping and unscrupulous power which her enemies represent her to be.

3. The latest intelligence received from Central Asia confirms the announcement of General Kauffman's occupation of Samarcand and advance upon Bokhárá, and foreshadows, as

---

* (A still more striking instance of the impunity with which military officers in Russia can overstep or disregard their instructions has recently occurred in the case of General Kauffman, the successful leader of the expedition against Khiva. It is believed that he was absolutely forbidden to annex territory in accordance with the Emperor's assurances to that effect communicated to the British Government through Count Schouvaloff before the commencement of the campaign; and yet when it was found that he had concluded a treaty at its termination, incorporating the whole Delta of the Oxus in the Russian Empire, and thus falsifying his sovereign's promise, no further notice was taken of his contumacy than was implied by a temporary absence from his command, to which it is understood he is now returning armed with almost plenary powers. —1874.)

the inevitable fate of the government of the Amír, that gradual absorption into the Russian Empire* which, in spite of disclaimers—in spite perhaps of real disinclination—has already been carried out to its full accomplishment in regard to the greater portion of the territory of Kokand. In fact, whatever may be the policy for the moment of the Court of St. Petersburg, it is the "manifest destiny" of Russia to absorb the Uzbeg states.

Her present position is another illustration of the old doctrine that when civilization and barbarism come in contact, the latter must inevitably give way. She has advanced to a point from which retreat is impossible; and thus, whether the final consummation occur this year, or next year, or five years hence, or even ten years hence—come it soon or come it late—we may take it for granted that nothing can prevent the extinction of the three independent governments of Kokand, Bokhárá, and Khiva, and the consequent extension of the Russian frontier to the Oxus.

The question then arises, How will this new distribution of power in Central Asia affect our interests in India? Will it strengthen us or weaken us? Is it, in fact, to be encouraged or opposed? A large portion of the thinking public, including the optimist class of Anglo-Indian politicians to a man, will declare in favour of the Russian advance. On general grounds they hold that the substitution of order and civilization and a Christian government for the ignorance, the cruelty, the anarchy of the fanatical Uzbegs must be advantageous; and they further point to the impetus that would be given to trade by an increased security and facility of communication as well as by the increased wants of a settled and improving community. But in such a view of the case sufficient weight seems

---

* (The actual absorption of Bokhárá has not yet taken place, though it is in gradual process of accomplishment. The treaty indeed that was imposed on the Amír at the conclusion of the war in 1868, and which is still in force, is of so stringent a nature that it scarcely leaves him a shadow of independence. He has been in fact ever since a mere vassal of the Empire, and Russia has thus enjoyed the full benefits, politically and commercially, of a domination of the country without incurring the cost of its administration.—1874.)

hardly to be given to special political considerations. Public opinion in Russia, with a truer instinct, has declared itself in a different sense. It is, indeed, well worthy of our notice that whilst the press in this country, with a few exceptions, has expressed satisfaction at the Russian progress in Central Asia, and has encouraged her to continue in the same course, the Russian press has decided with an equal unanimity that such an advance must be distasteful, if not dangerous, to England, and has accordingly been speculating on the steps that we are likely to take in order to arrest the movement, or, at any rate, to neutralise its effects.

It is not worth while, perhaps, to quote leading articles from the Russian papers, as they may be supposed merely to represent the views of a party, but the letters of M. Grigorief, the late Governor of Western Siberia, who has been personally and practically connected with the Eastern question for the last twenty years, are a more serious authority, and may be regarded indeed almost as an official exposition of the sentiments and policy of the Government. The following extracts, therefore, from these letters, which were published in the "Moscow Gazette" of last year, may be read with interest:—

" England is the only country that can assist the Bokhárians in a war with Russia. It is therefore very probable that the Amír, preferring a remote to an impending danger, will apply for co-operation against us to the British Government in India. According, indeed, to our most recent intelligence, envoys have been actually sent to Calcutta with solicitations for money, guns, artillerymen, and even troops, offering in return the most sincere attachment to British interests, an acknowledgment of an English protectorate over Bokhárá, and in fact anything else that may be thought desirable. Such a line of action on the part of Bokhárá may affect our relations with England; for the English being thus applied to, and having a real interest in the independence of Bokhárá, will hardly refrain from interfering between us and that country, if not materially, at any rate diplomatically; but however probable that interference may be, it is no less probable that any diplomatic action of England in favour of Bokhárá, would meet with the same fate which some years ago befell their intervention in favour of the Polish insurgents. If they charged us with aggression on Bokhárá, we could retort on them with a reference to their own conduct in India; we could read them a lesson in this respect that would be exceedingly bitter to them; and happily too the time has passed when we regarded diplomatic notes with the same terror as we regarded the approach of the cholera, and when we were prepared to sacrifice the material interests of the Empire rather than be subjected to them. Our Foreign Office is now sufficiently "fire-proof" in this respect: it is accustomed to hostile remonstrances from European Governments, and will be well able to answer any fresh attempt of such a nature with becoming dignity.

"Or it is possible that England may content herself with affording underhand assistance to the Bokhárians in arms and money. Against this we cannot guard, and it is useless therefore to discuss the question; but we may remind the English that exciting or fostering revolt is a game that two can play at, and that if underhand assistance should be rendered to the dissatisfied Bokhárians, we might retaliate by applying the same disturbing agency to various weak points upon the Indian frontier. Such a mode of conflict would be possible, but it would be advantageous to neither one party nor the other. It would involve a large expenditure, would be derogatory to the dignity of two great nations, and would after all lead to very poor results; for by no such means could the Uzbegs be enabled to cope with the Russians nor the Indians to cope with the English."

* * * * * * * *

"It is hardly to be expected that England will assist Bokhárá with troops; not that there is any physical obstacle to prevent this, for the road from Peshawer to the valley of the Oxus has been found to be practicable not only for light forces, but even for heavy artillery; but the route lies through the yet independent country of Cabul, and the Afgháns would never permit the march of a foreign army through their territory. And the English have not yet forgotten the terrible lesson of 1842. They will think seven times, therefore, before venturing on such a step and risking its consequences."

* * * * * * * *

"But that Bokhárá, furnished with moral support and encouragement from the South, may endeavour to stir up a general and combined Mohammedan movement against us, is more than probable. Khiva and Kokand may be expected under certain circumstances to unite their forces with her; but this will only lead to the more speedy destruction of the whole three provinces. In every contest, a portion of the Uzbeg territory will be lost, until their independence is entirely gone, and they are ultimately swallowed up in the Russian Empire."

Now these extracts are of value not only because they show the impression which prevails in Russia, that we shall regard her advance as a hostile movement, but because they also indicate the danger which any such advance may have to encounter. M. Grigorief, no doubt, gives us credit for too much sensitiveness in supposing that we shall either resort to an unavailing diplomatic protest, or that we shall assist the Uzbegs by force of arms in resisting their invaders; but at the same time he really suggests a serious matter for our reflexion in hinting at the possibility of an Uzbeg defensive league; more especially as the continued restlessness of Russia may be expected to incline the neighbouring independent states in favour of such a league, and as the three Uzbeg principalities—if they were supported on one side by Yakúb Beg, of Kashgar, whose power is daily on the increase, and on the other side by Persia, and if they were backed by the Afgháns, whose relations with Bokhárá have long been of the most intimate character—would present a truly formidable and, whilst maintained, an unassailable confederacy.

Before we can form any sound opinion, however, as to the advisability of promoting such a confederacy, or adopting any other precautions, we must be satisfied as to the present and proximate position of Russia in Central Asia, and to this point accordingly an inquiry will be now directed.

Russia has proceeded throughout this Central Asian movement with the utmost caution and temper. Although steadfastly making progress year by year—whether from accident or design is immaterial—she has never placed her foot beyond that point from which she could, if required, conveniently withdraw it. A demonstration has been sometimes made in advance, as on the occasion of General Tchernaief's invasion of the Bokhárá territory in February, 1866, but permanent occupation has only resulted from slow and careful arrangement. Russia has always had her reserves in readiness, and has not only secured her communications with her base, but has also looked to her lateral supports, so as to combine the whole forward movement in one harmonious operation. It thus happened that nearly a year elapsed between the capture of Tashkend and the attack upon Khojend, the interval being occupied in establishing communication between the new settlements in Turkestán and the old colonies of Fort Vernöe and Kopál, near the Mongolian frontier, to the eastward; and in the same way now that Samarcand has been occupied, we may be sure that Russia's first care will be to strengthen and support that occupation by opening out lines of communication to the west.

General Romanofski, indeed, the conqueror of Khojend, who was removed from his command last year, in consequence, as it was said, of his aggressive tendencies, and who is supposed to have been immersed ever since in the drudgery of a notary public's office at Moscow, has just brought out a pamphlet on the Central Asian question, which has made a most profound impression in military and political circles at St. Petersburg.* In this "brochure" he points out the brilliant future that is opening to the enterprise of Russia, settled as she now is on the Oxus and Jaxartes, in the very "garden of Asia," provided that no administrative or strategic errors are committed; and he suggests various measures for improving and strengthening the position.

The point, however, on which he mainly insists, as the pivot on which the whole question turns, is the immediate establishment of direct communication between the Caucasus and Turkestán, by which means the latter government, instead of remaining as an outlying and unimportant dependency, would become an integral portion of the Empire, and through which also the military resources accumulated in the Western province, and now no longer required there, might be utilised by being transferred to the Oxus and Jaxartes.† Romanofski suggests three different routes for this line of communication, the object of which would be to connect the Caspian with the Aral. The southern line would leave the Caspian in Krasnovodsk Bay and would follow up the old bed of the Oxus, in

* (An English translation of Romanofski's pamphlet has been recently published in this country, and is well worth perusal.—1874.)

† (In all probability the essential object aimed at in the recent Khiva expedition was the establishment of this strategical communication between the Caucasus and Turkestán. The reconnaissances, pushed into the Turcomán Steppe in all directions between 1869 and 1873, seem to have convinced the Russian authorities that it would be impossible to utilise for military or commercial purposes the routes leading from the Caspian to the Aral and the Oxus, so long as Khiva retained its independence; and hence arose the necessity for Kauffmann's expensive and apparently unproductive expedition.—1874.)

which water is always found, to the present embouchure of that river in the Aral. This line would be the easiest of all in respect to the physical character of the country; but before it could become a safe route for traffic, Khiva must be absorbed into the Empire and the Turcoman tribes must be brought under subjection. The northern line would be drawn from the mouth of the Emba, at the north-east corner of the Caspian, and would circle round the north of the Aral to Cazala on the Jaxartes. It would present no natural difficulties, but the route would be long and circuitous, and a considerable outlay would be required in providing water along the skirts of the Kara-kúm desert. According to Romanofski's view, by far the most eligible route would be a middle line which would cross the '*Ust-'Urt* waste between the Caspian and the Aral at its narrowest point, from Mertvi-Kultuk Bay on the one sea to Chernishef Bay on the other. The distance across this neck of land scarcely exceeds 200 miles, and it has long been in the contemplation of the Russian Government to carry out a plan, suggested in the first instance and recommended by Prince Bariatinski, of laying down a line of rails over this interval. Were the waterless waste of the 'Ust-'Urt to be thus bridged over by a railroad, the military position of the Russians in Turkestán would be entirely altered.* At present, as Romanofski remarks, it requires nearly two years to move troops and stores from the Volga across the Kirghiz Steppes to the advanced posts beyond the Bokhárá frontier, whereas with steamers on the Caspian and the Aral, a railroad connecting the two seas, and boats of light draught navigating the

* (A strong confirmation of the view that Kauffmann's expedition was undertaken—not as asserted for the vindication of the national honour, nor in support of the interests of humanity and commerce, but rather as part and parcel of a great system of military aggrandisement—is furnished by the fact that the first serious operations undertaken by the Russian Engineers, since the conquest of Khiva rendered their execution possible, are preliminary studies for those very works, to which Romanofski drew attention as the "desiderata" of the Russian position in Central Asia. A line of levels, indeed, has just been run across the Steppe between the Caspian and the Aral on the two precise tracks indicated by Romanofski, with a view to the excavation of a ship-canal on the southern line and the construction of a railway on the northern.—1874.)

Oxus and Jaxartes, a few weeks would suffice for the transport of a force from the overcrowded camps of the Caucasus into the heart of Asia, the one river being practicable for steamers as high as Khojend and the other to the neighbourhood of Balkh.

Now this is certainly no visionary scheme. On the contrary, so practical is it considered to be, that it is thought likely at St. Petersburg that Romanofski, who has been restored to favour, will be sent out again to Turkestán to work out his own recommendations; and in the mean time, in order to prepare the way for this junction of the Caucasus with Turkestán, so as to present a continuous Russian front to the South, extending from the Black Sea to the frontier of China, great efforts are being made to conciliate the Turcomans, who hold all the lower part of the desert between the Caspian and the Aral, and who, if they are ever reclaimed from brigandage and brought under military control, will furnish a far more formidable cavalry to a Russian army than even the Cossacks of the Ukraine and the Don.

4. The position, then, which on the soberest calculation Russia may be expected to occupy at the close of ten years from the present time, and supposing that during this period we abstain from all active interference against her,* will be something as follows:

The Caspian and the Aral will be connected either by a canal or railway, or by military roads, protected by forts and amply furnished with water and supplies. Turkestán will thus be brought into easy and direct communication, not only with the Caucasus but with the Russian cities on the Volga, and even with St. Petersburg. The independent Uzbeg governments will have ceased to exist, and in their place will have been established Russian provincial governors, the seat of central authority being probably at Bokhárá. The country

* (The ten years is not yet completed, but I think I may ask for the extension of the period to another ten years in order to test the accuracy of my views. It must be observed, moreover, that we have already interfered at Cabul to a certain extent, and probably shall interfere yet more actively in the sequel, so that the supposed case can hardly arise.—1874.)

will be administered under the joint control of Russian and native officials, according to the system which has long been successfully practised in the Trans-Caucasian provinces. Mohamedanism will be respected, though the extravagant bigotry and fanaticism of the Bokhárá priesthood will no doubt have been retrenched. Trade will prosper; man-stealing, the present bane of the country, will be suppressed; cultivation will be increased, and the condition of the people generally will be improved. The mouths of the Oxus and Jaxartes will have been dredged and deepened, and flotillas of steam-boats will have been established on both rivers. The strength of the permanent garrison will be regulated by the wants of the country as well as by its resources. At present 16,000 men are sufficient to hold the extent of country which Russia has subdued, and which is scarcely a third of that which will ultimately come into her possession. The future garrison, therefore, when Khiva and Eastern Kokand have both fallen in, and Turkestán is bounded on the south by the Oxus, can hardly be estimated at less than 40,000 men, of which 5000 would be allotted to Khiva, 15,000 to Kokand, including the populous cities of the valley of Fergháneh, and 20,000 to Bokhárá and its dependencies; and there can be little doubt that the resources of the country would be ample to meet this amount of military expenditure.

5. Let us now consider the effect of this position upon India. As long as Russia remained in her present strength to the northward of the Oxus, and confined her attention to the consolidation and improvement of her newly-acquired territory, we should have no occasion to complain of her neighbourhood. In fact, beyond the gradual exclusion of our commerce from the markets of Central Asia, her neighbourhood would exert little or no influence on our affairs. But would it be possible for her, even with the best intentions, to maintain this passive and innocuous attitude? Could she, if she wished, divest herself of the responsibilities and obligations, the temptations to interference inseparably associated with her new position? This is what it may be permitted to doubt. Intermediate, it must be remembered, between her position beyond the Oxus

and our own frontier, broadly marked by the valley of the Indus, would be the strong and independent country of the Afgháns. To pretend that it is physically impossible for Russia, entrenched upon the Oxus and wielding the resources of Bokhárá, to exercise an influence on Afghanistán, as boldly asserted in a recent number of the "Invalide Russe," is simply false and fatuous. To apprehend, on the other hand, with the Indian alarmists, that while Cabul still maintains its independence, we shall be subjected to the full inconvenience of Russian contiguity, is equally unreasonable.

(a). The truth lies between the two extremes. We are no doubt exposed to a certain danger from the advance of Russia to the Oxus, and that danger approaches us through Afghanistán, but the danger is *not* immediate and it *is* evitable. The close connexion which exists, and has for a long time past existed, between Bokhárá and Cabul is not generally known in England; yet it is an important element in the consideration of the Central Asian question—the most important element, indeed, since it is this circumstance alone which forces us into contact with Russia. The connexion between Bokhárá and Cabul is both geographical and political. The two provinces march with each other for many hundred miles. The cities of Balkh, Khulum, and Kundúz, which for the last thirty years have been held by the Afgháns, belong properly to Bokhárá. Other districts, such as Mymeneh, Sir-i-Púl, and Andkhói, are in dispute between the two states.* Russia, in fact, in possessing herself of Bokhárá, will inherit a multitude of Afghán grievances and embarrassments from which she cannot shake herself free. The political relations again of the two countries are even more intimate than the geographical. For the last thirty years Bokhárá has largely influenced the fortunes of Cabul. When we drove Dost Mahomed Khán from power in 1839, he took refuge with the Amír, and it was from Bokhárá that he returned in 1841, and his son returned in 1842, to attack us in Cabul. In all the recent Afghán revolutions also,

* (It has been since decided that, without reference to nationality, everything south of the Oxus belongs to Cabul, as having formed part of the possessions of Dost Mahomed Khan at the period of his death in 1863.—1874.)

Bokhárá has played a prominent part. It was chiefly by means of an Uzbeg contingent that Abdur-Rahman Khán, who had married a daughter of the Amír of Bokhárá, expelled his uncle Shír Alí Khán from Cabul in 1865, and since that time Bokhárá has swarmed with Afghán refugees. It appears, indeed, that it was a body of these refugees, two or three hundred in number, who having transferred their allegiance to Russia in consequence of oppressive treatment by the Uzbegs, led the Russian troops to the recent attack upon the Amír's forces and fought in line with them at the battle of Samarcand.* The implication of Russia in Afghán affairs is therefore no longer a matter of speculation. She has an Afghán contingent in her service commanded by a grandson of Dost Mahomed Khán's. She is the mistress of a country which on more occasions than one has been the arbiter of the destinies of Cabul. It will depend on her discretion, therefore, supposing us to remain inactive, whether she interfere to the extent of regulating the succession and directing the government, or whether she merely offer friendly counsel and cultivate general relations of amity.

(b). The next point, then, to consider is, in what shape danger can come upon us from this Russian connection with Cabul. The idea of invasion from such a quarter, which used to be brandished before us *in terrorem*, may be dismissed as almost chimerical. If a foreign army ever does descend upon the Indian frontier, it will be by way of Herát and Candahar, where the roads are open and traverse districts that have been called "the granary of Asia," and not through the sterile and difficult passes between Cabul and Pesháwer; but it is not invasion from any quarter, or in any form, that we have at

* (These Afgháns, given as 280 men, were led by Iskender Khán, son of Sultan Ahmed Khán, of Herát. The subsequent fate of this young Afghán chief has been singular. When his services were no longer required in Turkestán, he was transferred to St. Petersburg and given a commission in the Guards, but he was obliged to leave the Russian capital in consequence of a breach of discipline, in which however his honour was unimpeached; and he has since resided in London on a small allowance granted him by the India Office. He is a young man of considerable abilities and force of character, and may yet play a not unimportant part in the arena of Afghán politics.—1874.)

CH. V.] MEMORANDUM ON CENTRAL ASIA QUESTION. 279

present to guard against. The presence of Russia will make itself felt in a less obtrusive, though perhaps in a not less effective, way. If she establishes a mission at Cabul—and she can hardly do less—should we fail to pre-occupy the ground,— the effect of such an establishment will be at once perceptible in India. The intrusion, indeed, of a foreign element within the restricted circle of our Indian relations will of itself exert a disturbing influence through the country of a most mischievous and even dangerous tendency. Already the Mahárájá of Cashmere, taking offence at our efforts to promote trade by insisting on a reduction of the transit duties in his dominions, is said to have been negociating with the authorities of Tashkend, and to have suggested to them to appoint commercial agents at Yarkend, on the immediate frontier of Thibet;* and if the Russians were more accessible, his example would be followed by scores of others. There can, indeed, be no doubt but that if Russia once assumes a position which, in virtue either of an imposing military force on the Oxus, or of a dominant political influence in Afghanistán, entitles her, in native estimation, to challenge our Asiatic supremacy, the disquieting effect will be prodigious. Every chief throughout Northern India who either has, or fancies he has, a grievance, or who is even cramped or incommoded by our orderly Government, will at once commence intriguing in the hopes of relieving himself from our oppressive shadow. It is not that the natives of India, whether Mohamedans or Hindoos, have any particular affection for the Russians, or believe that their rule would be more kindly and beneficial than our own. On the contrary, the followers of the Prophet everywhere regard the

* (It is only fair to the Mahárájá of Cashmere to extract from the late Sir D. Macleod's Minute on this Memorandum the following remarks, exculpating His Highness from all blame in regard to his alleged communications with Russia. Referring to the passage to which this note is attached, Sir Donald says: "In point of fact, whatever rumours to the above effect may have arisen—and I do not believe they ever assumed any very definite form—date from a period anterior to the action on our part which is supposed to have given offence; and I myself entirely disbelieve those rumours, which in all probability resulted from the fact that the Mahárájá, at our request, made inquiries through traders and confidential agents as to the state of matters at Tashkend and elsewhere."—1874.)

Russians as more incorrigible infidels than the English from their uncleanly habits and their supposed worship of pictures; but, on the other hand, the approach of a rival European power betokens change, and to the active, gambling, reckless spirit of Asiatics, change is always exciting and agreeable.

(c). There is, however, a still more important point of view from which the subject must be regarded. Hitherto the argument has proceeded on the assumption that Russia is friendly to England, and has not contemplated the acquisition of any direct advantage over us from her career of Asiatic conquest. She must, of course, be conscious that her new position gives her a means of political leverage against us which she did not before possess, and that she is thus relatively so much stronger than she was at the time of the Crimean war; but it would be unfair to impute this result to her as the motive of her recent aggressions. Supposing, however, that owing to complications in Turkey, or elsewhere, it should be the policy of Russia to weaken and embarrass us— to find indeed such employment for our armies in the East as should prevent our active interference in Europe—let us consider under this altered aspect of affairs how her position at Bokhárá and her relations with Cabul would affect us. Now, in order to appreciate the danger which might thus beset us, it is necessary to look our position in India fairly in the face, and for this purpose we cannot have a better or more authentic guide than the series of Reports recently presented to Parliament under the title of "(East India) Systems of Government." Here, amid much that is satisfactory—amid a mass of evidence of the highest character, which tends to show that the agricultural populations of India are in general contented and prosperous, and that with these classes our administration is popular—there is also much of a very different complexion, much that furnishes abundant food for reflexion and uneasiness. To quote a single statement from the report of Sir Richard Temple, who is now Financial Member of the Governor-General's Council,* and than whom no one has greater experience of India or a keener insight into the native cha-

* (At present Lieut. Governor of Bengal. 1874.)

racter, it is asserted that there are four classes "who are necessarily our enemies, and are not open to any conciliation that we could reasonably use." These are—1st. The priestly class, whether Hindoo or Mohamedan. 2ndly. The military and political class. 3rdly. The native princes and chiefs whom we have superseded; and 4thly. "The mob, the *canaille*, the blackguardism of the whole population." Now if this statement be correct—and there seems no reason to doubt it—it may truly be said that we are living upon a volcano in India, which at any minute may explode and overwhelm us; and what is of especial importance to the present argument is, that the class which would be first exposed to Afghán intrigue, set on foot by Russian propagandism, is of all others the most inflammable and the most virulent. "This hostility," says Sir R. Temple, "is even stronger in the Mohamedan priesthood; with them it literally burns with an undying flame. From what I knew of Delhi in 1857-58—from what I am authentically informed of in respect to Hyderabad at that time—I believe that not more fiercely does the tiger hunger for his prey than does the Mussulman fanatic throughout India thirst for the blood of the white infidel. All this may be very sad, but it is no use disguising a fact which is inevitable." *

There is unfortunately too at the present time in the Afghán territory a machinery of agitation singularly well adapted for acting on what Sir R. Temple calls the "seething, fermenting, festering mass" of Mohamedan hostility in India. The fanatics of Sittána, who gave us so much trouble a few years back, are now showing signs of renewed vitality. They have been joined by the notorious Fíroz Shah, who, as the last representative of the House of Delhi, assumes the title of

* (It must be well understood that this Memorandum is not an official document. Had I been weighted with the responsibilities of office in 1868, it is probable that I should have hesitated to adopt language which I regard as alarmist in tone and as exaggerated in substance; but as an outsider anxious merely to arouse the attention of the Indian Government, it was quite allowable for me to quote the words of one of their most tried and valued officers. At the same time I must record my opinion of the indiscretion, almost the culpability, of publishing despatches of this very delicate and confidential nature.— 1874.)

"King of Hindustán," and proclaims himself our implacable enemy; and they are known to be in active communication with the Wahabís and other Mohamedan malcontents in Upper India. It is certain, then, that if Russia desired to embarrass us, and were sufficiently strong at Cabul to require the governor of that city to set in motion against us the Sittána confederacy, directing and encouraging the movement through the Akhond of Swát and other Afghán spiritual chiefs, and supporting it by inroads and forays of the mountain tribes along the whole line of frontier, we might be placed in a position of very considerable difficulty—of such difficulty indeed as to require extensive reinforcements from England, and thus to fulfil the very object which Russia had in view from the commencement.

6. With this prospect before us—with the knowledge that we present a vulnerable front, and that if Russia were so disposed she might in the natural course of events be enabled severely to injure us, are we justified in maintaining what has been sarcastically, though perhaps unfairly, called Sir John Lawrence's policy of " masterly inaction ? " Are we justified in allowing Russia to work her way on to Cabul unopposed, and there to establish herself as a friendly power, prepared to protect the Afgháns against the English? It has been said by the advocates of inaction that in competing for the goodwill of the Afgháns, the power which appears last in the field will be the most successful—that the first comers will be naturally regarded as enemies and those who follow as deliverers; but this leaves out of sight the fact that there is already a national feud between the English and the Afgháns, which has been rather deepened of late years by our withdrawal of the subsidy and our persistent refusal to mingle in their internecine quarrels; while, on the other hand, the Russians having never exerted any military pressure on the country or otherwise offended the pride of the mountaineers, are regarded by them, if not with friendly feelings, at any rate without animosity or fear. The main argument, however, against interference of any sort in the affairs of Afghanistán has hitherto been that the country is a hot-bed of anarchy and disorder; that in sup-

porting one candidate we provoke the enmity of his rivals, and throw them into the arms of Russia, whose appearance on the scene would be thus accelerated rather than retarded; but this is hardly a fair representation of the case. If we do nothing, Russia is sure in due course of time to secure a political footing at Cabul, as a necessary consequence of her occupation of Bokhárá. By some, indeed, it is suspected that the pending revolution in Afghanistán is due to her instigation, Shír Alí Khán having been launched from Herát as a sort of pilotballoon, preparatory to her own advance on Bokhárá; and if this be true, it may be difficult, in the event of Shír Alí's success, which seems now almost certain, to prevent a very rapid.development of her plans; but if, as is more probable, she is at present merely watching the progress of affairs, nursing her little nucleus of Afghán refugees, and expecting by their means at some future time to establish an influence at Cabul, then it would seem to be our bounden duty at once to step forward and forestall her. No one probably will dispute that Lord Auckland's famous doctrine of "establishing a strong and friendly power on our North-west frontier," has always been the true policy for India, though of late years too often neglected, and once fatally mismanaged in execution. No. one will question but that this policy would be advantageous at present, if it could be carried out without any considerable risk or expense. And why should there be any serious risk? Is it true that our intervention in Afghanistán would lead to "confusion worse confounded?" Is it borne out by experience that disorder is the normal condition of the country? Is it not notorious, on the contrary, that from the time of our evacuation of Cabul in 1842 to the year 1863, a period of more than twenty years, Afghanistán was perfectly tranquil and contented under the strong and friendly rule of Dost Mahomed Khan? This chief, having a firm belief in our power, and a scrupulous regard to his own engagements, repressed on all occasions the turbulence and unfriendliness of his subjects, and, in fact, conducted himself towards us, throughout his long career, with such perfectly good faith and orderly prudence as to make us doubt whether the revolution and counter-revolution which have distracted the country ever since his decease, to the injury of trade and the constant disturbance of our own frontier, may not be owing as much to our persistent non-interference as to the incompetence of the old chief's successors, or the natural indocility of the Afgháns. It is asserted by many authorities, fully competent to form an opinion, that if, in deference to Dost Mahomed's nomination, we had acknowledged and assisted Shír Alí Khán from the commencement, continuing to him the same subsidy which we had granted to his father, and according him our general support, he would have summarily suppressed the opposition of his brothers and nephews, and would have retained his power unbroken to the present day.* Another opportunity now presents itself. The fortunes of Shír Alí Khán are again in the ascendant. He is already in possession of Herát, Candahar, and Ghizni, and is expected, either in person or as represented by his son, Mahomed Yacúb Khán, to be soon installed at Cabul. He should be secured in our interest without further delay. Provided that he is unentangled with Russia, the restoration of his father's subsidy and the moral support of the British Indian Government would probably be sufficient to place him above all opposition and to secure his fidelity. If he has been already tampered with, his expectations of course will be higher. It may indeed be necessary to furnish him with arms and officers, or even to place an auxiliary contingent at his disposal; but, whatever the price, it must be paid, of such paramount importance is it to obtain at the present time a dominant position at Cabul, and to close that avenue of approach against Russia. Whether the time is come for the re-establishment of a mission at Cabul charged with the distribution of the subsidy and the direction of our quasi-protectorate of the country, is a question that can only be decided on the spot. It is a position that we must inevitably occupy sooner or later, unless we are prepared to jeopardise our Indian Empire ; and when once we have acquired the good-

* (Sir John Lawrence, in his Minute on this Memorandum, disclaims the responsibility of the non-recognition of Shír Alí Khán as Amír of Cabul on the death of his father, observing that "the matter had been disposed of before he arrived in India in December, 1863;" but at the same time he approves of the policy as "justified by circumstances."—1874.)

will and confidence of the Governor, there can be no great risk attached to it.* The success, indeed, of Major Lumsden's mission in 1856 has already shown that British officers of firm but conciliatory bearing may traverse our old battle-fields without exciting any special or dangerous hostility; and the prestige of our recent Abyssinian triumph would no doubt give an additional personal security to our Envoy.

There is one other argument relating to this branch of the subject which it may be worth while to notice. Putting aside all consideration of the Russian advance and the danger of their establishment at Cabul, it would seem to be a duty which we owe to our subjects in the Punjáb to make serious efforts for the consolidation of a strong and friendly government in Afghanistán. Anarchy is contagious, and with the spectacle of constant bloodshed and rapine above the passes, it is impossible to preserve order and content among the frontier tribes. In the interests, then, of peace; in the interests of commerce; in the interests of moral and material improvement, it may be asserted that interference in Afghanistán has now become a duty, and that any moderate outlay or responsibility we may incur in restoring order at Cabúl will prove in the sequel to be true economy.

7. Hitherto the argument has been confined to a practical consideration of the effects upon India of Russia's present and proximate position in Central Asia; but if we look a little ahead, and take in a somewhat more general view of the subject, we shall find many topics of equal, or even greater, interest. Anyone who traces the movements of Russia towards India on the map of Asia cannot fail to be struck with the resemblance which these movements bear to the operations of

* (The question of re-establishing a Mission at the Court of Cabul has always been and still is a moot point among Indian officials. Sir J. Lawrence and his Council reported unanimously against the measure in 1868, as unnecessary and premature, and Lord Mayo confirmed their decision in 1869, out of deference to Shír Alí's scruples; but the question has been recently revived on more occasions than one, and it is now a matter for serious consideration whether in submitting to continued exclusion from Cabul we are not sacrificing substantial interests to an undue regard for Afghán feeling.—1874.)

an army opening parallels against a beleaguered fortress. The first parallel would thus be the Russian frontier of twenty years back, stretching from the upper end of the Caspian by the Orenburg and Siberian lines northward of the Steppe to the Irtish. This may be considered strategically as a mere line of observation. The second parallel, which would constitute her line of demonstration, would be the frontier which she is now preparing to take up, and which, according to Romanofski's plan, would be drawn from Krasnovodsk Bay, about the centre of the Caspian, south of Khiva to the Oxus, and along the course of that river to the Pamír plateau, thus including the whole of the Uzbeg territory, and placing at her command the entire water way of the Oxus and Jaxartes. This parallel is above 1000 miles in advance of the first line, but it does not directly menace India, inasmuch as the intervening Afghán mountains constitute a strong military defence. The third parallel, which would be the natural result of the preceding preliminary operations, and which, if Russia survive revolution in Europe and catastrophe in Asia, she will assuredly some day attempt, would be drawn from Asterabád at the south-east corner of the Caspian along the Persian frontier to Herát, and from thence through the Hazáreh uplands to the Oxus, or possibly by Candahar to Cabul. Established upon such a line, her position would indeed be formidable. Troops, stores, and material might be concentrated to any extent at Asterabád. The country between that port and Herát is open and admirably supplied. A line of military posts would connect the two positions and effectually control the Turcománs, thereby conferring an essential benefit on Persia and securing her good-will and co-operation. Herát has been often called "the key of India," and fully deserves its reputation as the most important military position in Central Asia. The earthworks which surround the town are of the most colossal character, and might be indefinitely strengthened. Water and supplies abound, and routes from all the great cities to the north, which would furnish the Russian supports, meet in this favoured spot. In fact, it is no exaggeration to say that if Russia were once established in full strength at Herát, and her communications were secured in one direction with Asterabád through Meshed, in another with Khiva through Merv, and in a third with Tashkend and Bokhárá through Mymeneh and the passage of the Oxus, all the native forces of Asia would be inadequate to expel her from the position. Supposing, too, that she were bent on mischief—and it is only hostility to England that would be likely to lead her into so advanced and menacing a position—she would have the means of seriously injuring us, since, in addition to her own forces, the unchallenged occupation of Herát would place the whole military resources of Persia and Afghanistán at her disposal. It is not in general sufficiently considered that in a political struggle with Russia of this nature we should not engage her upon at all equal terms. We have no natural claim on the affections or allegiance of the intermediate nations, no inducement to hold out to them, as affecting their own interests, which should lead them to prefer our alliance to that of our rivals; whereas Russia has only to point to India as the traditional plunderground of Central Asia, as the prize which has ever rewarded the victorious hordes rushing down from the northern mountains, and she at once enlists their sympathies in her behalf. The pleasant memories of the sack of Delhi by Nadir Shah, and of Ahmed Khán Abdallí's successful campaign against the Mahrattas, have hardly faded from the minds of the present generation of Persians and Afgháns. Such visions possess irresistible attractions for them, and would always, unless counterbalanced by some special considerations, incline them to side with the invader rather than the invaded. It is thus quite within the bounds of possibility that some years hence, if Russia found herself engaged in another war with us, she might launch upon India from her Herát base a force of 50,000 Persian "Sirbáz," disciplined and commanded by Russian officers, and thus fully competent to cope with our best native troops; supporting such a force with 20,000 Turcoman and Afghán horse, than whom there is no better irregular cavalry in the world; and if she were really in earnest, detaching also a small auxiliary body of her own picked troops to give strength and consistency to the invading army. Now an attack of this nature might not lead to any serious result, might not jeopardise, that is, our hold upon India, for our garrisons, reinforced from England, would probably be equal to the emergency; but at any rate we should have to fight for our lives, and should be quite powerless to strike a blow against Russia in return.

8. Are we justified, then, in disregarding this danger merely because it is remote? Ought we not rather, while there is yet time, to provide against the possibility of being thus taken at a disadvantage? Russia could never establish herself at Herát and keep up her communications with Asterabád without the co-operation of Persia, and against the risk of that co-operation our efforts should be accordingly directed.

(a). The doctrine which prevails at present in our Eastern diplomacy is simply this, that Persia is too weak and faithless to justify any extraordinary expense in keeping up cordial relations with the Shah. We are content for a while to occupy a subordinate position to Russia at Teherán, trusting that when the time comes for action we may regain our lost ground by increased expenditure and redoubled activity; but this is after all a very short-sighted policy. The good-will of a nation,—that which we once possessed, but have now lost in Persia,—is not to be purchased in a day. It is the growth of time; of steady, unremitting attention. If we desire then to check the advance of Russia towards India—if we desire above all to render impossible, or at any rate indefinitely to postpone, her occupation of Herát, it is indispensable that we should bestir ourselves in Persia at once. The vast expenditure that we incurred in the days of Harford Jones, and Malcolm in expelling the French from Teherán is no longer required. What is required is an indication of renewed interest in the country and a disposition to protect it against Russian pressure. Our officers should be again placed in positions of confidence and power with the Persian troops, as in the days of Christie, of Lindsay, and of Hart. Presents of improved arms, and perhaps artillery, would testify to our awakened interest. The Persian nobles should be encouraged to send their sons for education to London rather than to Paris. Investments of English capital in banks, in railways, in mining operations, and other commercial enterprises are freely proffered, and if supported by our authorities would create a further bond of union between the countries. Among a people, again, who are so fond of display, and attach so much value to outward forms, it is of the first importance that our mission should be kept up on a very liberal scale, and that presents should be freely distributed—that the diplomatic establishment in fact at Teherán should be Oriental rather than European. A further opportunity has occurred for creating a very favourable impression, and, in fact, inaugurating the new system which is recommended, in the Shah's application for our aid in creating and keeping up a Persian naval force in the Gulf. Considering the singular maritime inaptitude of the Persians, it is not likely that this scheme, even if accorded our full countenance and support, would ever realise the Shah's expectations, but our acquiescence in the proposal would at any rate very much strengthen our influence at Court, and might aid even in developing that community of interests which our joint telegraphic establishment has already initiated.*

In connexion with these suggested reforms in our Persian diplomacy, it is important to consider whether our relations with that country ought not to be again placed under the India Office. Now there can be no doubt that Persian diplomacy is essentially an Eastern question, and mainly dependent on considerations of Indian policy. It is the advance of Russia towards India, and her demonstrations against Cabul and Herát, which seem now to require our more active interference at Teherán. Every measure of defence, referring either to Persia or Afghanistán, must be organised *in* India and executed *from* India. If troops were required, they would

* (These suggestions in regard to our Persian policy did not find favour at the time either in England or in India. They have been left to ferment and germinate for the last six years, and in the interim have assumed various incipient shapes of development—notably in the Reuter concession; but there is still an unaccountable hanging back and half-heartedness on our part, the result of excessive caution, which, if persisted in, may yet land us in the most serious difficulties. The subject is treated more at length in the concluding part of Chapter 2.—1874.)

U

be supplied from Peshâwer or Sinde. Officers for the Shah's forces would be drawn from the Indian army. Bombay would furnish the naval material for the Gulf. The Persian telegraph is an Indian establishment. The Indian revenues contribute a sum of £12,000 per annum towards the expenses of the Persian mission. There is no single element, indeed, of European diplomacy connected with Persia except the relations of that country with Turkey; and even these relations, referring almost exclusively to frontier grievances, come more naturally under the jurisdiction of Baghdad, or of Erzeroum, than of Constantinople. It may further be questioned whether the traditions and practice of the Foreign Office, admirably adapted as they are to European diplomacy, are fitted to deal with the peculiarities of Eastern character. Teherán is an Oriental Court of the same type and temper as the Courts of Cabul, of Lahore, of Delhi, Lucknow, or Hyderabad, where the eye must be addressed rather than the reason, and where individual character is of so much more importance and effect than the forms and precedents of office. It may be doubted if the duties of the Teherán mission, recognised as a powerful machine of Indian defence, could be carried out by an ordinary staff of Foreign Office *attachés*. At any rate it would be infinitely better to employ Indian officers, accustomed to the native character, acquainted with the language, and who would look to Persian and Afghán service as their career in life instead of pining for the luxuries and leisure of Paris and Vienna. One thing may be confidently predicted, that if we neglect the present occasion for retransferring the Persian mission to the India Office, the growth of Indian interests, and complications arising from the continued extension of Russia towards India, will render such a transfer obligatory at a later period, and probably after we are involved in difficulties from which it will require all the vigour and practised skill of our Indian authorities to effect our extrication.*

(*b*). In conclusion, the remedial measures recommended for

* (My views on this subject have been somewhat modified by the increasing gravity of the Russian question, as connected with her advances in Central Asia, with which the Foreign Office would seem to be

adoption in the present state of the Central Asian question may be briefly recapitulated. They are few, but not unimportant. Shír Alí Khán should be subsidised and strengthened at Cabul, our position at that capital being rendered as secure and paramount as would have been Burnes's position at the Court of Dost Mahomed Khán in 1847, if he had been supported by the full weight of Lord Auckland's authority and resources. The next step should be to recover our lost ground in Persia, so as to prevent the possibility of Russia making use of that country as an instrument to facilitate her own advances towards India. Locally also our communications with the Afghán frontier, considered especially as military lines, should be completed and improved. It is a crying reproach to us that up to the present day no progress should have been made in laying down a railway from Lahore to Pesháwer, and that we should still be dependent on the dilatory and uncertain Indus navigation for our communications between Multán and the sea.*

The only other point refers to the proposed establishment of a fortified outwork at Quetta above the Bolán Pass, a measure which has been strongly advocated in some quarters, and as strongly opposed in others. No one will be inclined to question the military advantage of such a work. As a "place d'armes" it would cover the frontier, and being held in too great strength to admit of being masked, would in the event of invasion delay our enemy sufficiently to enable us to mass our full forces in the rear. Perhaps also, under present circumstances, the creation of such a fortress would have a salutary effect upon the native mind in India. Our friends are now said to be dispirited at our inactivity, while

alone competent to deal. The whole subject, however, has been fully discussed in Chapter 2, sect. 6; and I have nothing to add to the views that are there recorded.—1874.)

* (At length this blot is being removed from our escutcheon, and in the course of the next few years we may expect to have a continuous railway on a uniform gauge, from the two bases of Calcutta and Karachí, extending in one direction to Pesháwer and in the other to the foot of the Bolán pass; but this is, alas! the only one of my proposed remedial measures that has been fairly carried out. Persia is still unreclaimed, and the support of Shír Alí has been so spasmodic that our position at Cabul is still unsecured.—1874.)

our enemies acquire fresh confidence and power. Breaking ground at Quetta would cheer the one class and would check the others. It would show that our repose had been the repose of strength, that we were fully alive to the gravity of the situation, and prepared to move immediately that the occasion arose. But, on the other hand, it is doubtful how such a proceeding would be regarded at Candahar and Cabul. If our position were already secured with Shír Alí Khán, and he could thus be led to look upon the Quetta post as a support to his own power, then we should hardly be deterred from undertaking the work by mere considerations of expense; but if, as is more probable, the tribes in general regarded this erection of a fortress—above the passes, although not on Afghán soil,*—as a menace, or as a preliminary to a further hostile advance, then we should not be justified, for so small an object, in risking the rupture of our friendly intercourse.

LONDON, *July* 20, 1868.

* (It must be explained that Quetta belongs to Kelat, and not to Cabul; and that we are permitted by treaty "to station British troops in any part of the territory of Kelat, as may be thought advisable by the British authorities." See Aitchison's Treaties, vol. vii. p. 77.—1874.)

CHAPTER VI.

THE LATER PHASES OF THE CENTRAL ASIA QUESTION.

1. Lord Mayo's Afghán policy: *a*. the Amballa Conference; *b*. the proposed Neutral zone.—2. Negociations with Russia with regard to the Afghán frontier.—3. The expedition to Khiva, considered politically, its origin and results.—4. The Turcoman question and Merv.—5. A few words on Eastern Turkestán.—6. Present position of Russia in Central Asia.—7. The present relations of England with Afghanistán.—8. Review of the general question and our future policy considered.

1. I NOW proceed to trace in outline the further progress of Central Asian affairs from 1868 to the present day; and I commence the sketch with a brief narrative of the events in Afghanistán which led to the famous Amballa Conference in March, 1869. As early as the autumn of 1867, while Azím Khán was still Amír of Cabul, the danger of prolonged isolation from Afghán politics—for a formal recognition of the *de facto* ruler could hardly be called interference—had become so apparent that Sir John Lawrence consulted the Secretary of State as to the propriety of furnishing our neighbour above the passes with arms and a subsidy from India. He would have accorded this support to the *de facto* ruler of the day, whoever he might be, observing that in the event of revolution " he should be prepared to renew with the successful chief the same terms and favourable conditions as obtained under his predecessor"; but Sir Stafford Northcote, whilst approving of the general principle of intervention, distinctly repudiated a fluctuating support, the effect of which would have virtually been to offer a premium on insurrection. "He had no objection," he said, "to ally ourselves with one chief, so far as to support him with arms and subsidies, should occasion require it, but he would not consent to the proposal that we should subsidize first one and then the other, according as accident brought up Shír Alí or Abdur Rahmán to the head of affairs." Sir John Lawrence, being thus armed with

authority to interfere under certain circumstances, waited on events; and the crisis came almost sooner than was expected. I had already anticipated in my Memorandum of July, 1868, that Shír Alí, who under his father's nomination was the rightful heir to the Afghán throne, would in due course recover his position at Cabul; and had recommended in that event that he should be secured at once in our interests, whatever might be the cost and risk of the operation. These suggestions reached Calcutta during the first week of September, 1868, and at almost the same moment of time intelligence arrived from Pesháwer, announcing that Azím Khán had been signally discomfited, and that Shír Alí was marching victoriously on Cabul. The opportunity which thus offered for interference was all the more favourable as Shír Alí, after his long exclusion from power, was naturally pressed for means, and our aid was essential to his complete success. Sir John Lawrence, therefore, no longer hesitated, but cast to the winds at once and for ever the famous policy of "masterly inaction." A friendly correspondence was opened between Calcutta and Cabul. Arrangements were even proposed for a personal interview between the Viceroy and the Amír with a view to the removal of past misunderstanding and the inauguration of a new policy, the object of which should be to place Shír Alí Khán beyond competition in respect to his rivals, while he was held in grateful, but not humiliating, dependence upon the British Government. Ultimately, on the 9th of January, 1869, three days before the arrival of Lord Mayo in India—pecuniary aid having in the interim been furnished to a limited extent—it was officially announced to the Amír that 12 lakhs of rupees would in all be forwarded to Cabul, together with a considerable supply of arms; and that in future years at the discretion of the Government he would receive further "practical assistance in the shape of money and materials of war," the only return which was expected by the Governor-General for such liberal aid being " abiding confidence, sincerity, and good will."

When Lord Mayo landed in Calcutta on January 13, 1869, he thus found the Government of India committed to a policy which was based on affording moral and material support to the reigning Amír of Cabul, the object being the same which governed the opening of our relations with Dost Mahomed Khán, and which afterwards impelled Lord Auckland to undertake the Afghán War, namely, "the establishment of a strong, friendly, and independent power in Afghanistán, as a permanent barrier against schemes of aggression on our north-west frontier." But Lord Mayo had a much less favourable field of action in 1869 than Lord Auckland had enjoyed in 1837. At the earlier period Afghanistán was diplomatically a virgin soil, and might have been secured in our interests if we could have obtained for the Amír the restoration of Peshawer from the Government of the Punjáb. Now the ruler of Cabul was swayed by a multitude of considerations, personal and political, which greatly complicated the question of an English alliance. His feelings indeed on many points conflicted with his interests, and the uncertainty of his character added a further difficulty to our establishment of relations with him on a basis of mutual confidence.

Lord Clarendon was justified, perhaps—in so far as he possessed any knowledge of the intentions of the Indian Government—in assuring Prince Gortchakoff at Heidelberg that Sir John Lawrence's policy in assisting Shír Alí Khán "had no reference to the advances of Russia in Central Asia;" but no one conversant with the negociations which preceded the Amballa Conference can doubt that these advances did exercise a very important influence on the feelings and conduct of the Amír of Cabul. Shír Alí Khán, it must be remembered, owed us no gratitude prior to 1869. On the contrary, he had always denounced our temporising policy, which subordinated all other considerations to success, as mischievous in the extreme; and he bore us an especial grudge for our successive recognition of Afzal Khán and Azím Khán as *de facto* rulers of Afghanistán while he himself still held possession of Herát.* So keen,

* He expressed his discontent on this occasion in very forcible language. "The English," he said, "look to nothing but their own interests, and bide their time. Whosoever's side they see strongest for the time they turn to him as their friend. I will not waste precious life in entertaining false hopes from the English, and will enter into friendship with other

indeed, were his feelings on this subject that, notwithstanding his necessities, he hesitated for some time after reaching Cabul to follow the suggestion of the British Agent, that he should apply to the Viceroy for assistance, resenting on the one hand our previous neglect, and suspicious on the other that our sudden and unexpected generosity was rather due to the neighbourhood of the Russians than to a real interest in his welfare. The urgency of the danger, however, with which he was himself threatened overcame his scruples. When he found that General Kaufmann had settled down at Samarcand, and that the shadow of the Russian eagle darkened along the line of the Oxus, while his own two inveterate enemies, Azím Khán and Abdur Rahmán, were still at large, and would not improbably take refuge beyond the Oxus, the Amír fairly gave in. Minor grievances now vanished, and Shír Alí courted our alliance as eagerly as he had before avoided it.

(a) Lord Mayo, informed of the change of feeling at Cabul, proposed at once to resume the arrangements for a personal interview which had been initiated under Sir J. Lawrence's viceroyalty, judging with much discrimination of the native character that the impressions which Shír Alí would carry back of the wealth, the power, and good intentions of the British Government would tend more to restore his confidence and confirm his loyalty than any amount of complimentary correspondence or any amount even of treasure, tendered as a retaining fee. It was accordingly arranged that a meeting should take place at Amballa at the end of March, 1869, and preparations were made for the reception of the Amír on a scale of unusual magnificence. Now it must not be supposed that Lord Mayo and Shír Alí Khán met on this famous occasion with identical views. On the contrary, with the exception of a general desire for friendly union, their views were divergent on all points. Lord Mayo on the one side, while he adopted Sir J. Lawrence's later policy to its full extent, and was thus prepared to increase, if necessary, the

Governments." This last threat referred to Persia, to which Government accordingly he made overtures for an alliance in the summer of 1867.— Wyllie's Precis, No. 2, par. 153.

amount of material assistance by which it was hoped to strengthen the Amír's position and to secure his fidelity, was equally determined to contract no obligations that should impose on India a liability to support the Cabul ruler with an armed force against internal or external foes. Shír Alí, on the other hand, looked to this guarantee of protection as the main object of his visit to India. He dreaded the advance of Russia; he dreaded the intrigues of Abdur Rahmán, and still more the pretensions of his elder son, Yacúb Khan, who had already risen into notice, to succeed to the " musnud," which even at that early period he seems to have destined for his younger but favourite boy, Abdullah Ján. For these reasons he was bent upon forming an offensive and defensive alliance with the British Government, whatever might be the conditions imposed on him. It is understood indeed—though perhaps the propositions never took any definite form—that he was prepared to admit British Agents freely throughout the country, excepting only in the city of Cabul; and also to fortify and, if necessary, to garrison with British troops the frontier posts, provided only that he were assured against foreign invasion and domestic disorder, and that the succession were guaranteed to that son whom he might nominate as heir-apparent. Entering on the conference with such very different views and expectations, it is not surprising that the negociators encountered difficulties as they proceeded to explain themselves; nor that the terms which were ultimately agreed on have since been productive of misunderstanding and embarrassment. Lord Mayo positively refused to be bound by any treaty obligation either to support Shír Alí against his competitors, or to grant him a fixed annual subsidy. What he did concede after a full and frank explanation was a written declaration that the British Government " would view with severe displeasure any attempt on the part of his rivals to disturb his position;" and inasmuch as Sir John Lawrence had led the Amír to expect that "practical assistance in the shape of money and materials of war" would be periodically furnished to him in the future " at the discretion of the head of the administration in India," Lord Mayo further confirmed this promise by assuring Shír Alí that "any representation he might make would always be treated with consideration and respect." It is believed that, owing to a certain freedom of translation, these expressions of general interest in his welfare were understood by Shír Alí in a more liberal sense than was intended; that he considered, indeed, the threat of "severe displeasure" to be equivalent to an assurance of armed support against his rivals, while the promised consideration of his future demands amounted in his view to an almost unlimited credit on the Indian Exchequer. At any rate the brilliant reception accorded to Shír Alí at Amballa, coupled with Lord Mayo's strong assurances of support—an earnest of which was at once afforded by the transfer to the Amír of 10,000 stand of arms and two batteries of guns—obliterated for the time all remembrance of previous disappointment; so that Shír Alí returned to Cabul, not only satisfied but deeply impressed with the interview, and so completely identified with our political interests that he was immediately suspected by Russia and Persia of aggressive designs in support of them.

When the report of Lord Mayo's proceedings at Amballa reached the authorities in England there was much difference of opinion regarding the character of his policy. The bolder spirits would have preferred that he had taken a more decided line, that he had at once indeed accepted the liability of an armed intervention by giving the Amír a direct guarantee of protection against insurrection as well as invasion, full advantage being taken of the favourable position we should have thus obtained to secure the Afghán frontiers and to establish our influence permanently throughout the country. My own feelings inclined to this policy, but the more cautious statesmen with whom the decision rested were, on the contrary, of opinion that Lord Mayo had already gone too far, the threat of "severe displeasure" launched upon Shír Alí's domestic rivals committing us to a more active interference in Afghán politics than had ever before been contemplated, or than was consistent in their view with the interests of India. Lord Mayo explained, however, that without risking the shipwreck of the whole scheme of our Afghán relations he had no alternative but to use the language complained of, and he further pointed, in justification of his policy, to the results which immediately followed on the Amír's return to Cabul, where faction for the time was hushed, and the discontented nobles, who had hitherto held aloof, now eagerly thronged to offer homage to the honoured guest of the Viceroy of Hindustán.*

(b) On the very day of the Amballa Conference, Lord Clarendon commenced that remarkable correspondence with St. Petersburg on Central Asian affairs which has been recently submitted to Parliament, and which certainly forms an im-

* The following extract from a private letter of Lord Mayo's to myself fully explains his views and justifies his policy:—
"I was much disappointed to find that some exception had been taken to our use of the words "severe displeasure" in our letter to the Amír. I fear that the difficulty of the situation at Amballa has not been appreciated. The Amír had sought the interview. To have refused it would have been insanity. Foreign agents would have been by this time powerful at Cabul. Shír Alí made many requests and suggestions, to not one of which would I accede. It was of the last importance then to put something in writing which would by being useful to him give some tangible shape to our repeated professions of friendship and good will. With this view he suggested two phrases, both of which I rejected. The words used express the simple truth. We are sincerely desirous that he should maintain his position. We would use any influence we possess to prevent his rivals from attacking him again. It was repeatedly explained to him that we should never send a British soldier to assist him against his rebellious subjects. Understanding the words fully in their real sense, he professed himself perfectly satisfied, and he went away contented. The effect has been, as far as we can see, good. Had I taken the other course, and sent him back without a single word that could have been of the least use to him, we should have lost the only opportunity that perhaps will offer for a long time of gaining the friendship of Afghanistán. Our twelve lakhs would have been thrown into the fire, and a fair field opened for foreign intrigue and annoyance. . . . . . . After full deliberation, much thought, and with the unanimous approbation of my Council, I used the only words that were suitable to the occasion; and as far as we have seen, the course of events has amply justified what was done. I agree with you that there may still be some difficulty about money; and though his Minister in his interview with the Foreign Secretary threw out many strong hints that a further grant would be very acceptable, he was plainly told that nothing of the kind would be listened to. I am sorry that when the twelve lakhs were given he was not told that it was a *donation*, not a *subscription*, but I think he is pretty well aware of that now. It is, however, possible that such a state of circumstances may arise that will necessitate some more help, but this is all for future consideration." June 10, 1869.

portant chapter in the political history of the East. The increasing disquietude of the Native States along the north-west frontier of India, which was caused by the persistent approaches of Russia, had for some years past given rise to discussions both in London and Calcutta as to the advisability of our coming to an understanding with the Emperor's Government, with a view to fixing some territorial limits which neither party should overstep. A general view of the question will be found in a previous chapter of this volume, written in 1865, the result which is there arrived at being that no arrangement involving mutual responsibility was practicable, nor, if practicable, desirable. This was not, however, the view of Lord Clarendon. He seems to have really thought it for the interest of both Governments "to recognise some territory as neutral between the possessions of England and Russia which should be the limit of those possessions, and should be scrupulously respected by both powers;" and he made a proposition accordingly to the Russian Minister in London.* But the Russian authorities, before replying, required to be informed as to the political geography of the countries beyond their frontier, and to this end obtained from Sir Roderick Murchison, President of the Royal Geographical Society, a map which had been recently compiled by Mr. Weller, a cartographer of some note, and which, being coloured according to ethnic rather than political divisions, gave rise to much embarrassment in the sequel.† In Weller's map, indeed, Afghanistán proper was bounded to the north by the line of the Indian Caucasus, while the whole of Afghán-Turkistán between the mountains and the Oxus, and extending east and west from Badakhshán to Mymeneh, was coloured yellow, as if it constituted an independent territory. The first proposal accordingly of Russia, in answer to Lord Clarendon's suggestion, was that Afghanistán, limited as to its northern frontier by the Indian Caucasus in accordance with the coloured map, should be the

* Parliamentary Papers, Central Asia, No. 2 (1873), page 1.
† "Weller's Map of Persia, Afghanistan and Beloochistan, published by Philips and Son, 32, Fleet Street, 1868."

neutral zone within which neither Government should exercise any intervention or interference opposed to the independence of that State; the effect of such an arrangement being that Russia from her Samarcand base might absorb not only Bokhárá and its dependent States of Hissár, Kuláb, and Darwáz, north of the Oxus, but all Afghán-Turkistán also south of the river to within one hundred miles of Herát, without England being permitted to address to her a word of remonstrance; while on our side we could not punish a raid of the Wazíris or Momands, or even address expostulations to Cabul without a quasi-violation of our engagements. Lord Clarendon, who was probably not alive to the full extravagance of this proposal, consulted the India Office as to its acceptance, and was at once advised that it was utterly unsuitable;* and although Russia afterwards modified her terms in so far as to offer to include the yellow territory of the map—that is, all Afghán-Turkistán between the Oxus and the mountains— within the neutral zone, the notion of concluding an arrangement on any such basis was never again seriously entertained.

Lord Mayo's Government, indeed, had regarded the proposals for a neutral zone almost as an attack on their independent action. "It is," they said, "in our opinion

* Lord Mayo's views on the "Neutral Zone" question are well stated in the following extract from the private letter, of June 10, 1869, which has been already quoted:—

"I may say that though we discussed the question of a neutral zone very fully in Council, there was not a shadow of a difference of opinion in respect to it. Indeed the feeling amongst us was very strong as to the danger that would arise if any foreign power could remonstrate against any action taken by us with regard to our frontier States or tribes. . . . If Russia would only consent to place herself in the same position as regards Khiva, the unconquered part of Bokhárá, and the independent tribes along her frontier (if she has a frontier), as we are willing to do as regards Kelat,

Afghanistán, and the territories of the Kushbegí—that is to say, to re-recognise and secure their independence, but to continue to exercise over them friendly influence with an unquestioned power of punishing them or their subjects if they misbehaved— if Russia would consent to this and agree to a joint solemn public declaration with us to that effect, binding on the honour and the good faith of the two Governments, I am inclined to believe that the 'Central Asia question' would cease to exist for your time and mine. If the present Government could effect this, it would confer on them immense honour, and would create a sense of security both in England and India that would give to us at once an incalculable addition to our strength."

essential to our strength and power in this country that we should be responsible to no foreign potentate for any of our dealings with the peoples who inhabit our frontiers." If Russia, they suggested, was really anxious to postpone indefinitely her contact with India, the simple course would be to establish a margin of independent States along her southern border, conterminous with a similar margin of independent States along our northern border. In India they were fully prepared to give a definite form to this policy by supporting the independence of Kelat, Afghanistán, and Yarkend, and they wished that Russia should be invited to adopt the same action in regard to Khiva, Bokhárá, and Kokand.* Lord Mayo's Government was undoubtedly quite sincere in suggesting this thoroughly unselfish policy, but the project was nevertheless hardly practical. To have proposed, indeed, to Russia that she should strengthen and subsidise the Uzbeg Khanates in the same manner as we were strengthening and subsidising Afghanistán, would have seemed like irony; for her aim was notoriously to weaken rather than to strengthen, with a view to eventual absorption; and she had never, moreover, appeared to understand that the States to the north and to the south of the Oxus were at all in the same condition of relationship to their European neighbours.

* The passages of the despatch in which these views are expressed, and which was sent to me by Lord Mayo at the time, are quite worthy of being quoted. They are as follows :—
"We believe that, as it is for the interests of both countries that a wide border of independent States should exist between the British frontier and the Russian boundary, it would be desirable that Russia should be invited to adopt the policy with regard to Khiva and other kindred States (Bokhárá and Kokand) that we are willing to pledge ourselves to adopt towards Kelat, Afghanistán, and the districts around Yarkend."
"A pledge of mutual non-interference of this kind, unratified by treaty, would be alike honourable to both nations, and would be better suited to the position in which civilised powers must ever stand with regard to wild and savage tribes than specific treaty engagements could ever be."
"Let Russia and England declare to the world that they have a common mission in Asia, namely, the establishment of good government and the civilisation of the mighty nations committed to their care, and that as a pledge of good faith it was desirable that a line of independent States should exist between their respective frontiers. Were this effected, we believe that public opinion, which is daily growing more and more powerful in every part of the world, would be amply satisfied." June 3, 1870.

There was in reality a very remarkable similarity between the Russian and English positions in Central Asia, both politically and geographically. The frontier capital of Tashkend, for instance, on the Russian side answered precisely to Lahore on the Indian side, their extreme military post of Samarcand, also, beyond the Jaxartes, corresponding with our military post of Peshawer beyond the Indus. Again the independent capitals of Bokhárá on the one side and of Cabul on the other were about equidistant from these advanced military posts, while in the region beyond, as Bokhárá ruled the outlying states of Hissár, Kuláb, and Darwáz, so Cabul held sway over Balkh, Kundúz, and Badakhshán, the Oxus being the ultimate and common boundary. But this parallelism of position had been systematically ignored by Russia in all her negociations, whether referring to a neutral zone or to a fixed Afghán frontier. She had assumed —and we had rarely challenged the assumption—to exercise an exclusive control over all the territory to the north of the Oxus, in virtue of her quasi-protectorate of Bokhárá and Kokand; and she had claimed accordingly to restrict international discussion to the districts south of the river. It would be well perhaps, if any future question should arise regarding frontier relations, to restore the true political status, and to show that we have as much right to interfere with the affairs of Bokhárá and Kokand as Russia has to interfere with those of Cabul and Herát. It is, indeed, neither consistent with our dignity nor our interests to admit that we are indebted to the forbearance of Russia for the exemption of Afghanistán from political intrigue, unless she also admits that she is indebted to our forbearance for the continued tranquillity of Bokhárá and Kokand. No one will question the truth of the remark that has been already quoted from Gregorief, that "it would be derogatory to the dignity of two great nations like England and Russia" to engage in a contest of petty intrigue, or to strive at mutual injury "by exciting and fostering revolt" among each others' subjects,* but it must always be remembered that Russia is far more vulnerable than England in this respect,

* See *ante*, page 271.

and that we could instigate a great anti-Russian Mahomedan movement north of the Oxus with much greater facility than she could stir up the Sikhs and Hindús beyond the Indus. For the sake however of civilisation, in the interests of human progress, of peaceful commerce, and of religion, it is to be hoped that we may never be forced into such an unnatural path of retaliation.

2. When the notion had been finally rejected of a neutral zone —that is, of an agglomeration of independent States, intermediate between the Russian and British possessions, and within the limits of which both powers should be prohibited by treaty from interfering—Lord Mayo's Government, still earnestly desiring to substitute certainty for uncertainty along the northwestern frontier of India, adopted as the basis of further negociation the assurance which Russia had spontaneously and almost ostentatiously offered, that "Afghanistán was completely outside the sphere within which she might be called upon to exercise her influence." There can be little doubt that when this declaration was originally made, it was not intended to apply to the whole country subsequently recognised as Afghanistán. Misled by Weller's map, and relying on marked ethnical distinctions, Gortchakoff seems to have thought, in the first instance, that the Amír of Cabul could not establish a right to any portion of the territory between the mountains and the Oxus, inhabited by Uzbegs or by tribes of Persian descent. He would willingly have seen Balkh, Kundúz, and Badakhshán annexed to Bokhárá, or, if possible, formed into independent States; and indeed Russian prejudice was so strong against the so-called territorial extension which the surrender of Afghán-Turkistán would secure for the Afghán power, that it was not until after three years of negociation, supported by unusually strong language on the part of our Foreign Office, and aided at last by the desire of Russia to secure our acquiescence in her Khivan expedition, that the line of the Oxus which we had from the outset asserted to be the true Afghán frontier to the north, was formally and irrevocably accepted. It must be clearly understood that in this determination of the course of the Oxus for the northern boundary of Afghanistán, there was no thought on our part of initiating a new territorial distribution or of in-

troducing any modification of existing obligations. It is true that the line of the Oxus had been from remote antiquity a great national and political boundary. It had separated Irán and Turán, the two ethnic divisions of the early East. It had limited the great Mohamedan satrapy of Máwer-ennahr. It had bounded the conquests of Ahmed Shah on the first institution of an Afghán monarchy; but these were not the considerations that impelled the Government of Lord Mayo to insist on the recognition of the Oxus as the Afghán boundary of the present day. The Calcutta authorities were not concerned to revive an old tradition, nor had they undertaken a new delimitation. All they looked to was the simple verification of an historical fact. The one point, indeed, to which their inquiries had been directed was the true definition of Shír Alí Khan's patrimonial estate; the identification, that is, of the various principalities and states which had paid allegiance to Dost Mahomed Khan at the time of his death in 1863, and which his son might thus claim to inherit as his father's full and only representative. Now it is not to be denied but that there were difficulties in ascertaining the exact line of frontier which Shír Alí might thus claim. When the course of the Oxus was first propounded as the limit of Russian interference, Gortchakoff pointed out that, as Khiva was on the left side of the river, such a limitation would protect her from punishment, however much it might be merited, and might thus be exceedingly inconvenient to Russia; while it would also interfere with the well-established claims of Bokhárá to the districts of Charjúí and Kirkí, which were both on the Southern or Afghán bank of the Oxus. These difficulties it is true were removed by the admission of Shír Alí Khan—and it was only as the interpreter of his wishes and the guardian of his interests that we engaged in a diplomatic contest at all,—that the Afghán dominion had never extended farther down the river than the passage of Khoja Sáleh on the high road from Bokhárá to Balkh, so that Kirkí and Charjúí and the entire oasis of Khiva, which were considerably to the north of that point, were excluded from the argument. But an irregularity of more importance was afterwards noticed, and one which, had the objections to it been pressed, might have shipwrecked the entire negociation. The petty states of Mymeneh and Andkhöi, the most westernly of the dependencies that were claimed by Cabul, had always been of a very fluctuating allegiance. Of the former chiefship, indeed, Vambéry had stated that "Mymeneh alone, at the death of Dost Mohamed Khan, of all the neighbouring States had refused to do homage to the flag of the Afgháns," and certainly when the Hungarian traveller passed through that region in 1864, he found the Uzbeg chief in direct dependence on Bokhárá. If, therefore, Russia had objected to include in Afghanistán this outlying district, the geographical position of which—commanding as it does the only access to Herát from Bokhárá—renders it of much political importance, we should have found it impossible to substantiate Shír Ali's hereditary claim to it, and must have rested his title upon other grounds; but fortunately although objection was taken *pro formâ*, the point was not seriously contested, as it was notorious that the present ruler of Mymeneh, who was a staunch personal adherent of Shír Ali's and had followed him through all his fortunes, would not be reannexed to Bokhárá except under compulsion, for which the means were wanting on the spot, and which moreover, if attempted, would probably have brought on a general collision between the Afgháns and Uzbegs. Accordingly after a very brief discussion it was agreed that a line should be drawn from the passage of Khoja Saleh towards the Persian frontier, so as to include Andkhöi and Mymeneh in the Afghán territory,* but

---

* The Government of India stated originally, in reference to this frontier line, that "the north-western boundary, of what, in our opinion, ought to be considered Shír Alí's dominions, runs in a south-westerly direction from a point on the Oxus, between Khoja Saleh and Kirki, skirting and including the provinces of Balkh, Mymeneh with its dependencies of Andkhöi, &c., and Herat with its dependencies between the Murgháb and the Heri-rud." Ultimately the territories and boundaries of the Amír of Cabúl in this quarter were defined as follows:—

"(2). Afghán Turkestán, comprising the districts of Kunduz, Khulm and Balkh, the northern boundary of which would be the line of the Oxus from the junction of the Kokcha river to the post of Khoja Saleh inclusive, on the high road from Bokhárá to Balkh. Nothing to be claimed by the Afghán Amír on the left bank of the Oxus below Khoja Saleh.

"(3) The internal districts of Akcheh, Siripúl, Mymeneh, Shib-

the Russian Government added the significant remark that great care must be observed in the protraction of this line, so as to exclude from Afghán dependency "the old city of Merv and the adjacent Turcoman districts, which were becoming of much commercial importance."* Further to the eastward the course of the Oxus from Khoja Saleh as far as the junction of the Kokcha was admitted on both sides to be an unexceptionable frontier, the whole of this portion of Afghán Turkestán having been undoubtedly in the hands of the Afgháns at the time of Dost Mohamed's death, and having been administered by them without interruption ever since; but beyond that point serious obstacles arose which were discussed with more or less activity for three years, and which are not definitively settled at the present day. There was admittedly a weak point in the Afghán tenure of Badakhshán. It was never contended by us

bergan and Andkhöi, the latter of which would be the extreme Afghán frontier possession to the north-west, the desert beyond belonging to independent tribes of Turcomans." Parliam. Papers. Correspondence with Russia respecting Central Asia. 1873. Page 1.

It may be inferred from this detail that it was intended to exclude Merv from Afghanistan, and to include it in the independent territory of the Turcomans, though the point of junction of the Persian, Turcoman and Afghán territories is nowhere stated, and owing to this want of precision, Stanford in his last map of Central Asia (Arrowsmith's, 1872) has drawn the line of political frontier as high as 38°, considerably to the north of Merv, which he thus leaves "debateable" between Persia and Afghanistán. In the map prefixed to this volume, which is Arrowsmith's map amended, and without Stanford's colouring, the point of junction of the three territories is placed a degree more to the south, Merv being thus assigned to the independent Turcoman Steppe,

while Serakhs, which is held by a Persian garrison, is included within the limits of Khorassan; and although perfect accuracy cannot be expected in the delineation of a frontier which has never been scientifically surveyed, such may be considered the normal political distribution at the present day.

* See Parliamentary Papers. Central Asia, No. 2. (1873) p. 51. This was the first indication that Russia took any particular interest in Merv, the letter being dated September, 1870. Later, in September, 1871, we were assured that Russia "could have little inducement to occupy Merv," and in all subsequent negotiations the occupation has been alluded to, as a mere possible eventuality, rendered necessary by the continued hostility of the Tekkeh Turcomans. In replying to Lord Grauville's last declaration that a Russian expedition against Merv might lead to serious difficulties, Prince Gortchakoff evaded the question, and merely spoke of punishing the Turcomans. Central Asia, No. 2. (1874). Page 11.

that Dost Mahomed had possessed Badakhshán in the same sense that he had possessed Kundúz and Balkh; it was merely asserted that he had rendered the Mír tributary,* that his "suzeraineté" had been acknowledged by the payment of "*nuzzeràna*," by the surrender of the ruby and lapis-lazuli mines and by the obligation of military service; and it was fairly asked if in the present territorial settlement Badakhshán and its dependencies were not assigned to Cabul to what power could they properly be attached? Russia, had throughout founded her objections to Shír Alí's claim to Badakhshán on two grounds,—1stly, on the incompleteness of the title, and 2ndly, on the danger of local complications, if the Cabul dominion should be extended into the northern bend of the Oxus adjoining Darwáz and eastward into Wakhán. She pointed out at an early period of the negociations that her ally the Khan of Kokand intended to attack Kuláb, conterminous with Badakhshán; afterwards that Bokhárá had undertaken hostilities against the same state—which was so far true that the Bokhárá troops did actually occupy Kuláb, and even crossed the river into Badakhshán territory in 1870 to the dismay of the Afgháns, who however soon forced them to withdraw;—and finally that Bokhárá and Kokand were preparing a joint expedition against Kara-tegín in order to form it into a neutral state; and she insisted with some show of reason that if Shír Alí were in military occupation of Badakhshán during these troubles, the Afgháns could not fail to be drawn into the fray. But although the arguments and remonstrances of Russia, commenced during Mr. Forsyth's visit to St. Petersburgh in 1869 and only finally withdrawn in 1873, were in some respects technically and perhaps diplomatically sound, still they were so thoroughly unpractical, leading to no result and admitting of no remedy—since Bokhárá repudiated the Badakhshán connexion, and the establishment of the province in isolated independence was of all possible experiments the most hazardous and unwise—that we were constrained to look

* The terms imposed by Dost Mahomed Khan, on the submission of the Mír of Badakhshán in 1859, are given in detail in the Central Asia Parliamentary Papers, No. 2 (1873). Page 17.

beyond the natural limits of the question at issue in order to account for the Russian persistency. It was difficult to believe, for instance, that Russia really contemplated as a substantive danger aggression on the part of Shír Alí Khan against her allies of Bokhárá and Kokand (as stated in General Kaufmann's report), if the Afghán claim to Badakhshán were realised. Still less could we admit the risk of a collision with Russia (to which the General also alluded), in consequence of Wakhán, a dependency of Badakhshán, being conterminous with the territories of Yacúb Khan of Kashgar.* What we did see was that the high road of trade in all ages between Western and Central Asia had passed through Badakhshán and Wakhán to Yarkand and Kashgar, and that it was therefore not unreasonable that a great power like Russia, powerfully interested in the extension of her commerce, should look with disfavour on the permanent control of this line being vested in the hands of the Afgháns, the allies and instruments of her great commercial rival in the East. There was also another political consideration which, although remote and shadowy, might have entered into the calculation of a far-seeing Government like that of Russia; namely, that as the two best routes conducting respectively from Cashmere and the Punjáb, by the Gilgít and Chitrál valleys, crossed the great range by open passes and descended on Wakhán, it was desirable with a view to future contingencies that that district, easily accessible from Kokand, should be independent of British control or supervision. There are some circumstances, indeed, which have led us to believe that Russia takes a special interest in the district of Sarík-kul or Tashkurghán,† immediately beyond the Wakhán boundary,

---

* Kaufmann says in his report of November, 29, 1872. "By the acquisition of Badakhshán and Wakhán he would prolong his line of contact with Bokhárá, and would find himself side by side with Karategín, whence Kokand is within easy reach. Finally his north-eastern boundary would touch the possessions of Yacúb Bey. Here is a road which would lead him straight into collision with Russia."

Correspondence with Russia respecting Central Asia. 1873. Page 9.

† Among other significant facts, it may be noted that Alif Beg, the native ruler of Sarík-kul, who was expelled from his government by Yacúb Bey in 1868, has been ever since honourably entertained by the Russians at Tashkend, where he forms one of that band of political refugees, whose services may be of much use in the future.

and a position of undoubted strategical value as commanding the passes in the neighbourhood, and if this be true it furnishes a further clue to explain the serious and sustained efforts made by the Russian diplomatists to obtain the independence of Badakhshán and its tributary districts.

It may now be convenient to say a few words regarding the territorial settlement as it was ultimately agreed on. Unfortunately our notions of the geography of the upper Oxus in 1872 were somewhat hazy. We knew little or nothing of the bend of the river to the northward, between the two points explored by Wood—namely the passage at Yengi-Kileh and the Ruby mines,—and our delineation of the upper feeders descending from Pamír was also far from accurate. When her Majesty's Government therefore, after hanging up the question for two years in the vain expectation of receiving General Kaufmann's promised report on the Afghán boundaries, determined to notify to Russia the extent of territory which Shír Alí claimed on the upper Oxus, and to which they were prepared to recognise his right, they could only follow native authority in defining the limitary line, and did not thus express themselves with the geographical precision that should have been observed in such a case. There was moreover a clerical error, caused by the omission of a line in the copy of the dispatch defining the limits of Badakhshán which occasioned further obscurity. The passage in question (with the restored line in italics) was as follows: "(1) Badakhshán with its dependent district of Wakhán from Sarík-kul on the east to the junction of the Kokcha river with the Oxus (or Penjah) *on the west; the stream of the Oxus* thus forming the northern boundary of this Afghán province through its entire extent." Now such a description, although sufficiently precise in claiming by name the two districts of Badakhshán and Wakhán, was in so far defective that it did not define which among the several feeders of the Oxus was to be considered the main stream of the river. In the criticisms to which the arrangement was subjected, both in the press and in Parliament, it was generally assumed that Wood's river, or the stream issuing from Lake Victoria, was the line indicated; and the English negociators were accordingly blamed for thus abandoning to Russia the section of the district of Wakhán to the north of this feeder; but in reality the main stream of the Oxus now appears from Colonel Gordon's inquiries to be the river which rises in the little Pamír Lake, running in the first instance to the east till it joins the Aktash, then turning to the north-west and circling round the elevated plateau of the "Great Pamír," where it is joined by an effluent from the Kara-kul Lake, and from whence, under the name of the Murghábi, it flows down the great Shignán valley, and unites with the southern branch of the Oxus at Wamír on the confines of Roshán. This river is well known at the present day to form the northern boundary of Wakhán, and from its size as well as its length has every right to be regarded as the main stream of the Oxus; so that it is to be hoped that in all future maps it will be adopted as the definite frontier of Afghanistán.* Politically considered, it is of course immaterial whether the Afghán territory be limited by one Oxus feeder or the other—the intervening Pamír Steppe to the northward being an equally effective barrier in either case;—but it might give rise to local inconvenience if Badakhshán were curtailed of its acknowledged dependencies of Shákhdereh, Gharán, and Shignán, which lie between the two feeders; and, indeed, as Russia has conceded the main question of the Afghán right to Badakhshán and Wakhán she is of course bound to accept the established frontiers of these districts as the line of demarcation which limits her own dependencies of Kokand and Bokhárá to the South.

A few observations are now required on the moot question of responsibility which arose out of this frontier settlement. When Prince Gortchakoff finally admitted the claim of Shír Alí to Badakhshán and Wakhán,—terming the admission "an act of courtesy" rather than the recognition of a right—he coupled the surrender with an implied obligation on the part of England "to maintain Shír Alí's peaceful attitude, and to restrain him from all measures of aggression or further conquest;" and as

* The Wakhán frontier as amended is laid down approximately in the map prefixed to this volume, though the surveys of Colonel Gordon's officers have not yet reached this country.

an obligation of this nature, if it really existed, committed us in case of necessity, to an armed intervention for the preservation of peace, it not unnaturally alarmed timid politicians in England, who were not well acquainted with the localities, and was made the subject of interpellations in Parliament. The matter being thus forced upon the notice of the Government, Mr. Gladstone was obliged formally to repudiate the responsibility which Russia had sought to impose on us,* explaining that we had never proposed to employ anything more than moral influence in keeping the peace between Shír Alí and his neighbours; and although this explanation was not well received by the Russian official press, there is no doubt but that it was fully justified by the correspondence that had passed upon the subject. But in real truth it may be questioned if Russia ever seriously meant to hold us responsible for Shír Alí's good behaviour. It is more probable that in reminding us of our "indisputable influence," and of the good effects that might be expected from it, she was merely giving expression to a diplomatic platitude, intended to soothe her own ruffled feelings and to cover her retreat from an untenable position. At any rate the controversy which arose as to whether we were, or were not, responsible was essentially unreal, for there never had been, and never could be, any prospect of aggression on the part of Shír Alí against the allies of Russia on the Badakhshán

* Mr. Gladstone closed his remarkable speech of April 23, 1873, with the following condensed statement of the points at issue. "The engagement referred solely to the moral influence possessed by England and Russia in the East, Russia engaging to abstain from any attempt to exercise it in Afghanistán, and England engaging to exercise it for a pacific purpose." The Government of India in considering the same subject, observed, "We have never desired to interfere with the independence of Afghanistán, and therefore, we can undertake no further responsibility with regard to the action of the Amír, than to press upon him, in case of need, in the strongest manner our friendly advice, and to govern our relations with him in accordance with the action he may take, in the same way as the Russian Government have engaged to act with regard to Bokhárá." June 30, 1873. In Russia, the *Gazette* observed somewhat testily, that "Mr. Gladstone's exposition shows that if England has preserved her freedom of action, Russia has preserved her own, and that consequently the two Governments have in reality not pledged themselves to any inconvenient obligations which might have the effect of placing them in false relations."

and Wakhán frontier, and there was nothing therefore to be responsible for. The Afghán ruler, indeed, had neither the means nor the wish to interfere directly in this remote corner of his dominions. It taxed his resources to the utmost to maintain his hold on Central Badakhshán by keeping up a small Afghán contingent at Fyzabád. For what possible reason then should he desire to invade the barren rocks and inhospitable wastes of Kuláb and Darwáz? If there was any danger of aggression it came entirely from the other side. As the dispossessed chief of Badakhshán, Jehandár Sháh, was ever oscillating like an uneasy spirit between Chitrál, Shignán, and Kuláb, seeking "per fas et per nefas" to embroil the frontier authorities in the vain hope of recovering his power, there certainly was a risk of Uzbeg forces crossing over from the right to the left bank of the Oxus,—as indeed actually occurred in 1870;—but that Afghán or Badakhshán soldiers should cross in an opposite direction for hostile purposes was to the last degree improbable. An interval, indeed, of two years has now elapsed since the terms of the Oxus frontier settlement were promulgated in the country, and nothing has occurred to give the least colour to Russia's pretended mistrust of Shír Alí's moderation. His frontier has been menaced by Abd-ur-Rahman and by Isbák Khan, the refugee sons of his brothers Afzal and Azím; and Jehandár Sháh, on more occasions than one, has excited troubles in the Eastern districts, but there has been no symptom of retaliation. Shír Alí's original instructions to his officers were to defend his frontier from Mymeneh to Badakhshán, and to that defensive policy he adheres, confirmed in his pacific attitude by our friendly counsels, and having no possible inducement to overstep the boundaries allotted to his kingdom.

3. The history of the Khivan expedition affords an apt illustration of the normal course of Russian progress in the East. Up to the year 1869 there was no special grievance against Khiva. The Khan did not, it is true, encourage trade nor cultivate very close relations with Russia; but, on the other hand, he had carefully held aloof, whilst Kokand and Bokhárá had been successively humbled and dismembered, and, indeed,

had studiously avoided giving cause of offence to his powerful neighbour. When the first Russian detachment, accordingly, crossed the Caspian from Petrofsk to Krasnovodsk, in Nov. 1869, and established itself at the latter place, there was no question of punishing Khiva for past transgressions. The object of the expedition was stated "to be entirely commercial, as it would open a shorter caravan route to Central Asia, and also give increased security to trade by restraining the predatory practices of the Turcomans;"* and this explanation was repeated whenever questions were asked, either by Persia, who not unnaturally took alarm at the sudden appearance of a Russian force within an easy distance of the Khorassan frontier, or by England, who in a new base of operations on the east shore of the Caspian foresaw danger to Khiva immediately and to India more remotely.

Russian explanations are not always to be relied on, but there seems no reason to doubt that it really was, as stated, a paramount object with the Russian government at this time to open a road into the interior of Asia; and we are, perhaps, therefore justified in regarding the occupation of Krasnovodsk as intended to be the first step towards the realization of a policy which had recently been put forward by General Romanofski, and which pointed to the establishment of direct and assured lines of communication between the Caspian and the Aral as indispensible to the prosperity—almost to the retention—of the new province of Turkestán; the only difference indeed between the two programmes, as set forth by Romanofski and the Government, being that in the one the strategical value of such lines in connecting Turkestán with the Caucasus was mainly insisted on, and in the other the commercial value.†

---

* See Parl. Pap. Central Asia, No. 2 (1873). Page 11.

† A more detailed notice of Romanofski's project, and of the arguments by which it is supported, has been given in the preceding chapter, page 273. It will, of course, take many years to execute the two great engineering works which were indicated by Romanofski as essential to the success of his plan, namely, the construction of a ship canal in the old bed of the Oxus to its *embouchure* in the Caspian, and the laying down a railway from the Caspian to the Aral, between the 45th and 46th parallels of north latitude, but both of these operations are now occupying the

But whatever may have been the proximate object of the Russian government in 1869—whether they were conscious that in sending troops across the Caspian they were initiating the most important movement that had been yet made in a great scheme of Central Asiatic Empire, or whether they merely looked to the extension of trade and the better protection of their commercial interests,—one thing is certain, that the descent of Russian troops on the Turcoman coast was an arbitrary act of power which, according to the law of nations, admitted of no justification. In an international point of view, indeed, Russia had no more right to appropriate the eastern shores of the Caspian than she had to appropriate Ghilán and Mazenderán. The coast was independent territory, inhabited by tribes who owed no allegiance either to Russia or Persia, and were only partially under the sway of Khiva. These tribes had given Russia no provocation, nor had they solicited her protection. It was simply their misfortune to be encamped upon a line of country which was required for other purposes, and from which, accordingly, it was necessary to remove them.

During the three years which followed the settlement of the Russians at Krasnovodsk, their progress was slow but continuous. A certain portion of the neighbouring Turcoman population was conciliated and subsidized. Dependent military posts were established at convenient distances in the interior, and direct negotiations were opened with the Khan of Khiva, requiring his co-operation in organizing a trade route between the Caspian and his dominions. But the Khan naturally regarded the appearance of the Russians in the Bay of Balkán, and the demands which were subsequently made on him in General Kaufmann's letters, as a menace to his independence; and it is not surprising therefore if he declined to be drawn into a correspondence, or if he even went so far as to endea-

serious attention of the Russian Government; and as the late careful survey has shown the delta of the Oxus to be 250 feet above the level of the Caspian, there can be no doubt as to the feasibility of deflecting the river to the westward, though, perhaps, if such a canal were once opened, it would lead to the gradual desiccation of the Aral.

vour to concert measures with his Kirghiz neighbours to the north for their mutual defence. His country had, in fact, been invaded, and he was fully justified in retaliating on the invaders, but political logic rarely stoops to considerations of this nature. The Khan's continued silence was construed into an affront, and became in due course a direct ground of offence, and when he was further convicted of intriguing with the Kirghiz,—being implicated, indeed, according to Russian statements, in an attack upon the fort at Mangishlak, in which Colonel Rukin and a portion of the garrison were carried off into captivity—the measure of his sins was full. From henceforward the tone of the Russian government became minatory in the extreme, and we were duly notified that, unless the Khan atoned for his transgressions, encouraged trade, repressed disorder, and gave security for his future good conduct, he would be attacked and punished.

In the meantime reconnoissances on a scale of considerable magnitude were pushed into the desert, with the undisguised object of testing the practicability to the march of troops of the various routes conducting to Khiva from the Caspian. A new military post was also established at Chikishlar, on the sea-coast near the mouth of the Atrek, from whence in the autumn of 1872 an expeditionary column issued, which marched along the northern skirts of the Kuren-dágh—the range bounding Khorassán to the north—as far as Beurm, forty miles beyond Kizil-Arvát, and which on several occasions was engaged in direct hostilities with the Tekkeh Turcomans. The consequence of these various demonstrations was of course to keep the Steppe in a constant state of turmoil and excitement, and to increase those disorders which it was the professed object of the Russian authorities to repress. Several vain attempts were now made by the Khan at negotiation, but the time for compromise was passed. An expedition in imposing force had been decided on,—partly, perhaps, to gratify the thirst of military ambition, which was so important an element in the political life of Russia, partly to strengthen the national prestige in Central Asia,—but more especially, to give effect to the great scheme of consolidating

Turkestán by dominating Khiva and rendering the valleys of the Oxus and Jaxartes directly accessible from the Caspian. It may be presumed, from the magnitude of the means employed, that the original plan included the incorporation in the Russian empire of the entire Khanate of Khiva, which, indeed, was a part of Romanofski's programme, but the Emperor was notoriously opposed to any such wholesale annexation, and, moreover, it was necessary to avoid creating serious differences with England; so that ultimately a more moderate course was decided on, which was announced to us by Count Schouvaloff during his special mission to England in January, 1873. No official manifesto, explaining how the "casus belli" with Khiva had arisen, was ever published, but we were told by Schouvaloff that "the object of the expedition was to punish acts of brigandage, to recover fifty Russian prisoners, and to teach the Khan that such conduct on his part could not be continued with the impunity in which the moderation of Russia had led him to believe"; and in continuation of this important declaration we were further informed, that "not only was it far from the intention of the Emperor to take possession of Khiva, but positive orders had been prepared to prevent it, and directions given that the conditions imposed should be such as would not in any way lead to the prolonged occupation of Khiva." *

When Lord Granville, on the direct authority of the Emperor's most trusted minister, gave this positive assurance to Parliament, great satisfaction was expressed throughout England, but I ventured to point out at the time the extreme difficulty of giving practical effect to his Imperial Majesty's benevolent intentions. To evacuate the country indeed imme-

* See Parliamentary Papers, Central Asia, No. 1, 1873, p. 12. It is understood that the Foreign Office at St. Petersburg, was disinclined from the commencement to offer any explanation to England on the subject of the Khiva expedition, alleging that it was an affair of Russian frontier police with which England had no right whatever to interfere. The Emperor's instructions to Count Schouvaloff on his mission to England, as well as the injunctions to Kauffmann against annexing any portion of the Khiva territory, being thus given in opposition to the views of the Foreign Office, it was foreseen by the politicians of St. Petersburg, at an early period, that they would be rendered nugatory.

diately after its occupation, and to retire within the old limits of the Empire, would be not only to sacrifice all the prestige of success, all the advantages indeed of the advance, but to compromise very seriously the whole Russian position in Central Asia; and I was confident, therefore, whatever might be the Emperor's personal feelings on the question, that such an impotent conclusion could never have entered into the calculations of the astute politicians who planned the enterprise.* The result abundantly confirmed the view which was thus expressed, for when Khiva fell before the united efforts of four converging columns, any single one of which would have amply sufficed for its subjugation, terms were imposed, positions were occupied, and finally territory was permanently ceded to Russia, which reduced the country to a perfect state of vassalage, and thus fully secured access to those strategic lines across the Steppe which were essential to Russia's further progress, and which had been, in fact, the primary object of the expedition.† When the terms of the Khivan treaty were published in England the reaction in public opinion was complete. It was felt that we had been grievously deceived, that public faith had been broken, that an Emperor's word had been weighed in the balance and found wanting;‡ but no practical means of

---

* See Appendix No. VIII. Extracts from "Notes on Khiva," read before the Royal Geographical Society of London, March 24, 1873.

† The following report of a conversation with General Kaufmann in December, 1873, explains how and why the Emperor's wishes were not complied with.

"In reference to the late expedition to Khiva, His Excellency said, that His Imperial Majesty had most strictly commanded him to retire from the Khanate immediately after the conquest of the place, and the infliction of a penalty on the Khan and his people, and under no circumstances to annex to Russia any portion of the Khiva territory. The General had however found that he could not possibly evacuate the Khanate at once without sacrificing all the advantages, resulting from the expedition, and without leaving the Khanate a prey to the Turcomans and to internal commotions. His Excellency, therefore, wrote to the Emperor, explaining the circumstances which compelled him to remain there a month, and to act as he had done, and the Emperor in reply, approved of his conduct, and of the annexation of the lands along the right bank of the Oxus."

‡ Count Schouvaloff is said to have been greatly shocked at the publication of the Khivan Treaty, and to have requested the Emperor either to disavow the promises which he had made to Lord Granville in his Majesty's

vindicating our offended feelings was open to us. Officially we were told that the necessities of the case had overridden all other considerations. Unofficially we heard that the Emperor, despotic as he was, had been forced to yield to Ministerial influence. It was assumed by the public that we had no substantive interests of any moment at stake warranting our further interference, and when the treaty accordingly was communicated to Lord Granville in January, 1874, he merely replied in cold and measured terms that "her Majesty's Government saw no practical advantage in examining too minutely how far the Khivan arrangements were in strict accordance with the assurances given by Count Schouvaloff as to the intentions with which the expedition was undertaken."

The political provisions of the treaty, independently of those which virtually abolish the Khan's independence, are well worthy, however, of a brief consideration.* By obtaining the whole of the right bank of the river, from Gugertli downwards, Russia entirely isolates Khiva from Bokhárá,—as in a former instance her possession of Samarcand had dissevered Bokhárá from Kokand; and she is further enabled to connect her extreme post on the Oxus by an arbitrary line with the Samarcand frontier to the north of Bokhárá so as to include the whole area of the Kizil-kúm Steppe in the province of Turkestán. Why she should have given up the left bank of the Talduk,

name or to repudiate the course pursued by General Kaufmann in annexing Khivan territory to Russia. The Emperor, however, under pressure from the Foreign Office, decided on adopting a middle course, which consisted in publishing in the Official Gazette, under date November 30, 1873, an explanation of the circumstances under which Russia had been compelled to retain in her own hands the territory on the right bank of the river, and to establish the military post of Petro-Alexandrofsk for its protection. It is probable that had it been left to the Emperor's personal discretion, he would have disavowed the Khiva Treaty; but as General Kaufmann was vested with full powers, there was diplomatically no necessity for ratification, and it further so happened, as if to obviate the chance of his arrangements being interfered with, that the text of the treaty was published in the Turkestan Gazette before it was seen at St. Petersburg, an irregularity which the General afterwards described as an "affaire de bureau" for which he was not responsible.

* For the text of the Russian treaty with Khiva, see Appendix No. VI.

the most westernly branch of the delta of the Oxus, as far as the sea, instead of running the line direct from Kongrad across the Aibugír morass to the Ust-urt is not apparent, nor is it defined in the treaty how far down in the direction of the Caspian, the old bed of the Oxus (now called the Usböi) is to form the boundary between Russian and Khivan territory, precision on this point having no doubt been designedly avoided in order to obtain an elastic frontier for the Trans-Caspian Military Government, which has been since formed in dependence on Krasnovodsk. But the war indemnity is probably the most important article of the treaty. A fine of 2,200,000 roubles (or about £250,000), to be paid by instalments in eighteen years, would not appear a very heavy penalty in European warfare; but in a petty principality like Khiva, where the sedentary population is scanty and the nomades are hardly accessible to taxation, it is impossible that an extraordinary annual levy of about £15,000 can be raised and paid with any regularity, so that there will always be an available ground for renewed interference whenever Russian interests may seem to require it. Serious difficulties, indeed, have already arisen in regard to the payment of the annual instalment, and the Khan is said to have declared his utter inability to enforce payment from the outlying Turcoman tribes, whose allegiance to him, never very willingly paid, has been further shattered by the abolition of the slave trade in the Khiva market and the consequent suppression of their means of livelihood.

It is not very easy to forecast the future of Khiva. A Russian force has been intrenched for the last eight months in the new fort of Petro-Alexandrofsk, on the right bank of the Oxus, within an easy distance (about thirty miles) of the capital. The military position, which in its inception was not only hazardous but almost meaningless, has been recently rendered somewhat more secure by the establishment of a second post at Núkús, half way between the advanced station and the Aral; but even with this support and with the prospect of steamers plying on the river so as to keep up a regular communication with the sea, the maintenance of a small isolated garrison in such an exposed situation is neither dignified nor useful. The lines, indeed, across the Kizil-kum waste, connecting Petro-Alexandrofsk with the Turkestán base either at Cazala, or Fort Petrofski, or Jizákh, are exposed at present to constant interruption, while caravans are plundered almost within sight of the Cossack patrols; and although the Khan is believed to be personally loyal, it has been nevertheless found necessary to undertake operations on an extensive scale against his Turcoman subjects, who encamp around the skirts of Khiva, in order to prevent the fortress from being beleaguered.

It would thus seem to be impossible to maintain affairs on their present footing. Either the position must be strengthened by lateral lines of communication connecting the Oxus with the Caspian on one side* and with the Samarcand frontier on the other, or Petro-Alexandrofsk must be abandoned and Russia must be content for the present to hold Kongrad and Núkús, and to restrict her operations to the navigable delta of the river. Which of these two courses she will be most likely to pursue, will be considered in the next section, which treats of the Turcomans and the various important questions arising from the attempts which are now being made to bring them under Russian control.

4. In the general question of British and Russian relations in the East, the Turcomans play a much more important part than Khiva. Although indeed the expedition against Khiva had a certain bearing on the general politics of Central Asia, in the support which it rendered to the consolidation of Russian power in Turkestán, it only immediately affected British interests by serving as a stepping-stone to the subjugation of the Turcomans. This source of danger and the particular direction it would take was detected at a very early period of the Khivan difficulties by the observant and expe-

* To connect Petro-Alexandrofsk with Krasnovodsk on the Caspian, the line of communication must traverse the Khivan oasis to the old bed of the Oxus, which would hardly be compatible with the continued existence of Khiva as an independent state. The only other available line of communication would pass by Merv and the Tekkeh country to Chikishlar, and could not be established until after the complete reduction of the Turcoman tribes.

Y

rienced officer, Mr. R. Thomson, who was then in charge of her Majesty's Mission at Teherán, and who, in reporting to the Foreign Office the arrival of the first Russian detachment at Krasnovodsk in November, 1869, and the consequent alarm of the Persian Government, stated as follows:—"This danger would appear to be imminent, for in order to open a road to the Oxus from the Caspian the Russians would have to construct forts and station troops within the Turcoman country, through which it will pass, and this being done, the Turcoman tribes will all, sooner or later, be brought under the protection and authority of Russia. The desert across which the Russians now propose to establish a line of communication with Central Asia is ill adapted for the purpose, the supply of water being insufficient for caravans traversing the plains, and the heat in summer being excessive. It is possible before long that they will find these difficulties insurmountable; and they may then seek a more practicable route, which will be found by starting from Hassan-Kooli at the embouchure of the Atrek in the bay of Asterabad near Ashoor-ada, the Russian naval station in the south-east of the Caspian; following the course of that river eastward and then skirting along the hills to the north of Boojnoord and Kochán in the direction of Merv, which is not more than four marches from the Oxus and within ten easy stages of Herat. By that line the road would pass for nearly the whole distance from the Caspian through an inhabited tract of country, where an abundant supply of water exists, together with rich pasturage and a salubrious climate at all seasons."*

I would only supplement this pregnant passage by suggesting that the advantages of the Attock route from the Caspian to Merv could hardly require to be discovered by accident, as Mr. Thomson charitably supposes, but were in all probability thoroughly well known to Russian strategists long before troops were despatched from Petrofsk, and in fact had great weight in determining the Government, in the first instance, to send forth so serious an expedition. At any rate, whether this suggestion be true or not, from the first moment the troops

* Parliamentary papers, Central Asia, No. 2 (1873). Page 20.

landed at Krasnovodsk there was a manifest tendency to the south east. A military post was at once established at Chikishlar, near the site of the old Hassan-Kooli station mentioned by Mr. Thomson, and entirely away from the Khivan line, while reconnaissances were pushed along the skirts of the hills in the direction of Merv with even greater boldness and persistency than along the direct route by the old bed of the Oxus towards Khiva. Without going into any details of Turcoman statistics it may here be sufficient to state that the total number of Turcoman tents,—for the entire race is nomade, —are about 200,000, which gives, perhaps, a million of souls for the aggregate population. Of this vaste horde the only tribes with which the Russians have hitherto come in contact are the Chádurs between the Caspian and Khiva; the Yomút on the Atrek and south-eastern shore of the Caspian and also on the outskirts of the Khivan oasis; the Goklan between the Atrek and Gurgán, and the western Tekkeh along the skirts of the hills from the Atrek towards Merv.*

* The following extract from "Notes on Khiva" read at the Geographical Meeting of March 24, 1873, conveys the views I had formed of the Turcomans and their probable future relations with Russia, previously to the Khivan expedition.

"A few observations must now be made on the Turcomans. These tribes are in their origin of the same family as the Uzbegs, though the two races have been long separated. At present the Turcomans number about 200,000 tents, or at five persons to a tent, a million souls. The chief tribes are the Chádur, of 12,000 tents, between the Caspian and the Aral; the Ersari, of 50,000 tents, along the Oxus; the Salor and Sarúk, of about 20,000 tents, on the Murgháb and Tejend; the Tekkehs, along the 'Attock' or skirts of the hills from Merv to the Caspian, numbering 60,000 tents, and the most warlike of all the branches of the race; and, lastly, the Yomúts

and Goklans, of about 50,000 tents, who dwell along the Persian border, and on the shores of the Caspian, and for the most part own allegiance to Persia. Now there can be no doubt but that the disposition of the Turcomans, and especially of the Tekkehs, will be of the utmost importance to Russia, both in the advance on Khiva from Chikishlar, and in arranging future relations with the Khanate. If the Turcomans could be conciliated and utilised like the Kirghiz-Kazaks, they would form a most valuable auxiliary force—indeed I should look on a body of 50,000 Turcoman horse of the Tekkeh, Salor and Sarúk tribes, under Russian officers, as the most formidable light cavalry in Asia; but I see little chance, I confess, of thus converting these hereditary brigands and man-stealers into orderly soldiers. It is far more likely that they will remain for ages the scourge of Eastern Persia, and the inveterate enemy to

Now it must be well understood that these four tribes, as well as the other five divisions camping more to the eastward, although belonging to one Turcoman nationality are entirely independent of each other. They are under different chiefs; they inhabit different localities, and pursue different avocations of pastoral and agricultural life. It was necessary therefore that Russia, aiming as she did at bringing them all under her sway, should pursue a distinct line of policy with each division. The Chádurs to the north, and the Yomúts to the south, soon became more or less amenable to her influence, but the western Tekkehs proved more intractable. Resisting all conciliatory overtures they held themselves aloof, until in 1870 a reconnoitring party from Krasnovodsk attacked and took their most westernly station at Kizil-Arvat on the skirts of the Kuren-dágh. From this time forward a desultory war was kept up with the Tekkehs, until in 1872 a considerable engagement took place between a portion of the tribe and a Russian column which had been sent under Colonel Markosof from Chikishlar to explore the southern route across the Steppe, the Tekkehs oeing subsequently punished severely for their temerity in opposing the Russian advance by the destruction of a large number of their camps and villages and the plunder of their camels and cattle. It was on this occasion that the Russians first gained a practical knowledge of the line conducting to Merv along the skirts of the southern mountains, where in the space of 265 miles there were found to be fifty-nine Tekkeh settlements and forts, including the towns of Kizil-arvat, Kahríz, and Ashkabád.

The Tekkehs appear to have been so disheartened by the punishment received from Markosof on this occasion that when in the following spring the substantive expedition against

civilisation and commerce. If Russia, indeed, judged it necessary to keep them under control so as to ensure uninterrupted communication between the Caspian and the Oxus, it would be necessary to build a line of forts along the 'Attock,' and to occupy in force both Serakhs and Merv, measures which would certainly be resented by Persia, if she still retained her independence, and which would further involve the Russian Government in political complications with this country which might compromise her whole position in Central Asia."

Khiva was set on foot and the same General attempted to lead a co-operating column by the southern route, they hardly took any part in the campaign, leaving it, indeed, to the Atabäi Yomúts to oppose and harass Markosof's detachment, both on its advance to Igdy and during its subsequent retirement, baffled, but not subdued, to Krasnovodsk. Had the Tekkehs, indeed, supported the Atabäis and pressed on the Russians in their retreat,—utterly exhausted as the soldiers were by the heat and by want of water,—it is probable that the entire column would have perished in the desert. Nor did the Tekkehs come to the assistance of the Yomúts on their next encounter with the Russians, when after the capture of Khiva—for some unexplained reason—the camps of that tribe along the south-western border of the oasis were attacked by Kauffmann, and fire and sword were carried through the country;* but this forbearance on the part of the Tekkehs was not held to atone for their previous offences. They were in fact the special objects of Russian hostility, because apparently they held the line of country of which she most coveted the possession; and it is thus of interest to observe how, although their camping grounds are far removed from any of the commercial or military lines now followed by the Russians, they have been, nevertheless, held accountable for all excesses committed in the Turcoman Steppe, and their misdeeds have been duly registered to form a bill of indictment, should the Russian right to attack them be ever questioned. For instance, immediately after the Khivan settlement, they were accused of maltreating the emissaries of the Khan, who had been sent down to Akhál and Merv to collect the Tekkeh share of the war indemnity. Again it is

* This attack on the unfortunate Yomúts, encamped along the south-western skirts of the Khivan oasis, is one of the most unpleasant incidents of the late campaign. It seems clearly established that the nomades had given no just cause of offence, but whether the attack was planned in order to give Kauffmann's column, which had hitherto been eclipsed by the Orenburg detachment under Veref- kin, an opportunity of distinguishing itself, or whether, as has often been stated on Russian authority, the object was to exasperate the tribes, and thus lead them to commit disorders which might justify ulterior measures of subjugation, has never been determined. The animadversions of the Russian press on Kauffmann's conduct in this matter, have been severe and have never been answered.

made a serious ground of offence that they rejected the overtures of the Russian authorities in Khiva, who wished to enter into friendly relations with them. In September, 1873, they were stated to have crossed the Oxus and pillaged certain stores which were being conveyed from the abandoned fort of St. George at Irkabäi to Petro-Alexandrofsk, the same party after extensive plundering being intercepted by a cavalry force from the Russian garrison in their attempt to recross the Oxus and being nearly exterminated in the conflict which ensued. During the winter they are further said to have repeated their raids from Merv along both banks of the Oxus and to have carried off a Russian soldier into captivity—and again in last May they are reported to have plundered a Russian caravan passing under Yomút escort from Khiva to Krasnovodsk.

The unfortunate Tekkehs having thus accumulated on their own heads a responsibility for all the disorders of the inner Steppe since the first occupation of Krasnovodsk, it was generally understood, in the autumn of 1873, that, with the avowed purpose of punishing these so-called incorrigible marauders, a Russian force was to be marched from the Caspian along the "Attock," or "skirts" of the Kuren-dágh, to Akhál and Merv; and the co-operation of Persia, who had many wrongs to avenge on the same ruthless tribes, was believed to have been promised by the Shah when he passed through Teflis on his return to Teherán from his European tour. At any rate the Tekkehs were thoroughly alarmed by these rumours and by the threatening messages received from Col. Ivanoff at Petro-Alexandrofsk, and began to cast about for assistance. They first offered their allegiance to Persia, to escape further persecution by Russia, and when repelled in this quarter they invoked the protection of Afghanistán. Shír Ali being thus obliged to consider the troubles which menaced the Merv and Herat frontier, sought counsel of the Viceroy of India, and in due course at his suggestion we represented the case to Russia, pointing out in firm but courteous language that a Russian expedition against Merv, such as was generally reported to be in preparation, would almost infallibly lead to complications on the Herat frontier, and very possibly to our intervention in support of the integrity of the Afghán territory. Gortchakoff, in replying to Lord Granville's letter on this subject, took no notice whatever of the eventualities that were thus hinted at, but simply said that "Russia had no intention of undertaking at present any expedition against the Turcomans," but that "if these turbulent tribes were to commit acts of aggression or brigandage against us we should be compelled to punish them."* Now, as it was well known that such a pretext for interference would never be wanting, the mere disclaimer of any present intention to attack the tribes could not be considered reassuring; and in real truth, having advertence to the whole course of Russian policy subsequent to the debarcation of the troops at Krasnovodsk, it could scarcely be doubted but that the subjugation of the Tekkeh Turcomans and subsequent occupation of Akhál and Merv was a mere question of time, which it behoved us to consider and make preparations for meeting, irrespective of useless explanations, and without further hesitation or delay. In anticipation, however, of the Emperor's arrival in England during last spring, we were informed that the Turcoman expedition was deferred at any rate for the year, in order not to allow a shadow of misunderstanding to dim the lustre of so auspicious a visit, and that announcement, regarded in the light of a respite, was so far satisfactory; but in the meantime local affairs have been leading up to the denouement with steady and unfailing precision.

A Trans-Caspian military government was instituted on the 10th of May, 1874, under General Lomakin, who established his head-quarters at Krasnovodsk, and has been ever since engaged in sowing dissensions among the Turcoman tribes, and attaching to the Russian cause all whom he can influence by threats, or promises, or substantial favours. A recent proclamation indeed, addressed by this officer to the Turcomans of the Atrek and Gurgán, calling on them to give in their allegiance to Russia, has occasioned some umbrage to

* See the letters from Earl Granville to Lord A. Loftus of January 7, 1874, and from Prince Gortchakoff to Baron Brunnow, of January 21, 1874, in Parliamentary Papers, Russia, No. 2 (1874).

Persia as interfering with her territorial rights, which are admitted to extend to the former river, and explanations even have been demanded as to the General's intentions;* but there seems no reason to doubt that in spite of small interruptions of this nature, Lomakin is making good way in the country by his persistent pressure, and that, in fact, at present not only the Yomúts and Goklans generally,—in so far as they can withdraw themselves from Persian supervision,—but that the western Tekkehs also, reaching to Kahríz, nearly half-way to Merv, are more or less inclined to welcome the Russian troops and assist them in their onward march. The eastern Tekkehs, however, still hold out in their dogged determination to resist the Russian advance, and have recently attacked the villages of their apostate brethren to the west, to mark their hatred of the invaders—extending their raids even, it is said, to the Yomút villages round Khiva, who since Ivanof's last winter's campaign, in which they were severely punished, have paid unfaltering fealty to the Khan and his Russian protectors.

A further element of confusion has been introduced into the Turcoman question by the pretensions of Persia. There is no doubt but that she has suffered grievously from the raids of the Tekkehs. Ever since Nadír Sháh, in the last century, placed a colony of warlike Kurds along the frontier to arrest irruption from the "Attock," there has been a chronic state of warfare in Khorassán, from Merv to Asterabád. Whole districts have been ravaged and depopulated; trade has been suspended; the high road has been rendered impassable to travellers; while many thousands of unfortunate Persians have been yearly carried off to the slave-markets of Khiva and Bokhárá. Even during the present year, while the Tekkehs,

* The explanation, which was given in due course, stated that Lomakin's proclamation was addressed to the Turcomans of the Gurgán by mistake, and that there was no intention of calling in question the right of Persia to the territory between the two rivers. The incident was thus of no political significance, and was only remarkable in testifying to the extreme sensitiveness of Russia as to any interference from without in support of Persian interests, notwithstanding that the Governments of England and Russia are bound by a sort of mutual understanding equally to respect the integrity of the Shah's dominions.

distracted apparently with terror at the imminency of a Russian invasion, have been appealing for succour to Cabul, they have on two occasions burst, 4000 strong, across the border and harried the country to the gates of Meshed. Persia has therefore substantial grievances to redress, and cannot be expected to remain passive while the fate of her implacable enemies is in the balance ; but the danger now is that she may further complicate the position by premature activity. Acting, indeed, as much, perhaps, under the impulse of her old besetting sin of territorial greed, as from a legitimate desire to protect her frontiers, she is now inclined to reassert her rights upon Merv and to anticipate the Russian movement by throwing forward an efficient body of her own troops from Serakhs,—as she did in 1857 and 1860,—and establishing herself in strength upon the Murgháb. Experience has shown that Persia can thus occupy Merv whenever she finds it necessary to do so, but that the retention of the position, unless the Turcomans are controlled in other quarters, is difficult and costly. If then she insists on pushing her claims at the present time it will be very unwise both in her own interests and in those of the neighbouring countries. A failure to make good her position at Merv would stimulate the warlike ardour of the Turcomans and encourage them in those acts of brigandage which would justify foreign interference, while on the other hand the most complete success would only facilitate the Russian advance and thus accelerate the crisis of Russia's contact with the Afghán frontier. The probable issue of the Turcoman difficulty, which is now daily increasing in importance, will be considered further in the summing up on the general question of the Anglo-Russian position in Central Asia.

5. A survey of our political position in Central Asia would be incomplete without a brief notice of Eastern Turkestán, though the country is hardly of the same importance in regard to India as the regions more to the westward. We were first introduced to an acquaintance with this province of the "six cities," or "seven cities," as it is indifferently named, by the visit of Mr. Johnson, of the Survey Department to Khoten in 1865,

followed by the visit of Messrs. Shaw and Hayward as private travellers to Yarkend and Kashgar in 1869. In the interval between these visits Yacúb Beg, an adventurer from Kokand, had raised himself to power on the ruins of the old Chinese dominion, which had been in the first instance, shattered by the Tungan rebellion. He had already, before the arrival of the English travellers at Kashgar, been in communication with Russia, a certain Capt. Reinthal having been deputed to him from Tashkend on commercial business, in October 1868, and a return mission under Mirza Shadí having been immediately despatched by Yacúb Beg to St. Petersburg. The Russian government however, at this period, were not prepared to recognize Yacúb Beg as an independent Sovereign; nor, though they required from him the same protection and privileges for their trade which they had enjoyed under the Chinese, would they even permit the Foreign Office at St. Petersburg to treat directly with the Kashgar envoy. As late indeed as December 1869, when Mr. Forsyth was in Russia, Prince Gortchakoff still regarded Yacúb Beg merely as a "successful insurgent," and maintained that to open friendly diplomatic relations with him, or to send a force across the Thian-Shan range against him, would be equally to break solemn treaty engagements with China; but notwithstanding this assumption of indifference, and notwithstanding that Mr. Forsyth was authorized to assure Yacúb Beg that he need be under no apprehension of Russian hostility,* there can be no doubt that the two parties did in reality regard each other from the commencement with a mutual

---

* Prince Gortchakoff's language is thus reported by Sir A. Buchanan in his despatch to Lord Clarendon of November 2, 1869.

"He then said that Mr. Forsyth had also spoken to him of the expediency of establishing friendly relations with Kashgaria and the government of the Ataligh Ghazí; but he said, though that ruler might have established a government 'de facto,' Russia had treaties with China and would not enter into diplomatic relations with a successful insurgent against the authority of the Chinese Emperor. His Excellency further said that the Ataligh Ghazí had nothing to fear from Russia; but 'as the Government have no relations with him, and the Government of India, appear to have dealings with him, you can assure him on my authority, that Russia has no hostile intentions towards him, or any desire to make conquests in his territories." Parliamentary Papers, Central Asia, No. 2 (1873), p. 11.

and a deep-seated mistrust. Yacúb Beg had witnessed the Russian encroachments in Kokand and Bokhárá, and he naturally anticipated a similar fate for Kashgar in due course of time, regarding, indeed, the commercial ventures which were sent by Russian merchants in spite of all discouragement into the country, and the urgent requisitions addressed to him, to protect and encourage trade, as mere preliminaries to an active interference; while Russia, on the other hand, could not but look with jealousy at the establishment of a powerful and independent state, under a Mahomedan ruler, on her immediate frontier, stimulating disaffection among the recently annexed populations on the Jaxartes, and impeding her own extension further to the East. It is probable, therefore, that the fitful anxiety which Yacúb Beg has displayed at intervals, ever since Mr. Shaw's first visit to Kashgar in 1869, to cultivate relations with British India, has been in a great measure owing to real apprehensions of Russia, not unmixed, however, with the usual Oriental disposition to play off one power against the other, and further, perhaps, tempered by a natural desire to deprecate the hostility of his powerful Northern neighbour. Our own dealings with him may be described in a few sentences.

As soon as Mirza Shadí returned in 1869 from St. Petersburg, where he had been indifferently received, he was despatched by his master to Calcutta to prosecute those relations which Mr. Shaw had unofficially commenced; and as it consisted with Lord Mayo's policy at this time that India should be surrounded with a "cordon" of strong, friendly and independent states, the Kashgar overtures, supported by Mr. Shaw's very favourable report of the country, were cordially welcomed, and a public mission was at once organized to accompany Mirza Shadí on his return. This first attempt, however, to open diplomatic relations turned out a failure, not through any fault of Mr. Forsyth's, but because Lord Mayo, from an excess of caution, had absolutely prohibited the envoy from wintering beyond the mountains—a prohibition which, as Yacúb Beg was then employed in battling with the Tungans on the eastern frontiers of the province, rendered it impossible for the English party to reach his camp within the prescribed limits of time, and thus obliged them to return bootless from Yarkend. It is probable that Yacúb Beg—or the Ataligh Ghází, as he was then called—resented this abortive proceeding, which being unexplained, must have appeared as an affront. At any rate, beyond sending an envoy with letters to the Queen and the Viceroy at the end of 1871, he attempted no further communication with Calcutta till the summer of 1873, when Syud Yacúb Khan, a near relation of the Ataligh's, who had been deputed on a confidential mission to Constantinople, presented himself at Calcutta with formal offers of friendship.

In the interval, negociations of some importance had passed between the Ataligh and the Russian Government. The Russians having occupied Kulja in June, 1871, after expelling and crushing the Taranchis, and having subsequently extended their frontier along the crest of the Thian-Shan considerably to the eastward, appeared to menace the towns of Turfán, Urumchí and Manass which the Ataligh at about the same period of time had captured from the Tungans. The construction of a Russian fort on the Naryn within an easy distance of Kashgar, seems to have still further discomposed the Ataligh, who accordingly in April 1872, invited Baron Kaulbars from Tashkend, to give an opportunity for explanation, and in fact, as it turned out, to negociate a formal treaty of peace and friendship. Russia had still some scruples as to acknowledging the Ataligh's independence. In the Official Journal of the period, he was designated as the "*de facto* chief of the Seven Cities," and was said to have merely confirmed the Chinese engagements; but at the same time, in his personal capacity he was considered by signing the treaty, and by his unreserved communications with Baron Kaulbars, to have fairly given in his adhesion to the Russian cause.* The

---

* The Russian Official Journal of October 31, 1872, contains a remarkable notice of Baron Kaulbars' mission, and of the treaty concluded with Yacúb Beg. The article finishes with the following passage :—

"There is reason to believe that Yacúb Beg has accepted these conditions in all sincerity, and that he will be guided by them in all matters concerning our merchants. He has been able to judge by the example of the Sultan of Kulja, of the consequences of obstinacy and bad faith in regard to us. The example of his neighbour, the Khan of Kokand, has,

treaty, which in so far as it was made public was confined to commercial matters, was ratified in due course;* another Russian Officer (Stcherbinski) having returned with it to Kashgar in December 1872, and finally an Ambassador was sent to St. Petersburg with an autograph letter to the Emperor in July 1873, and Kashgar was formally recognized by Russia as an independent state.

But notwithstanding these outward appearances of cordiality, it may be doubted if the Ataligh's confidence in Russian promises or Russian forbearance, was ever very deep or very lasting. The deputation at any rate of Syud Yacúb Khan to Constantinople in 1873 indicated renewed suspicion, and the result of that mission was certainly unfavourable for a time to the further development of Russian influence at Kashgar. In the Turkish capital, the envoy found the antagonism of Russia to the interests of Islam to be a standard article of faith, while her boundless ambition was the theme of universal comment, and was deplored by all true believers. The reactionary party, who were straining every nerve to sustain the interests of Mahomedanism, hailed with eagerness the prospect of a "revival" in the far East. The Ataligh, through their influence, was granted by the Sultan the title of Amír-el-Múmenein (or "commander of the faithful") formerly held by the Caliphs of Baghdad, and it was agreed that the Kashgar money should in future bear the Sultan's superscription, as the head of the Mahomedan world. Personally also, the envoy was treated with every mark of consideration, and presents of rifled guns and improved arms were sent for his master, not so much for military use, as to gratify and attach this new champion of Islam. It was only natural that General Ignatief, who has a large personal experience of Central Asia, and has always denounced the danger of Mahomedan propagandism, should endeavour to check this growing intimacy

on the other hand, served, as he himself said in his letter to General Kauffmann, to show that whoever has come to terms of peace with Russia, and has secured her friendship, has suffered neither from prejudice nor oppression,

but that, on the contrary, all the small states enjoy security by the grace of potent Russia."

* The text of the treaty is given in Appendix No. IX.

between the West and East, by the ordinary arts of diplomacy. Attempts were probably made by him to tamper with the Syud's fidelity to his master, and to instill into his mind suspicions of the sincerity of his English allies, but it is not believed that any such efforts were successful. The Syud returned from Constantinople with his guns and arms in the autumn of 1873, just in time to join Mr. Forsyth who had been a second time appointed Envoy to Kashgar, and who was then in full march for Yarkend. They travelled together to the court of the Amír, and by their joint efforts a treaty was negociated on February 2, 1874, the object of which was stated in the preamble to be "to confirm and strengthen the good understanding which exists" (between England and Kashgar), and "to promote commercial intercourse between their respective subjects."*

It will be observed that commercial interests have been put in the first rank both by Russia and England in all negociations with Kashgar, and this definition of the Amír's relations with the European powers has been generally accepted as sufficiently correct; but it is impossible to overlook the fully equal importance of the political aspect of the country. Whatever may be the extent of the importation of Russian goods into Kashgar—and in native, if not in European hands, it is no doubt considerable,—the trade with India, at any rate, across Thibet is utterly insignificant.† It never indeed has been and never can be, owing to the physical

* See, for text of Kashgar Treaty, Appendix No. X.

† The following extracts from the Proceedings of the Lieutenant-Governor of the Punjab, dated May 26, 1874, are sufficient authority for the unfavourable opinions here expressed as to the British trade with Kashgar:—

"It is to be remembered that though the development of trade between Yarkend and British India has received the careful attention of the British Government for upwards of six years; though transit duties have been abolished, and special officers appointed to watch over the interests of traders, the total value of the trade with Eastern Turkestán, though the greatest on record, amounted last year to less than £60,000, a great increase compared with what it was; but, after all, an amount which must be considered altogether insignificant.

* * * * *

"Again, it must be confessed, that the greater our experience of the routes between India and Yarkend, the greater do the difficulties appear in the way of establishing a satisfac-

CH. VI.] LATER PHASES OF CENTRAL ASIA QUESTION. 335

difficulties of the route, of sufficient magnitude to produce any perceptible effect on the revenues or the prosperity of the Empire. Without contesting, therefore, the good faith of our sanguine commercial negociators, I shall here dwell more particularly on the political features of the question, which they would seem rather to have neglected, but which are, in my view, of vastly superior importance to any trade interests that can be possibly involved. Russia has certainly always dreaded the effect on her inflammable Asiatic subjects of the formation of a strong and prosperous Mahomedan power in their immediate neighbourhood, and she has thus looked with intense jealousy on any assistance, moral or material, that might be furnished by England to this end. For some time she tried the effect of intimidation on Kashgar. She called the Amír "a bad neighbour," complained that in spite of treaty-engagements he opposed and hampered trade; that he intrigued with her disaffected subjects, with the Kirghiz on one side, the Turcomans on the other; that he was in fact thoroughly unfriendly to her, and that the more his power was consolidated the more would his unfriendliness be felt. She asked even for explanations as to the guns and arms contributed by Turkey, which accompanied Mr. Forsyth's last mission, and also as to the military instructors and artificers which were said to have been furnished from India, and the whole tenor of her conduct and language led us to expect that she was preparing to put pressure on the Amír, with a view of preventing the further development of his power, and of rendering him more amenable to her influence. Quite recently, however, a change seems to have come " o'er the spirit of her dream." So far from using a threatening tone, the

tory trade-route, owing to the length of the journey, the enormous altitudes to be traversed, the arid and unproductive character of a large portion of the country, the absence of population, and the deficiency of carriage and supplies.

" The expedition of last year, though aided by all the influence of the Government officials of British India and Cashmere, met with no small difficulties, and taxed the resources of the country, both as regards carriage and supplies, to the utmost. If such were the case with an expedition proceeding with all the prestige and advantages of an Imperial Embassy, the successful performance of the journey by large caravans under less favourable circumstances must be considered problematical."

Russian press now speaks approvingly of the Amír's conduct; but whether this change of tone be owing to an altered policy, or whether the relations between Russia and Kashgar may really have improved, it is impossible to say. No doubt the uninterrupted success which attended the march of the several Russian columns across the Steppes in the late expedition against Khiva must have powerfully impressed the native mind throughout the East, whilst the unexpected moderation of Russia, in forbearing to take any part in the recent Kokand disturbances, may have also reassured Amír Yacúb as to his own position, and have thus rendered him more docile and considerate.

The policy of England in the mean time in regard to Kashgar has never altered; though negative in its object, it is clearly defined, and needs neither concealment nor excuse. It would undoubtedly be inconvenient to us if Russia, either by force of arms or at the invitation of the native ruler, succeeded in establishing a protectorate over Eastern Turkestán—similar to her protectorate of the Usbeg Khanates,—and were thus brought into contact, through Thibet with Cashmere, and through Wakhán with Cabul. Our interest, therefore, irrespective of commercial considerations, is clearly to maintain the Amír in independent power. We desire to see him ruling over a contented and orderly population, giving offence neither to Russia nor to China, contracting his frontiers within manageable limits, devoting himself to the improvement of his country, and laying the foundations of a permanent dynasty. Fortunately we have not the same dread as Russia of the contagion of Mahomedan influence, the Musselmans of India, prone as they may be to mischief, being outnumbered and controlled by Hindoos and Sikhs. Turkestán, indeed, like Afghanistán and Persia, may help to buttress our Indian Empire ; but it can never, so long as it retains its independence, be to us a source of danger or uneasiness. Our envoys, therefore, to Kashgar have invariably counselled prudence and moderation. We have recommended the Amír, as a measure of precaution, to withdraw his garrisons from Urumchí and Manass, and to remain content with the submission and tribute of the Tungans.

Above all things we have insisted that he should strictly fulfil his treaty-engagements with Russia, and leave no opening for reprisals.

It is not possible of course to see very far ahead in this region of nebulous politics. There are difficulties, both external and internal, which may shipwreck the most carefully considered plans. If China, for instance, should recover from the military paralysis, which for some years past has stricken her extremities, she might possibly reassert her claim to Kashgar, and thus necessitate a European armed intervention, the result of which it would be impossible to foresee. Or Kokand and Bokhárá, inspired from without, might follow up the call they are said to have already made on Amír Yacúb's allegiance, by invading his territories, which would certainly embroil Kashgar with Russia. But the most serious indications of danger come from within. The Amír Yacúb has been by no means single-minded in his dealings with us. His experience of Russia had rendered him suspicious of all Europeans; and as an Oriental prince, moreover, cannot understand the meaning of a commercial mission, but always supposes there is some deep political design shrouded under the mask of trade, so in the Amír's reception of Mr. Forsyth—notwithstanding that it was marked with a lavish hospitality and much personal attention—still there was from the commencement an undercurrent of mistrust, which it required the nicest circumspection not to rouse into activity. There was in fact no reason why the Amír should especially affect our friendship except as a defence against Russia, and when the suspicion therefore crossed him,—partly perhaps from the recent matrimonial alliance of the two Royal families, and partly from our interposition in favour of Russian interests,—that the two powers might have coalesced to compass his ruin, he showed undoubted signs of recalcitration. With the intuitive love also for duplicity which characterises all Orientals, he has apparently desired to steer his course midway between Scylla and Charybdis, concluding treaties of friendship with both powers, but never committing himself irretrievably with either.*

* In support of this charge of duplicity, I place in juxtaposition the two accounts of Amír Yacúb's language to the Russian and English missions

z

As he has made known his communications with Russia to us, so, if we had exposed our hands, or had had any hands to expose, he might have made known our communications to Russia. Passing then from this shadowy ground of intrigue and deception to practical life, we can at any rate repose with satisfaction on our own honesty of intention, and take further consolation from the knowledge that under no circumstances can we incur real danger from the hostility of Kashgar; since invasion through a country like Thibet, entirely destitute of supplies, and seamed with passes 18,000 feet in height, is beyond the scope of modern warfare, while the only other access to India from Turkestán, by the Chitrál route, is closed by stubborn mountaineers who have never succumbed to an invader since the days of Timúr, as well as by the proud and stern resistance of the free-born tribes of Afghanistán.

6. There is a difficulty, which it would be affectation to ignore, in seizing the leading features of Russia's policy in Central Asia, and tracing in broad lines, as we should in regard to other countries, the natural course of its future progress and development; and this difficulty arises not so much from her movements being shrouded in mystery, or from any uncertainty as to their scope and direction, as from the many conflicting influences which control her policy, and

respectively. When Baron Kaulbars in his first interview with the Amír explained the object of his mission, and alluded to the possibility of a good understanding between Russia and Kashgar, "Yacúb's countenance wore an expression of lively satisfaction which he could not conceal." On a second occasion, Yacúb said to Baron Kaulbars, "I consider you (Russians) as my friends"; and being afterwards left alone with the Baron, he told him "that the English had already sent plenipotentiaries to him, but that he preferred the protection of the sovereign of Russia, his nearest and most potent neighbour."—"Journal de St. Pétersbourg," August, 23, 1872.

Eighteen months later, when Sir D. Forsyth was presented to the Amír at Kashgar, on December 11, 1873, the following speech was addressed to him:—

"The Queen of England has shown me great favour, and done me very high honour. I look mainly to England, and I consider myself most fortunate in obtaining the friendship of the English nation. The Queen of England is a great sovereign, whose friendship is to be greatly desired, for it is always most beneficial to those who possess it. I look to the English for favour and good will. I prefer their friendship. The Queen of England is as the sun to me, making poor people like me happy, when shining on them."

which, being for the most part arbitrary and abnormal, baffle any determinate calculation. On one side, his Majesty the Emperor, who, being at the head of a despotic government, must be supposed to have the ultimate decision on all disputed points in his hands, has repeatedly declared that he considered "extension of territory to be extension of weakness," and that "he was directly opposed to any further conquests"; and in corroboration of these sentiments we know that he proposed in 1869 to restore Samarcand to Bokhárá, that in 1863 he distinctly forbade the annexation of any portion of the Khivan territory, and that still more recently he suspended the preparations for an expedition against the Turcomans. But, on the other side, all such good intentions have proved in practice to be mere temporary interruptions in one uniform career of extension and aggrandizement. And in addition to the results of our own experience, which, as we are interested parties might be supposed to incline rather to the side of suspicion, we have further been assured by sagacious foreign observers, free from all national prejudice, but who have watched the progress of events, and have been more or less admitted behind the scenes, that the continued advance of Russia in Central Asia is as certain as the movement of the sun in the heavens. Whether it be from a natural law of increase, or from the preponderating weight of the military classes, thirsting for distinction, or from the deliberate action of a government which aims at augmented power in Europe through extension in Asia, or from all these causes combined, we are told on high authority that, in spite of professions of moderation, in spite of the Emperor's real pacific tendencies, in spite even of our remonstrances and possibly our threats, Russia will continue to push on towards India until arrested by a barrier which she cannot remove or overstep. If this programme be correct, it means of course contact and collision, and such I believe, as far as my own means of observation extend, to be the inevitable result in due course of time. The only uncertain element in the calculation seems to me to be the interval that may elapse before the crisis, an interval to be employed by us in active, but well-considered, preparation.

Premising, then, that I am alone responsible for the views that I am about to enunciate, I will commence with a review of the Russian position from the Caucasus in the west to the Thian-shan in the east.

In Persia quite recently there has been unwonted activity. The plan of a railway from the frontier to Tabriz, originated by a private company, has been pressed on the acceptance of the Shah's government by the full weight of Russian official influence, against his Majesty's wishes, and in flagrant disregard of the rights of Baron Reuter, the annulment of whose concession, although formally notified by Persia, has never been accepted either by the individual or by his protecting government. There can be no question that the interference of the Russian government in this matter has far transcended the limits of advice or even solicitation tendered by a friendly power, and has given a rude shock to the Shah's independent authority; but the incident is not likely to lead to serious misunderstanding, since the Reuter privileges cannot certainly be maintained in their entirety, and if they are annulled, either partially or wholly, it is probable that a compromise will be effected between the Baron and the Russian company. Considerable uneasiness at the same time is felt by Persia at the facilities which such a railway would afford for the military occupation of Tabriz by Russia in the event of war between the two countries; but this question is, in my opinion, hardly worth considering, since the northern Persian capital has always been and still is completely at the mercy of the Russian forces cantoned on the frontier, within a week's march of the city, and the danger therefore of such an operation is not in any essential degree augmented by the railway. Of far more importance is the eventual destination of this line, which, it is understood, is to be protracted through Kurdistán towards Baghdad, so as to give access to a part of the Turkish Empire where the Porte is, in a political point of view, especially vulnerable, but which has been hitherto supposed by its remote position to be secured from attack from the northward.

The most important negociations, however, on which Russia

CH. VI.] LATER PHASES OF CENTRAL ASIA QUESTION. 341

is now engaged with Persia refer, no doubt, to the Turcomans. General Lomakin, the new governor of the Trans-Caspian military district, is making strenuous efforts to withdraw the Yomúts and Goklans from their Persian allegiance, with a view, no doubt, to employing them as auxiliaries against the recalcitrant Tekkehs, and Persia is thus subjected to the danger of not only losing her subjects, but of seeing her Asterabád frontier completely exposed. As the Turcoman campaign, however, proceeds, and Persian interests become more and more involved in the contest of Russia with the nomades, it is not at all improbable that important territorial adjustments may take place on this frontier. The advance of Russia, indeed, along the Caspian has been so steady and persistent, and the possession of Asterabád is so manifestly necessary to the further extension of her power to the eastward, that I can hardly doubt but that in the course of a few years, unless we interfere actively to prevent it, the territory at the south-east corner of the Caspian will have become, either by conquest, or cession, or exchange, the property of the Russian crown.

A scheme of territorial settlement is said to have been much discussed in influential quarters in the early part of the present year, by which it was thought the Turcoman respite might be indefinitely prolonged, so as to remove all future cause of disagreement between England and Russia, so indeed as to restore peace permanently to Central Asia. According to this scheme, Russia was to declare her territory between the Caspian and the Aral to be bounded on the south by the old bed of the Oxus throughout its course, recognizing all the region beyond as the "independent Turcoman Steppe." Now it seemed incredible that Russia should voluntarily consent to a surrender of this nature, which would compromise the safety of the military and commercial lines that she had been at such pains to establish across the Steppe, and would further necessitate a withdrawal from Petro-Alexandrofsk, which could not be permanently held without lateral support from the Caspian; but we were nevertheless assured that the project had been approved by the peace party in Russia, and that a moderate degree of pressure on the part of England was alone required to ensure its adoption. That pressure certainly was not exerted, and the project, if it ever existed, except in the imagination of certain enthusiastic politicians, accordingly fell through. In its place we are now informed that the long contemplated expedition against the Turcomans is on the eve of accomplishment, a double column of attack having been organized, with instructions to advance simultaneously into the country of the Tekkehs from Chikishlar and the bay of Michaelofski, south of Krasnovodsk, and to commence serious operations against the nomades. By many, no doubt, this movement will be regarded as "the beginning of the end;" but, for my own part, I venture to think that "the end is not yet." The present expedition may pave the way to important results, but time is required before anything serious can be accomplished. Large preparations indeed must be made: stores and supplies must be concentrated both to the east and west; and, above all, grave explanations must take place with England, and negociations with Persia, before Russia can settle down in Merv, throw up intrenchments, found a colony, draw in populations, and directly threaten the Afghán frontier. What is proposed at present is probably to sweep up the Yomúts and Goklans as the force marches to the eastward, and thus make a strong demonstration against the Tekkehs.* The western division of this

* As these last sheets are passing through the press, it is announced that operations have commenced, the Russian column from Chikishlar having appeared on the Atrek, with the avowed intention of attacking and occupying the Yomút post of Kari-kileh, on the Simbar, which is the most westerly affluent of the Atrek on its right bank. This demonstration then raises the frontier question in a direct and tangible form. Persia maintains her frontier to be marked not by the main stream, but by the watershed of the Atrek, the valleys of all the affluents of that river from the north, of which the Simbar, often called the Kari-kileh, is one, belonging to her, and the Yomúts who inhabit those valleys being accounted her subjects. If Russia overrule this claim, and insist on her right to regard the main stream of the Atrek from its embouchure to its source as the boundary between Russian and Persian territory, the Shah will lose some of the fairest districts of Khorassan, and Russia will command not only the Attock route to Merv, but the high-road to Meshed from the Caspian. Of course the protest of Persia against what she calls a violation of frontier would be unavailing unless warmly supported by England, and Russia does not seem disposed to admit of our right of interference in such a matter. (According to still more recent intelligence, the expedition alluded to, which

tribe, already more or less demoralized, is not likely to offer any sustained resistance—though desultory skirmishes may be expected to occur—and General Lomakin will accordingly be able as he advances to establish along the skirts of the hills a line of posts, connecting the advanced station at Kahríz—or possibly at Ashkabád—with the Russian base on the Caspian. At the extreme point to which the columns may penetrate, a fort will no doubt be erected, from whence the same influences, both of conciliation and pressure, will be directed against the Tekkehs of Akhál and Merv that have already been so successfully employed against their western brethren from Krasnovodsk and Chikishlar. Disunion will be introduced amongst the Eastern Tekkehs as amongst the Western; portions of the tribe will give in their allegiance, while the stubborn who elect to fight for their ancestral pastures will be denounced as rebels and marked down for future chastisement. But Russia will no doubt proceed in this matter with the same wariness and skill that have characterized her previous movements. The first expedition is always tentative. A second expedition will in all probability be organized next year, but even that effort may perhaps extend Russia's dominion no further than Akhál, and a third expedition may thus be necessary before the great and crowning success be attained in the capture and occupation of Merv; the Oxus, in the meantime, however, being thoroughly opened up to navigation, and regular communication being established by means of a line of wells and military posts between the Oxus and the Murgháb.* This last-named precaution, indeed, is absolutely necessary, with a view of connecting Petro-Alexandrofsk with Merv, and thus forming a continuous frontier; and it will be not less important both to the growth of Merv as

seems to have been a mere reconnaissance, has returned to the sea-coast after selecting a suitable position for a Russian fortified post on the right bank of the Atrek at the distance of 80 miles from the mouth of the river.)

* This hiatus between the Murgháb

and the Oxus will ultimately prove in all probability to be the weakest point in the whole line of the Russian frontier towards India, the water supply at present in the intervening desert being very limited, without any visible means of increasing it.

a commercial emporium and to its strength and stability as the extreme Russian post to the south that there should be a thorough understanding with Persia and a secure passage across the desert which intervenes between Merv and Serakhs.

If these auxiliary measures should be fully executed, and Merv, whose natural advantages are of the highest order, should thus, in due course of time, take rank with Samarcand and Tashkend as one of the bulwarks of the Russian position towards India, then, and not till then, would the danger of collision with England assume a tangible form. The Amír, Shír Alí, has already foreseen under such circumstances that the Eastern Tekkehs, together with the Sarúk and Salor tribes, who encamp to the south of Merv, would be driven up the valley of the Murgháb and be thus forced to take refuge across the border in the Afghán district of Badgheis, from whence they would continue to raid and plunder as is their wont, throwing the whole frontier into confusion and provoking pursuit and punishment. But retribution exacted from the Turcomans on Afghán soil would inevitably lead to collision with Afghán subjects, with the Jamshídís and Tymúrís especially, who guard the north-western frontier, and any such aggression on Herat territory would be the sure prelude to our own interference. Putting aside, indeed, the obligation on our part to protect Afghanistán from invasion—an obligation which was indicated by Lord Derby in his very important speech of last May—the mere fact of Russian troops being stationed in any considerable number at Merv—although drawn to that point in their legitimate pursuit of the Tekkehs and detained there in order to hold the tribes permanently in check—would be fraught with such peril to our Indian interests that we could not remain passive, even if we wished. There is one point, indeed, the pivot of the whole Eastern Question, which must never be lost sight of—*we cannot afford to expose Herat to the risk of being taken by a Russian coup-de-main.* If a Russian force is sufficiently near to threaten the safety of the key of India, we must also have a British force sufficiently near to protect it.

All other questions relating to the Russian position in Central Asia are, as far as British interests are concerned, of much inferior importance to the Turcoman expedition and its results. At the present moment, indeed, it may be assumed that the attention of Russia is steadily turned in the direction of Merv and Herat, and that she will be mainly guided in her general Asiatic policy by considerations affecting this special question. Whether, for instance, the Khán of Khiva be continued in the nominal chiefship, or whether he be superseded by a Russian governor, will depend upon which arrangement promises best for the control of the Turcoman tribes; and even the great engineering works, the ship-canal and railway between the Caspian and the Aral, which are about to be commenced, are probably regarded by Russia as of more value in strengthening her position on the Oxus, with a view to the occupation and restoration of Merv, than as improving the communications with Turkestán.

Her further relations again with Bokhárá and Kokand will no doubt await the issue of the Turcoman crisis. No one questions but that the general feeling at Bokhárá is intensely hostile to Russia, and that the Amír has had, and still has, the utmost difficulty in preventing his subjects from breaking out and declaring a holy war against the Infidels.* Repeated rumours, indeed, have been circulated of the intention of Muzeffer-ed-dín to abdicate in favour of his son—weary of the perpetual conflict between his feelings and his interests, and despairing of the future of his country; and it is not at all improbable that such may be the result of the pending troubles at Bokhárá; but a revolution of this nature, unless accompanied with direct outrage upon the Russians, will hardly precipitate their occupation of the Khanate. It is, indeed, so manifestly to their advantage to procrastinate until their lines of communication are completed that no amount of mere provocation

* It is rarely that Russian officers venture to criticize the political conduct of the Government, or to publish remarks disparaging to the national interests. In November 1872, however, some very interesting letters appeared in the St. Petersburg *Goloss*, from the pens of M. Raeffski, who had resided some time in Tashkend, and of M. Maeff, the editor of the *Turkestán Gazette*, which gave an alarming account of the state of public feeling among the Mahomedan subjects of Russia in Central Asia at that period; and as far as our means of information extend, the situation, instead of improving, has since then become still more precarious.

will probably induce them at present to interfere. By retaining in their hands a complete command of the water supply of Bokhárá, as well as by exhibiting an imposing military force upon the Samarcand frontier, they are enabled to control the government almost as effectively as if they maintained a garrison in the capital city, whilst at the same time they avoid the expense as well as the dangers of occupation. But it is well understood that this vicarious government cannot be permanent. As soon as there is rapid and direct communication between the Caucasus and Turkestán, a Russian governor-general will take the place of the Amír, and then, if we may judge by our own Afghán experience, the Russian difficulties will commence. On one side the military expenses will be prodigious, with a very poor set-off from trade or revenue; on another side the friction and irritation which must arise from the Russian soldiery being brought into daily contact with a fanatical Mahomedan population will neutralize all efforts at improvement, and finally Russia will find the mountaineers of Hissár and Dehinow and Shahr-i-Sebz at least as impatient of control as her old enemies the Lezghies and Daghestánís, and insurrection will thus be chronic along the southern frontier.

In Kokand the prospect is better, inasmuch as the inhabitants generally are neither so fanatical nor so warlike, while the upper valley of the Jaxartes, studded with populous and important cities, is far better able to repay the expense of occupation. Even in that quarter, however, Russia is not yet prepared for intervention. If she had had troops available to garrison the large towns of Kokand, Nemengán, Andiján, Oosh, and Marghilán, it is incredible that she should have resisted the temptation to enter in and take possession which was afforded in the recent civil war between the Kirghiz and Kipchak parties, when either side invited her interference, and would have willingly submitted to her rule. For the moment it is believed that Khodayár Khán has silenced his opponents, and that he will thus be allowed to continue in power, acting, when necessary, as a lever against Amír Yacúb in virtue of the old money claims of Kokand upon Kashgar,* until railways and steam

The precise conditions are unknown under which the rulers of vessels have brought the military resources of European Russia into the heart of Turkestán, and have thus rendered the annexation of the whole province a mere question of administrative expediency. But even with all the impulsive force of civilization and all the appliances of modern warfare, which may thus be brought to bear on the position, it is not clear that Russia, although she may be in complete possession of the Jaxartes valley, will be able to realise her sway over the southern dependencies of Kokand, any more than over the mountain ranges of Bokhárá. It is far more likely that for long years Kuláb, Darwáz, and Karategín will be virtually independent, and that whatever may happen to the westward, we shall thus, at any rate, escape the inconvenience of direct Russian contact with Afghán territory along the borders of Badakhshán and Wakhán.

It only remains to consider the future Russian relations with Kashgar. It is said that ever since Mr. Forsyth's last visit to Kashgar, the Amír Yacúb has assiduously cultivated the friendship of Russia, treating her merchants with exceptional liberality, and showing a becoming deference to her counsels and her wishes. In fact he is now emphatically called a "good neighbour," as he was formerly called a "bad neighbour." Russia is not inclined at the same time to attribute this change of conduct in any great degree to the advice of the British Envoy; she rather explains it as the result of the Amír's conviction that England is unwilling—perhaps unable—to afford him material support, and that his only chance of safety, therefore, consists in his disarming Russian jealousy and proving himself the obedient vassal of the Emperor. Under present circumstances this recantation of his errors—this truce, if it may so be called—coincides sufficiently well with Russian interests. She is certainly not prepared for a direct rupture with Kashgar. Her objects, political as well as commercial, are better served by securing through moral pressure

Kokand, through their Ak-Sakals, or resident consuls, levied tribute from the Mahomedan inhabitants of Kashgar during the Chinese dominion, but the amount is stated to have been as much as £16,000 per annum, obtained from this single city.

a dominant influence at the court and in the country at large, by means of which she may exclude, or curtail, British commerce, check the contagion of Mahomedan success, and improve the general security of her Turkestán frontier. Of course if this subservience of the Amír were carried too far, it might lead to unpleasant consequences, as England could not allow her treaty rights to be disregarded, and might even be obliged in case of necessity to employ pressure through Cashmere or Afghanistán. But it is not likely that any such extreme measures can ever be required. Our new Envoy, Mr. Shaw, who is thoroughly acquainted with the country and enjoys much personal popularity, is now proceeding to Kashgar, where it is to be hoped by tact and address he may tide over the present period of difficulty, waiting with patience till the Amír reassert his natural confidence, and set himself to redress the balance between his European allies.*

7. We must now look nearer home. When Lord Northbrook reached Calcutta in May, 1872, the only Afghán questions then under discussion were the definition of the northern frontier along the Oxus, and the Seistán arbitration. Russia's acquiescence in the line of the Oxus and her recognition of Shír Alí's right to Badakhshán and Wakhán were communicated to the British Government in January, 1873, and soon afterwards the Seistán negociations terminated

---

* The special object of Mr. Shaw's deputation was to convey to Kashgar the Viceroy's ratification of the Commercial Treaty, but he was also instructed amongst other matters, "in the event of questions arising between the Amír and the Russian Government, to take care, if the opportunity arises, to impress on the Amír the risk of complications with that Government, and the importance of avoiding any step that might unnecessarily prejudice amicable relations with its representatives."

These instructions were formed, no doubt, in the most benevolent spirit, and with a view to promoting general amity at Kashgar, but their execution would require the nicest care, since there is nothing probably more distasteful to Russia—as she showed on the occasion of the Russian captives at Khiva being liberated by Shakespeare in 1841—than the sense of being indebted to English intercession for any political success in Central Asia, where she aims at being supreme, and claims to confer obligations instead of receiving them. Mr. Shaw's residence at Kashgar will not, however, in all probability be sufficiently protracted to occasion much jealousy or irritation.

in the withdrawal of the Persian protest, and the final acceptance of General Goldsmid's arbitral award. In September of the same year, Shír Alí's confidential agent, Syud Núr Mahomed Sháh, who had been associated with General Pollock in the Seistán commission, waited on the Viceroy at Simlah to discuss the general question of the Indo-Afghán relations. Matters of great importance are understood to have been brought forward at this interview, and the Afghán alliance may be considered from the date in question to have entered on a new, and a not altogether satisfactory, phase. The Amír was pleased at the territorial settlement on the Oxus, but was displeased with the settlement in Seistán, and as injuries notoriously make a deeper impression than favours, he was thus on the whole rather prepossessed against us at the opening of the negociations. But graver matters followed for discussion, and it soon became apparent that the Amír of 1873, speaking through his Envoy, was a very different individual from the Amír of 1869. His four years of unchallenged rule had relieved him from all apprehension of competitors, and had made him proud and self-reliant. It had also given him an insight into foreign politics which rendered him not only extravagant in his demands, but stubborn in pressing those demands, and sullen when they were negatived. The Viceroy, who was fully prepared to support Lord Mayo's policy, and who earnestly desired to strengthen the Afghán alliance, announced a programme of unexampled liberality. The Amír, in the spring of 1872, had received a present of two lakhs of rupees, to enable him to carry out certain administrative reforms. He was now promised ten lakhs in addition, of which one half was to be expended in compensating his subjects for losses sustained through the Seistán arbitration, and the other half was to meet the urgent wants of the Government at Cabul. Still more valuable assistance was tendered in the allotment of 10,000 Enfield and 5000 Snider rifles for the armament of the Afghán troops; but it soon appeared that the Amír's expectations went far beyond a mere temporary and regulated scale of relief. His contention was that the British Government was bound by the terms of Lord Mayo's Amballa letter to comply with any request that he might prefer, and as he now believed, or affected to believe, that his country was in danger from the advances of Russia, he would have thrown on us the whole expense and responsibility of placing Afghanistán in a position to meet the contingency of invasion. Whether the Amír really felt the alarm that he expressed, or whether he magnified the danger in order to give increased force to his demands, has never been ascertained. He certainly made out a very fair case to justify his present appeal. He had been told, he said, by Lord Mayo that Russia had pledged herself not to interfere with Afghanistán, and he regarded this assurance at first as almost equivalent to a treaty engagement, but as time wore on, he began to lose faith in the promises of Russia, which were so often evaded or falsified. His right to Badakhshán, for instance, had been acknowledged when Mr. Forsyth was at St. Petersburg in 1869,* yet it was not till January 1873 that Russia finally withdrew her opposition. The promised restoration also of Samarcand to the Amír of Bokhárá had been formally announced to him, yet Russian troops were still in possession. His anxiety, again, at the time of the Khivan expedition, had been met by the assurance that no part of the territory would be annexed, and yet he now found the Russians permanently established on the Oxus within hail almost of his own frontier. The famous case even was cited in which Russia took advantage of the Franco-German war to escape from the Black Sea clauses of the treaty of Paris. Over and over again he had been told there would be no further extension of Russian territory to the south, and yet her troops were ever moving on, resistless as fate. It was clear to all the world that the Turcomans would now be attacked in succession to the Uzbegs, that they would be projected on Afghán territory, that a quarrel would thus arise between him and the Russians, and that the old assurance of the inviolability of Afghanistán would then be scattered to the winds. There was much in this catalogue of grievances that was unanswerable. In some respects, as we, no doubt, pointed out,

---

* Sir A. Buchanan sent a telegram, No. 235, of Nov. 7, 1869, "announcing Mr. Forsyth's departure from St. Petersburg; Amír of Cabul's right to Badakhshán having been acknowledged."

he had not done justice to the good faith of Russia, especially as regarded her refusal to sanction or encourage the intrigues of Abdur Rahman, or to allow Bokhárá to disturb the Afghán frontier. On the essential question of invasion, we could only say that there appeared to us to be no sufficient ground for the Amír's apprehension, certainly not sufficient grounds to justify any large expenditure on preparations for defence; that we did not anticipate any foreign interference with Afghanistán, but that, "if, in the event of any aggression from without, British influence were invoked and failed by negociation to effect a satisfactory settlement, it was probable that the British Government would afford the Amír material assistance in repelling an invader."*

If the Amír had been actuated by no other feeling than one of genuine alarm at the advance of Russia, and a desire to be shielded from danger, it is hardly conceivable but that this implied promise of protection would have satisfied and reassured him. As events turned out, however, it seems to have entirely failed in restoring his confidence and good feeling towards us. His Envoy left Simlah disappointed and complaining, and from that time to the present our relations with Cabul have become daily more strained and disagreeable. For many months the Amír hesitated to receive either our money or the arms which had been sent to Peshawer for his acceptance. He refused to permit any English officer to visit Cabul, extending the prohibition even in a most ungracious manner to Mr. Forsyth's party, who were desirous of returning to India from Kashgar by that route. He further interfered—apparently, however, under a misconception—with the transit of our native Agents,

* It was in reference to this communication that Lord Derby at the close of his important speech in the House of Lords of May 8, 1874, made use of the following significant language:—

"To maintain the integrity and territorial independence of Afghanistán is in our judgment a most important object of English feeling; and any interference with the national independence of Afghanistán would be regarded by Her Majesty's Government as a very grave matter, requiring their most careful and serious consideration; and as one which might involve serious danger to the peace of India. I think if such an interference occurred, to put the matter mildly, *it is highly probable that this country would interfere.*"

who have hitherto been allowed to pass freely throughout Asia. His nomination of Abdullah Ján as heir-apparent towards the close of last year was promulgated independently of any consultation with his British allies, although they were naturally much interested in the question of the succession, while his recent arrest of Yacúb Khán, who had been summoned to Cabul under a promise of safe conduct, shows a reckless disregard of our good opinion, which augurs most unfavourably for the maintenance of even formal relations of amity. Finally, the British Agent at Cabul does not occupy that position of independence and authority to which he is entitled as the representative of the Government of India, being unable, it is believed, either to obtain or to communicate any trustworthy information of a confidential character.

It may be assumed, then, that the Amír of Cabul is for the time being displeased with his English allies, and it is further evident that an estrangement of this nature may lead to serious consequences, unless we can fathom the grounds of his ill-humour and bring him to a better sense of his duties and his interests. To follow the course of thought in an Asiatic mind is always difficult, and in this case the difficulty is enhanced by the presumed multiplicity as well as complicity of the agencies at work. It was the spectacle of Russian activity as contrasted with English inertness which in the first place probably arrested his attention and disturbed his judgment. He could not understand why Russia should advance year by year from conquest to conquest with unvarying success, while England remained inactive within her ancient limits, except on the supposition that we were the weaker power of the two. An Oriental again always desires to have an alternative resource, and it is thus not at all improbable that Shír Alí, like Amír Yacúb, may have proposed to steer a middle course, and may have even thought he saw his advantage in playing off one power against the other. At any rate he has openly exchanged correspondence with General Kaufmann as a neighbouring friendly potentate,*

---

* The Russian press has often alluded to this correspondence, which after all seems to have been of a very common place character, in terms of ostentatious self-satisfaction. In one of his letters General Kaufmann expressed his abhorrence of Yacúb Khán's rebellion, and congratu-

and it is not impossible that the location at some future time of Russian Agents at Cabul, and at other points in Afghanistán, to which the Amír's Envoy alluded at Simlah, may have been discussed confidentially between them.* But the Amír, no doubt, further considers that he has special grievances against England. He certainly believed Lord Mayo to have promised him unlimited support, and he thought that the present time, when we were supposed to be thoroughly alarmed at Russia's approach through the Turcoman country, was favourable for urging his pretensions. When he found accordingly that he had misunderstood the Viceroy's language, and that, in engaging to treat his requests "with respect and consideration," it was intended that the Government should decide in the first instance on the propriety of those requests, he was disappointed and irritated. It must be remembered also that the Amír has never thoroughly trusted us from the beginning. He bore us an ancient grudge—not without reason, as is thought by many—for our time-serving policy during his early struggles with his brothers, and though he may have been captivated for a season by Lord Mayo's frank and cordial bearing, and may have honestly desired to reciprocate the attentions which he then received, still when the novelty of the situation wore off, he could not but remember that the English were his hereditary enemies, the people who had, in times gone by, invaded his country and proscribed his family, and who were still viewed with deep hostility by a large and powerful section

lated the Amír on having at length received his submission. This language, it appears, gratified the Amír exceedingly, and was contrasted by him with the Viceroy's intercession in Yacúb Khán's behalf, "the English," as he remarked, " supporting sons against fathers, while the Russians upheld the authority of fathers over sons." It is possible that this trivial circumstance may have further contributed to the Amír's ill humour with his English allies.

* The Envoy was informed on this subject that Prince Gortchakoff had officially intimated (as recorded in the Parliamentary Blue Book) that while he saw no objection to English officers going to Cabul, he agreed with Lord Mayo that Russian agents should not do so. It is quite possible, however, in the sequel, if matters should become at all complicated, that this subject may be revived, and that Russia may wish to have a mission at Cabul. Diplomatically perhaps, we could hardly object to such an arrangement, but we might at any rate insist on sending at the same time a British mission to Bokhárá.

A A

of the priests and nobles of his court. The same misgiving, too, which had prevailed at Kashgar, as to the chance of our coalescing with Russia with a view to the extinction of the independent Asiatic States, seems to have been not unknown at Cabul, being fostered, perhaps, by the otherwise unaccountable union of the royal families of Russia and England, as well as by the programme of "a friendly partition of Asia, leaving no intermediate zone," which was advocated by an influential portion of the Russian press.

At the same time it is difficult to believe that this estrangement can be other than temporary. The Viceroy, we may be sure, has been most careful not to aggravate the misunderstanding. A dignified and distant tone has marked, no doubt, his sense of the Amír's ungracious attitude, but he has never condescended to reproach or threaten. Exhibiting, indeed, the most perfect temper and a very sound discretion, he would seem to have treated Shír Alí's rudeness as the petulance of a spoilt child rather than the deliberate provocations of an enemy. At any rate, it is satisfactory to know that it is not owing to his strained relations with England that those domestic differences have arisen in the Amír's family, which are now causing us so much anxiety and which threaten, sooner or later, to convulse the country. The nomination of Abdullah Ján as heir-apparent was probably due to female influence rather than to any political motive, and the recent arrest of Yacúb Khan, though imprudent, and under the circumstances most regretable, appears to have been dictated by a sense of personal insecurity rather than by any desire to give offence to England. Although, indeed, we have often counselled the Amír to consolidate his power and to make such timely arrangements in his family as should ensure the transmission of that power undivided to his heir, we have never interfered in the succession question, in so far as to identify ourselves with the claims of either candidate, or even to indicate a decided preference for one over the other. Since Abdullah Ján was proclaimed the position of the elder brother, Yacúb Khan, at Herát, has been no doubt intolerable, and even dangerous. Deprived of what he regarded as his birthright, and menaced with deposition from his government, he could hardly fail to renew the old intrigues with Persia, which had never, indeed, entirely ceased, and these unlawful dealings with the enemy have been the ostensible cause of his present disgrace. How the dead-lock which at present exists, owing to the antagonistic interests of the two princes, is to terminate no one can pretend to foresee, and it is useless therefore to discuss the question; but there are certain general principles connected with Afghán government, which these troubles have brought into prominent notice, and to which our attention must be directed as seriously affecting our future relations with the country. It should be remembered, then, that Afghanistán never has had, and never can have, the cohesion and consistency of a regular monarchical government. The nation consists of a mere collection of tribes, of unequal power and with divergent habits, which are held together, more or less closely, according to the personal character of the chief who rules them. The feeling of patriotism, as known in Europe, cannot exist among the Afgháns, for there is no common country. In its place is found a strong, turbulent love of individual liberty, which naturally rebels against authority, and would be equally impatient of control, whether exercised by English or Russians, or Persians, or even Duránis. There is no natural or ethnical reason why Herát and Candahar should be attached to Cabul. Herát is inhabited by races entirely alien to the Afgháns, by Jamshídis, Eymáks, and Hazárehs; while at Candahar, though the lands were parcelled out by Nadir Shah in the middle of the last century among the Dúráni aristocracy, and their descendants still exist as a privileged class, the peasantry are everywhere of Persian, or Tájik, or Turkish descent, and have no community of feeling with the northern and eastern Afgháns, who are the dominant party at Cabul, and who are especially opposed to the English alliance. Looking, then, to the natural incoherency and indocility of this heterogeneous population, looking especially to the discord now introduced into the administration by the jealousies of Shír Alí's sons, to the serious disturbance threatened on the north-western frontier by the inroads of the Turcomans, the pursuit of the Russians, and the pressure of the Persians,—looking also to the probability of further troubles in Afghan-Turkestán from the renewed intrigues of Abdur Rahman and other pretenders, I confess that, however the present embroglio at Cabul may terminate, I see little prospect of any settled government in the country during Shír Ali's further tenure of power. It has never hitherto consisted with our interests nor our wishes to draw attention to the evils of Afghán maladministration, after the fashion of Russia, who is in the habit of advertizing the disorganized condition of the Uzbeg Khanates and the Turcoman Steppe: on the contrary, we have sought to extenuate rather than to accuse, because we desire to avoid, not to court, intervention; but if we were to chronicle all the frontier raids that we have had for years past to endure, if we were to show how long the Bolán and Khyber passes have been absolutely closed to trade, if we were to record the many injuries and indignities we have received, our bill of indictment against the Afgháns would be at least as heavy as that which heralded the Khivan expedition, or which now threatens to bring retribution on the Tekkehs. The principles of our policy, no doubt, remain the same as ever. We desire to have a strong, friendly, and independent power on our north-western frontier; but, of course, forbearance has its limit. We are quite able to right ourselves, if pushed beyond endurance, and above all, we cannot under present circumstances afford to leave an unfriendly power at liberty to create mischief unobserved upon our Indian border.

8. It remains to consider the general question and briefly to suggest what should be our policy in the future. Our position in India is strong and flourishing. The social condition of the people is rapidly improving. The revenue is increasing. New paths of industry are being opened up, in the advantages of which the governors and the governed equally participate. The interests, indeed, of the two classes are becoming identified. Education in the mean time is spreading—perhaps too rapidly. Crime is being repressed, and even-handed justice is everywhere administered. Since the mutiny, insurrection has been

rendered impossible, and the embers of discontent, save in some of the native states, are hardly to be seen; not that the elements of mischief are extinct, but that they are checked for the time by moral and material prosperity. All that we want is rest— rest from foreign wars, rest from political disturbance; and this is precisely what we are not likely to obtain. The power which scares away our confidence, and obliges us to embark on the troubled waters of political strife, is Russia. If we were assured that Russia would remain within the limits of her present frontiers, or would stir no further than was necessary to protect those frontiers, we might fold our hands in peace, careless of the Turcomans, careless of Kashgar, careless even of the repellent attitude of Cabul; but past experience tells us that it would be folly to pin our faith on such an issue. Observation shows that whether it be from accident or from design, the continuous advance of Russia towards India is certain, and that we must prepare, therefore, for the contact. The present expedition against the Turcomans is merely one of a series of movements that will almost infallibly lead the Russians to Merv. The stereotyped mode of proceeding in such cases would be to ask for explanations, and, if necessary, to protest; but knowing as we do that we have no means of effectually arresting the march of the troops, is it wise or dignified thus to commit ourselves to a mere "brutum fulmen?" We have already pointed out the complications that are almost certain to arise if the Turcomans are driven up the Murgháb into the Afghán hills, and our representations have been treated with a studied indifference, which certainly does not encourage their repetition. We might possibly, by interference in Persia, retard, or even frustrate, a Russian movement upon Merv; but such an intervention would be costly in its conduct, and uncertain in its issue, besides entailing on us the possible responsibility of defending Persia from subsequent attack.

Our proper course, then, as it seems to me, is in the first place to assure ourselves of the principles of the policy that we are in future to pursue in Central Asia, and in the second place to keep the execution of that policy exclusively under our own control, and as far as possible in our own hands.

There have been—I know not if there are—politicians who, in considering the possible invasion of India by a Russian army, have advised us to fight upon the Indus. Their argument is simply this, that the further Russia advances from her base the weaker she becomes, owing to extended communications and the awakened hostility of the nations on whom she tramples in her progress; while, of course, the nearer we remain to our resources, to our depôts, our magazines, and especially to our sea base, the stronger is our military position; but this view of the question entirely leaves out of consideration the discouraging—nay, the disastrous—moral effect that would be produced in India by our remaining inactive and apparently paralysed until called on to stake our empire on a frontier battle ; and it equally ignores the danger of our fair provinces being desolated under such circumstances by hordes of barbarians, who, in thirst of plunder, would accompany the European invaders,—the descendants of those wild warriors who rode with Nadir Shah to Delhi. There is not, of course, at present— and probably there never will be—any question of such an extreme alternative ; but as a mere matter of argument it seems like fatuity to pretend to set off the vital danger of defeat on our immediate frontier against the possible inconvenience of incurring the hostility of the mountain tribes by a forward movement.

Taking it for granted, then, that we shall never wait to be attacked, in which case the troubles in our rear would probably be more serious than those in front, the next point to consider is how and where we are to meet the enemy. At what point are we prepared to say to Russia, " Thus far shalt thou go and no further ? " Along the northern limits of India and its dependencies Russia has herself drawn a line—the line of the Oxus—which she is bound not to transgress ; but this limitation hardly meets the general question, since the road into India from Russia's European base is not from the northward across the Hindú-kúsh to Cabul, but from the north-westward by Merv, Herát, and Candahar, and upon this line there has been hitherto no understanding as to a finality of advance, nor perhaps is it advisable that there should be an understanding which would hamper England but leave Russia free. Without, therefore, making any offensive notification to Russia about the limitation of her advance, and reserving to ourselves the right, in the interests of the Afgháns, to impede her occupation of Merv if it seem advisable, I submit that we should at any rate make up our own minds that she shall not follow up the Murgháb valley from Merv into the Afghán territory unopposed. In fact the facility of taking Herát by a "coup-de-main" from Merv is so patent, while the consequences of that movement to British India might be so fatal, that it seems a fair matter for consideration whether the Russian occupation of the one city should not be immediately followed by the British occupation of the other. Should the crisis be delayed for another year or two—and it seems only a fair surmise that it will be so delayed—the clouds that now obscure the Cabul horizon will in all probability be blown away, and Shír Alí will then be the first to suggest the necessity of holding the "key of India" with a British garrison.

To some Indian statesmen,—and especially to those who have been bred up in the modern school of political puritanism,—the notion of occupying Herát with a British force, under any conceivable circumstances, may appear wild and extravagant. Visions will arise on their troubled imaginations of murdered envoys, of imprisoned ladies, of decimated legions, of England's honour trailed in the dust, of defeat, of bankruptcy, of ruin. It is time that all this puerile absurdity, the stale refuse of a bygone period of panic, should cease. I am not insensible to the gravity of the step suggested, to the many weighty objections that may be urged against sending another British army above the passes, on the score of expense, and especially on account of the danger of reviving dormant enmities and bringing on political complications both with Persia and with Cabul; but, in a professional point of view, the movement on Herát would be a mere bagatelle. If the Amír of Cabul, indeed, concurred in the operation, as an auxiliary measure of Afghán defence, the expedition, advancing from Scinde by Quetta and Candahar to Herát, would realize probably what was formerly promised to Lord Keane's army, "a military promenade," with just enough variety to break the monotony of a march, but hardly enough to provoke a sense of danger. The distance, it must be remembered, from our base in Upper Scinde to Herát is considerably less than the distance from Orenburg to Khiva or from the Caspian to Merv, while the country to be traversed is far better provided with carriage and supplies, and the tribes on the line of march, even if they were disposed to resist, would be less formidable opponents than the Kirghiz and Turcomans. Of course, if the perversity of the Amír were to continue, and he were inclined to thwart the expedition from feelings of jealousy or from a mistrust of our intentions, the difficulties of the march would be much increased, and our preparations would require to be made upon a larger scale, including, perhaps, a demonstration at the mouth of the Khyber; but under no circumstances need the expeditionary column, as far as I can form an opinion, exceed a strength of 10,000 men (the greater part being, of course, Europeans), 5000 being allotted to the garrison of Herát, and 3000 to Candahar, while 1000 men might occupy Quetta and Pishín, keeping up the communications in the lower section of the line, and the remaining 1000 would be distributed between Girishk and Farreh, so as to connect Candahar with Herát.

It would be premature, perhaps, at present to discuss in any detail the political arrangements that might be rendered necessary in order to support this large military operation, since so very much must depend on the contemporary march of events both in Russia and in India. I would not propose, under existing circumstances, that a British force should occupy Cabul, or that we should interfere with the Government of the Amír. It should be rather understood that we had no views of aggrandizement or territorial conquest, but, on the contrary, that the occupation of Candahar and Herát was purely a measure of military defence forced upon us by the aggressive attitude of Russia. If the Amír went along with us in this policy, and placed the resources of Western Afghanistán at our disposal for the purposes of the expedition,—as was the case in our former occupation of the country,—there would be no occasion to supersede the ordinary civil administration, or, in fact, to behave otherwise than as temporary visitors in a friendly country.

The Amír's officers would collect the revenues and be responsible for the maintenance of discipline and order, merely attending to our requisitions, and treating us as an auxiliary army of occupation; or if it were found that this double jurisdiction produced friction and tended to disorder, we might lease Candahar and Herát from the Amír for the time being, paying him a liberal sum as rental, and administering the districts through our own officers. I can see no reason why we should not remain on terms of perfect amity and good will with the Amír under such an arrangement. Our jurisdiction would be restricted to the districts which comprised or flanked our lines of communications, to Shawl and Pishín, the plain of Candahar, the lower valleys of the Turnuk and Arghandáb, Girishk and Zamín-Dáwer, Farreh, Sabzár, and the fertile plain of Herát. The Amír would rule over all the rest of Afghanistán, from Mymeneh to Wakhán, from Kelat-i-Ghilzye to the Khyber, and he would receive for the first time since he rose to power a good surplus revenue from Candahar and Herát.

What this occupation might lead to it is impossible to say. Russia might recoil from contact with us, or we might mutually retire to a convenient distance from each other, or in our respective positions at Merv and Herát, Russia being able to draw on her European resources through the Oxus and the Caspian, while a railway through Candahar connected our advanced garrison with the Indus, we might lay the foundation of that limitary relationship along the whole line of frontier, which, although unsuited to the present state of affairs in Central Asia, must inevitably be the ultimate condition of our joint dominion in the East.

And here I might conclude this outline sketch of our proposed policy in Central Asia were it not that the argument seems imperfect without a brief notice of some of the drawbacks and objections which may be used on the other side. The first question that is likely to be asked is, What is the particular evil or danger to be apprehended from the presence of the Russians at Merv, or even at Herát, which can require to be counteracted by so enormously expensive a measure of defence?

The answer to this question would be to the following effect.

Russia by advancing on Merv evidently means mischief. She would never embark on an enterprise of so perilous a nature for mere purposes of trade or police. Political objects of high import could alone justify the movement. Those objects necessarily point to Herát, which would lie at the mercy of a European power holding Merv, and from whence India would be seriously threatened. Herát possesses natural advantages of quite an exceptional importance. It is the frontier town between Persia and India. It is connected by high roads with the capitals of all the surrounding countries, with Cabul through the Hazáreh hills, with Balkh and Bokhárá through Mymeneh, with Khiva through Merv, with Meshed, with Yezd and Isfahán, with Seistán and with Candahar. It enjoys an admirable climate, and is situated in the midst of one of the most fertile and populous valleys in Asia. Above all, the city itself is surrounded by earth works of the most colossal character, dating from pre-historic times, and which, with the adaptations and improvements of modern science, might be rendered quite impregnable to an Asiatic force.* Russia in possession of Herát would have a gripe on the throat of India. She would, indeed, in virtue of the position, command the military resources, both of Persia and Afghánistán, and would thus oblige us at once to increase our frontier army by at least 20,000 fresh British troops. Viewing, then, the question as merely one of finance, it may be assumed that our advance above the passes and occupation of Herát would be the cheapest insurance against Russia that we could effect for the benefit of our great Indian estate. Let it be further remembered that all these considerations have been already discounted by our statesmen in regard to the smaller question of a Persian occu-

* The city of Herát occupies an area of nearly a mile square, and is surrounded by an earth-work, which measures about 250 feet in width at the base, and from 50 to 60 feet in height, and which is surmounted by a wall, 14 feet thick at the base, 9 feet thick at the top, aud 18 feet high, exclusive of the parapet. There is also a wet ditch of 45 feet in width and 16 feet in depth ; and an ark or citadel of considerable strength. A most elaborate report on the defences of Herát, extending over 30 pages, by Major Sanders, Bengal Engineers, who visited the place in 1838, after the Persian siege, is to be found in M'Gregor's Central Asia, Part II. p. 341.

pation of Herát. We sent a considerable expedition to the Gulf in order to oblige Persia to raise the siege of Herát in 1838, and when Persian troops occupied the place in 1856, we actually went to war with the Shah for the purpose of compelling their withdrawal. If, then, such measures were justifiable in order to prevent the Western Afghán capital from falling into the hands of Persia, who was only to be feared as the minion or precursor of Russia, much more must they be required when the danger comes directly from Russia herself. I will not pretend to calculate the cost of sending an expedition to Herát. Any estimate, based on the uncertain premises which are alone at present available would be fallacious; but I may point out that the expenses of our defensive position, however great, must be far less than those encountered by Russia in constructing and maintaining her elaborate system of attack. For when Russia is established at Merv, and has completed the communications of that post with the Caspian on one side and with the Oxus and Turkestán on the other, she will have at least 50,000 soldiers in Central Asia, and it is not too much to assume that the main object of bringing that large body of troops into the field, towards whose support the conquered Uzbeg States contribute little or nothing, will have been to enable her to threaten India.

There is one other aspect of the question that requires explanation. Some of our best authorities on Central Asian politics maintain that not only should we incur an enormous and useless expenditure in advancing to meet Russia above the passes, but that we should be intensifying tenfold the difficulties of our position. They believe that we should everywhere meet with hatred and resistance, that we should thus throw the Afgháns into the hands of Russia, who would, in fact, when she advanced, be hailed by them as a deliverer rather than opposed as an invader. My own experience points in an exactly contrary direction, and I am happy to find my views corroborated by the independent testimony of our latest travellers.* Be-

---

* The following extracts from Dr. Bellew's recent work, entitled "From the Indus to the Tigris," page 148, convey his impressions derived from

lieving, as I do, the Western Afgháns to be the most contemptible of enemies, and hardly, therefore, caring to consider the possibility of a skirmish in the Bolán or Khojek passes, the only defensible positions on the line from Scinde to Herát, I still feel satisfied that we should generally receive the warm support of the great mass of the population in the districts that we traversed. The Syuds of Pishín, the Atchikzyes of the Khojek, who adhered to us in all our troubles in 1841-42, the Parsiwán peasantry of Candahar, the mercantile and agricultural classes throughout the country, would one and all throng to us for support and protection. Mindful of past benefits, hopeful of future favours, they would bring in their camels from the desert and empty their granaries of corn to supply our wants, as they did in those days when, although Ghizni and Cabul were lost and an army had perished in the passes, we were safe and strong and triumphant at Candahar. The only parties from whom we should experience ill-will would be the priesthood and a few of the Duráni chiefs; and they might be called upon to retire to Cabul. Most assuredly, as far as the disposition of the natives is concerned, we should not have more difficulty in governing Candahar and Herát than the Russians encounter in governing Tashkend and Samarcand; whilst our long familiarity with Eastern administration, our special knowledge of Western Afghánistán, our consideration

personal observation of the present feelings of the inhabitants of Candahar.

"The discontent of the people is universal, and many a secret prayer is offered up for the speedy return of the British, and many a sigh expresses the regret that they ever left the country. Our just rule and humanity, our care of the friendless sick, our charitable treatment of the poor, and the wealth we scattered amongst the people, are now remembered with gratitude, and eager is the hope of our return. This is not an exaggerated picture, and speaks well for the philanthropic character of the short-lived British rule in this province when we consider that our occupation of the country was but a military aggression.

"But even if they had never had a practical experience of British rule, the desire of the Kandaharis for the establishment of our authority, and extension of the British government to their province, is explained by the glowing accounts they receive from their returning merchants of the prosperity, happiness, and liberty that reign in India, whilst such accounts render them more impatient of the tyranny under which they are forced to groan."

for Mahomedan prejudices, our prestige, our high reputation for justice and good faith, ought to make the task of maintaining the position far more easy to us than to our less experienced Northern neighbours.*

I will only say one word in conclusion, that I counsel nothing rash or premature. If Russia remained encamped on the Caspian, we should not, of course, leave the valley of the Indus. So long as she held aloof from Merv, we should hold aloof from Herát; but if she deliberately threw down the gauntlet, she must expect it to be taken up. We could not, as the guardians of the interests of India, permit her, on the pretext of curbing the Turcomans or establishing a trade route through Asia, to take up a position unopposed on the Murgháb, which would compromise the safety of Herát. That city is both strategically and politically an indispensable bulwark of India, and we cannot and will not allow its future fate to be at the disposition of a foreign power.

December, 1874.

* The recently discovered gold field of Candahar, though comparatively worthless in the hands of the Afgháns, who have no mining experience whatever, and employ only the rudest process in extracting the metal, would, according to Dr. Bellew (p. 140), who examined the locality, yield a very considerable revenue, if worked by skilful European miners, duly furnished with the improved machinery of the present day. The auriferous region, indeed, along the hills to the north of Candahar, is apparently so extensive that the produce of this single district in our hands might very well pay the whole expense of the Western Afghán occupation.

APPENDIX.

TABLE OF CONTENTS.

1. Engagement of the Persian Government regarding Herát, Jan. 25, 1853.—2. Preliminary Treaty of Peshawer, March 30, 1855.—3. Definitive Treaty of Peshâwer, Jan. 26, 1857.—4. Treaty of Paris with the Shah of Persia, March 4, 1857.—5. Abstract of Reuter's Concession, July 25, 1872.—Russian Treaty with Khiva, August 25, 1873.—7. Russian Treaty with Bokhárá, Sept. 28, 1873.—8. Extracts from "Notes on Khiva," March 25, 1873.—9. Russian Treaty with Yaoûb Beg of Kashgar, June 8, 1872.—10. English Treaty of Commerce with the Amír of Kashgar, Feb. 2, 1874.

I.

ENGAGEMENT OF THE PERSIAN GOVERNMENT REGARDING HERAT.

TRANSLATION.*

15th Rebbel-oo-Sanee, 1269 (January 25, 1853).

THE Persian Government engages not to send troops on any account to the territory of Herát, excepting when troops from without attack that place, that is to say, troops from the direction of Cabul or from Candahar, or from other foreign territory; and in case of troops being despatched under such circumstances, the Persian Government binds itself that they shall not enter the city of Herát, and that immediately on the retreat of the foreign troops to their own country, the Persian force shall forthwith return to the Persian soil without delay.

The Persian Government also engages to abstain from all interference whatsoever in the internal affairs of Herát, likewise in (regard to) occupation or taking possession, or assuming the sovereignty or government, except that the same amount of interference which took place between the two in the time of the late Zuheer-ood-Dowlah, Yar Mahomed Khan, is to exist as formerly. The Persian Government therefore engages to address a letter to Syed Mahomed Khan, acquainting him with these conditions, and to forward it to him (by a person) accompanied by some one belonging to the English Mission who may be in Meshed.

The Persian Government also engages to relinquish all claim or pre-

---

* This translation was made in 1857 from the original Persian, as some doubt was raised as to the correctness of the translation made in 1853.

tension to the coinage of money and to the " Khootbeh," or to any other mark whatever of subjection or of allegiance on the part of the people of Herát to Persia. But if, as in the time of the late Kamrán and in that of the late Yar Mahomed Khan, they should, of their own accord, send an offering in money and strike it in the Shah's name, Persia will receive it without making any objection. This condition will also be immediately communicated to Syed Mahomed Khan. They also engage to recall Abbas Koolee Khan, Peeseean, after four months from the date of his arrival, so that he may not reside there permanently ; and hereafter no permanent agent will be placed in Herát, but intercourse will be maintained as in the time of Yar Mahomed Khan. Neither will they maintain a permanent agent on the part of Herát in Tehrán. There will be the same relations and privileges which existed in Kamrán's time, and in that of the late Yar Mahomed Khan. For instance, if at any time it should be necessary for the punishment of the Toorkomans, or in case of disturbance or rebellion in the Shah's dominions, that the Persian Government should receive assistance from the Herátees, similar to that afforded by the late Yar Mahomed Khan, they may, as formerly, render assistance of their own accord and free will, but not of a permanent nature.

The Persian Government further engages, unconditionally and without exception, to release and set free all the chiefs of Herát who are in Meshed or in Tehrán or in any other part of Persia, and not to receive any offenders, prisoners, or suspected persons whatsoever from Syed Mahomed Khan, with the exception of such persons as having been banished by Syed Mahomed Khan from Herát, may come here and themselves desire to remain, or to enter the service. These will be treated with kindness and favour, as formerly. District orders will be issued immediately to the Prince Governor of Khorassán to carry out these engagements.

The above six engagements on the part of the Persian Government are to be observed and to have effect ; and the Persian Ministers, notwithstanding the rights which they possess in Herát solely out of friendship, and to satisfy the English Government, have entered into these engagements with the English Government, so long as there is no interference whatsoever on its part in the internal affairs of Herát and its dependencies ; otherwise these engagements will be null and void, and as if they never had existed or been written. And if any foreign (State), either Afghán or other, should desire to interfere with or encroach upon the territory of Herát, or its dependencies, and the Persian Ministers should make the request, the British Government are not to be remiss in restraining them and in giving their friendly advice, so that Herát may remain in its own state of independence.

Seal and autograph of the SADR AZIM.

Translated by

(Signed)   RONALD THOMSON.

II.

TREATY CONCLUDED BETWEEN SIR JOHN LAWRENCE, CHIEF COMMISSIONER OF THE PUNJAB AND SIRDAR GHOLAM HYDER KHAN AT PESHAWUR, March 30, 1855.

ARTICLE I.—There shall be perpetual peace and friendship between the Honourable East India Company and His Highness Dost Mahomed Khán, The Amír of Kábul, his heirs and successors.

ARTICLE II.—The Honourable East India Company engages to respect and never interfere with the territories now in possession of His Highness the Amír.

ARTICLE III.—His Highness Dost Mahomed Khán engages, on his own part, and on the part of his heirs and successors, to respect the territories belonging to the Honourable East India Company ; to be the friends of its friends, and the enemies of its enemies.

III.

Articles of Agreement made, at Pesháwur, on the 26th January 1857 (corresponding with Jámadi-ul-awwal, A.H. 1273) between Amír Dost Muhammad Khán, Ruler of Kabul, and of those countries of Afghánistán now in his possession, on his own part, and Sir John Lawrence, K.C.B., Chief Commissioner of the Punjáb, and Lieut.-Colonel H. B. Edwards, C.B., Commissioner of Pesháwur, on the part of the Honourable East India Company, under the authority of the Right Honourable Charles John Viscount Canning, Governor-General of India in Council.

1.—Whereas the Shah of Persia, contrary to his engagement with the British Government, has taken possession of Herát, and has manifested an intention to interfere in the present possessions of Amír Dost Muhammad Khán, and there is now war between the British and Persian Governments ; therefore, the Honourable East India Company, to aid Amír Dost Muhammad Khán to defend and maintain his present possessions in Balkh, Kabul and Kandahár against Persia, hereby agrees, out of friendship, to give the said Amír one lákh of Company's rupees monthly during the war with Persia, on the following conditions :—

2.—The Amír shall keep his present number of cavalry and artillery, and shall maintain not less than 18,000 infantry, of which 13,000 shall be regulars, divided into 13 regiments.

3.—The Amír is to make his own arrangements for receiving the money at the British treasuries, and conveying it through his own country.

4.—British officers, with suitable establishments, and orderlies, shall be deputed, at the pleasure of the British Government, to Kábul or Kandahár or Bálkh, or all three places, or wherever an Afghán army be assembled to act against the Persians. It will be their duty to see generally that the subsidy granted to the Amír be devoted to the military purposes for which it is given, and to keep their own Government informed of all affairs. They will have nothing to do with the payment of the troops, or advising the Kabul Government, and they will not interfere in any way in the internal administration of the country. The Amír will be responsible for their safety and honourable treatment while in his country, and for keeping them acquainted with all military and political matters connected with the war.

5.—The Amír of Kábul shall appoint and maintain a vakíl at Peshawur.

6.—The subsidy of one lákh per mensem shall cease from the date on which peace is made between the British and Persian Governments, or at any previous time, at the will and pleasure of the Governor-General of India.

7.—Whenever the subsidy shall cease, the British officers shall be withdrawn from the Amír's country; but, at the pleasure of the British Government, a vakíl, not a European officer, shall remain at Kábul, on the part of the British Government, and one at Peshawur on the part of the Government of Kábul.

8.—The Amír shall furnish a sufficient escort for the British officers from the British border when going to the Amír's country, and to the British border when returning.

9.—The subsidy shall commence from 1st January, 1857, and be payable at the British treasury, one month in arrears.

10.—The five lákhs of rupees which have been already sent to the Amír (three to Kandahár and two to Kábul) will not be counted in this agreement. They are a free and separate gift from the Honourable East India Company; but the sixth lákh, now in the hands of the Mahájans of Kábul, which was sent for another purpose, will be one of the instalments under this agreement.

11.—This agreement in no way supersedes the treaty made at Peshawur on 30th March, 1855 (corresponding with the 11th of Rajjab 1271), by which the Amír of Kábul engaged to be the friend of the friends, and enemy of the enemies, of the Honourable East India Company; and the Amír of Kábul, in the spirit of that treaty, agrees to communicate to the British Government any overtures he may receive from Persia, or the allies of Persia, during the war, or while there is friendship between the Kábul and British Governments.

12.—In consideration of the friendship existing between the British Government and Amír Dost Mahomed Khán, the British Government engages to overlook the past hostilities of all the tribes of Afghánistan, and on no account to visit them with punishment.

13.—Whereas the Amír has expressed a wish to have 4000 muskets given him in addition to the 4000 already given, it is agreed that 4000 muskets shall be sent by the British Government to Tall; whence the Amír's people will convey them with their own carriage.

IV.

TREATY OF PEACE BETWEEN HER MAJESTY THE QUEEN OF THE UNITED KINGDOM OF GREAT BRITAIN AND IRELAND, AND HIS MAJESTY THE SHAH OF PERSIA.—MARCH 4, 1857.

In the name of God, the Almighty, the All-Merciful, Her Majesty the Queen of the United Kingdom of Great Britain and Ireland, and His Majesty the Shah of Persia, being both equally and sincerely animated by a desire to put a stop to the evils of a war, which is contrary to their friendly wishes and dispositions, and to re-establish on a solid basis the relations of amity, which had so long existed between the two exalted States, by means of a peace calculated for their mutual advantage and benefit, have appointed as their Plenipotentiaries for carrying into effect this desired object the following, that is to say :—

Her Majesty the Queen of the United Kingdom of Great Britain and Ireland—the Right Hon. Henry Richard Charles, Baron Cowley, &c.

And His Majesty the Shah of Persia—His Excellency the Abode of Greatness, the Favourite of the King, Ferokh Khan, &c.

Who, having exhibited and exchanged their full powers, and found them to be in due form, have agreed upon and concluded the following Articles :—

ARTICLE I.—From the day of the exchange of the ratifications of the present treaty there shall be perpetual peace and friendship between Her Majesty the Queen of the United Kingdom of Great Britain and Ireland on the one part, and His Majesty the Shah of Persia on the other, as likewise between their respective successors, dominions, and subjects.

ARTICLE II.—Peace being happily concluded between their said Majesties, it is hereby agreed that the forces of Her Majesty the Queen shall evacuate the Persian territory, subject to conditions and stipulations hereafter specified.

ARTICLE III.—The high contracting parties stipulate that all prisoners taken during the war, by either belligerent, shall be immediately liberated.

APPENDIX. 371

ARTICLE IV.—His Majesty the Shah of Persia engages further, immediately, on the exchange of the ratifications of this treaty, to publish a full and complete amnesty absolving all Persian subjects who may have in any way been compromised by their intercourse with the British forces during the war, from any responsibility for their conduct in that respect, so that no persons, of whatever degree, shall be exposed to vexation, persecution, or punishment on that account.

ARTICLE V.—His Majesty the Shah of Persia engages further to take immediate measures for withdrawing from the territory and city of Herát, and from every other part of Afghánistán, the Persian troops and authorities now stationed therein; such withdrawal to be effected within three months from the date of the exchange of the ratifications of this treaty.

ARTICLE VI.—His Majesty the Shah of Persia agrees to relinquish all claims to sovereignty over the territory and city of Herát and the countries of Afghánistán, and never to demand from the chiefs of Herát, or of the countries of Afghánistán, any marks of obedience, such as the coinage, or "Khotbeh," or tribute.

His Majesty further engages to abstain hereafter from all interference with the internal affairs of Afghánistán. His Majesty promises to recognize the independence of Herát, and of the whole of Afghánistán, and never to attempt to interfere with the independence of those States.

In case of differences arising between the Government of Persia and the countries of Herát and Afghánistán, the Persian Government engages to refer them for adjustment to the friendly offices of the British Government, and not to take up arms unless those friendly offices fail of effect.

The British Government, on their part, engage at all times to exert their influence with the States of Afghánistán to prevent any cause of umbrage being given by them, or by any of them to the Persian Government; and the British Government, when appealed to by the Persian Government, in the event of difficulties arising, will use their best endeavours to compose such differences in a manner just and honourable to Persia.

ARTICLE VII.—In case of any violation of the Persian frontier by any of the states referred to above, the Persian Government shall have the right, if due satisfaction is not given, to undertake military operations for the repression and punishment of the aggressors; but it is distinctly understood and agreed to, that any military force of the Shah which may cross the frontier for the above-mentioned purpose, shall retire within its own territory as soon as its object is accomplished, and that the exercise of the above-mentioned right is not to be made a pretext for the permanent occupation by Persia, or for the annexation to the Persian dominions, of any town or portion of the said States.

ARTICLE VIII.—The Persian Government engages to set at liberty without ransom, immediately after the exchange of the ratifications of this treaty, all prisoners taken during the operations of the Persian troops in Afghánistán and all Afgháns who may be detained either as hostages or as captives on political grounds in any part of the Persian dominions, shall, in like manner be set free; provided that the Afghāns, on their part, set at liberty, without ransom, the Persian prisoners and captives who are in the power of Afghāns.

Commissioners on the part of the two contracting powers shall, if necessary, be named to carry out the provisions of this Article.

ARTICLE IX.—The high contracting parties engage that in the establishment and recognition of Consuls, General Consuls, Vice-Consuls, and Consular Agents, each shall be placed in the dominions of the other on the footing of the most favoured nation; and that the treatment of their respective subjects and their trade, shall also, in every respect, be placed on the footing of the treatment of the subjects and commerce of the most favoured nation.

ARTICLE X.—Immediately after the ratifications of this treaty have been exchanged, the British Mission shall return to Teherán, when the Persian Government agrees to receive it with the apologies and ceremonies specified in the separate note signed this day by the Plenipotentiaries of the high contracting parties.

ARTICLE XI.—The Persian Government engages, within three months after the return of the British Mission to Teherán, to appoint a Commission, who, in conjunction with a Commissioner to be appointed by the British Government, shall examine into, and decide upon, the pecuniary claims of all British subjects upon the Government of Persia, and shall pay such of those claims as may be pronounced just, either in one sum or by instalments, within a period not exceeding one year from the date of the award of the Commissioners. And the same Commissioners shall examine into and decide upon, the claims upon the Persian Government of all Persian subjects, or the subjects of other powers, who, up to the period of the departure of the British Mission from Teherán, were under British protection, which they have not since renounced.

ARTICLE XII.—Saving the provisions in the latter part of the preceding Article, the British Government will renounce the right of protecting hereafter any Persian subject not actually in the employment of the British Mission, or of British Consuls, General Consuls, Vice-Consuls or Consular Agents, provided that no such right is accorded to or exercised by, any other foreign powers; but in this as in all other respects, the British Government requires, and the Persian Government engages, that the same privileges and immunities shall in Persia be conferred upon, and shall be enjoyed by the British Government, its servants, and its subjects, and that the same respect and consideration shall be shown for them, and shall be enjoyed by them, as are conferred upon and enjoyed by, and shown to the most favoured foreign Government, its servants, and its subjects.

ARTICLE XIII.—The high contracting parties hereby renew the agreement entered into by them in the month of August 1851 (Shawal 1267), for the suppression of the slave trade in the Persian Gulf, and engage further that the said agreement shall continue in force after the date at which it expires, that is after the month of August 1862, for the further space of ten years, and for so long afterwards as neither of the high contracting parties shall, by a formal declaration, annul it; such declaration not to take effect until one year after it is made.

ARTICLE XIV.—Immediately on the exchange of the ratifications of this treaty, the British troops will desist from all acts of hostility against Persia; and the British Government engages, further, that as soon as the stipulations in regard to the evacuation, by the Persian troops, of Herát and the Afghán territories, as well as in regard to the reception of the British Mission at Teherán, shall have been carried into full effect, the British troops shall, without delay, be withdrawn from all ports, places, and islands belonging to Persia; but the British Government engages that, during this interval, nothing shall be designedly done by the commander of the British troops to weaken the allegiance of the Persian subjects towards the Shah, which allegiance it is, on the contrary, their earnest desire to confirm; and, further, the British Government engages that, as far as possible, the subjects of Persia shall be secured against inconvenience from the presence of the British troops, and that all supplies which may be required for the use of those troops and which the Persian Government engages to direct its authorities to assist them in procuring, shall be paid for at the fair market price by the British commissariat, immediately on delivery.

ARTICLE XV.—The present treaty shall be ratified, and the ratifications exchanged at Baghdad, in the space of three months, or sooner, if possible.

In witness whereof the respective Plenipotentiaries have signed the same, and have affixed thereto the seal of their arms.

Done at Paris, in quadruplicate, this Fourth day of the month of March, in the year of our Lord One Thousand Eight Hundred and Fifty Seven.

     (Signed)   COWLEY.

     (Signed)   FEROKH (in Persian.)

V.

CONCESSION OF THE PERSIAN GOVERNMENT TO BARON REUTER (ABSTRACT),
July 25, 1872.

I. Authorises Baron Reuter to establish in London a company, or any number of companies, for carrying out the works specified in the concession.

II. Authorises Baron Reuter, or his associates, or representatives, to construct a railway between the Caspian and the Persian Gulf, as well as any other railways he may think fit. This important privilege excludes competition, and is awarded for a period of seventy years.

III. Extends the railway privilege to tramways, referring to Articles IV. V. VI. for the rules to be observed in establishing and working these two kinds of lines.

IV. Relates to the land required for the construction of railways, tramways, and the buildings and works connected with them. The Government land wanted will be handed over free of expense; the land belonging to private persons may be appropriated at current prices. In the land required for the line is included the permanent way wide enough for a double set of metals, and a space of thirty mètres on either side.

V. Allows the concessionaire (who is throughout identical with the company or companies representing him), the gratuitous use of the stone, sand, gravel, &c., on the Government domains, which may be required in the construction and maintenance of the works. The Government also engages to see that the persons employed by the company be supplied with provisions, beasts of burden, &c., charges not exceeding the ordinary prices of the country.

VI. Enacts that all the "matériel" imported by the concessionaire, or company or companies, both for railway or other purposes, shall be exempt from any duty, toll, custom, or excise whatsoever. All the concessionaire's lands, works, and employés will be free from any impost whatever; all business will be conducted free from impost; all his products, manufactures, &c., will be allowed to circulate in the country, or to be exported from the country, free of impost.

VII. Stipulates that the details of the construction and working of the line shall be laid down in a "cahier de charge," to be appended to the concession.

VIII. Demands that the sum of 40,000l. be deposited as caution money in the Bank of England, in the name of the Persian Government and the concessionaire. Should the works not be begun within fifteen months of the date of the concession, the caution money will be forfeited to the Persian Government. If the works are begun within the time specified, the caution money reverts to the concessionaire, in exchange for a certificate from the Government of Resht, confirming the arrival at Enzeli of the quantity of rails necessary for the construction of the line between Resht and Teheran.

IX. Allots to the Government 20 per cent. of the net profits resulting from the working of the line.

X. The line, or lines, after a period of seventy years, revert to the Government free of charge, unless another agreement has been previously concluded between the Government and the concessionaire or concessionaires. As to the buildings, &c., belonging to the line, or lines, they will have to be paid for under any circumstances by the Government at the prices accorded by the most liberal governments on such occasions.

XI. and XII. Introduces the subject of mines. With the exception of gold, silver and precious stones, any mine situate on Government land may be appropriated and worked by the concessionaire free of charge, his sole obligation consisting in handing over to the Government 15 per cent. of the net proceeds. Any mine situate on private property, unless it has been worked five years previous to the concessionaire expressing a wish to acquire it, will have likewise to be handed over to him. Any mine discovered by the concessionaire may be bought by him at the price currently paid for the mere superfices of the grounds in which it is situate.

XIII. The land required to work the mines, as well as the land to put them in communication with railway, tramway, or high road, if belonging to the State, is handed over gratis to the concessionaire. The exemptions accorded to railway and tramway in Article VI. are expressly extended to the mines, which likewise come under the seventy years' clause contained in X.

XIV. Accords to the concessionaire for seventy years the sole and exclusive privilege of making the most of the Government forests, all the land not cultivated up to the date of the concession being expressly included in this clause ; 15 per cent. of the proceeds of the forests belong to the Government. If the concessionaire cuts down a wood, the land thus gained must be sold to him in preference to other buyers.

XV. Passes on to canals, wells, and other subjects connected with the natural and artificial water-courses of the country. All such works are the exclusive privilege of the concessionaire who receives the necessary land without payment, but undertakes to indemnify those proprietors who are injured by the innovation. Any cultivated land made productive by these works, belongs to the concessionaire, who will enter into an understanding with the Government respecting the price of the water to be sold. 15 per cent. of the net profits of the works belong to the Government.

XVI. Empowers the concessionaire and his associates to raise a capital of 6,000,000*l.* by means of shares and obligations to commence the construction of the railway and other works. The concessionaire to be left at liberty to determine the mode of raising the sum.

XVII. Contains a guarantee of the Persian Government to undertake to pay an interest of 5 per cent., and an additional 2 per cent. as a sinking fund on all capital raised or to be raised by the concessionaire, his associates or representatives.

XVIII. Pledges the income of the Government mines, forests, watercourses, and customs for the payment of the 7 per cent. accorded. The guarantee comes into force only after the construction of the line between Resht and Isfahâw, the concessionaire, his associates, and representatives undertaking to pay interest upon the capital issued up to that time.

XIX. The Government engage to hand over the management of their customs to the concessionaire or concessionaires for a period of twenty-five years, beginning March 1, 1874. The concessionaires engage to pay for this privilege 20,000*l.* a year in excess of what the Government now receive. The price thus fixed will hold good for the first five years, after that period the Government to receive for the remainder of the term 60 per cent. of the difference between the annual net proceeds and the amount realized at present.

XX. Records that if the Persian Government should determine to permit the establishment of a bank or any other credit institution in their country, the concessionaire or concessionaires will be allowed the first refusal, in preference to any other parties.

XXI. Extends this right of preference enjoyed by the concessionaire to all enterprises connected with the providing gas, roads, telegraphs, mills, manufactures, forges, pavement, &c. Improvements in the capital and post-offices are also included in this clause.

XXII. Provides that the right accorded in this concession can be transferred to other parties at any time.

XXIII. Stipulates that the works connected with the mines, forests, and water courses shall be begun simultaneously with the construction of the line; the Government engaging to supply the requisite amount of manual labour at current prices, and to protect the agents, employés, and property of the company.

XXIV. The French text of the concession, in preference to the Persian text, is declared the one by which all difficulties shall be decided.

An additional Article stipulates that the 7 per cent. shall not be paid by the Government direct, but be taken from the proceeds of the customs, mines, forests, and water courses in case of need.

VI.

TREATY OF PEACE CONCLUDED BETWEEN GENERAL VON KAUFMANN AND THE KHAN OF KHIVA UNDER DATE AUGUST 25, 1873 :—

CLAUSE I.—Seid Muhammed Rachim Bahadur Khan professes himself the obedient servant of the Emperor of All the Russias. He renounces the right of entertaining direct relations with neighbouring sovereigns and Khans. He will neither conclude commercial nor any other treaties with these sovereigns and Khans, nor will he engage in hostile operations against them without the cognizance and sanction of the supreme Russian authorities in Central Asia.

CLAUSE II.—From Kukertli to the point where the most westerly branch of the Amu Darya leaves the main stream, that river is to form the frontier between the Russian and Khivese territories. Further down the frontier runs along the most westerly branch of the river to the shore of Lake Aral, then proceeds along the shore to the Promontory of Urgu and from the latter point follows the southern slope of the Ust Urt plateau along the so-called ancient bed of the Amu.

CLAUSE III.—All the land on the right bank of the Amu, as well as the territories belonging to it, and hitherto regarded as Khivese, with all inhabitants both sedentary and nomad, are ceded by the Khan to Russia. In this cession are included any districts which may have been conferred by the Khan upon private persons or dignitaries. The former proprietors of these districts shall be entitled to no indemnity from the Russian Government, but the Khan is at liberty to indemnify them by lands on the left bank of the Amu.

CLAUSE IV.—In the event of the Emperor of Russia surrendering a portion of the territory on the right bank of the Amu to the Khan of Bokhara, the Khan of Khiva will acknowledge the latter sovereign as the legitimate proprietor of the districts thus ceded, and will refrain from all attempts to restore his authority in these districts.

CLAUSE V.—Russian steamers and other ships, whether belonging to the Government or to private persons, will enjoy the right of free navigation on the Amu ; the said right will belong exclusively to the said ships. Khivese or Bokharese ships will be permitted to navigate the Amu only with the special sanction of the supreme Russian authorities in Central Asia.

CLAUSE VI.—The Russians will have the right of constructing harbours and piers at any points on the left bank of the Amu which they may regard as necessary or convenient for their purposes. The Government of the Khan of Khiva will be responsible for the security of these harbours and piers. In the event of any such points being selected by the Russians, the choice will require to be confirmed by the Russian supreme authorities in Central Asia.

CLAUSE VII.—Besides these harbours and piers, the Russians will be entitled to have factories and storehouses on the left bank of the Amu. Any lands near these factories which may be selected by the Russian supreme authorities in Central Asia will have to be given up by the Khivese Government. Such lands are to be unencumbered with any population, and to be sufficiently extensive to admit of the construction of harbours and piers, of magazines and offices, as also of dwelling-houses for those serving in the factories or having business there. It shall likewise be legal for the Russians to establish farms and carry on agriculture on these lands. The factories, with all their inhabitants, chattels, and merchandise are placed under the immediate protection of the Khan's Government, which will be responsible for their safety.

CLAUSE VIII.—All towns and villages of the Khanate of Khiva will henceforth be open to Russian trade. Russian caravans and merchants will be at liberty to travel in all parts of the Khanate, and will enjoy the direct and special protection of the local authorities. The Khivese Government will be responsible for the security of the caravans and stores.

CLAUSE IX.—Considering that Khivese merchants have never paid zakát on the Kasalinsk road, or at Orenburg and the Caspian ports, Russian merchants trading in the Khanate will be likewise exempt from the payment of the zaket or any other impost on trade levied in Khiva.

CLAUSE X.—The right of sending their goods across the Khanate free of any transit dues, is expressly accorded to Russian merchants.

CLAUSE XI.—For the better supervision of their trade, and the maintenance of direct relations with the local authorities, the Russian merchants will be entitled to keep agents in the town of Khiva, as well as in the other towns of the Khanate.

CLAUSE XII.—Russian subjects are accorded the right of possessing real property in the Khanate. Real property of this description may, with the sanction of the Russian supreme authorities in Central Asia, be subjected to the land tax.

CLAUSE XIII.—Commercial obligations mutually contracted by Russians and Khivese must be conscientiously fulfilled by both parties.

CLAUSE XIV.—Any complaints or claims against Khivese subjects preferred by Russian subjects will be inquired into at once by the Khivese Government, and if just, satisfied without delay. In the event of mutual claims being made on each other by Russian and Khivese subjects, the Russian claim shall be first inquired into and adjusted before the claim of the Khivese is proceeded with.

CLAUSE XV.—Any complaints or claims on Russian subjects living in the Khanate which may be preferred by Khivese, are to be inquired into and decided upon by the nearest Russian authorities.

CLAUSE XVI.—No persons arriving from Russia, whatever nationality they may belong to, will be admitted by the Khan's Government, within the Khivese frontiers unless provided with a Russian permit. Should a Russian criminal attempt to evade pursuit by hiding in the Khivese territory the Khan's Government will be obliged to take measures for his apprehension, and to deliver him to the nearest Russian authorities.

CLAUSE XVII.—The manifesto published on July 25, by Seid Muhammed Rachim Bahadur Khan, setting at liberty all slaves in the Khanate and abolishing for ever slavery and the traffic in human beings remains in full force, the Khan's Government expressly engaging with all its might to compel the strict and conscientious fulfilment of the provisions here detailed.

CLAUSE XVIII.—A fine of 2,200,000 roubles is hereby imposed upon the Khivese Government, to cover the expenses of the Russian Exchequer in the last war, kindled by the Khivese Government and people. Considering, however, the scarcity of ready money in the Khanate, and more especially in the coffers of the Government—considering also the difficulty the Government would have in paying the fine within a brief period—the Government is allowed the option to pay the sum exacted in instalments, with five per cent. interest thereon, on condition that in the first two years the Khivese Government is to pay 100,000 roubles annually, in the second two years 125,000 roubles annually in 1877 and 1878, 150,000 roubles each year after that, 175,000 roubles annually during the two succeeding years, and in the year 1881—that is, nine years hence— 200,000 roubles; and every succeeding year till the final liquidation of the debt, 200,000 roubles, at the very least. The instalments to be made in Russian "*billets de credit*" or in current Khivese coin, at the option of the Khivese Government, and the first instalment to be handed over on the 13th of December, 1873. To facilitate the payment of the first instalment, the Khan will be allowed to levy this year's taxes on the inhabitants of the right bank of the Amoo, the amount of these taxes being calculated in accordance with the existing standard of taxation, and the collection to cease on December 13, unless another date should be fixed by the local Russian and Khivese authorities. Subsequent instalments to be paid annually on November 13, till the final liquidation of capital and interest. In nineteen years after the payment of 200,000 roubles on November 13, 1892, there will remain still a rest of 70,054 roubles for the Government of the Khan to pay, and on November 13, 1893, he will have to pay the last 73,557 roubles.

Should the Khan's Government wish to shorten the term of payment, it will enjoy the right of making the annual instalments greater than fixed in the above.

All these stipulations have been laid down and accepted for constant guidance and conscientious fulfilment by the Governor-General of Turkistan, Adjutant-General Kaufmann, and by the Ruler of Khiva, Seid I. Muhammed Rachim Bahadur Khan, in the gardens of Gendemain, the site of the Russian camp at Khiva, on August 25, 1873, being the 1st day of the month of Radshab of the year 1290.

(Signature and seal)   VON KAUFMANN.

(Signature and seal)   SEID MUHAMMED RACHIM BAHADUR KHAN.

VII.

TEXT OF THE NEW RUSSIAN TREATY WITH THE AMEER OF BOKHARA, DATED SEPTEMBER 28, 1873.

CLAUSE I.—The frontiers between the possessions of His Imperial Majesty the Emperor of all the Russias, and His Worship the Ameer of Bokhárá remain unchanged.

The Khivese territory on the right bank of the Amoo having been embodied with the Russian Empire, the former frontier between Khiva and Bokhárá, from the Oasis of Kholat to Gugertli, is altered in this wise :—The possessions of the Ameer of Bokhárá are augmented by the addition to them of the lands between the former Khiva-Bokhárá frontier on the right bank of the Amoo, from Gugertli to Meschekli, and from Meschekli to the point where the former Khiva-Bokhárá frontier met the frontier of the Russian Empire.

CLAUSE II.—In consequence of the right bank of the Amoo being severed from Khiva, the caravan roads going from Bokhárá north to the Russian possessions, traverse Bokharese and Russian territory exclusively. The Russian and Bokharese Governments, each in its own territory, will watch over the safety of these caravan roads and the commerce along them.

CLAUSE III.—Russian steamers and other vessels, whether belonging to the Government or to private persons, will have the right to navigate without let or hindrance the Bokharese portion of the Amoo, equally with Bokharese ships.

CLAUSE IV.—Any locality on the Bokharese banks of the Amoo which the Russians may select for the construction of piers or storehouses may be used by them for this purpose, the Bokharese Government being responsible for the safety of the erections thus established. The final and definitive selection of these localities depends upon the supreme Russian authorities in Central Asia.

CLAUSE V.—All the towns and villages of the Khanate of Bokhárá will be open to Russian commerce. Russian merchants and caravans will be allowed to travel freely in the whole Khanate, and will enjoy the special protection of the local authorities. The safety of the Russian caravans on Bokhárese territory is expressly guaranteed by the Bokhárá Government.

CLAUSE VI.—On all merchandise belonging to Russian traders, whether imported from Russia to Bokhárá, or from Bokhárá to Russia, an *ad valorem* tax of $2\frac{1}{2}$ per cent. will be levied in Bokhárá. In the Russian province of Turkestan the goods mentioned in the preceding sentence are to pay a tax amounting to one-fortieth of their value. No other tax, duty, or impost whatsoever will be levied upon merchandise of the description mentioned.

CLAUSE VII.—Russian merchants will be entitled to send their goods through Bokhárá free of transit dues.

CLAUSE VIII.—Russian merchants will be entitled to have caravan-series for the storing of merchandise in all Bokhárese towns. The same right is accorded to the Bokhárese merchants in the towns of the province of Turkestan.

CLAUSE IX.—The better to direct the course of commerce, insure the levying of the above tax, and regulate their relations with the local authorities in mercantile matters, Russian merchants are accorded the right of keeping commercial agents in all towns of the Khanate. The same right is accorded to the Bokhárese merchants in the towns of the province of Turkestan.

CLAUSE X.—Commercial engagements between Russians and Bokhárese must be considered as sacred, and be unconditionally carried out by both parties. The Bokhárá Government promises to look after the honest fulfilment of commercial engagements, and the fair and conscientious conduct of commercial affairs generally.

CLAUSE XI.—Russian subjects will enjoy an equality of right with Bokhárese subjects in carrying on in Bokhárese territory all branches of industry and handicraft allowed by the law of Sharígat. A corresponding right is accorded to Bokhárese subjects on Russian territory, with regard to the exercise of all trades and handicrafts permitted by the Russian law.

CLAUSE XII.—Russian subjects are permitted to possess houses, gardens, arable land, and every species of real property in the Khanate, such property to be subject to the land-tax assessed on Bokhárese property. A corresponding privilege is accorded to Bokhárese subjects in the whole territory of the Russian Empire.

CLAUSE XIII.—Russian subjects are admitted to the Bokhárese territory when provided with permits signed by the Russian authorities. They may travel freely in the whole Khanate, and are placed under the special protection of the Bokhárese authorities.

CLAUSE XIV.—In no case will the Bokhárese Government receive on Bokhárá territory persons arriving from the Russian territory, whatever nationality they may belong to, unless provided with a special permit duly and satisfactorily signed by the Russian authorities. If criminals who are Russian subjects should take refuge on Bokhárese territory, they will be arrested by the Bokhárese authorities and delivered to the nearest Russian authorities.

CLAUSE XV.—With a view to the maintenance of direct and permanent relations with the supreme Russian authorities in Central Asia, the Ameer of Bokhárá will appoint one of his intimate counsellors to be his resident envoy and plenipotentiary at Tashkend. This plenipotentiary will live at Tashkend in the house and at the expense of the Ameer.

CLAUSE XVI.—If it chooses to do so, the Russian Government may keep a permanent representative at Bokhárá, attached to the person of his worship the Ameer. As the Ameer's representative at Tashkend, so the Russian plenipotentiary at Bokhárá will live in the house and at the expense of the Russian Government.

CLAUSE XVII.—To please the Emperor of all the Russias and enhance the future glory of His Imperial Majesty, His Worship the Ameer Seid Mustafar, of Bokhárá, has determined as follows :—The traffic in human beings, being contrary to the law which commands man to love his neighbour, is abolished for ever in the territory of the Khanate. In accordance with this resolve, the strictest injunctions will be given by the Ameer to all his Beys to enforce the new law, and special orders will be sent to all border towns where slaves are transported for sale from neighbouring countries that, should any such slaves be brought there they shall be taken from their owners and set at liberty without loss of time.

CLAUSE XVIII.—His Worship the Ameer Seíd Mustafa being sincerely desirous to strengthen and develope the amicable relations established five years for the benefit of Bokhárá, approves and accepts for his constant guidance the above 17 clauses, constituting an agreement relative to the friendship between Russia and Bokhárá. This agreement has been made out in two copies, each copy in the two languages—Russian and Turkish. In proof of his having sanctioned this agreement and accepted it for his own guidance, as well as for the guidance of his successors, the Ameer Seíd Mustafa has affixed to it his seal.

Done at Shaar on the 28th of September, 1873, A.D., being the 19th day of the month of Shayban of the year 1290, A.H.

VIII.

EXTRACTS FROM "NOTES ON KHIVA," READ BEFORE THE ROYAL GEOGRAPHICAL SOCIETY OF LONDON, MARCH 24, 1873.

(See "Times" March 25, 1873.)

I abstain from any speculations as to the immediate issue of the expedition. If the four columns, numbering 12,000 men, and having 40 pieces of artillery, concentrate in Khiva without mishap, the military success of the expedition is assured; but it is important to remember that the more complete this success may be, the more inevitably will Russia be lodged on the horns of a political dilemma. If, indeed, by the mere pressure of a powerful demonstration the Khan were brought to submit without a struggle, yielding to such terms as Russia might choose to impose in the interests of her policy, as well as of her commerce, then would she indeed have achieved a great result, honourable to herself and beneficial to humanity at large; but if hostilities once supervene, and after defeating the Uzbeg troops in two or three decisive engagements, she proceed to occupy the country, her difficulties will then commence. To retreat indeed, or to remain in the country, will be equally injurious. She has volunteered a declaration—and apparently in all honesty—that her object is a mere vindication of her honour, and that she has no intention to annex the country, or hold it as a conquered province; but she has not sufficiently considered, I think, that by thus evacuating the country after having once occupied and ruled it, she will lose far more than she gained before. Orientals can only explain such evacuations—and not altogether wrongly—as the result of weakness, and let me ask what effect such a serious blow to her prestige would be likely to have on the kindred communities of Tashkend and Samarcand? We have had ourselves bitter experience of thus trifling with Oriental feeling. Although we fully retrieved our Afghán disasters in 1842, and did not evacuate Cabul and Candahar till the whole country lay completely at our mercy, yet it is still generally believed throughout Asia that we were driven out of the country, and the Seikh invasion of India, and more remotely the great

Indian mutiny, were both attributable to the blow which our political credit thus sustained. In the same way the disgrace of a retreat from Khiva would obliterate all the glory of the advance, and hold out a most dangerous example to other subject races impatient of a foreign yoke.

But if this danger of a loss of prestige were patent to Russia, and induced her to disregard her promises in regard to evacuating Khiva, as cognate circumstances have induced her to forfeit her pledges for the restoration of Samarcand to Bokhárá, then, by remaining in the country, she would be committed to an enormous expenditure, as far as I can see, for no commensurate object, and she would seriously weaken, I think, her general political position in Central Asia. It is quite certain that Turkestán costs Russia half a million a year, and, considering the peculiar condition of Khiva, the impoverished state of the country, the paucity of inhabitants, and the difficulty of obtaining an immigrant population to supply the requirements of irrigation and agriculture, considering also the necessity of sustained vigilance against the Turcomans, and the expense of constructing and garrisoning forts and sinking wells in order to keep up the communication with the Caspian, I cannot suppose that Khiva could possibly be retained as a subject province at a less cost than Turkestán. What is there, then, to compensate Russia for throwing away a million a year, not to speak of the sacrifice of the lives of many thousand soldiers? Those, I believe, who wish her ill, would desire that she should hold on in this career of improvidence and territorial extension. Her friends would rather see her relegated to her old position on the northern border of the Kirghiz Steppe. At any rate, if she does advisedly maintain her position in Khiva and Turkestán, regardless of the burden which it entails on her finances, it will show the excessive value which she attaches to her commercial and political rivalry with England, and it will give some colour to the opinions of those who suspect her of important ulterior designs. For my own part, I will only say that though I should have preferred, in the interest of peace that Russia had not entered on a career of conquest along the Jaxartes and the Oxus, yet I see no reason at present to feel any anxiety about the advance towards India. Asia is large enough for both of us, and we may well pursue our respective paths and fulfil our respective missions, without jostling or jealousy. Our position in Asia is at present quiescent while hers is progressive. Our position improves daily in solidity, whilst hers becomes daily more insecure. We can, therefore, well afford to wait, forbearing but vigilant, and conscious that if real danger approaches at any time, we are strong enough to arrest and crush it.

IX.

CONDITIONS OF FREE TRADE PROPOSED BY GENERAL AIDE-DE-CAMP VON KAUFMANN TO YAKUB-BEK, CHIEF OF DJETY-SHAHR.

I. All Russian subjects, of whatsoever religion, shall have the right to proceed for purposes of trade to Djety-Shahr, and to all the localities and towns subjected to the Chief of Djety-Shahr, which they may desire to visit, in the same way as the inhabitants of Djety-Shahr have hitherto been and shall be in the future entitled to prosecute trade throughout the entire extent of the Russian Empire. The Honourable Chief of Djety-Shahr undertakes to keep a vigilant guard over the complete safety of Russian subjects within the limits of his territorial possessions, and also over that of their caravans, and in general over everything that may belong to them.

II. Russian merchants shall be entitled to have caravanseries, in which they *alone* shall be able to store their merchandise, in all the towns of Djety-Shahr in which they may desire to have them.

III. Russian merchants shall, if they desire it, have the right to have commercial agents (*caravan-bashis*) in all the towns of Djety-Shahr, whose business it is to watch over the regular courts of trade and over the legal imposition of customs dues. The merchants of Djety-Shahr shall enjoy the same privilege in the towns of Turkestan.

IV. All merchandise transported from Russia to Djety-Shahr, or from that province into Russia, shall be liable to a tax of $2\frac{1}{2}$ per cent. *ad valorem*. In every case this tax shall not exceed the rate of the tax taken from Mussulmans being subject to Djety-Shahr.

V. Russian merchants and their caravans shall be at liberty, with all freedom and security, to traverse the territories of Djety-Shahr in proceeding to countries conterminous with that province. Caravans from Djety-Shahr shall enjoy the same advantages for passing through territories belonging to Russia.

These conditions were sent from Tashkend on the 9th of April, 1872.

General von Kaufmann I., Governor General of Turkestan, signed the treaty and attached his seal to it.

In proof of his assent to these conditions, Mahommed Yakub, Chief of Djety-Shahr, attached his seal to them at Yangy-Shar on the 8th of June 1872.

X.

TREATY OF COMMERCE WITH THE AMIR OF KASHGAR.

Treaty between the British Government and His Highness the Ameer Mahommed Yakoob Khan, Ruler of the territory of Kashgar and Yarkund, his heirs and successors, executed on the one part by Thomas Douglas Forsyth, C.B., in virtue of full powers conferred on him in that behalf by His Excellency the Right Honourable Thomas George Baring, Baron Northbrook, of Stratton, and a Baronet, Member of the Privy Council of Her Most Gracious Majesty the Queen of Great Britain and Ireland, Grand Master of the Most Exalted Order of the Star of India, Viceroy and Governor General of India in Council, and on the other part by Syud Mahomed Khan Toorah, Member of the First Class of the Order of Medjidie, &c., in virtue of full powers conferred on him by His Highness.

Whereas it is deemed desirable to confirm and strengthen the good understanding which now subsists between the high contracting parties, and to promote commercial intercourse between their respective subjects, the following Articles have been agreed upon :—

ARTICLE I.—The high contracting parties engage that the subjects of each shall be at liberty to enter, reside in, trade with, and pass with their merchandise and property into and through all parts of the dominions of the other, and shall enjoy in such dominions all the privileges and advantages with respect to commerce, protection, or otherwise, which are or may be accorded to the subjects of such dominions, or to the subjects or citizens of the most favoured nation.

ARTICLE II.—Merchants of whatever nationality shall be at liberty to pass from the territories of the one contracting party to the territories of the other with their merchandise and property, at all times and by any route they please. No restriction shall be placed by either contracting party upon such freedom of transit, unless for urgent political reasons to be previously communicated to the other, and such restriction shall be withdrawn as soon as the necessity for it is over.

ARTICLE III.—European British subjects entering the dominions of His Highness the Ameer for purposes of trade or otherwise, must be provided with passports certifying to their nationality. Unless provided with such passports they shall not be deemed entitled to the benefit of this Treaty.

ARTICLE IV.—On goods imported into British India from territories of His Highness the Ameer by any route over the Himalayan passes which lie to the south of His Highness's dominions, the British Government engages to levy no import duties. On goods imported from India into the territories of His Highness the Ameer no import duty exceeding

2½ per cent. *ad valorem* shall be levied. Goods imported as above into the dominions of the contracting parties may, subject only to such excise regulations and duties, and to such municipal or town regulations and duties as may be applicable to such classes of goods generally, be freely sold by wholesale or retail, and transported from one place to another within British India, and within the dominions of His Highness the Ameer respectively.

ARTICLE V.—Merchandise imported from India into the territories of His Highness the Ameer will not be opened for examination till arrival at the place of consignment. If any disputes should arise as to the value of such goods, the Customs officer or other officer acting on the part of His Highness the Ameer shall be entitled to demand part of the goods, at the rate of one in 40, in lieu of the payment of duty. If the aforesaid officer should object to levy the duty by taking a portion of the goods, or if the goods should not admit of being so divided, then the point in dispute shall be referred to two competent persons, one chosen by the aforesaid officer, and the other by the importer, and a valuation of the goods shall be made, and if the referees shall differ in opinion they shall appoint an arbitrator, whose decision shall be final, and the duty shall be levied according to the value thus established.

ARTICLE VI.—The British Government shall be at liberty to appoint a representative at the Court of His Highness the Ameer, and to appoint commercial agents subordinate to him in any towns or places considered suitable within His Highness's territories. His Highness the Ameer shall be at liberty to appoint a representative with the Viceroy and Governor General of India, and to station commercial agents at any places in British India considered suitable. Such representatives shall be entitled to the rank and privileges accorded to ambassadors by the law of nations, and the agents shall be entitled to the privileges of Consuls of the most favoured nation.

ARTICLE VII.—British subjects shall be at liberty to purchase, sell, or hire land or houses or depôts for merchandise in the dominions of His Highness the Ameer, and the houses, depôts, or other premises of British subjects shall not be forcibly entered or searched without the consent of the occupier, unless with the cognizance of the British representative or agent, and in presence of a person deputed by him.

ARTICLE VIII.—The following arrangements are agreed to for the decision of civil suits and criminal cases within the territories of His Highness the Ameer in which British subjects are concerned :—

(*a.*) Civil suits in which both plaintiff and defendants are British subjects, and criminal cases in which both prosecutor and accused are British subjects, or in which the accused is a European British subject mentioned in the Third Article of this Treaty, shall be tried by the British representative, or one of his agents, in the presence of an agent appointed by His Highness the Ameer.

(*b.*) Civil suits, in which one party is a subject of His Highness the Ameer and the other party a British subject, shall be tried by the Courts of His Highness in the presence of the British representative, or one of his agents, or of a person appointed in that behalf by such representative or agent.

(*c.*) Criminal cases, in which either prosecutor or accused is a subject of His Highness the Ameer, shall, except as above otherwise provided, be tried by the Courts of His Highness in presence of the British representative, or of one of his agents, or of a person deputed by the British representative or by one of his agents.

(*d.*) Except as above otherwise provided, civil and criminal cases in which one party is a British subject and the other the subject of a Foreign Power, shall, if either of the parties is a Mahommedan, be tried in the Courts of His Highness. If neither party is a Mahommedan, the case may, with consent of the parties, be tried by the British representative, or one of his agents. In the absence of such consent, by the Courts of His Highness.

(*e.*) In any case disposed of by the Courts of His Highness the Ameer to which a British subject is party, it shall be competent to the British representative, if he considers that justice has not been done, to represent the matter to His Highness the Ameer, who may cause the case to be re-tried in some other Court, in the presence of the British representative, or of one of his agents, or of a person appointed in that behalf by such representative or agent.

ARTICLE IX.—The rights and privileges enjoyed within the dominions of His Highness the Ameer by British subjects under this Treaty shall extend to the subjects of all Princes and States in India in alliance with Her Majesty the Queen ; and if, with respect to any such Prince or State, any other provisions relating to this Treaty, or to other matters, should be considered desirable, they shall be negotiated through the British Government.

ARTICLE X.—Every affidavit and other legal document filed or deposited in any Court established in the respective dominions of the high contracting parties, or in the Court of the Joint Commissioners in Ladakh, may be proved by an authenticated copy, purporting either to be sealed with the seal of the Court to which the original document belongs, or in the event of such Court having no seal, to be signed by the Judge or by one of the Judges of the said Court.

ARTICLE XI.—When a British subject dies in the territory of His Highness the Ameer, his movable and immovable property situate therein shall be vested in his heir, executor, administrator, or other representative in interest, or (in the absence of such representative) in the representative of the British Government in the aforesaid territory. The person in whom such charge shall be so vested shall satisfy the claims outstanding against the deceased, and shall hold the surplus (if any) for distribution among those interested. The above provisions, *mutatis mutandis*, shall apply to the subjects of His Highness the Ameer who may die in British India.

ARTICLE XII.—If a British subject residing in the territories of His Highness the Ameer becomes unable to pay his debts, or fails to pay any debt within a reasonable time after being ordered to do so by any Court of Justice, the creditors of such insolvent shall be paid out of his goods and effects; but the British representative shall not refuse his good offices, if needs be, to ascertain if the insolvent has not left in India disposable property which might serve to satisfy the said creditors. The friendly stipulations in the present Article shall be reciprocally observed with regard to His Highness's subjects who trade in India under the protection of the laws.

This Treaty having this day been executed in duplicate, and confirmed by His Highness the Ameer, one copy shall, for the present, be left in the possession of His Highness, and the other, after confirmation by the Viceroy and Governor General of India, shall be delivered to His Highness within twelve months in exchange for the copy now retained by His Highness.

> Signed and sealed at Kashgar, on the 2nd day of February, in the year of our Lord 1874, corresponding with the 15th day of Zilhijj 1290 Hijri.
>
> (Signed) T. DOUGLAS FORSYTH,
> Envoy and Plenipotentiary.

Whereas a Treaty for strengthening the good understanding that now exists between the British Government and the Ruler of the Territory of Kashgar and Yarkund, and for promoting commercial intercourse between the two countries, was agreed upon and concluded at Kashgar on the 2nd day of February in the year of our Lord 1874, corresponding with the 15th day of Zilhijj 1290 Hijree, by the respective plenipotentiaries of the Government of India and of His Highness the Ameer of Kashgar and Yarkund duly accredited and empowered for that purpose. I, the Right Honourable Thomas George Baring, Baron Northbrook, of Stratton, &c., &c., Viceroy and Governor General of India, do hereby ratify and confirm the Treaty aforesaid.

> Given under my hand and seal at Government House in Calcutta, this 13th day of April, in the year of our Lord 1874.
>
> (Signed) NORTHBROOK.

INDEX.

ABBOTT.

Abbott, James, exceeds his instructions at Khiva, 153
Abu Rihán, an early Arab writer, 244
Afghán war, The, 56–59; frontier, negotiations with Russia concerning, 304, 310
Afghanistán, revolutions and counter-revolutions in, 187; present relations of England with, 348
———, or South-western section of Central Asia, 254
Ak-Mesjed on the Jaxartes taken by assault, 166
Alison, Mr., appointed to Teherán, 99
Amballa Conference, 296
Amír-Nizám, Prime Minister of Persia, 81; impartiality of his political conduct, 82; his downfall and death, 83
Aralsk, fort erected at, 160; steamers launched, 164
Arian civilization in Central Asia, 246
Army, Persian, training of, by English officers, 37, 49, 100, 288
Ashoor Ada, Russian naval arsenal at, 70, 137, *note*
Ataligh Gházi, 332; *see* Yacúb Beg
Atrek frontier, the Russians' claim to the, 118, 342, *note*

Badakhshán, Afghán possession of, disputed by Russia, 308; conceded, 311
Bahrein, island of, blockade, 109
Baker's, Col. Valentine, services to geography, 220
Bellew, Dr., "From the Indus to the Tigris," 363
Bokhárá, its standing army, 196; intensely hostile to Russia, 345; Russian treaty with, 379
——— and Cabul, close connection between, 277
Boutakoff, Adm., report of his ascent of the Jaxartes, 168
British policy in Central Asia after the Afghán war, review of, 178
Burckhardt, the most accomplished European Arab, 220

DOST MAHOMED.

Burnes, Sir A., prejudice against Persia, 45
Butenef, Col., head of the Russian mission to Bokhárá, 156, 209

Candahar gold field, 365
Cashmere and Thibet, south-east section of Central Asia, 251
Caspian, steady advance of Russia along, 341
Caucasus, rebellion in the, 68
——— with Turkestán, junction of the, 275
Central Asia, its geography, 205; German and Russian travellers in, 207–209; English and other travellers, 210–220; apocryphal travels, 221–231; native explorers, 231–235; general description of, 235; early civilization, 242; ethnological sketch, 247; political condition, 251; and considerations, 260
Central Asian commercial question, 197–200
Circassian nationality, extinction of, 264
Clarendon, Lord, correspondence with St. Petersburg, 299
Coal, found in large quantities in the Kara-tán and Ala-tán ranges, 193
Conolly, Arthur, sent to Bokhárá, 153; his execution, 157
———, Edward, shot in Cabul, 210

Danibeg, Raphael, journey from India to Semipolatinsk, 216
Danilevski, Col., concludes a direct treaty between Russia and Khiva, 159
D'Arcy Todd, killed at the battle of Firoz-shahar, 210
Dost Mahomed friendly to the Indian government, 45; concludes a treaty with England at Pesháwer, 88; appropriates Farrah, 100; death, 101

D D

East India, systems of government, quotation from Report on, 280
Ellis, Mr., sent on an embassy of condolence to Persia, 52
Ephraimoff's adventures in Central Asia, 215
Erzeroom, Conference at, 66

Farrah appropriated by Dost Mahomed Khan, 100; re-annexed to Herát by Sultan Ahmed Khan, 101
Ferrier, Gen., in Central Asia, 211
Ferrukh Khan sent to England on Mr. Murray's retirement, 93
Forbes, Dr., murdered at Seistán, 210
France, opening of relations with Persia, 18
Futteh Ali Shah, his campaign of 1799, 7; his second expedition, 9; treaty with the French, 16; death, 49

Gardanne, Gen., Minister at Teherán, 18
Gardiner, Col., "Travels in Central Asia," 221
George Ludwig, von ———, "Travels through Upper Asia," 224–231
Gladstone, Mr., speech of, on the Afghán and Russian question, 312
Gokchah, occupation of, by Russia, 39, 40
Goldsmid, Sir Fred., appointed to mediate between the Persians and Beloochees, 111; his Seistán arbitration, 112–116; services to geography, 220
Gortchakoff's, Prince, Circular, 173; see Manifesto
Grigorief's, M., letters published in the "Moscow Gazette," 270
Gulistan, Treaty of, 33

Hajee Mirza Aghassee, Prime Minister of Persia, 71; escapes the popular fury by taking sanctuary, 73
Haji Khalil Khan, his unfortunate death, 13, *note*
Herát, Persian expedition against, 47; siege raised, 57; our convention with Persia with regard to, 84, 85, 366; surrendered to Persia, 89; evacuated by the Persians, 92; natural advantages of, 362; to be protected against Russia at all risks, 365

Immigration, Scythian, 248; Turkish, 249

Iranians, the Eastern, founders of Central Asian civilization, 244, 247
Iskender Khan, 278
Issi-kul, or the "Warm Lake," 169; Armenian monastery on the north side, said to contain the body of St. Matthew, 169

James, Major, valuable report on the Kokand embassy, 234
Jaxartes, The, progress of the Russians up, 163; remarkable physical features, 168; affords great facilities for successful colonization, 193
Johnson's, Mr., report on Khoten, extract from, 214
Jones, Sir Harford, Envoy Extraordinary to Persia, 20; brief sketch of his remarkable career, 23; his "coup" and preliminary treaty, 24; Resident Minister at Teherán, 26

Kara Kalpáks, or "black bonnets," 162
Karrack, island of, occupation of, by British troops, 58; removal of, 65
Kashgar, the aim and limit of Russian commercial policy in Central Asia, 177; recognized by Russia as an independent state, 333; policy of England towards, 336; future Russian relations with, 347
Kaufmann's, Gen., occupation of Samarcand, 268; report on Afghán frontier, 309; conduct towards the Yomúts, 325
Kaye, "History of the Afghán War," quotation from, 201
Keane's, Lord, expedition to Cabul, 147, 359
Khanikoff, M., visit to Bokhárá, 156; to Herát, 184, 185; travels in Central Asia, 208
Khiva, expedition to, in 1839, translated by Mr. Michell, reviewed, 136; failure of, 151; Russian expedition against, in 1873; considered politically, 313, 321; treaty with, 319, 376; notes on, 382
Khojend, taken by the Russians, 259
Khorassan campaign, Abbas Mirza's in 1832, 46; rebellion in, crushed, 1851, 82
Kirghiz tribe, The, 249
Klaproth, suspected author of the Russo-German manuscript, 231
Kokand territory, invasion of the, by the Russians, 171; capture of Tur-

kestán and Chemkend, 172 ; present Chief of, 177, *note* ; present condition of, 346

Lawrence, Sir John, tribute to him, 190 ; his later Afghán policy, 293
Lomakin, Gen., strenuous efforts to withdraw the Yomúts and Goklans from their Persian allegiance, 341
Lumley's, Mr., report on Central Asian trade, 199
Lumsden's, Major, mission to Candahar, 92, 212, 285

Macdonald, Sir J., modification of the Teherán treaty by, 42
Macleod, Sir D., on the Maharájá of Cashmere, 279
Mahomed Shah, accession of, 49 ; forms an alliance with Russia, 53 ; death, 72
Mahomed Yussouf succeeds Said Mahomed at Herát, 88 ; hoists the English flag, 89 ; deposed and sent as prisoner to the Persian camp, 89
Malcolm, Sir John, his mission and treaty, 8, 9 ; prejudicial effect of his prodigality, 11 ; his fears of the French establishing themselves on the shores of the Persian Gulf, 12 ; nominated envoy to Persia by Lord Minto, 20 ; his discomfiture, 20 ; resumes his functions, 26
Manifesto, Prince Gortchakoff's Russian, explaining her Central-Asian policy, 161, 173, 265
Mayo's, Lord, Afghán policy, 294 ; conference at Amballa with Shír Alí Khán, 296 ; views on the "Neutral Zone," 301
McNeill, Sir J., "The Progress of Russia in the East," 4 ; sent to England, 52 ; returns to Persia with further supplies of arms, &c., 53 ; compelled by ill-health to leave, 65
Mehdi Alí Khan opens a correspondence with Teherán, 6
Menzikoff, Prince, his mission to Teherán, 39
Merv, great natural advantages of, 120, *note ;* position of, 307
Michel, Mr., "Expedition to Khiva," 145, 150 ; "Russians in Central Asia," 164 ; both reviewed in Chap. III.
Minto, Lord, appoints Malcolm envoy to Persia, 20 ; repudiates in anticipation Sir H. Jones's treaty, 26
Mír Izzet Ollah, itinerary of, 188, 232

Mirza Hussien Khan appointed Grand Vizier, 121 ; his enlightened policy, 122 ; accompanies the Shah to Europe, 124 ; his fall, and appointment as foreign minister, 132
Mirza Reza, ambassador to Napoleon, 16
Mirza Robat, skirmish at, between Russians and Uzbegs, 258
Mirza Shadi despatched to St. Petersburg, 330 ; sent to Calcutta, 331
Moutgomerie's, Capt., maps of Cashmere and Ladakh, 213
Murray, Mr., suspends relations with the Persian Court, 89

Nassar-ed-din, Mirza, Shah of Persia, accession of, 73 ; visits the European capitals, 124 ; disaffection and intrigues on his return, 131
Naval strength of Russia in the East, 141
"Neutral Zone," The, Lord Mayo's views on, 301

Orenburg and Siberian Lines, The, 138, *note*
Ouseley, Sir Gore, ambassador extraordinary to Teherán in 1811, 33
Oxus, The line of the, a national and political boundary, 305 ; negociations concerning, 305-313

Paris, Treaty of, with Russia, 90, 370
Pattinson, Lieut., murdered at Candahar, 210
Perofski's expedition against Khiva, 149 ; failure of, 151
Persia, opening of relations with, 1 ; gradually sinking before the power of Russia, 14 ; origin of French connexion, 15 ; want of system in the army, 31 ; failure in the improvement of her military resources, 37 ; summary of our relations with, 38, 41 ; state of, under Hajee Mirza Aghassee, 71 ; England declares war with, 89 ; her present condition, 132
Persian diplomacy, suggested reforms in our, 135, 289
Persian Gulf, British force in the, 61
Pesháwer, Treaty of, 88, 308
Policy, our future, towards Russia, 356-365
Pottinger, Lieut., at Herát, 59 ; dies of fever at Hong Kong, 211
Press agitation on the Eastern question, 52

Quetta, proposed establishment of a fortified post at, 291

Race, antagonism of, in Persia, 60
Raverty's, Capt., papers in the Calcutta Asiatic Journals, 233
Reuter Concession, The, 373; opposition of Russia, 125; annulled, 127; annulment not accepted by England, 340
Romanofski, Gen., takes Khojend, 266; *brochure* on the Central Asian question, 273; his views on the junction of the Caucasus with Turkestán, 274, 314
Romieu, Col., Envoy from Napoleon to Teherán, 15
Russia, successes in Persia, 14; gradual encroachments, 29; contemptuous bearing, 38; demands the payment of ten crores, 41; becomes the ally of Persia, 53; tries to effect a reconciliation between Engand and Persia, 64; reasons for her inactivity, 67; her interference more guarded, but not less progressive, 70; naval strength in the East, 141; extension of her territory, 141; her policy in Central Asia from the period of the Afghán War, 144; maintains her right to the Khanat of Khiva, 145; position of, in regard to the Uzbeg States in 1865, 191-197; probable position of, in Central Asia if unchecked by England, 275; present position of, in Central Asia, 338-348
Russians, The, expedition to Khiva, 118; found a military post at Chikeslar, 118; in Central Asia, article on, 136-204
Russophobia in 1838-39, 136; change to apathy in 1865, 142; causes of, 142, 143

Said Mahomed proffers his allegiance to the Shah, 84; deposed, 88
Sanders, Col., killed at battle of Maharajpoor, 211
Sartiges, Comte de, at Teherán, 72
Schlagentweit, the Brothers, 218
Scythian immigration, 248
Seistán, province of, conflicting claims to, by Persian and Afghán crowns, 102; England refuses to mediate, 103; General Goldsmid employed as arbitrator, 112; scheme of partition, 114; its political bearings, 115
Semenoff's report from the top of Záúkú Pass, extract from, 214
Shamil, Sheik, 69
Shakespeare, Richmond, his mission to Khiva, 154; releases the Russian prisoners, 154
Shaw, Mr., visits Yarkend in 1869, 330; again with Mr. Forsyth in 1870, 331; Envoy to Kashgar in 1874, 348
Shír Alí Khán succeeds to the crown of Cabul, 103; expelled from power, 254; recovers his position, 294; reception at Amballa, 296; defensive policy, 313; relations with England strained, 351
Steppe, The, operations of the Russians in, 160
Stoddart, Col., sent to Bokhárá, 152; his execution, 157; his travels in Central Asia, 210
Sultan Ahmed Khan assumes the government of Herát, 94, 184; recovers Farrah from Dost Mohamed, 101; death, 101
Sutherland's, Col., opinion of the Malcolm treaty, 10

Tabriz, Russian plan of a railway from the frontier to, 340
Tashkend, capture of, 176
Teherán, Treaty of, concluded by Messrs. Morier and Ellis, 34; modification of, by Sir J. Macdonald, 42; mission transferred to India Office, 96; restored to the Foreign Office, 98; Report of the Committee of the House of Commons on the subject, 98; further remarks, 289
Tchernaieff, Gen., sends four Russian officers to Bokhárá, 257
Telegraph, the Electric, in Persia, history of, 105
———— the Indo-European line, 107
Telegraphic convention, The, 106
Temple's, Sir R., Report on Systems of Government in East India, extract from, 281
Thomson, Dr. Thomas, the first Englishman who determined the geographical position of the Kara-Koram range, 218
———— Mr. R., despatch on the arrival of the first Russian detachment at Krasnovodsk, 322
Tilsit, Conference at, discussion of the Eastern question, 18
Toorks and Persians, antipathy between, 61
Trans-Caspian military government under General Lomakin, 327
Trans-Ili region, Russian occupation of the, 169

Treaty of commerce, English, with the Amír of Kashgar, 385

Treaty, Russian, with Bokhárá, 379; with Yacúb Beg, 384

Turcoman tents, number of, 323

Turcomans, expeditions of the Russians against, 119, 321-329

Turkestán, creation of the government of, 175; our unofficial relations with, 188

———— Eastern, or North-east section of Central Asia, 252; brief notice of, 329-338

———— Russian, or North-western section of Central Asia, 256

Turkish immigration, 249

Uzbegs, The, of Khiva, Russian grievances against, 149; of Kokand, appeal to Sir John Lawrence for assistance, 189

Vambéry, M., Travels in Central Asia, 219, 316

Vernoë, a Russian military agricultural colony for veteran soldiers, 169

Vitkevitch, the Russian emissary, 148

Weller's map of Persia, Afghanistán, and Beloochistan, 300, 304

Wellesley's, Marquis of, administration in India, 5, 8

Wood, Lieut., journey from Cabul to the sources of the Oxus, 219

Yacúb Beg, of Kashgar, 330; his independence acknowledged by Russia, 332; granted by the Sultan the title of "Commander of the Faithful," 333; his variable policy, 337; friendship with Russia, 347

Yar Mohamed Khan, his death, 84

Zeman, Shah, hostility of, 6

THE END.

BRADBURY, AGNEW, & CO., PRINTERS, WHITEFRIARS.

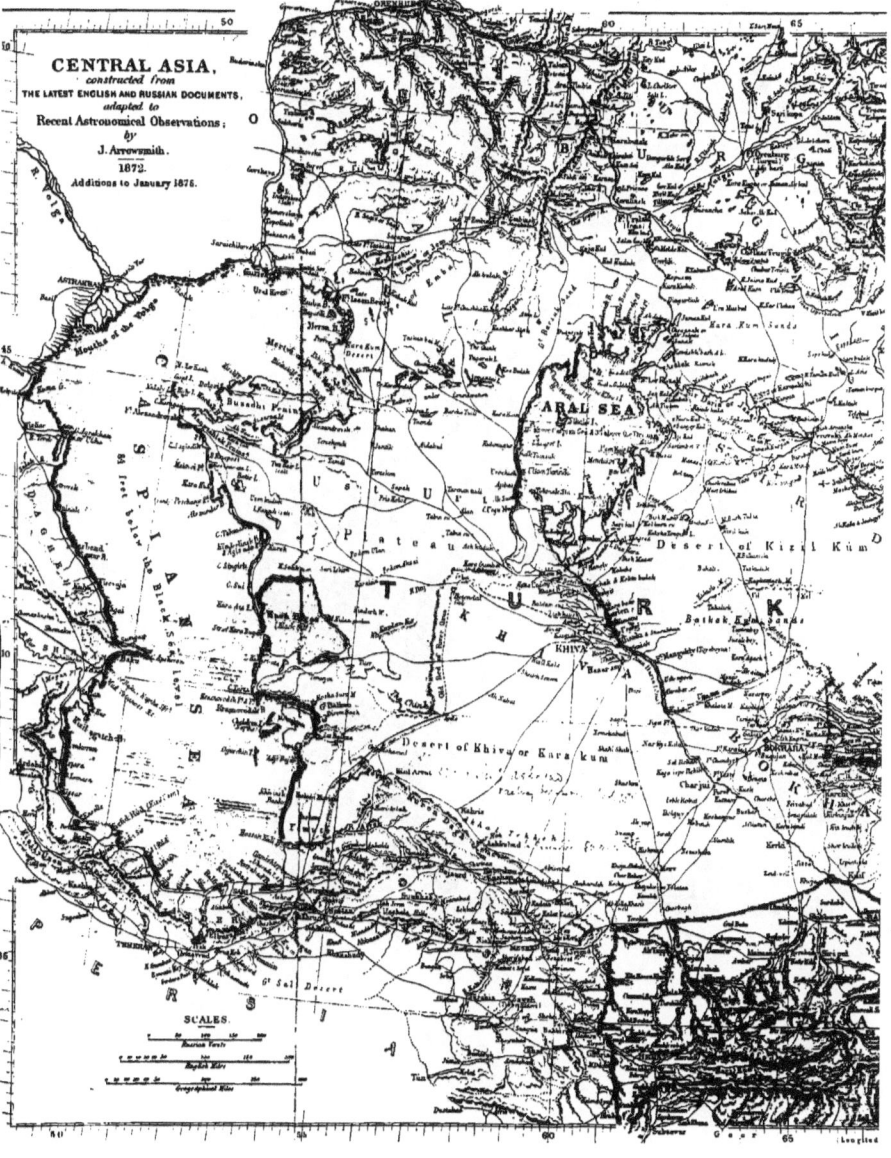

RECENT TRAVELS.

THE LAST JOURNALS OF DAVID LIVINGSTONE

in CENTRAL AFRICA from 1865 to within a FEW DAYS OF HIS DEATH. Continued by a NARRATIVE of his LAST MOMENTS and SUFFERINGS, obtained from his faithful servants, CHUMAH and SUSI. By HORACE WALLER, F.R.G.S., Rector of Twywell, Northampton. With Portrait, 2 Maps, and 44 Illustrations, 2 vols., 8vo, 28s.

"The last journals of David Livingstone have come before us like a voice from the dead. The fidelity of a small portion of his people has enabled us to bury his withered remains in Westminster Abbey, and has saved to the world the record of his labours. There is no British name more widely known, or more universally respected, than that of Livingstone. The greatest among African travellers, he has shown a persistence and devotion to his work which has not only upheld the reputation of his country throughout the world, but has infused a new spirit into African exploration, and by his high example he has stimulated others to follow upon the same course, which will eventually result in the opening of that hitherto mysterious region."—*Sir Samuel Baker.*

TROY AND ITS REMAINS.—A NARRATIVE OF DISCOVERIES AND RESEARCHES MADE ON THE SITE OF ILIUM AND IN THE TROJAN PLAIN. By DR. HENRY SCHLIEMANN, Translated with the Author's Sanction and Co-operation. Edited by PHILIP SMITH, B.A., with Maps, Plans, Views, and 500 Illustrations of Objects of Antiquity, &c., Royal 8vo.

"It is questionable if any archæological discovery of greater interest was ever made than that which Dr. Schliemann has accomplished. Our interest in Nineveh and Babylon pales before that which we feel in Troy. Dr. Schliemann has rescued the City of Priam from the iconoclasts. He has brought to light courts and walls and palaces; he has discovered over one hundred thousand objects of antiquity, including shields, gold cups, some sixty gold ear-rings, and half a dozen gold bracelets."—*Standard.*

TRAVELS OF A PIONEER OF COMMERCE ON AN OVERLAND JOURNEY FROM CHINA TOWARDS INDIA. By T. T. COOPER, late Agent for the Chamber of Commerce at Calcutta. With Maps and Illustrations, 8vo, 16s.

"Mr. Cooper made an attempt to traverse the unknown region between the Chinese province Szechuen and Assam, but was turned back by the Chinese authorities at Bathang, after making a successful journey up the Yang-tse and Taitow-ho rivers, and through the frontier town of Tai-tsian-loo. He then endeavoured to cross to Burmah *via* Yunnan, but found this also impracticable. His narrative is one of those racy descriptions of exciting adventure which we can only look for from men of high pluck, and not too often from them. His narrative illustrates Marco Polo's story."—*Quarterly Review.*

A JOURNEY TO THE SOURCE OF THE RIVER OXUS, BY THE INDUS, KABUL, AND BADAKHSHAN. By CAPTAIN JOHN WOOD (Indian Navy). A new Edition with an Essay on the Geography of the Valley of the Oxus. By COL. YULE, C.B., Editor of "Marco Polo." New Edition, with Map, 8vo, 12s.

"Captain Wood accompanied Alexander Burnes in his mission to Cabool, and afterwards performed one of the most remarkable journeys ever undertaken in Central Asia. He made a survey of the Indus, from its mouth to Attock. After reaching Cabool, he crossed the mountains to Khunduz, and was eventually the first European, after Marco Polo and Benedict Goës, who ever reached the Bam-i-dunya, or Roof of the World. Captain Wood's narrative presents the most brilliant confirmation in detail of Marco Polo's descriptions."—*Quarterly Review.*

RECENT TRAVELS.

THE BOOK OF SER MARCO POLO, THE VENETIAN.
Concerning the KINGDOMS AND MARVELS OF THE EAST. A new English Version. Illustrated by the light of Oriental Writers and Modern Travels. By COL. HENRY YULE, C.B., late Royal Engineers (Bengal). With Maps and Illustrations, 2 vols., Medium 8vo, 42s.

"The book of Marco Polo is one which can never lose its interest and its value. It brought the West into some contact with the East at a time when it had only the memory of the Crusades to make the confusion of its ignorance of these unknown regions worse confounded. It impressed on the European imagination the notion of the boundless wealth of those distant lands, and the idea that they might be reached by sailing westwards from the shores of Europe led directly to the discoveries of Columbus, who lighted on a new continent, although he died in the firm belief that he had reached the coasts of Cathay. More than this, it weakened the traditions of internecine hatred by associations of peaceful and profitable trade."—*Saturday Review.*

TRAVELS IN THE EASTERN CAUCASUS, ON
THE CASPIAN AND BLACK SEAS, especially in DAGHESTAN AND ON THE FRONTIER OF PERSIA AND TURKEY. By LIEUT.-GEN. SIR ARTHUR CUNYNGHAME, K.C.B., F.R.G.S., with Map and Illustrations, 8vo, 18s.

"This book contains descriptions of the new Russian fortifications on the Black Sea and elsewhere, of Sebastopol and the Crimean fields in their present condition, and of the scenes of Schamyl's patriotic resistance to the Russians. Much in reference to these matters is worth reading, in connection with the talk of Russian advances towards India, in which apparently, the author does not believe. His descriptions of the great Eastern cities, Tiflis, Astrakan, Bucharest, &c., are interesting, as are also his remarks on the condition and disposition of the various races with whom he came in contact—Roumanians, Turks, Russians, Cossacks, and Georgians."—*Scotsman.*

TRAVELS IN CENTRAL ASIA, from TEHERAN
across the TURKOMAN DESERT to KHIVA, BOKHARA, and SAMARCAND. By ARMINIUS VAMBÉRY, Member of the Hungarian Academy of Pesth. With Map and Illustrations, 8vo, 16s.

"A more perilous undertaking in the interest of science was, perhaps, never entered on. The very names of Khiva, Bokhara, and Samarcand are so associated with danger and difficulty, that no European who is not prepared to take his life in his hand can venture to visit them."—*Westminster Review.*

NEW JAPAN; THE LAND of the RISING SUN;
its ANNALS and PROGRESS during the past TWENTY YEARS, recording the remarkable PROGRESS of the JAPANESE in WESTERN CIVILIZATION. By SAMUEL MOSSMAN, Author of "China, its History and Inhabitants." With Map, 8vo, 15s.

Nearly Ready, 2 vols., Post 8vo.

THE CAUCASUS, PERSIA, AND TURKEY IN ASIA;
A JOURNEY THROUGH THE CAUCASUS TO TABREEZ, KURDISTAN, DOWN THE TIGRIS AND EUPHRATES TO NINEVEH AND BABYLON, AND ACROSS THE DESERT TO PALMYRA. By BARON MAX VON THIELMANN. Translated by CHARLES HENEAGE, of Her Majesty's Diplomatic Service.

JOHN MURRAY, ALBEMARLE STREET.

ALBEMARLE STREET, LONDON,
January, 1875.

MR. MURRAY'S

GENERAL LIST OF WORKS.

ALBERT (THE) MEMORIAL. A Descriptive and Illustrated Account of the National Monument erected to the PRINCE CONSORT at Kensington. Illustrated by Engravings of its Architecture, Decorations, Sculptured Groups, Statues, Mosaics, Metalwork, &c. With Descriptive Text. By DOYNE C. BELL. With 24 Plates. Folio. 12l. 12s.

——— (PRINCE) SPEECHES AND ADDRESSES with an Introduction, giving some outline of his Character. With Portrait. 8vo. 10s. 6d.; or *Popular Edition*, fcap. 8vo. 1s.

ABBOTT'S (REV. J.) Memoirs of a Church of England Missionary in the North American Colonies. Post 8vo. 2s.

ABERCROMBIE'S (JOHN) Enquiries concerning the Intellectual Powers and the Investigation of Truth. 19th Edition. Fcap. 8vo. 3s. 6d.

——— Philosophy of the Moral Feelings. 14th Edition. Fcap. 8vo. 2s. 6d.

ACLAND'S (REV. CHARLES) Popular Account of the Manners and Customs of India. Post 8vo. 2s.

ÆSOP'S FABLES. A New Version. With Historical Preface. By Rev. THOMAS JAMES. With 100 Woodcuts, by TENNIEL and WOLF. 64th Thousand. Post 8vo. 2s. 6d.

AGRICULTURAL (ROYAL) JOURNAL. (*Published half yearly.*)

AIDS TO FAITH: a Series of Theological Essays. 8vo. 9s.

CONTENTS.

Miracles	DEAN MANSEL.
Evidences of Christianity	BISHOP FITZGERALD.
Prophecy & Mosaic Record of Creation.	Dr. MCCAUL.
Ideology and Subscription	Canon COOK.
The Pentateuch	CANON RAWLINSON.
Inspiration	BISHOP HAROLD BROWNE.
Death of Christ	ARCHBISHOP THOMSON.
Scripture and its Interpretation	BISHOP ELLICOTT.

AMBER-WITCH (THE). A most interesting Trial for Witchcraft. Translated by LADY DUFF GORDON. Post 8vo. 2s.

ARMY LIST (THE). *Published Monthly by Authority.*

ARTHUR'S (LITTLE) History of England. By LADY CALLCOTT. *New and Cheaper Edition*, continued to 1872. With 36 Woodcuts. Fcap. 8vo. 1s. 6d.

AUSTIN'S (JOHN) LECTURES ON GENERAL JURISPRUDENCE; or, the Philosophy of Positive Law. 5th Edition. Edited by ROBERT CAMPBELL. 2 Vols. 8vo. 32s.

——— Student's Edition, compiled from the above work. By ROBERT CAMPBELL. Post 8vo.

ARNOLD'S (THOS.) Ecclesiastical and Secular Architecture of Scotland: The Abbeys, Churches, Castles, and Mansions. With Illustrations. Medium 8vo. [*In Preparation.*

B

LIST OF WORKS

ADMIRALTY PUBLICATIONS; Issued by direction of the Lords Commissioners of the Admiralty:—

A MANUAL OF SCIENTIFIC ENQUIRY, for the Use of Travellers. Edited by Sir JOHN F. HERSCHEL and ROBERT MAIN, M.A. *Fourth Edition.* Woodcuts. Post 8vo. 3s. 6d.

GREENWICH ASTRONOMICAL OBSERVATIONS 1841 to 1846, and 1847 to 1871. Royal 4to. 20s. each.

MAGNETICAL AND METEOROLOGICAL OBSERVATIONS. 1840 to 1847. Royal 4to. 20s. each.

APPENDICES TO OBSERVATIONS.
    1837. Logarithms of Sines and Cosines in Time. 3s.
    1842. Catalogue of 1439 Stars, from Observations made in 1836 to 1841. 4s.
    1845. Longitude of Valentia (Chronometrical). 3s.
    1847. Description of Altazimuth. 3s.
    Twelve Years' Catalogue of Stars, from Observations made in 1836 to 1847. 4s.
    Description of Photographic Apparatus. 2s.
    1851. Maskelyne's Ledger of Stars. 3s.
    1852. I. Description of the Transit Circle. 3s.
    1853. Refraction Tables. 3s.
    1854. Description of the Zenith Tube. 3s.
    Six Years' Catalogue of Stars, from Observations. 1848 to 1853. 4s.
    1862. Seven Years' Catalogue of Stars, from Observations. 1854 to 1860. 10s.
    Plan of Ground Buildings. 3s.
    Longitude of Valentia (Galvanic). 2s.
    1864. Moon's Semid. from Occultations. 2s.
    Planetary Observations, 1831 to 1835. 2s.
    1868. Corrections of Elements of Jupiter and Saturn. 2s.
    Second Seven Years' Catalogue of 2760 Stars for 1861 to 1867. 4s.
    Description of the Great Equatorial. 3s.
    1856. Descriptive Chronograph. 3s.
    1860. Reduction of Deep Thermometer Observations. 2s.
    1871. History and Description of Water Telescope. 3s.

Cape of Good Hope Observations (Star Ledgers). 1856 to 1863. 2s.
——————————— 1856. 5s.
——————————— Astronomical Results. 1857 to 1858. 5s.
Report on Teneriffe Astronomical Experiment. 1858. 5s.
Paramatta Catalogue of 7385 Stars. 1822 to 1826. 4s.

ASTRONOMICAL RESULTS. 1847 to 1871. 4to. 3s. each.

MAGNETICAL AND METEOROLOGICAL RESULTS. 1847 to 1871. 4to. 3s. each.

REDUCTION OF THE OBSERVATIONS OF PLANETS. 1750 to 1830. Royal 4to. 20s. each.

——————————— LUNAR OBSERVATIONS. 1750 to 1830. 2 Vols. Royal 4to. 20s. each.
——————————— 1831 to 1851. 4to. 10s. each.

BERNOULLI'S SEXCENTENARY TABLE. 1779. 4to. 5s.

BESSEL'S AUXILIARY TABLES FOR HIS METHOD OF CLEARING LUNAR DISTANCES. 8vo. 2s.

ENCKE'S BERLINER JAHRBUCH, for 1830. *Berlin,* 1828. 8vo. 9s.

HANSEN'S TABLES DE LA LUNE. 4to. 20s.

LAX'S TABLES FOR FINDING THE LATITUDE AND LONGITUDE. 1821. 8vo. 10s.

ADMIRALTY PUBLICATIONS—continued.

LUNAR OBSERVATIONS at GREENWICH. 1783 to 1819. Compared with the Tables,.1821. 4to. 7s. 6d.

MACLEAR ON LACAILLE'S ARC OF MERIDIAN. 2 Vols. 20s. each·

MAYER'S DISTANCES of the MOON'S CENTRE from the PLANETS. 1822, 3s.; 1823, 4s. 6d. 1824 to 1835. 8vo. 4s. each.

———— TABULÆ MOTUUM SOLIS ET LUNÆ. 1770. 5s.

———— ASTRONOMICAL OBSERVATIONS MADE AT GOTTINGEN, from 1756 to 1761. 1826. Folio. 7s. 6d.

NAUTICAL ALMANACS, from 1767 to 1877. 2s. 6d. each.

———————— SELECTIONS FROM, up to 1812. 8vo. 5s. 1834-54. 5s.

———————— SUPPLEMENTS, 1828 to 1833, 1837 and 1838. 2s. each.

———————— TABLE requisite to be used with the N.A. 1781. 8vo. 5s.

SABINE'S PENDULUM EXPERIMENTS to Determine the Figure of the Earth. 1825. 4to. 40s.

SHEPHERD'S TABLES for Correcting Lunar Distances. 1772. Royal 4to. 21s.

———— TABLES, GENERAL, of the MOON'S DISTANCE from the SUN, and 10 STARS. 1787. Folio. 5s. 6d.

TAYLOR'S SEXAGESIMAL TABLE. 1780. 4to. 15s.

———— TABLES OF LOGARITHMS. 4to. 60s.

TIARK'S ASTRONOMICAL OBSERVATIONS for the Longitude of Madeira. 1822. 4to. 5s.

———— CHRONOMETRICAL OBSERVATIONS for Differences of Longitude between Dover, Portsmouth, and Falmouth. 1823. 4to. 5s.

VENUS and JUPITER: Observations of, compared with the Tables. London, 1822. 4to. 2s.

WALES' AND BAYLY'S ASTRONOMICAL OBSERVATIONS. 1777. 4to. 21s.

———— REDUCTION OF ASTRONOMICAL OBSERVATIONS made in the Southern Hemisphere. 1764–1771. 1788. 4to. 10s. 6d.

BARBAULD'S (Mrs.) Hymns in Prose for Children. With 112 Illustrations. Crown 8vo. 5s.

BARROW'S (Sir John) Autobiographical Memoir, from Early Life to Advanced Age. Portrait. 8vo. 16s.

———— (John) Life, Exploits, and Voyages of Sir Francis Drake. Post 8vo. 2s.

BARRY'S (Sir Charles) Life and Works. By Canon Barry. Second Edition. With Portrait and Illustrations. Medium 8vo. 15s.

BATES' (H. W.) Records of a Naturalist on the River Amazon during eleven years of Adventure and Travel. Third Edition. Illustrations. Post 8vo. 7s. 6d.

BEAUCLERK'S (Lady Diana) Summer and Winter in Norway. Third Edition. With Illustrations. Small 8vo. 6s.

BELCHER'S (Lady) Account of the Mutineers of the 'Bounty,' and their Descendants; with their Settlements in Pitcairn and Norfolk Islands. With Illustrations. Post 8vo. 12s.

BELL'S (Sir Chas.) Familiar Letters. Portrait. Post 8vo. 12s.

LIST OF WORKS

BELT'S (THOS.) Naturalist in Nicaragua, including a Residence at the Gold Mines of Chontales; with Journeys in the Savannahs and Forests; and Observations on Animals and Plants. Illustrations. Post 8vo. 12s.

BERTRAM'S (JAS. G.) Harvest of the Sea: an Account of British Food Fishes, including sketches of Fisheries and Fisher Folk. *Third Edition.* With 50 Illustrations. 8vo. 9s.

BIBLE COMMENTARY. EXPLANATORY and CRITICAL. With a REVISION of the TRANSLATION. By BISHOPS and CLERGY of the ANGLICAN CHURCH. Edited by F. C. COOK, M.A., Canon of Exeter. Medium 8vo. VOL. I., 30s. VOLS. II. and III., 36s. VOL. IV., 24s.

Vol. I. { GENESIS	Bishop of Ely.
EXODUS	Canon Cook; Rev. Sam. Clark.
LEVITICUS	Rev. Samuel Clark.
NUMBERS	Canon Espin; Rev. J. F. Thrupp.
Vols. II. and III. { DEUTERONOMY	} Canon Espin.
JOSHUA	
JUDGES, RUTH, SAMUEL.	Bishop of Bath and Wells.
KINGS, CHRONICLES, EZRA, NEHEMIAH, ESTHER	} Canon Rawlinson.
Vol. IV. { JOB	Canon Cook.
PSALMS	{ Dean of Wells, Canon Cook; Rev. C. I. Elliott.
PROVERBS	Rev. E. H. Plumptre.
ECCLESIASTES	Rev. W. T. Bullock.
SONG OF SOLOMON	Rev. T. Kingsbury.
Vol. V. { ISAIAH	Rev. W. Kay, D.D.
JEREMIAH	Dean of Canterbury.

BICKMORE'S (A. S.) Travels in the Eastern Archipelago, 1865-6; a Popular Description of the Islands, with their Natural History, Geography, Manners and Customs of the People, &c. With Maps and Illustrations. 8vo. 21s.

BIRCH'S (SAMUEL) History of Ancient Pottery and Porcelain: Egyptian, Assyrian, Greek, Roman, and Etruscan. *Second Edition.* With Coloured Plates and 200 Illustrations. Medium 8vo. 42s.

BIRD'S (ISABELLA) Hawaiian Archipelago; or Six Months Among the Palm Groves, Coral Reefs, and Volcanoes of the Sandwich Islands. With Illustrations. Crown 8vo.

BISSET'S (ANDREW) History of the Commonwealth of England, from the Death of Charles I. to the Expulsion of the Long Parliament by Cromwell. Chiefly from the MSS. in the State Paper Office. 2 vols. 8vo. 30s.

BLUNT'S (REV. J. J.) Undesigned Coincidences in the Writings of the Old and New Testament, an Argument of their Veracity: containing the Books of Moses, Historical and Prophetical Scriptures, and the Gospels and Acts. *Eleventh Edition.* Post 8vo. 6s.

—— History of the Church in the First Three Centuries. *Fifth Edition.* Post 8vo. 6s.

—— Parish Priest; His Duties, Acquirements and Obligations. *Sixth Edition.* Post 8vo. 6s.

—— Lectures on the Right Use of the Early Fathers. *Third Edition.* 8vo. 9s.

—— University Sermons. *Second Edition.* Post 8vo. 6s.

—— Plain Sermons. *Sixth Edition.* 2 vols. Post 8vo. 12s.

BLOMFIELD'S (BISHOP) Memoir, with Selections from his Correspondence. By his Son. *Second Edition.* Portrait, post 8vo. 12s.

BOSWELL'S (JAMES) Life of Samuel Johnson, LL.D. Including the Tour to the Hebrides. By Mr. CROKER. *A new and revised Library Edition.* Portraits. 4 vols. 8vo. [*In Preparation.*

BRACE'S (C. L.) Manual of Ethnology; or the Races of the Old World. Post 8vo. 6s.
BOOK OF COMMON PRAYER. Illustrated with Coloured Borders, Initial Letters, and Woodcuts. 8vo. 18s.
BORROW'S (GEORGE) Bible in Spain; or the Journeys, Adventures, and Imprisonments of an Englishman in an Attempt to circulate the Scriptures in the Peninsula. Post 8vo. 5s.
——— Zincali, or the Gypsies of Spain; their Manners, Customs, Religion, and Language. With Portrait. Post 8vo. 5s.
——— Lavengro; The Scholar—The Gypsy—and the Priest. Post 8vo. 5s.
——— Romany Rye—a Sequel to "Lavengro." Post 8vo. 5s.
——— WILD WALES: its People, Language, and Scenery. Post 8vo. 5s.
——— Romano Lavo-Lil; Word-Book of the Romany, or English Gypsy Language; with Specimens of their Poetry, and an account of certain Gypsyries. Post 8vo. 10s. 6d.
BRAY'S (MRS.) Life of Thomas Stothard, R.A. With Portrait and 60 Woodcuts. 4to. 21s.
——— Revolt of the Protestants in the Cevennes. With some Account of the Huguenots in the Seventeenth Century. Post 8vo. 10s. 6d.
BRITISH ASSOCIATION REPORTS. 8vo.

York and Oxford, 1831-32, 13s. 6d.
Cambridge, 1833, 12s.
Edinburgh, 1834, 15s.
Dublin, 1835, 13s. 6d.
Bristol, 1836, 12s.
Liverpool, 1837, 16s. 6d.
Newcastle, 1838, 15s.
Birmingham, 1839, 13s. 6d.
Glasgow, 1840, 15s.
Plymouth, 1841, 13s. 6d.
Manchester, 1842, 10s. 6d.
Cork, 1843, 12s.
York, 1844, 20s.
Cambridge, 1845, 12s.
Southampton, 1846, 15s.
Oxford, 1847, 18s.
Swansea, 1848, 9s.
Birmingham, 1849, 10s.
Edinburgh, 1850, 15s.
Ipswich, 1851, 16s. 6d.
Belfast, 1852, 15s.
Hull, 1853, 10s. 6d.
Liverpool, 1854, 18s.
Glasgow, 1855, 15s.
Cheltenham, 1856, 18s.
Dublin, 1857, 15s.
Leeds, 1858, 20s.
Aberdeen, 1859, 15s.
Oxford, 1860, 25s.
Manchester, 1861, 15s.
Cambridge, 1862, 20s.
Newcastle, 1863, 25s.
Bath, 1864, 18s.
Birmingham, 1865, 25s.
Nottingham, 1866, 24s.
Dundee, 1867, 26s.
Norwich, 1868, 25s.
Exeter, 1869, 22s.
Liverpool, 1870, 18s.
Edinburgh, 1871, 16s.
Brighton, 1872, 24s.
Bradford, 1873, 25s.

BROUGHTON'S (LORD) Journey through Albania, Turkey in Europe and Asia, to Constantinople. Illustrations. 2 Vols. 8vo. 30s.
——— Visits to Italy. 2 Vols. Post 8vo. 18s.
BROWNLOW'S (LADY) Reminiscences of a Septuagenarian. From the year 1802 to 1815. Third Edition. Post 8vo. 7s. 6d.
BRUGSCH'S (PROFESSOR) History of Ancient Egypt. Derived from Monuments and Inscriptions. New Edition. Translated by H. DANBY SEYMOUR. 8vo. [In Preparation.
BURGON'S (REV. J. W.) Christian Gentleman; or, Memoir of Patrick Fraser Tytler. Second Edition. Post 8vo. 9s.
——— Letters from Rome. Post 8vo. 12s.
BURN'S (COL.) Dictionary of Naval and Military Technical Terms, English and French—French and English. Fourth Edition. Crown 8vo. 15s.
BURROW'S (MONTAGU) Constitutional Progress. A Series of Lectures delivered before the University of Oxford. 2nd Edition. Post 8vo. 5s.

BUXTON'S (CHARLES) Memoirs of Sir Thomas Fowell Buxton, Bart. With Selections from his Correspondence. Portrait. 8vo. 16s.
Popular Edition. Fcap. 8vo. 5s.
——— Notes of Thought. With Biographical Sketch. By Rev. LLEWELLYN DAVIES. With Portrait. Crown 8vo. 10s. 6d.

BURCKHARDT'S (DR. JACOB) Cicerone; or Art Guide to Painting in Italy. Edited by REV. DR. A. VON ZAHN, and Translated from the German by MRS. A. CLOUGH. Post 8vo. 6s.

BYLES' (SIR JOHN) Foundations of Religion in the Mind and Heart of Man. Post 8vo. [*Nearly ready.*

BYRON'S (LORD) Life, Letters, and Journals. By THOMAS MOORE. *Cabinet Edition.* Plates. 6 Vols. Fcap. 8vo. 18s.; or One Volume, Portraits. Royal 8vo., 7s. 6d.
——— ——— and Poetical Works. *Popular Edition.* Portraits. 2 vols. Royal 8vo. 15s.
——— Poetical Works. *Library Edition.* Portrait. 6 Vols. 8vo. 45s.
——— ——— *Cabinet Edition.* Plates. 10 Vols. 12mo. 30s.
——— ——— *Pocket Edition.* 8 Vols. 24mo. 21s. *In a case.*
——— ——— *Popular Edition.* Plates. Royal 8vo. 7s. 6d.
——— ——— *Pearl Edition.* Crown 8vo. 2s. 6d.
——— ——— Childe Harold. With 80 Engravings. Crown 8vo. 12s.
——— ——————————— 16mo. 2s. 6d.
——— ——————————— Vignettes. 16mo. 1s.
——— ——————————— Portrait. 16mo. 6d.
——— Tales and Poems. 24mo. 2s. 6d.
——— Miscellaneous. 2 Vols. 24mo. 5s.
——— Dramas and Plays. 2 Vols. 24mo. 5s.
——— Don Juan and Beppo. 2 Vols. 24mo. 5s.
——— Beauties. Poetry and Prose. Portrait. Fcap. 8vo. 3s. 6d.

BUTTMAN'S LEXILOGUS; a Critical Examination of the Meaning of numerous Greek Words, chiefly in Homer and Hesiod. By Rev. J. R. FISHLAKE. *Fifth Edition.* 8vo. 12s.
——— IRREGULAR GREEK VERBS. With all the Tenses extant—their Formation, Meaning, and Usage, with Notes, by Rev. J. R. FISHLAKE. *Fifth Edition.* Post 8vo. 6s.

CALLCOTT'S (LADY) Little Arthur's History of England. *New and Cheaper Edition, brought down to 1872.* With Woodcuts. Fcap. 8vo. 1s. 6d.

CARNARVON'S (LORD) Portugal, Gallicia, and the Basque Provinces. *Third Edition.* Post 8vo. 3s. 6d.
——— Reminiscences of Athens and the Morea. With Map. Crown 8vo. 7s. 6d.
——— Recollections of the Druses of Lebanon. With Notes on their Religion. *Third Edition.* Post 8vo. 5s. 6d.

CASTLEREAGH (THE) DESPATCHES, from the commencement of the official career of Viscount Castlereagh to the close of his life. 12 Vols. 8vo. 14s. each.

CAMPBELL'S (LORD) Lord Chancellors and Keepers of the Great Seal of England. From the Earliest Times to the Death of Lord Eldon in 1838. *Fifth Edition.* 10 Vols. Crown 8vo. 6s. each.

——————— Chief Justices of England. From the Norman Conquest to the Death of Lord Tenterden. *Third Edition.* 4 Vols. Crown 8vo. 6s. each.

——————— Lords Lyndhurst and Brougham. 8vo. 16s.

——————— Shakspeare's Legal Acquirements. 8vo. 5s. 6d.

——————— Lord Bacon. Fcap. 8vo. 2s. 6d.

——————— (SIR NEIL) Account of Napoleon at Fontainebleau and Elba. Being a Journal of Occurrences and Notes of his Conversations, &c. Portrait. 8vo. 15s.

——————— (SIR GEORGE) India as it may be: an Outline of a proposed Government and Policy. 8vo.

——————— (THOS.) Essay on English Poetry. With Short Lives of the British Poets. Post 8vo. 3s. 6d.

CATHCART'S (SIR GEORGE) Commentaries on the War in Russia and Germany, 1812-13. Plans. 8vo. 14s.

CAVALCASELLE AND CROWE'S History of Painting in Italy, from the 2nd to the 16th Century. With Illustrations. 5 Vols. 8vo. 21s. each.

——————— Early Flemish Painters, their Lives and Works. Illustrations. Post 8vo. 10s. 6d.; or Large Paper, 8vo. 16s.

CHILD'S (G. CHAPLIN, M.D.) Benedicite; or, Song of the Three Children; being Illustrations of the Power, Beneficence, and Design manifested by the Creator in his works. 10th Thousand. Post 8vo. 6s.

CHISHOLM'S (Mrs.) Perils of the Polar Seas; True Stories of Arctic Discovery and Adventure. Illustrations. Post 8vo. 6s.

CHURTON'S (ARCHDEACON) Gongora. An Historical Essay on the Age of Philip III. and IV. of Spain. With Translations. Portrait. 2 Vols. Small 8vo. 12s.

——————— New Testament. Edited with a Plain Practical Commentary for the use of Families and General Readers. With 100 Panoramic and other Views, from Sketches and Photographs made on the Spot. 2 vols. 8vo. 21s.

CICERO'S LIFE AND TIMES. His Character as a Statesman, Orator, and Friend, with a Selection from his Correspondence and Orations. By WILLIAM FORSYTH, M.P. *Third Edition.* With Illustrations. 8vo. 10s. 6d.

CLARK'S (SIR JAMES) Memoir of Dr. John Conolly. Comprising a Sketch of the Treatment of the Insane in Europe and America. With Portrait. Post 8vo. 10s. 6d.

CLIVE'S (LORD) Life. By REV. G. R. GLEIG. Post 8vo. 3s. 6d.

CLODE'S (C. M.) Military Forces of the Crown; their Administration and Government. 2 Vols. 8vo. 21s. each.

——————— Administration of Justice under Military and Martial Law, as applicable to the Army, Navy, Marine, and Auxiliary Forces. *2nd Edition.* 8vo. 12s.

COLCHESTER (THE) PAPERS. The Diary and Correspondence of Charles Abbott, Lord Colchester, Speaker of the House of Commons 1802-1817. Portrait. 3 Vols. 8vo. 42s.

CHURCH (THE) & THE AGE. Essays on the Principles and Present Position of the Anglican Church. 2 vols. 8vo. 26s. Contents:—

VOL. I.
Anglican Principles.—Dean Hook.
Modern Religious Thought.—Bishop Ellicott.
State, Church, and Synods.—Rev. Dr. Irons.
Religious Use of Taste.—Rev. R. St. John Tyrwhitt.
Place of the Laity.—Professor Burrows
Parish Priest.—Rev. Walsham How.
Divines of 16th and 17th Centuries. —Rev. A. W. Haddan.
Liturgies and Ritual, Rev. M. F. Sadler.
Church & Education.—Canon Barry.
Indian Missions.—Sir Bartle Frere.
Church and the People.—Rev. W. D. Maclagan.
Conciliation and Comprehension.— Rev. Dr. Weir.

VOL. II.
Church and Pauperism.—Earl Nelson.
American Church.—Bishop of Western New York.
Church and Science. — Prebendary Clark.
Ecclesiastical Law.—Isambard Brunel.
Church & National Education.— Canon Norris.
Church and Universities.—John G. Talbot.
Toleration.—Dean Cowie.
Eastern Church and Anglican Communion.—Rev. Geo. Williams.
A Disestablished Church.—Dean of Cashel.
Christian Tradition.—Rev. Dr. Irons.
Dogma.—Rev. Dr. Weir.
Parochial Councils. — Archdeacon Chapman.

COLERIDGE'S (SAMUEL TAYLOR) Table-Talk. Portrait. 12mo. 3s. 6d.

COLLINGWOOD'S (CUTHBERT) Rambles of a Naturalist on the Shores and Waters of the China Sea. Being Observations in Natural History during a Voyage to China, &c. With Illustrations. 8vo. 16s.

COLONIAL LIBRARY. [See Home and Colonial Library.]

COOK'S (Canon) Sermons Preached at Lincoln's Inn. 8vo. 9s.

COOKERY (MODERN DOMESTIC). Founded on Principles of Economy and Practical Knowledge, and adapted for Private Families. By a Lady. Woodcuts. Fcap. 8vo. 5s.

COOPER'S (T. T.) Travels of a Pioneer of Commerce on an Overland Journey from China towards India. Illustrations. 8vo. 16s.

CORNWALLIS (THE) Papers and Correspondence during the American War,—Administrations in India,—Union with Ireland, and Peace of Amiens. *Second Edition.* 3 Vols. 8vo. 63s.

COWPER'S (COUNTESS) Diary while Lady of the Bedchamber to Caroline Princess of Wales, 1714—20. Edited by Hon. SPENCER COWPER. *Second Edition.* Portrait. 8vo. 10s. 6d.

CRABBE'S (REV. GEORGE) Life and Poetical Works. With Illustrations. Royal 8vo. 7s.

CROKER'S (J. W.) Progressive Geography for Children. *Fifth Edition.* 18mo. 1s. 6d.

———— Stories for Children, Selected from the History of England. *Fifteenth Edition.* Woodcuts. 16mo. 2s. 6d.

———— Boswell's Life of Johnson. Including the Tour to the Hebrides. *New and revised Library Edition.* Portraits. 4 vols. 8vo.
[*In Preparation.*

———— Essays on the Early Period of the French Revolution. 8vo. 15s.

———— Historical Essay on the Guillotine. Fcap. 8vo. 1s.

PUBLISHED BY MR. MURRAY.   9

CUMMING'S (R. GORDON) Five Years of a Hunter's Life in the Far Interior of South Africa. *Sixth Edition.* Woodcuts. Post 8vo. 6s.

CROWE'S AND CAVALCASELLE'S Lives of the Early Flemish Painters. Woodcuts. Post 8vo, 10s. 6d.; or Large Paper, 8vo, 15s.

—————— History of Painting in Italy, from 2nd to 16th Century. Derived from Researches into the Works of Art in that Country. With 100 Illustrations. 5 Vols. 8vo. 21s. each.

CUNYNGHAME'S (SIR ARTHUR) Travels in the Eastern Caucasus, on the Caspian, and Black Seas, in Daghestan and the Frontiers of Persia and Turkey. With Map and Illustrations. 8vo. 18s.

CURTIUS' (PROFESSOR) Student's Greek Grammar, for the Upper Forms. Edited by DR. WM. SMITH. Post 8vo. 6s.

—————— Elucidations of the above Grammar. Translated by EVELYN ABBOT. Post 8vo. 7s. 6d.

—————— Smaller Greek Grammar for the Middle and Lower Forms. Abridged from the larger work. 12mo. 3s. 6d.

—————— Accidence of the Greek Language. Extracted from the above work. 12mo. 2s. 6d.

—————— Principles of Greek Etymology. Translated by A. S. WILKINS, M.A., and E. B. ENGLAND, B.A. 8vo. *Nearly Ready.*

CURZON'S (HON. ROBERT) ARMENIA AND ERZEROUM. A Year on the Frontiers of Russia, Turkey, and Persia. *Third Edition.* Woodcuts. Post 8vo. 7s. 6d.

—————— Visits to the Monasteries of the Levant. *Fifth Edition.* Illustrations. Post 8vo. 7s. 6d.

CUST'S (GENERAL) Lives of the Warriors of the 17th Century—The Thirty Years' War. 2 Vols. 16s. Civil Wars of France and England. 2 Vols. 16s. Commanders of Fleets and Armies before the Enemy. 2 Vols. 18s.

—————— Annals of the Wars—18th & 19th Century, 1700—1815. With Maps. 9 Vols. Post 8vo. 5s. each.

DAVIS'S (NATHAN) Ruined Cities of Numidia and Carthaginia. Illustrations. 8vo. 16s.

DAVY'S (SIR HUMPHRY) Consolations in Travel; or, Last Days of a Philosopher. *Seventh Edition.* Woodcuts. Fcap. 8vo. 3s. 6d.

—————— Salmonia; or, Days of Fly Fishing. *Fifth Edition.* Woodcuts. Fcap. 8vo. 3s. 6d.

DARWIN'S (CHARLES) Journal of Researches into the Natural History of the Countries visited during a Voyage round the World. *Eleventh Thousand.* Post 8vo. 9s.

—————— Origin of Species by Means of Natural Selection; or, the Preservation of Favoured Races in the Struggle for Life. *Sixth Edition.* Post 8vo. 7s. 6d.

—————— Variation of Animals and Plants under Domestication. With Illustrations. 2 Vols. 8vo. 28s.

—————— Descent of Man, and Selection in Relation to Sex. With Illustrations. Crown 8vo. 9s.

—————— Expressions of the Emotions in Man and Animals. With Illustrations. Crown 8vo. 12s.

—————— Fertilization of Orchids through Insect Agency, and as to the good of Intercrossing. Woodcuts. Post 8vo. 9s.

—————— Fact and Argument for Darwin. By FRITZ MULLER. With numerous Illustrations and Additions by the Author. Translated from the German by W. S. DALLAS. Woodcuts. Post 8vo. 6s.

DELEPIERRE'S (Octave) History of Flemish Literature. 8vo. 9s.
——————— Historic Difficulties & Contested Events. Post 8vo. 6s.
DENISON'S (E. B.) Life of Bishop Lonsdale. With Selections from his Writings. With Portrait. Crown 8vo. 10s. 6d.
DERBY'S (Earl of) Iliad of Homer rendered into English Blank Verse. 7th Edition. 2 Vols. Post 8vo. 10s.
DE ROS'S (Lord) Young Officer's Companion; or, Essays on Military Duties and Qualities: with Examples and Illustrations from History. Post 8vo. 9s.
DEUTSCH'S (Emanuel) Talmud, Islam, The Targums and other Literary Remains. 8vo. 12s.
DOG-BREAKING; the Most Expeditious, Certain, and Easy Method, whether great excellence or only mediocrity be required. With a Few Hints for those who Love the Dog and the Gun. By Lieut.-Gen. Hutchinson. Fifth Edition. With 40 Woodcuts. Crown 8vo. 9s.
DOMESTIC MODERN COOKERY. Founded on Principles of Economy and Practical Knowledge, and adapted for Private Families. Woodcuts. Fcap. 8vo. 5s.
DOUGLAS'S (Sir Howard) Life and Adventures. Portrait. 8vo. 15s.
——————— Theory and Practice of Gunnery. Plates. 8vo. 21s.
——————— Construction of Bridges and the Passage of Rivers, in Military Operations. Plates. 8vo. 21s.
——————— (Wm.) Horse-Shoeing; As it Is, and As it Should be. Illustrations. Post 8vo. 7s. 6d.
DRAKE'S (Sir Francis) Life, Voyages, and Exploits, by Sea and Land. By John Barrow. Third Edition. Post 8vo. 2s.
DRINKWATER'S (John) History of the Siege of Gibraltar, 1779-1788. With a Description and Account of that Garrison from the Earliest Periods. Post 8vo. 2s.
DUCANGE'S MEDIÆVAL LATIN-ENGLISH DICTIONARY. Translated by Rev. E. A. Dayman, M.A. Small 4to. [In preparation.
DU CHAILLU'S (Paul B.) EQUATORIAL AFRICA, with Accounts of the Gorilla, the Nest-building Ape, Chimpanzee, Crocodile, &c. Illustrations. 8vo. 21s.
——————— Journey to Ashango Land; and Further Penetration into Equatorial Africa. Illustrations. 8vo. 21s.
DUFFERIN'S (Lord) Letters from High Latitudes; an Account of a Yacht Voyage to Iceland, Jan Mayen, and Spitzhergen. Fifth Edition. Woodcuts. Post 8vo. 7s. 6d.
DUNCAN'S (Major) History of the Royal Artillery. Compiled from the Original Records. Second Edition. With Portraits. 2 Vols. 8vo. 30s.
DYER'S (Thos. H.) History of Modern Europe, from the taking of Constantinople by the Turks to the close of the War in the Crimea. With Index. 4 Vols. 8vo. 42s.
EASTLAKE'S (Sir Charles) Contributions to the Literature of the Fine Arts. With Memoir of the Author, and Selections from his Correspondence. By Lady Eastlake. 2 Vols. 8vo. 24s.
EDWARDS' (W. H.) Voyage up the River Amazons, including a Visit to Para. Post 8vo. 2s.

PUBLISHED BY MR. MURRAY. 11

ELDON'S (LORD) Public and Private Life, with Selections from his Correspondence and Diaries. By HORACE TWISS. *Third Edition.* Portrait. 2 Vols. Post 8vo. 21s.

ELGIN'S (LORD) Letters and Journals. Edited by THEODORE WALROND. With Preface by Dean Stanley. *Second Edition.* 8vo. 14s.

ELLESMERE'S (LORD) Two Sieges of Vienna by the Turks. Translated from the German. Post 8vo. 2s.

ELLIS'S (W.) Madagascar, including a Journey to the Capital, with notices of Natural History and the People. Woodcuts. 8vo. 16s.

——————— Madagascar Revisited. Setting forth the Persecutions and Heroic Sufferings of the Native Christians. Illustrations. 8vo. 16s.

——————— Memoir. By HIS SON. With his Character and Work. By REV. HENRY ALLON, D.D. Portrait. 8vo. 10s. 6d.

——————— (ROBINSON) Poems and Fragments of Catullus. 16mo. 5s.

ELPHINSTONE'S (HON. MOUNTSTUART) History of India—the Hindoo and Mahomedan Periods. *Sixth Edition.* Map. 8vo. 18s.

——————— (H. W.) Patterns for Turning; Comprising Elliptical and other Figures cut on the Lathe without the use of any Ornamental Chuck. With 70 Illustrations. Small 4to. 15s.

ENGEL'S (CARL) Music of the Most Ancient Nations; particularly of the Assyrians, Egyptians, and Hebrews; with Special Reference to the Discoveries in Western Asia and in Egypt. *Second Edition.* With 100 Illustrations. 8vo. 10s. 6d.

ENGLAND. See CALLCOTT, CROKER, HUME, MARKHAM, SMITH, and STANHOPE.

ENGLISHWOMAN IN AMERICA. Post 8vo. 10s. 6d.

ESSAYS ON CATHEDRALS. With an Introduction. By DEAN HOWSON. 8vo. 12s.

CONTENTS.

Recollections of a Dean.—Bishop of Carlisle.
Cathedral Canons and their Work.—Canon Norris.
Cathedrals in Ireland, Past and Future.—Dean of Cashel.
Cathedrals in their Missionary Aspect.—A. J. B. Beresford Hope.
Cathedral Foundations in Relation to Religious Thought —Canon Westcott.
Cathedral Churches of the Old Foundation.—Edward A. Freeman.
Welsh Cathedrals.—Canon Perowne.
Education of Choristers.—Sir F. Gore Ouseley.
Cathedral Schools.—Canon Durham.
Cathedral Reform.—Chancellor Massingberd.
Relation of the Chapter to the Bishop. Chancellor Benson.
Architecture of the Cathedral Churches.—Canon Venables.

ETHNOLOGICAL SOCIETY'S TRANSACTIONS. Vols. I. to VI. 8vo.

ELZE'S (KARL) Life of Lord Byron. With a Critical Essay on his Place in Literature. Translated from the German, and Edited with Notes. With Original Portrait and Facsimile. 8vo. 16s.

FAMILY RECEIPT-BOOK. A Collection of a Thousand Valuable and Useful Receipts. Fcap. 8vo. 5s. 6d.

FARRAR'S (A. S.) Critical History of Free Thought in reference to the Christian Religion. 8vo. 16s.

——————— (F. W.) Origin of Language, based on Modern Researches. Fcap. 8vo. 5s.

FERGUSSON'S (JAMES) History of Architecture in all Countries from the Earliest Times. Vols. I. and II. Ancient and Mediæval. With 1,000 Illustrations. Medium 8vo. 63s.
———— Vol. III. Indian and Eastern. With 300 Illustrations. Medium 8vo. [In the Press.
———— Vol. IV. Modern. With 330 Illustrations. Medium 8vo. 31s. 6d.
———— Rude Stone Monuments in all Countries; their Age and Uses. With 230 Illustrations. Medium 8vo. 24s.
———— Holy Sepulchre and the Temple at Jerusalem. Woodcuts. 8vo. 7s. 6d.
FLEMING'S (PROFESSOR) Student's Manual of Moral Philosophy. With Quotations and References. Post 8vo. 7s. 6d.
FLOWER GARDEN. By REV. THOS. JAMES. Fcap. 8vo. 1s.
FORD'S (RICHARD) Gatherings from Spain. Post 8vo. 3s. 6d.
FORSYTH'S (WILLIAM) Life and Times of Cicero. With Selections from his Correspondence and Orations. *Third Edition*. Illustrations. 8vo. 10s. 6d.
———— Hortensius; an Historical Essay on the Office and Duties of an Advocate. *Second Edition*. Illustrations. 8vo. 12s.
———— History of Ancient Manuscripts. Post 8vo. 2s. 6d.
———— Novels and Novelists of the 18th Century, in Illustration of the Manners and Morals of the Age. Post 8vo. 10s. 6d.
FORTUNE'S (ROBERT) Narrative of Two Visits to the Tea Countries of China, 1843-52. *Third Edition*. Woodcuts. 2 Vols. Post 8vo. 18s.
FOSS' (Edward) Biographia Juridica, or Biographical Dictionary of the Judges of England, from the Conquest to the Present Time, 1066-1870. Medium 8vo. 21s.
———— Tabulæ Curiales; or, Tables of the Superior Courts of Westminster Hall. Showing the Judges who sat in them from 1066 to 1864. 8vo. 10s. 6d.
FRANCE. *** See MARKHAM, SMITH, Student's.
FRENCH (THE) in Algiers; The Soldier of the Foreign Legion— and the Prisoners of Abd-el-Kadir. Translated by Lady DUFF GORDON. Post 8vo. 2s.
FRERE'S (SIR BARTLE) Indian Missions. *Third Edition*. Small 8vo. 2s. 6d.
———— Eastern Africa as a field for Missionary Labour. With Map. Crown 8vo. 5s.
———— Bengal Famine. How it will be Met and How to Prevent Future Famines in India. With Maps. Crown 8vo. 5s.
———— (M.) Old Deccan Days; or Fairy Legends Current in Southern India. With Notes, by SIR BARTLE FRERE. With Illustrations. Fcap. 8vo. 6s.
GALTON'S (FRANCIS) Art of Travel; or, Hints on the Shifts and Contrivances available in Wild Countries. *Fifth Edition*. Woodcuts. Post 8vo. 7s. 6d.
GEOGRAPHICAL SOCIETY'S JOURNAL. (*Published Yearly.*)
GEORGE'S (ERNEST) Mosel; a Series of Twenty Etchings, with Descriptive Letterpress. Imperial 4to. 42s.
———— Loire and South of France; a Series of Twenty Etchings, with Descriptive Text. Folio. 42s.
GERMANY (HISTORY OF). See MARKHAM.

GIBBON'S (EDWARD) History of the Decline and Fall of the
Roman Empire. Edited by MILMAN and GUIZOT. *A New Edition.*
Edited, with Notes, by Dr. WM. SMITH. Maps. 8 Vols. 8vo. 60s.

—————— (The Student's Gibbon); Being an Epitome of the
above work, incorporating the Researches of Recent Commentators. By
Dr. WM. SMITH. Woodcuts. Post 8vo. 7s. 6d.

GIFFARD'S (EDWARD) Deeds of Naval Daring; or, Anecdotes of
the British Navy. Fcap. 8vo. 3s. 6d.

GLADSTONE'S (W. E.) Financial Statements of 1853, 1860, 63-65.
8vo. 12s.

GLEIG'S (G. R.) Campaigns of the British Army at Washington
and New Orleans. Post 8vo. 2s.

—————— Story of the Battle of Waterloo. Post 8vo. 3s. 6d.

—————— Narrative of Sale's Brigade in Affghanistan. Post 8vo. 2s.

—————— Life of Lord Clive. Post 8vo. 3s. 6d.

—————— Sir Thomas Munro. Post 8vo. 3s. 6d.

GOLDSMITH'S (OLIVER) Works. Edited with Notes by PETER
CUNNINGHAM. Vignettes. 4 Vols. 8vo. 30s.

GORDON'S (SIR ALEX.) Sketches of German Life, and Scenes
from the War of Liberation. Post 8vo. 8s. 6d.

—————— (LADY DUFF) Amber-Witch: A Trial for Witchcraft. Post 8vo. 2s.

—————— French in Algiers. 1. The Soldier of the Foreign
Legion. 2. The Prisoners of Abd-el-Kadir. Post 8vo. 2s.

GRAMMARS. See CURTIUS; HALL; HUTTON; KING EDWARD;
MATTHIÆ; MAETZNER; SMITH.

GREECE. *See* GROTE—SMITH—Student.

GREY'S (EARL) Correspondence with King William IVth and
Sir Herbert Taylor, from 1830 to 1832. 2 Vols. 8vo. 30s.

—————— Parliamentary Government and Reform; with
Suggestions for the Improvement of our Representative System.
Second Edition. 8vo. 9s.

GRUNER'S (LEWIS) Terra-Cotta Architecture of North Italy,
from careful Drawings and Restorations. With Illustrations, engraved
and printed in Colours. Small folio. 5l. 5s.

GUIZOT'S (M.) Meditations on Christianity, and on the Religious
Questions of the Day. Part I. The Essence. Part II. Present State.
Part III. Relation to Society and Opinion. 3 Vols. Post 8vo. 30s.

GROTE'S (GEORGE) History of Greece. From the Earliest Times
to the close of the generation contemporary with the death of Alexander
the Great. *Library Edition.* Portrait, Maps, and Plans. 10 Vols. 8vo.
120s. *Cabinet Edition.* Portrait and Plans. 12 Vols. Post 8vo. 6s. each.

—————— PLATO, and other Companions of Socrates. 3 Vols. 8vo. 45s.

—————— ARISTOTLE. Edited by Professors BAIN and ROBERTSON.
2 Vols. 8vo. 32s.

—————— Minor Works. With Critical Remarks on his
Intellectual Character, Writings, and Speeches. By ALEX.BAIN, LL.D.
Portrait. 8vo. 14s.

—————— Personal Life. Compiled from Family Documents,
Private Memoranda, and Original Letters to and from Various
Friends. By Mrs. Grote. Portrait. 8vo. 12s.

—————— (MRS.) Memoir of Ary Scheffer. Portrait. 8vo. 8s. 6d.

HALL'S (T. D.) School Manual of English Grammar. With Copious Exercises. 12mo. 3s. 6d.
———— Primary English Grammar for Elementary Schools. 16mo. 1s.
———— Child's First Latin Book, including a Systematic Treatment of the New Pronunciation, and a full Praxis of Nouns, Adjectives, and Pronouns. 16mo. 1s. 6d.
HALLAM'S (HENRY) Constitutional History of England, from the Accession of Henry the Seventh to the Death of George the Second. *Library Edition.* 3 Vols. 8vo. 30s. *Cabinet Edition,* 3 Vols. Post 8vo. 12s.
———— Student's Edition of the above work. Edited by WM. SMITH, D.C.L. Post 8vo. 7s. 6d.
———— History of Europe during the Middle Ages. *Library Edition.* 3 Vols. 8vo. 30s. *Cabinet Edition,* 3 Vols. Post 8vo. 12s.
———— Student's Edition of the above work. Edited by WM. SMITH, D.C.L. Post 8vo. 7s. 6d.
———— Literary History of Europe, during the 15th, 16th and 17th Centuries. *Library Edition.* 3 Vols. 8vo. 36s. *Cabinet Edition.* 4 Vols. Post 8vo. 16s.
———— (ARTHUR) Literary Remains; in Verse and Prose. Portrait. Fcap. 8vo. 3s. 6d.
HAMILTON'S (GEN. SIR F. W.) History of the Grenadier Guards. From Original Documents in the Rolls' Records, War Office, Regimental Records, &c. With Illustrations. 3 Vols. 8vo. 63s.
HANNAH'S (REV. DR.) Divine and Human Elements in Holy Scripture. 8vo. 10s. 6d.
HART'S ARMY LIST. (*Published Quarterly and Annually.*)
HAY'S (SIR J. H. DRUMMOND) Western Barbary, its Wild Tribes and Savage Animals. Post 8vo. 2s.
HEAD'S (SIR FRANCIS) Royal Engineer. Illustrations. 8vo. 12s.
———— Life of Sir John Burgoyne. Post 8vo. 1s.
———— Rapid Journeys across the Pampas. Post 8vo. 2s.
———— Bubbles from the Brunnen of Nassau. Illustrations. Post 8vo. 7s. 6d.
———— Emigrant. Fcap. 8vo. 2s. 6d.
———— Stokers and Pokers; or, the London and North Western Railway. Post 8vo. 2s.
———— (SIR EDMUND) Shall and Will; or, Future Auxiliary Verbs. Fcap. 8vo. 4s.
HEBER'S (BISHOP) Journals in India. 2 Vols. Post 8vo. 7s.
———— Poetical Works. Portrait. Fcap. 8vo. 3s. 6d.
———— Hymns adapted to the Church Service. 16mo. 1s. 6d.
HERODOTUS. A New English Version. Edited, with Notes and Essays, historical, ethnographical, and geographical, by CANON RAWLINSON, assisted by SIR HENRY RAWLINSON and SIR J. G. WILKINSON. *Third Edition.* Maps and Woodcuts. 4 Vols. 8vo.
HATHERLEY'S (LORD) Continuity of Scripture, as Declared by the Testimony of our Lord and of the Evangelists and Apostles. *Fourth Edition.* 8vo. 6s. *Popular Edition.* Post 8vo. 2s. 6d.
HOLLWAY'S (J. G.) Month in Norway. Fcap. 8vo. 2s.
HONEY BEE. By REV. THOMAS JAMES. Fcap. 8vo. 1s.
HOOK'S (DEAN) Church Dictionary. *Tenth Edition.* 8vo. 16s.
———— (THEODORE) Life. By J. G. LOCKHART. Fcap. 8vo. 1s.

PUBLISHED BY MR. MURRAY. 15

HOPE'S (T. C.) ARCHITECTURE OF AHMEDABAD, with Historical Sketch and Architectural Notes. With Maps, Photographs, and Woodcuts. 4to. 5*l*. 5*s*.
——— (A. J. BERESFORD) Worship in the Church of England. 8vo. 9*s*.

FOREIGN HANDBOOKS.

HAND-BOOK—TRAVEL-TALK. English, French, German, and Italian. 18mo. 3*s*. 6*d*.
——— HOLLAND,—BELGIUM, and the Rhine to Mayence. Map and Plans. Post 8vo. 6*s*.
——— NORTH GERMANY,—PRUSSIA, SAXONY, HANOVER, and the Rhine from Mayence to Switzerland. Map and Plans. Post 8vo. 6*s*.
——— SOUTH GERMANY,—Bavaria, Austria, Styria, Salzburg, the Austrian and Bavarian Alps, the Tyrol, Hungary, and the Danube, from Ulm to the Black Sea. Map. Post 8vo. 10*s*.
——— KNAPSACK GUIDE TO THE TYROL. 16mo. 6*s*.
——— PAINTING. German, Flemish, and Dutch Schools. Illustrations. 2 Vols. Post 8vo. 24*s*.
——— LIVES OF EARLY FLEMISH PAINTERS. By CROWE and CAVALCASELLE. Illustrations. Post 8vo. 10*s*. 6*d*.
——— SWITZERLAND, Alps of Savoy, and Piedmont. Maps. Post 8vo. 9*s*.
——— FRANCE, Normandy, Brittany, the French Alps, the Rivers Loire, Seine, Rhone, and Garonne, Dauphiné, Provence, and the Pyrenees. Maps. 2 Parts. Post 8vo. 12*s*.
——— ISLANDS OF THE MEDITERRANEAN—Malta, Corsica, Sardinia, and Sicily. Maps. Post 8vo.
——— ALGERIA. Map. Post 8vo. 9*s*.
——— PARIS, and its Environs. Map. 16mo. 3*s*. 6*d*.
⁎ MURRAY'S PLAN OF PARIS, mounted on canvas. 3*s*. 6*d*.
——— SPAIN, Madrid, The Castiles, The Basque Provinces, Leon, The Asturias, Galicia, Estremadura, Andalusia, Ronda, Granada, Murcia, Valencia, Catalonia, Aragon, Navarre, The Balearic Islands, &c. &c. Maps. 2 Vols. Post 8vo. 24*s*.
——— PORTUGAL, LISBON, Porto, Cintra, Mafra, &c. Map. Post 8vo. 9*s*.
——— NORTH ITALY, Piedmont, Liguria, Venetia, Lombardy, Parma, Modena, and Romagna. Map. Post 8vo. 10*s*.
——— CENTRAL ITALY, Lucca, Tuscany, Florence, The Marches, Umbria, and the Patrimony of St. Peter's. Map. Post 8vo. 10*s*.
——— ROME AND ITS ENVIRONS. Map. Post 8vo. 10*s*.
——— SOUTH ITALY, Two Sicilies, Naples, Pompeii, Herculaneum, and Vesuvius. Map. Post 8vo. 10*s*.
——— KNAPSACK GUIDE TO ITALY. 16mo.
——— PAINTING. The Italian Schools. Illustrations. 2 Vols. Post 8vo. 30*s*.
——— LIVES OF ITALIAN PAINTERS, FROM CIMABUE to BASSANO. By Mrs. JAMESON. Portraits. Post 8vo. 12*s*.
——— RUSSIA, ST. PETERSBURG, MOSCOW, POLAND, and FINLAND. Maps. Post 8vo. 15*s*.
——— DENMARK. Map. Post 8vo. 6*s*.

HAND-BOOK—SWEDEN. Map. Post 8vo. 6s.
————— NORWAY. Map. 6s.
————— GREECE, the Ionian Islands, Continental Greece, Athens, the Peloponnesus, the Islands of the Ægean Sea, Albania, Thessaly, and Macedonia. Maps. Post 8vo. 15s.
————— TURKEY IN ASIA—Constantinople, the Bosphorus, Dardanelles, Brousa, Plain of Troy, Crete, Cyprus, Smyrna, Ephesus, the Seven Churches, Coasts of the Black Sea, Armenia, Mesopotamia, &c. Maps. Post 8vo. 15s.
————— EGYPT, including Descriptions of the Course of the Nile through Egypt and Nubia, Alexandria, Cairo, and Thebes, the Suez Canal, the Pyramids, the Peninsula of Sinai, the Oases, the Fyoom, &c. Map. Post 8vo. 15s.
————— HOLY LAND—Syria Palestine, Peninsula of Sinai, Edom, Syrian Desert, &c. Maps. Post 8vo.
————— INDIA — Bombay and Madras. Map. 2 Vols. Post 8vo. 12s. each.

ENGLISH HANDBOOKS.

HAND-BOOK—MODERN LONDON. Map. 16mo. 3s. 6d.
————— ESSEX, CAMBRIDGE, SUFFOLK, AND NORFOLK, Chelmsford, Colchester, Maldon, Cambridge, Ely, Newmarket, Bury, Ipswich, Woodbridge, Felixstowe, Lowestoft, Norwich, Yarmouth, Cromer, &c. Map and Plans. Post 8vo. 12s.
————— CATHEDRALS of Oxford, Peterborough, Norwich, Ely, and Lincoln. With 90 Illustrations. Crown 8vo. 18s.
————— KENT AND SUSSEX, Canterbury, Dover, Ramsgate, Sheerness, Rochester, Chatham, Woolwich, Brighton, Chichester, Worthing, Hastings, Lewes, Arundel, &c. Map. Post 8vo. 10s.
————— SURREY AND HANTS, Kingston, Croydon, Reigate, Guildford, Dorking, Boxhill, Winchester, Southampton, New Forest, Portsmouth, and Isle of Wight. Maps. Post 8vo. 10s.
————— BERKS, BUCKS, AND OXON, Windsor, Eton, Reading, Aylesbury, Uxbridge, Wycombe, Henley, the City and University of Oxford, Blenheim, and the Descent of the Thames. Map. Post 8vo. 7s. 6d.
————— WILTS, DORSET, AND SOMERSET, Salisbury, Chippenham, Weymouth, Sherborne, Wells, Bath, Bristol, Taunton, &c. Map. Post 8vo. 10s.
————— DEVON AND CORNWALL, Exeter, Ilfracombe, Linton, Sidmouth, Dawlish, Teignmouth, Plymouth, Devonport, Torquay, Launceston, Truro, Penzance, Falmouth, the Lizard, Land's End, &c. Maps. Post 8vo. 12s.
————— CATHEDRALS of Winchester, Salisbury, Exeter, Wells, Chichester, Rochester, Canterbury. With 110 Illustrations. 2 Vols. Crown 8vo. 24s.
————— GLOUCESTER, HEREFORD, and WORCESTER, Cirencester, Cheltenham, Stroud, Tewkesbury, Leominster, Ross, Malvern, Kidderminster, Dudley, Bromsgrove, Evesham. Map. Post 8vo. 9s.
————— CATHEDRALS of Bristol, Gloucester, Hereford, Worcester, and Lichfield. With 50 Illustrations. Crown 8vo. 16s.
————— NORTH WALES, Bangor, Carnarvon, Beaumaris, Snowdon, Llanberis, Dolgelly, Cader Idris, Conway, &c. Map. Post 8vo. 7s.
————— SOUTH WALES, Monmouth, Llandaff, Merthyr, Vale of Neath, Pembroke, Carmarthen, Tenby, Swansea, and The Wye, &c. Map. Post 8vo. 7s.

HAND-BOOK—CATHEDRALS OF BANGOR, ST. ASAPH, Llandaff, and St. David's. With Illustrations. Post 8vo. 15s.
——— ——— DERBY, NOTTS, LEICESTER, STAFFORD, Matlock, Bakewell, Chatsworth, The Peak, Buxton, Hardwick, Dove Dale, Ashborne, Southwell, Mansfield, Retford, Burton, Belvoir, Melton Mowbray, Wolverhampton, Lichfield, Walsall, Tamworth. Map. Post 8vo. 9s.
——— SHROPSHIRE, CHESHIRE AND LANCASHIRE —Shrewsbury, Ludlow, Bridgnorth, Oswestry, Chester, Crewe, Alderley, Stockport, Birkenhead, Warrington, Bury, Manchester, Liverpool, Burnley, Clitheroe, Bolton, Blackburn, Wigan, Preston, Rochdale, Lancaster, Southport, Blackpool, &c. Map. Post 8vo. 10s.
——— YORKSHIRE, Doncaster, Hull, Selby, Beverley, Scarborough, Whitby, Harrogate, Ripon, Leeds, Wakefield, Bradford, Halifax, Huddersfield, Sheffield. Map and Plans. Post 8vo. 12s.
——— CATHEDRALS of York, Ripon, Durham, Carlisle, Chester, and Manchester. With 60 Illustrations. 2 Vols. Crown 8vo. 21s.
——— DURHAM AND NORTHUMBERLAND, Newcastle, Darlington, Gateshead, Bishop Auckland, Stockton, Hartlepool, Sunderland, Shields, Berwick-on-Tweed, Morpeth, Tynemouth, Coldstream, Alnwick, &c. Map. Post 8vo. 9s.
——— WESTMORLAND AND CUMBERLAND—Lancaster, Furness Abbey, Ambleside, Kendal, Windermere, Coniston, Keswick, Grasmere, Ullswater, Carlisle, Cockermouth, Penrith, Appleby. Map. Post 8vo. 8s.
⁎ MURRAY'S MAP OF THE LAKE DISTRICT, on canvas. 3s. 6d.
——— SCOTLAND, Edinburgh, Melrose, Kelso, Glasgow, Dumfries, Ayr, Stirling, Arran, The Clyde, Oban, Inverary, Loch Lomond, Loch Katrine and Trossachs, Caledonian Canal, Inverness, Perth, Dundee, Aberdeen, Braemar, Skye, Caithness, Ross, Sutherland, &c. Maps and Plans. Post 8vo. 9s.
——— IRELAND, Dublin, Belfast, Donegal, Galway, Wexford, Cork, Limerick, Waterford, Killarney, Munster, &c. Maps. Post 8vo. 12s.
——— FAMILIAR QUOTATIONS. From English Authors. *Third Edition.* Fcap. 8vo. 5s.
HORACE; a New Edition of the Text. Edited by DEAN MILMAN. With 100 Woodcuts. Crown 8vo. 7s. 6d.
——— Life of. By DEAN MILMAN. Illustrations. 8vo. 9s.
HOUGHTON'S (LORD) Monographs, Personal and Social. With Portraits. Crown 8vo. 10s. 6d.
HUME'S (The Student's) History of England, from the Invasion of Julius Cæsar to the Revolution of 1688. Corrected and continued to 1868. Woodcuts. Post 8vo. 7s. 6d.
HUTCHINSON (GEN.), on the most expeditions, certain, and easy Method of Dog-Breaking. *Fifth Edition.* With 40 Illustrations. Crown 8vo. 9s.
HUTTON'S (H. E.) Principia Græca; an Introduction to the Study of Greek. Comprehending Grammar, Delectus, and Exercise-book, with Vocabularies. *Sixth Edition.* 12mo. 3s. 6d.
IRBY AND MANGLES' Travels in Egypt, Nubia, Syria, and the Holy Land. Post 8vo. 2s.
JACOBSON'S (BISHOP) Fragmentary Illustrations of the History of the Book of Common Prayer; from Manuscript Sources (Bishop SANDERSON and Bishop WREN). 8vo. 5s.
JAMES' (REV. THOMAS) Fables of Æsop. A New Translation, with Historical Preface. With 100 Woodcuts by TENNIEL and WOLF. *Sixty-fourth Thousand.* Post 8vo. 2s. 6d.

c

LIST OF WORKS

HOME AND COLONIAL LIBRARY. A Series of Works adapted for all circles and classes of Readers, having been selected for their acknowledged interest, and ability of the Authors. Post 8vo. Published at 2s. and 3s. 6d. each, and arranged under two distinctive heads as follows :—

CLASS A.
HISTORY, BIOGRAPHY, AND HISTORIC TALES.

1. SIEGE OF GIBRALTAR. By JOHN DRINKWATER. 2s.
2. THE AMBER-WITCH. By LADY DUFF GORDON. 2s.
3. CROMWELL AND BUNYAN. By ROBERT SOUTHEY. 2s.
4. LIFE OF SIR FRANCIS DRAKE. By JOHN BARROW. 2s.
5. CAMPAIGNS AT WASHINGTON. By REV. G. R. GLEIG. 2s.
6. THE FRENCH IN ALGIERS. By LADY DUFF GORDON. 2s.
7. THE FALL OF THE JESUITS. 2s.
8. LIVONIAN TALES. 2s.
9. LIFE OF CONDÉ. By LORD MAHON. 3s. 6d.
10. SALE'S BRIGADE. By REV. G. R. GLEIG. 2s.
11. THE SIEGES OF VIENNA. By LORD ELLESMERE. 2s.
12. THE WAYSIDE CROSS. By CAPT. MILMAN. 2s.
13. SKETCHES OF GERMAN LIFE. By SIR A. GORDON. 3s. 6d.
14. THE BATTLE OF WATERLOO. By REV. G. R. GLEIG. 3s. 6d.
15. AUTOBIOGRAPHY OF STEFFENS. 2s.
16. THE BRITISH POETS. By THOMAS CAMPBELL. 3s. 6d.
17. HISTORICAL ESSAYS. By LORD MAHON. 3s. 6d.
18. LIFE OF LORD CLIVE. By REV. G. R. GLEIG. 3s. 6d.
19. NORTH - WESTERN RAILWAY. By SIR F. B. HEAD. 2s.
20. LIFE OF MUNRO. By REV. G. R. GLEIG. 3s. 6d.

CLASS B.
VOYAGES, TRAVELS, AND ADVENTURES.

1. BIBLE IN SPAIN. By GEORGE BORROW. 3s. 6d.
2. GYPSIES OF SPAIN. By GEORGE BORROW. 3s. 6d.
3 & 4. JOURNALS IN INDIA. By BISHOP HEBER. 2 Vols. 7s.
5. TRAVELS IN THE HOLY LAND. By IRBY and MANGLES. 2s.
6. MOROCCO AND THE MOORS. By J. DRUMMOND HAY. 2s.
7. LETTERS FROM THE BALTIC. By a LADY. 2s.
8. NEW SOUTH WALES. By MRS. MEREDITH. 2s.
9. THE WEST INDIES. By M. G. LEWIS. 2s.
10. SKETCHES OF PERSIA. By SIR JOHN MALCOLM. 3s. 6d.
11. MEMOIRS OF FATHER RIPA. 2s.
12 & 13. TYPEE AND OMOO. By HERMANN MELVILLE. 2 Vols. 7s.
14. MISSIONARY LIFE IN CANADA. By REV. J. ABBOTT. 2s.
15. LETTERS FROM MADRAS. By a LADY. 2s.
16. HIGHLAND SPORTS. By CHARLES ST. JOHN. 3s. 6d.
17. PAMPAS JOURNEYS. By SIR F. B. HEAD. 2s.
18. GATHERINGS FROM SPAIN. By RICHARD FORD. 3s. 6d.
19. THE RIVER AMAZON. By W. H. EDWARDS. 2s.
20. MANNERS & CUSTOMS OF INDIA. By REV. C. ACLAND. 2s.
21. ADVENTURES IN MEXICO. By G. F. RUXTON. 3s. 6d.
22. PORTUGAL AND GALLICIA. By LORD CARNARVON. 3s. 6d.
23. BUSH LIFE IN AUSTRALIA. By REV. H. W. HAYGARTH. 2s.
24. THE LIBYAN DESERT. By BAYLE ST. JOHN. 2s.
25. SIERRA LEONE. By A LADY. 3s. 6d.

*** Each work may be had separately.

JAMESON'S (Mrs.) Lives of the Early Italian Painters—
and the Progress of Painting in Italy—Cimabue to Bassano. *New Edition.* With 50 Portraits. Post 8vo. 12s.

JENNINGS' (L. J.) Eighty Years of Republican Government in the United States. Post 8vo. 10s. 6d.

JERVIS'S (Rev. W. H.) Gallican Church, from the Concordat of Bologna, 1516, to the Revolution. With an Introduction. Portraits. 2 Vols. 8vo. 28s.

JESSE'S (Edward) Gleanings in Natural History. Fcp. 8vo. 3s. 6d.

JOHNS' (Rev. B. G.) Blind People; their Works and Ways. With Sketches of the Lives of some famous Blind Men. With Illustrations. Post 8vo. 7s. 6d.

JOHNSON'S (Dr. Samuel) Life. By James Boswell. Including the Tour to the Hebrides. Edited by Mr. Croker. *New revised Library Edition.* Portraits. 4 Vols. 8vo. [*In Preparation.*
—— Lives of the most eminent English Poets, with Critical Observations on their Works. Edited with Notes, Corrective and Explanatory, by Peter Cunningham. 3 vols. 8vo. 22s. 6d.

JUNIUS' Handwriting Professionally investigated. By Mr. Chabot, Expert. With Preface and Collateral Evidence, by the Hon. Edward Twisleton. With Facsimiles, Woodcuts, &c. 4to. £3 3s.

KEN'S (Bishop) Life. By a Layman. Portrait. 2 Vols. 8vo. 18s.
—— Exposition of the Apostles' Creed. 16mo. 1s. 6d.

KERR'S (Robert) GENTLEMAN'S HOUSE; or, How to Plan English Residences, from the Parsonage to the Palace. *Third Edition.* With Views and Plans. 8vo. 24s.
—— Small Country House. A Brief Practical Discourse on the Planning of a Residence from 2000l. to 5000l. With Supplementary Estimates to 7000l. Post 8vo. 3s.
—— Ancient Lights; a Book for Architects, Surveyors, Lawyers, and Landlords. 8vo. 5s. 6d.
—— (R. Malcolm) Student's Blackstone. A Systematic Abridgment of the entire Commentaries, adapted to the present state of the law. Post 8vo. 7s. 6d.

KING EDWARD VIth's Latin Grammar. *Seventeenth Edition.* 12mo. 3s. 6d.
—— —————— First Latin Book. *Fifth Edition.* 12mo. 2s. 6d.

KING GEORGE IIIrd's CORRESPONDENCE WITH LORD NORTH, 1769-82. Edited, with Notes and Introduction, by W. Bodham Donne. 2 vols. 8vo. 32s.

KING'S (R. J.) Sketches and Studies; Historical and Descriptive. 8vo. 12s.

KIRK'S (J. Foster) History of Charles the Bold, Duke of Burgundy. Portrait. 3 Vols. 8vo. 45s.

KIRKES' Handbook of Physiology. Edited by W. Morrant Baker, F.R.C.S. *Eighth Edit.* With 240 Illustrations. Post 8vo. 12s. 6d.

KUGLER'S Handbook of Painting.—The Italian Schools. *Fourth Edition.* Revised and Remodelled from the most recent Researches. By Lady Eastlake. With 140 Illustrations. 2 Vols. Crown 8vo. 30s.
—— Handbook of Painting.—The German, Flemish, and Dutch Schools. *Third Edition.* Revised and in part re-written. By J. A. Crowe. With 60 Illustrations. 2 Vols. Crown 8vo. 24s.

LANE'S (E. W.) Account of the Manners and Customs of Modern Egyptians. *New Edition.* With Illustrations. 2 Vols. Post 8vo. 12s.

LAWRENCE'S (Sir Geo.) Reminiscences of Forty-three Years' Service in India; including Captivities in Cabul among the Affghans and among the Sikhs, and a Narrative of the Mutiny in Rajputana. Edited by W. Edwards, H.M.C.B.S. Crown 8vo. 10s. 6d.

LAYARD'S (A. H.) Nineveh and its Remains. Being a Narrative of Researches and Discoveries amidst the Ruins of Assyria. With an Account of the Chaldean Christians of Kurdistan; the Yezedis, or Devil-worshippers; and an Enquiry into the Manners and Arts of the Ancient Assyrians. *Sixth Edition.* Plates and Woodcuts. 2 Vols. 8vo. 36s.

*** A POPULAR EDITION of the above work. With Illustrations. Post 8vo. 7s. 6d.

—— **Nineveh and Babylon**; being the Narrative of Discoveries in the Ruins, with Travels in Armenia, Kurdistan and the Desert, during a Second Expedition to Assyria. With Map and Plates. 8vo. 21s.

*** A POPULAR EDITION of the above work. With Illustrations. Post 8vo. 7s. 6d.

LEATHES' (STANLEY) Practical Hebrew Grammar. With the Hebrew Text of Genesis i.—vi. and Psalms i.—vi. Grammatical Analysis and Vocabulary. Post 8vo. 7s. 6d.

LENNEP'S (REV. H. J. VAN) Missionary Travels in Asia Minor. With Illustrations of Biblical History and Archæology. With Map and Woodcuts. 2 Vols. Post 8vo. 24s.

LESLIE'S (C. R.) Handbook for Young Painters. With Illustrations. Post 8vo. 7s. 6d.

—— **Life and Works of Sir Joshua Reynolds.** Portraits and Illustrations. 2 Vols. 8vo. 42s.

LETTERS FROM THE BALTIC. By a LADY. Post 8vo. 2s.

—— MADRAS. By a LADY. Post 8vo. 2s.

—— SIERRA LEONE. By a LADY. Post 8vo. 3s. 6d.

LEVI'S (LEONE) History of British Commerce; and of the Economic Progress of the Nation, from 1763 to 1870. 8vo. 16s.

LEWIS'S (M. G.) Journal of a Residence among the Negroes in the West Indies. Post 8vo. 2s.

LIDDELL'S (DEAN) Student's History of Rome, from the earliest Times to the establishment of the Empire. With Woodcuts. Post 8vo. 7s. 6d.

LINDSAY'S (LORD) Lives of the Lindsays; Memoir of the Houses of Crawfurd and Balcarres. With Extracts from Official Papers and Personal Narratives. 3 Vols. 8vo. 24s.

—— **Etruscan Inscriptions.** Analysed, Translated, and Commented upon. 8vo. 12s.

LLOYD'S (W. WATKISS) History of Sicily to the Athenian War; with Elucidations of the Sicilian Odes of Pindar. With Map. 8vo. 14s.

LISPINGS from LOW LATITUDES; or, the Journal of the Hon. Impulsia Gushington. Edited by LORD DUFFERIN. With 24 Plates. 4to. 21s.

LITTLE ARTHUR'S HISTORY OF ENGLAND. By LADY CALLCOTT. *New and Cheaper Edition,* continued to 1872. With Woodcuts. Fcap. 8vo. 1s. 6d.

LIVINGSTONE'S (DR.) Popular Account of Missionary Travels and Researches in South Africa. Illustrations. Post 8vo. 6s.

—— **Narrative of an Expedition to the Zambezi and** its Tributaries, with the Discovery of the Lakes Shirwa and Nyassa. Map and Illustrations. 8vo. 21s.

—— **Last Journals in Central Africa,** from 1865 to his Death. Continued by a Narrative of his last moments and sufferings. By Rev. HORACE WALLER. Maps and Illustrations. 2 Vols. 8vo. 28s.

LIVONIAN TALES. By the Author of "Letters from the Baltic." Post 8vo. 2s.

LOCH'S (H. B.) Personal Narrative of Events during Lord Elgin's Second Embassy to China. *Second Edition.* With Illustrations. Post 8vo. 9s.

LOCKHART'S (J. G.) Ancient Spanish Ballads. Historical and Romantic. Translated, with Notes. *New Edition.* With Portrait and Illustrations. Crown 8vo. 5s.
———— Life of Theodore Hook. Fcap. 8vo. 1s.
LONSDALE'S (BISHOP) Life. With Selections from his Writings. By E. B. DENISON. With Portrait. Crown 8vo. 10s. 6d.
LOUDON'S (MRS.) Gardening for Ladies. With Directions and Calendar of Operations for Every Month. *Eighth Edition.* Woodcuts. Fcap. 8vo. 3s. 8d.
LUCKNOW : A Lady's Diary of the Siege. Fcap. 8vo. 4s. 6d.
LYELL'S (SIR CHARLES) Principles of Geology; or, the Modern Changes of the Earth and its Inhabitants considered as illustrative of Geology. *Eleventh Edition.* With Illustrations. 2 Vols. 8vo. 32s.
———— Student's Elements of Geology. *Second Edition.* With Table of British Fossils and 600 Illustrations. Post 8vo. 9s.
———— Geological Evidences of the Antiquity of Man, including an Outline of Glacial Post-Tertiary Geology, and Remarks on the Origin of Species. *Fourth Edition.* Illustrations. 8vo. 14s.
———— (K. M.) Geographical Handbook of Ferns. With Tables to show their Distribution. Post 8vo. 7s. 6d.
LYTTELTON'S (LORD) Ephemera. 2 Vols. Post 8vo. 19s. 6d.
LYTTON'S (LORD) Memoir of Julian Fane. With Portrait. Post 8vo. 5s.
McCLINTOCK'S (SIR L.) Narrative of the Discovery of the Fate of Sir John Franklin and his Companions in the Arctic Seas. *Third Edition.* With Illustrations. Post 8vo. 7s. 6d.
MACDOUGALL'S (COL.) Modern Warfare as Influenced by Modern Artillery. With Plans. Post 8vo. 12s.
MACGREGOR'S (J.) Rob Roy on the Jordan, Nile, Red Sea, Gennesareth, &c. A Canoe Cruise in Palestine and Egypt and the Waters of Damascus. *Cheaper Edition.* With Map and 70 Illustrations. Crown 8vo. 7s. 6d.
MACPHERSON'S (MAJOR) Services in India, while Political Agent at Gwalior during the Mutiny. Illustrations. 8vo. 12s.
MAETZNER'S ENGLISH GRAMMAR. A Methodical, Analytical, and Historical Treatise on the Orthography, Prosody, Inflections, and Syntax of the English Tongue. Translated from the German. By CLAIR J. GRECE, LL.D. 3 Vols. 8vo. 36s.
MAHON (LORD), see STANHOPE.
MAINE'S (SIR H. SUMNER) Ancient Law : its Connection with the Early History of Society, and its Relation to Modern Ideas. *Fifth Edition.* 8vo. 12s.
———— Village Communities in the East and West. *Second Edition.* 8vo. 9s.
———— Early History of Institutions. 8vo. 12s.
MALCOLM'S (SIR JOHN) Sketches of Persia. Post 8vo. 3s. 6d.
MANSEL'S (DEAN) Limits of Religious Thought Examined. *Fifth Edition.* Post 8vo. 8s. 8d.
———— Letters, Lectures, and Papers, including the Phrontisterion, or Oxford in the XIXth Century. Edited by H. W. CHANDLER, M.A. 8vo. 12s.
———— Gnostic Heresies of the First and Second Centuries. With a sketch of his life and character. By Lord CARNARVON. Edited by Canon LIGHTFOOT. 8vo. 10s. 6d.
MANUAL OF SCIENTIFIC ENQUIRY. For the Use of Travellers. Edited by SIR J. F. HERSCHEL & REV. R. MAIN. Post 8vo. 3s. 6d. (*Published by order of the Lords of the Admiralty.*)

MARCO POLO. The Book of Ser Marco Polo, the Venetian. Concerning the Kingdoms and Marvels of the East. A new English Version. Illustrated by the light of Oriental Writers and Modern Travels. By COL. HENRY YULE. *New Edition.* Maps and Illustrations. 2 Vols. Medium 8vo. 42s.

MARKHAM'S (MRS.) History of England. From the First Invasion by the Romans to 1867. Woodcuts. 12mo. 3s. 6d.

———— History of France. From the Conquest by the Gauls to 1861. Woodcuts. 12mo. 3s. 6d.

———— History of Germany. From the Invasion by Marius to 1867. Woodcuts. 12mo. 3s. 6d.

———— (CLEMENTS R.) Travels in Peru and India. Maps and Illustrations. 8vo. 16s.

MARRYAT'S (JOSEPH) History of Modern and Mediæval Pottery and Porcelain. With a Description of the Manufacture. *Third Edition.* Plates and Woodcuts. 8vo. 42s.

MARSH'S (G. P.) Student's Manual of the English Language. Post 8vo. 7s. 6d.

MATTHIÆ'S GREEK GRAMMAR. Abridged by BLOMFIELD, *Revised* by E. S. CROOKE. 12mo. 4s.

MAUREL'S Character, Actions, and Writings of Wellington. Fcap. 8vo. 1s. 6d.

MAYNE'S (CAPT.) Four Years in British Columbia and Vancouver Island. Illustrations. 8vo. 16s.

MEADE'S (HON. HERBERT) Ride through the Disturbed Districts of New Zealand, with a Cruise among the South Sea Islands. With Illustrations. Medium 8vo. 12s.

MELVILLE'S (HERMANN) Marquesas and South Sea Islands. 2 Vols. Post 8vo. 7s.

MEREDITH'S (MRS. CHARLES) Notes and Sketches of New South Wales. Post 8vo. 2s.

MESSIAH (THE) : The Life, Travels, Death, Resurrection, and Ascension of our Blessed Lord. By A Layman. Map. 8vo. 18s.

MILLINGTON'S (REV. T. S.) Signs and Wonders in the Land of Ham, or the Ten Plagues of Egypt, with Ancient and Modern Illustrations. Woodcuts. Post 8vo. 7s. 6d.

MILLS' (REV. JOHN) Three Months' Residence at Nablus, with an Account of the Modern Samaritans. Illustrations. Post 8vo. 10s. 6d.

MILMAN'S (DEAN) History of the Jews, from the earliest Period down to Modern Times. *Fourth Edition.* 3 Vols. Post 8vo. 18s.

———— Early Christianity, from the Birth of Christ to the Abolition of Paganism in the Roman Empire. *Fourth Edition.* 3 Vols. Post 8vo. 18s.

———— Latin Christianity, including that of the Popes to the Pontificate of Nicholas V. *Fourth Edition.* 9 Vols. Post 8vo. 54s.

———— Annals of St. Paul's Cathedral, from the Romans to the funeral of Wellington. *Second Edition.* Portrait and Illustrations. 8vo. 18s.

———— Character and Conduct of the Apostles considered as an Evidence of Christianity. 8vo. 10s. 6d.

———— Quinti Horatii Flacci Opera. With 100 Woodcuts. Small 8vo. 7s. 6d.

———— Life of Quintus Horatius Flaccus. With Illustrations. 8vo. 9s.

———— Poetical Works. The Fall of Jerusalem—Martyr of Antioch—Belshazzar—Tamor—Anne Boleyn—Fazio, &c. With Portrait and Illustrations. 3 Vols. Fcap. 8vo. 18s.

———— Fall of Jerusalem. Fcap. 8vo. 1s.

———— (CAPT. E. A.) Wayside Cross. Post 8vo. 2s.

MICHIE'S (ALEXANDER) Siberian Overland Route from Peking to Petersburg. Maps and Illustrations. 8vo. 16s.

MODERN DOMESTIC COOKERY. Founded on Principles of Economy and Practical Knowledge. *New Edition*. Woodcuts. Fcap.8vo. 5s.

MONGREDIEN'S (AUGUSTUS) Trees and Shrubs for English Plantation. A Selection and Description of the most Ornamental which will flourish in the open air in our climate. With Classified Lists. With 30 Illustrations. 8vo. 16s.

MOORE & JACKMAN on the Clematis as a Garden Flower. Descriptions of the Hardy Species and Varieties, with Directions for their Cultivation. 8vo. 10s. 6d.

MOORE'S (THOMAS) Life and Letters of Lord Byron. *Cabinet Edition*. With Plates. 6 Vols. Fcap. 8vo. 18s.; *Popular Edition*, with Portraits. Royal 8vo. 7s. 6d.

MOSSMAN'S (SAMUEL) New Japan; the Land of the Rising Sun; its Annals and Progress during the past Twenty Years, recording the remarkable Progress of the Japanese in Western Civilisation. With Map. 8vo. 15s.

MOTLEY'S (J. L.) History of the United Netherlands: from the Death of William the Silent to the Twelve Years' Truce, 1609. *Library Edition*. Portraits. 4 Vols. 8vo. 60s. *Cabinet Edition*. 4 Vols. Post 8vo. 6s. each.

―――― Life and Death of John of Barneveld, Advocate of Holland. With a View of the Primary Causes and Movements of the Thirty Years' War. Illustrations. 2 Vols. 8vo. 26s.

MOUHOT'S (HENRI) Siam, Cambojia, and Lao; a Narrative of Travels and Discoveries. Illustrations. 2 vols. 8vo.

MOZLEY'S (CANON) Treatise on Predestination. 8vo. 14s.

―――― Primitive Doctrine of Baptismal Regeneration. 8vo. 7s.6d.

MUNDY'S (GENERAL) Pen and Pencil Sketches in India. *Third Edition*. Plates. Post 8vo. 7s. 6d.

MUNRO'S (GENERAL) Life and Letters. By REV. G. R. GLEIG. Post 8vo. 3s. 6d.

MURCHISON'S (SIR RODERICK) Russia in Europe and the Ural Mountains. With Coloured Maps, &c. 2 Vols. 4to. 5l. 5s.

―――― Siluria; or, a History of the Oldest Rocks containing Organic Remains. *Fifth Edition*. Map and Plates. 8vo. 18s.

―――― Memoirs. With Notices of his Contemporaries, and Rise and Progress of Palæozoic Geology. By ARCHIBALD GEIKIE. Portraits. 2 Vols. 8vo.

MURRAY'S RAILWAY READING. Containing:—

WELLINGTON. By LORD ELLESMERE. 6d.	MAHON'S JOAN OF ARC. 1s.
NIMROD ON THE CHASE. 1s.	HEAD'S EMIGRANT. 2s. 6d.
MUSIC AND DRESS. 1s.	NIMROD ON THE ROAD. 1s.
MILMAN'S FALL OF JERUSALEM. 1s.	CROKER ON THE GUILLOTINE. 1s.
MAHON'S "FORTY-FIVE." 3s.	HOLLWAY'S NORWAY. 2s.
LIFE OF THEODORE HOOK. 1s.	MAUREL'S WELLINGTON. 1s. 6d.
DEEDS OF NAVAL DARING. 3s. 6d.	CAMPBELL'S LIFE OF BACON. 2s. 6d.
THE HONEY BEE. 1s.	THE FLOWER GARDEN. 1s.
ÆSOP'S FABLES. 2s. 6d.	TAYLOR'S NOTES FROM LIFE. 2s.
NIMROD ON THE TURF. 1s. 6d.	REJECTED ADDRESSES. 1s.
ART OF DINING. 1s. 6d.	PENN'S HINTS ON ANGLING. 1s.

MUSTERS' (CAPT.) Patagonians; a Year's Wanderings over Untrodden Ground from the Straits of Magellan to the Rio Negro. *2nd Edition*. Illustrations. Post 8vo. 7s. 6d.

NAPIER'S (SIR CHAS.) Life, Journals, and Letters. *Second Edition*. Portraits. 4 Vols. Post 8vo. 48s.

―――― (SIR WM.) Life and Letters. Portraits. 2 Vols. Crown 8vo. 28s.

―――― English Battles and Sieges of the Peninsular War. *Fourth Edition*. Portrait. Post 8vo. 9s.

NAPOLEON AT FONTAINEBLEAU AND ELBA. A Journal of Occurrences and Notes of Conversations. By Sir NEIL CAMPBELL, C.B. With a Memoir. By REV. A. N. C. MACLACHLAN, M.A. Portrait. 8vo. 15s.

NASMYTH AND CARPENTER. The Moon. Considered as a Planet, a World, and a Satellite. With Illustrations from Drawings made with the aid of Powerful Telescopes, Woodcuts, &c. Second Edition. 4to. 30s.

NAUTICAL ALMANAC (THE). (By Authority.) 2s. 6d.

NAVY LIST. (Monthly and Quarterly.) Post 8vo.

NEW TESTAMENT. With Short Explanatory Commentary. By ARCHDEACON CHURTON, M.A., and ARCHDEACON BASIL JONES, M.A. With 110 authentic Views, &c. 2 Vols. Crown 8vo. 21s. bound.

NEWTH'S (SAMUEL) First Book of Natural Philosophy; an Introduction to the Study of Statics, Dynamics, Hydrostatics, Optics, and Acoustics, with numerous Examples. Small 8vo. 3s. 6d.

———— Elements of Mechanics, including Hydrostatics, with numerous Examples. Fifth Edition. Small 8vo. 8s. 6d. Cloth.

———— Mathematical Examinations. A Graduated Series of Elementary Examples in Arithmetic, Algebra, Logarithms, Trigonometry, and Mechanics. Third Edition. Small 8vo. 8s. 6d. each.

NICHOLLS' (SIR GEORGE) History of the English, Irish and Scotch Poor Laws. 4 Vols. 8vo.

NICOLAS' (SIR HARRIS) Historic Peerage of England. Exhibiting the Origin, Descent, and Present State of every Title of Peerage which has existed in this Country since the Conquest. By WILLIAM COURTHOPE. 8vo. 30s.

NIMROD, On the Chace—Turf—and Road. With Portrait and Plates. Crown 8vo. 5s. Or with Coloured Plates, 7s. 6d.

NORDHOFF'S (CHAS.) Communistic Societies of the United States; including Detailed Accounts of the Shakers, The Amana, Oneida, Bethell, Aurora, Icarian and other existing Societies; with Particulars of their Religious Creeds, Industries, and Present Condition. With 40 Illustrations. 8vo. 15s.

OLD LONDON; Papers read at the Archæological Institute. By various Authors. 8vo. 12s.

ORMATHWAITE'S (LORD) Astronomy and Geology—Darwin and Buckle—Progress and Civilisation. Crown 8vo. 6s.

OWEN'S (LIEUT.-COL.) Principles and Practice of Modern Artillery, including Artillery Material, Gunnery, and Organisation and Use of Artillery in Warfare. Second Edition. With Illustrations. 8vo. 15s.

OXENHAM'S (REV. W.) English Notes for Latin Elegiacs; designed for early Proficients in the Art of Latin Versification, with Prefatory Rules of Composition in Elegiac Metre. Fifth Edition. 12mo. 3s. 6d.

PALGRAVE'S (R. H. I.) Local Taxation of Great Britain and Ireland. 8vo. 5s.

———— NOTES ON BANKING IN GREAT BRITAIN AND IRELAND, SWEDEN, DENMARK, AND HAMBURG, with some Remarks on the amount of Bills in circulation, both Inland and Foreign. 8vo. 6s.

PALLISER'S (MRS.) Brittany and its Byeways, its Inhabitants, and Antiquities. With Illustrations. Post 8vo. 12s.

———— Mottoes for Monuments, or Epitaphs selected for General Use and Study. With Illustrations. Crown 8vo. 7s. 6d.

PARIS' (DR.) Philosophy in Sport made Science in Earnest; or, the First Principles of Natural Philosophy inculcated by aid of the Toys and Sports of Youth. Ninth Edition. Woodcuts. Post 8vo. 7s. 6d.

PARKMAN'S (FRANCIS) Discovery of the Great West; or, The Valleys of the Mississippi and the Lakes of North America. An Historical Narrative. Map. 8vo. 10s. 6d.

PARKYNS' (MANSFIELD) Three Years' Residence in Abyssinia: with Travels in that Country. *Second Edition*, with Illustrations. Post 8vo. 7s. 6d.

PEEK PRIZE ESSAYS. The Maintenance of the Church of England as an Established Church. By REV. CHARLES HOLE—REV. R. WATSON DIXON—and REV. JULIUS LLOYD. 8vo. 10s. 6d.

PEEL'S (SIR ROBERT) Memoirs. 2 Vols. Post 8vo. 15s.

PENN'S (RICHARD) Maxims and Hints for an Angler and Chess-player. Woodcuts. Fcap. 8vo. 1s.

PERCY'S (JOHN, M.D.) Metallurgy. Vol. I., Part 1. Fuel, Wood, Peat, Coal, Charcoal, Coke, Refractory Materials, Fire-Clays, &c. *Second Edition*. With Illustrations. 8vo. 24s.

—— Vol. I., Part 2. Copper, Zinc, Brass. *Second Edition*. With Illustrations. 8vo. (*In the Press.*)

—— Vol. II. Iron and Steel. *New Edition*. With Illustrations. 8vo. (*In Preparation.*)

—— Vol. III. Lead, including Desilverization and Cupellation. With Illustrations. 8vo. 30s.

—— Vols. IV. and V. Gold, Silver, and Mercury, Platinum, Tin, Nickel, Cobalt, Antimony, Bismuth, Arsenic, and other Metals. With Illustrations. 8vo. (*In Preparation.*)

PERSIA'S (SHAH OF) Diary during his Tour through Europe in 1873. Translated from the Original. By J. W. REDHOUSE. With Portrait and Coloured Title. Crown 8vo. 12s.

PHILLIPS' (JOHN) Memoirs of William Smith. 8vo. 7s. 6d.

—— Geology of Yorkshire, The Coast, and Limestone District. Plates. 4to.

—— Rivers, Mountains, and Sea Coast of Yorkshire. With Essays on the Climate, Scenery, and Ancient Inhabitants. *Second Edition*, Plates. 8vo. 15s.

—— (SAMUEL) Literary Essays from "The Times." With Portrait. 2 Vols. Fcap. 8vo. 7s.

PICK'S (DR.) Popular Etymological Dictionary of the French Language. 8vo. 7s. 6d.

POPE'S (ALEXANDER) Works. With Introductions and Notes, by REV. WHITWELL ELWIN. Vols. I., II., VI., VII., VIII. With Portraits. 8vo. 10s. 6d. each.

PORTER'S (REV. J. L.) Damascus, Palmyra, and Lebanon. With Travels among the Giant Cities of Bashan and the Hauran. *New Edition*. Map and Woodcuts. Post 8vo. 7s. 6d.

PRAYER-BOOK (ILLUSTRATED), with Borders, Initials, Vignettes, &c. Edited, with Notes, by REV. THOS. JAMES. Medium 8vo. 18s. *cloth*; 31s. 6d. *calf*; 36s. *morocco*.

PRINCESS CHARLOTTE OF WALES. A Brief Memoir. With Selections from her Correspondence and other unpublished Papers. By LADY ROSE WEIGALL. With Portrait. 8vo. 8s. 6d.

PUSS IN BOOTS. With 12 Illustrations. By OTTO SPECKTER. 16mo. 1s. 6d. Or coloured, 2s. 6d.

PRINCIPLES AT STAKE. Essays on Church Questions of the Day. 8vo. 12s. Contents:—

Ritualism and Uniformity.—Benjamin Shaw.	Scripture and Ritual.—Canon Bernard.
The Episcopate.—Bishop of Bath and Wells.	Church in South Africa.—Arthur Mills.
The Priesthood.—Dean of Canterbury.	Schismatical Tendency of Ritualism.—Rev. Dr. Salmon.
National Education.—Rev. Alexander R. Grant.	Revisions of the Liturgy.—Rev. W. G. Humphry.
Doctrine of the Eucharist.—Rev. G. H. Sumner.	Parties and Party Spirit.—Dean of Chester.

PRIVY COUNCIL JUDGMENTS in Ecclesiastical Cases relating to Doctrine and Discipline. With Historical Introduction, by G. C. Brodrick and W. H. Fremantle. 8vo. 10s. 6d.

QUARTERLY REVIEW (The). 8vo. 6s.

RAMBLES in the Syrian Deserts.- Post 8vo. 10s. 6d.

RANKE'S (Leopold) History of the Popes of Rome during the 16th and 17th Centuries. Translated from the German by Sarah Austin. Third Edition. 3 Vols. 8vo. 30s.

RASSAM'S (Hormuzd) Narrative of the British Mission to Abysinia. With Notices of the Countries Traversed from Massowah to Magdala. Illustrations. 2 Vols. 8vo. 28s.

RAWLINSON'S (Canon) Herodotus. A New English Version. Edited with Notes and Essays. Third Edition. Maps and Woodcut. 4 Vols. 8vo.

—————— Five Great Monarchies of Chaldæa, Assyria, Media, Babylonia, and Persia. Third Edition. With Maps and Illustrations. 3 Vols. 8vo. 42s.

—————— (Sir Henry) England and Russia in the East; a Series of Papers on the Political and Geographical Condition of Central Asia. Map. 8vo.

REED'S (E. J.) Shipbuilding in Iron and Steel; a Practical Treatise, giving full details of Construction, Processes of Manufacture, and Building Arrangements. With 5 Plans and 250 Woodcuts. 8vo. 30s.

—————— Iron-Clad Ships; their Qualities, Performances, and Cost. With Chapters on Turret Ships, Iron-Clad Rams, &c. With Illustrations. 8vo. 12s.

REJECTED ADDRESSES (The). By James and Horace Smith. New Edition. Woodcuts. Post 8vo. 3s. 6d.; or Popular Edition, Fcap. 8vo. 1s.

RENNIE'S (D. F.) British Arms in Peking, 1860. Post 8vo. 12s.

—————— Narrative of the British Embassy in China. Illustrations. 2 Vols. Post 8vo. 24s.

—————— Story of Bhotan and the Dooar War. Map and Woodcut. Post 8vo. 12s.

RESIDENCE IN BULGARIA; or, Notes on the Resources and Administration of Turkey, &c. By S. G. B. St. Clair and Charles A. Brophy. 8vo. 12s.

REYNOLDS' (Sir Joshua) Life and Times. By C. R. Leslie, R.A. and Tom Taylor. Portraits. 2 Vols. 8vo.

RICARDO'S (David) Political Works. With a Notice of his Life and Writings. By J. R. M'Culloch. New Edition. 8vo. 16s.

RIPA'S (Father) Thirteen Years' Residence at the Court of Peking. Post 8vo. 2s.

ROBERTSON'S (Canon) History of the Christian Church, from the Apostolic Age to the Reformation, 1517. Library Edition. 4 Vols. 8vo. Cabinet Edition. 8 Vols. Post 8vo. 6s. each.

—————— How shall we Conform to the Liturgy. 12mo. 9s.

ROME. See Liddell and Smith.

ROWLAND'S (David) Manual of the English Constitution. Its Rise, Growth, and Present State. Post 8vo. 10s. 6d.

—————— Laws of Nature the Foundation of Morals. Post 8vo. 6s.

ROBSON'S (E. R.) SCHOOL ARCHITECTURE. Being Practical Remarks on the Planning, Designing, Building, and Furnishing of School-houses. With 300 Illustrations of School-buildings in all Parts of the World, drawn to scale. Medium 8vo. 31s. 6d.

RUNDELL'S (Mrs.) Modern Domestic Cookery. Fcap. 8vo. 5s.

RUXTON'S (GEORGE F.) Travels in Mexico; with Adventures among the Wild Tribes and Animals of the Prairies and Rocky Mountains. Post 8vo. 3s. 6d.

ROBINSON'S (REV. DR.) Biblical Researches in Palestine and the Adjacent Regions, 1838—52. *Third Edition.* Maps. 3 Vols. 8vo. 42s.

―――― Physical Geography of the Holy Land. Post 8vo. 10s. 6d.

―――― (WM.) Alpine Flowers for English Gardens. *New Edition.* With 70 Illustrations. Crown 8vo. [*Nearly ready.*

―――― Wild Garden; or, our Groves and Shrubberies made beautiful by the Naturalization of Hardy Exotic Plants. With Frontispiece. Small 8vo. 6s.

―――― Sub-Tropical Garden ; or, Beauty of Form in the Flower Garden. With Illustrations. Small 8vo. 7s. 6d.

SALE'S (SIR ROBERT) Brigade in Affghanistan. With an Account of the Defence of Jellalabad. By REV. G. R. GLEIG. Post 8vo. 2s.

SCHLIEMANN'S (DR. HENRY) Troy and Its Remains. A Narrative of Researches and Discoveries made on the Site of Ilium, and in the Trojan Plain. Edited by PHILIP SMITH, B.A. With Maps, Plans, Views, and 500 Illustrations of Objects of Antiquity, &c. Medium 8vo.

SCOTT'S (SIR G. G.) Secular and Domestic Architecture, Present and Future. 8vo. 9s.

―――― (DEAN) University Sermons. Post 8vo. 8s. 6d.

SHADOWS OF A SICK ROOM. *Second Edition.* With a Preface by CANON LIDDON. 16mo. 2s 6d.

SCROPE'S (G. P.) Geology and Extinct Volcanoes of Central France. Illustrations. Medium 8vo. 30s.

SHAW'S (T. B.) Manual of English Literature. Post 8vo. 7s. 6d.

―――― Specimens of English Literature. Selected from the Chief Writers. Post 8vo. 7s. 6d.

―――― (ROBERT) Visit to High Tartary, Yarkand, and Kashgar (formerly Chinese Tartary), and Return Journey over the Karakorum Pass. With Map and Illustrations. 8vo. 16s.

SHIRLEY'S (EVELYN P.) Deer and Deer Parks; or some Account of English Parks, with Notes on the Management of Deer. Illustrations. 4to. 21s.

SIERRA LEONE; Described in Letters to Friends at Home. By A LADY. Post 8vo. 3s. 6d.

SINCLAIR'S (ARCHDEACON) Old Times and Distant Places. A Series of Sketches. Crown 8vo.

SMILES' (SAMUEL) Lives of British Engineers ; from the Earliest Period to the death of the Stephensons. With Portraits and Illustrations. *Cabinet Edition.* 5 Vols. Crown 8vo. 7s. 6d. each.

―――― Lives of George and Robert Stephenson. *Library Edition.* With Portraits and Illustrations. Medium 8vo. 21s.

―――― Lives of Boulton and Watt. *Library Edition.* With Portraits and Illustrations. Medium 8vo. 21s.

―――― Self-Help. With Illustrations of Conduct and Perseverance. Post 8vo. 6s. Or in French, 5s.

―――― Character. A Companion Volume to /"SELF-HELP." Post 8vo. 6s.

―――― Industrial Biography : Iron-Workers and Tool-Makers. Post 8vo. 6s.

―――― Boy's Voyage round the World; including a Residence in Victoria, and a Journey by Rail across North America. With Illustrations. Post 8vo. 6s.

SMITH'S (Dr. Wm.) Dictionary of the Bible; its Antiquities, Biography, Geography, and Natural History. Illustrations. 3 Vols. 8vo. 105s.
—————————— Christian Antiquities. Comprising the History, Institutions, and Antiquities of the Christian Church. 2 Vols. 8vo. Vol. I. (*Nearly ready.*)
—————————— Biography and Doctrines; from the Times of the Apostles to the Age of Charlemagne. 8vo. (*In Preparation.*)
—————— Concise Bible Dictionary. With 300 Illustrations. Medium 8vo. 21s.
—————— Smaller Bible Dictionary. With Illustrations. Post 8vo. 7s. 6d.
—————— Atlas of Ancient Geography—Biblical and Classical. (5 Parts.) Folio. 21s. each.
—————— Greek and Roman Antiquities. With 500 Illustrations. Medium 8vo. 28s.
—————————— Biography and Mythology. With 600 Illustrations. 3 Vols. Medium 8vo. 4l. 4s.
—————————— Geography. 2 Vols. With 500 Illustrations. Medium 8vo. 56s.
—————— Classical Dictionary of Mythology, Biography, and Geography. 1 Vol. With 750 Woodcuts. 8vo. 18s.
—————— Smaller Classical Dictionary. With 200 Woodcuts. Crown 8vo. 7s. 6d.
—————— Greek and Roman Antiquities. With 200 Woodcuts. Crown 8vo. 7s. 6d.
—————— Latin-English Dictionary. With Tables of the Roman Calendar, Measures, Weights, and Money. Medium 8vo. 21s.
—————— Smaller Latin-English Dictionary. 12mo. 7s. 6d.
—————— English-Latin Dictionary. Medium 8vo. 21s.
—————— Smaller English-Latin Dictionary. 12mo. 7s. 6d.
—————— School Manual of English Grammar, with Copious Exercises. Post 8vo. 3s. 6d.
—————— Primary English Grammar. 16mo. 1s.
—————— History of Britain. 12mo. 2s. 6d.
—————— French Principia. Part I. A Grammar, Delectus, Exercises, and Vocabularies. 12mo. ?s. 6d.
—————— Principia Latina—Part I. A Grammar, Delectus, and Exercise Book, with Vocabularies. With the Accidence arranged for the "Public School Primer." 12mo. 3s. 6d.
—————————— Part II. A Reading-book of Mythology, Geography, Roman Antiquities, and History. With Notes and Dictionary. 12mo. 3s. 6d.
—————————— Part III. A Latin Poetry Book. Hexameters and Pantameters; Eclog. Ovidianæ; Latin Prosody. 12mo. 3s. 6d.
—————————— Part IV. Latin Prose Composition. Rules of Syntax, with Examples, Explanations of Synonyms, and Exercises on the Syntax. 12mo. 3s. 6d.
—————————— Part V. Short Tales and Anecdotes for Translation into Latin. 12mo. 3s.
—————— Latin-English Vocabulary and First Latin-English Dictionary for Phædrus, Cornelius Nepos, and Cæsar. 12mo. 3s. 6d.
—————— Student's Latin Grammar. Post 8vo. 6s.
—————— Smaller Latin Grammar. 12mo. 3s. 6d.

PUBLISHED BY MR. MURRAY. 29

SMITH'S (DR. WM.) Tacitus, Germania, Agricola, &c. With English Notes. 12mo. 3s. 6d.
——— Initia Græca, Part I. A Grammar, Delectus, and Exercise-book. With Vocabularies. 12mo. 3s. 6d.
——— Initia Græca, Part II. A Reading Book. Containing Short Tales, Anecdotes, Fables, Mythology, and Grecian History. 12mo. 3s. 6d.
——— Initia Græca, Part III. Greek Prose Composition. Containing the Rules of Syntax, with copious Examples and Exercises. 12mo. 3s. 6d.
——— Student's Greek Grammar. By PROFESSOR CURTIUS. Post 8vo. 6s.
——— Smaller Greek Grammar. 12mo. 3s. 6d.
——— Greek Accidence. Extracted from the above work. 12mo. 2s. 6d.
——— Plato. The Apology of Socrates, the Crito, and Part of the Phædo; with Notes in English from Stallbaum and Schleiermacher's Introductions. 12mo. 3s. 6d.
——— Smaller Scripture History. Woodcuts. 16mo. 3s. 6d.
——— Ancient History. Woodcuts. 16mo. 3s. 6d.
——— Geography. Woodcuts. 16mo. 3s. 6d.
——— Rome. Woodcuts. 16mo. 3s. 6d.
——— Greece. Woodcuts. 16mo. 3s. 6d.
——— Classical Mythology. With Translations from the Poets. Woodcuts. 16mo. 3s. 6d.
——— History of England. Woodcuts. 16mo. 3s. 6d.
——— English Literature. 16mo. 3s. 6d.
——— Specimens of English Literature. 16mo. 3s. 6d.
——— (PHILIP) History of the Ancient World, from the Creation to the Fall of the Roman Empire, A.D. 455. *Fourth Edition.* 3 Vols. 8vo. 31s. 6d.
——— (REV. A. C.) Nile and its Banks. Woodcuts. 2 Vols. Post 8vo. 18s.
SIMMONS' (CAPT.) Constitution and Practice of Courts-Martial; with a Summary of the Law of Evidence, and some Notice of the Criminal Law of England with reference to the Trial of Civil Offences. *Sixth Edition.* 8vo. 15s.
STANLEY'S (DEAN) Sinai and Palestine, in connexion with their History. *20th Thousand.* Map. 8vo. 14s.
——— Bible in the Holy Land; Extracted from the above Work. *Second Edition.* Woodcuts. Fcap. 8vo. 2s 6d
——— History of the Eastern Church. *Fourth Edition.* Plans. 8vo. 12s.
——— Jewish Church. *Fifth Edition.* 8vo. 24s.
——— Church of Scotland. 8vo. 7s. 6d.
——— Memorials of Canterbury Cathedral. *Fifth Edition.* Woodcuts. Post 8vo. 7s. 6d.
——— Westminster Abbey. *Third Edition.* With Illustrations. 8vo. 21s.
——— Sermons during a Tour in the East. 8vo. 9s.
——— on Evangelical and Apostolical Teaching. Post 8vo. 7s. 6d.
——— ADDRESSES AND CHARGES OF THE LATE BISHOP STANLEY. With Memoir. 8vo. 10s. 8d.

LIST OF WORKS

STUDENT'S OLD TESTAMENT HISTORY; from the Creation to the Return of the Jews from Captivity. Maps and Woodcuts. Post 8vo. 7s. 6d.
——— NEW TESTAMENT HISTORY. With an Introduction connecting the History of the Old and New Testaments. Maps and Woodcuts. Post 8vo. 7s. 6d.
——— ANCIENT HISTORY OF THE EAST; Egypt, Assyria, Babylonia, Media, Persia, Asia Minor, and Phœnicia. By PHILIP SMITH. Woodcuts. Post 8vo. 7s. 6d.
——— GEOGRAPHY. By REV. W. L. BEVAN. Woodcuts. Post 8vo. 7s. 6d.
——— HISTORY OF GREECE; from the Earliest Times to the Roman Conquest. By WM. SMITH, D.C.L. Woodcuts. Crown 8vo. 7s. 6d.
*** Questions on the above Work, 12mo. 2s.
——— HISTORY OF ROME; from the Earliest Times to the Establishment of the Empire. By DEAN LIDDELL. Woodcuts. Crown 8vo. 7s. 6d.
——— GIBBON'S Decline and Fall of the Roman Empire. Woodcuts. Post 8vo. 7s. 6d.
——— HALLAM'S HISTORY OF EUROPE during the Middle Ages. Post 8vo. 7s. 6d.
——— HUME'S History of England from the Invasion of Julius Cæsar to the Revolution in 1688. Continued down to 1868. Woodcuts. Post 8vo. 7s. 6d.
*** Questions on the above Work. 12mo. 2s.
——— HALLAM'S HISTORY OF ENGLAND; from the Accession of Henry VII. to the Death of George II. Post 8vo. 7s. 6d.
——— ENGLISH LANGUAGE. By GEO. P. MARSH. Post 8vo. 7s. 6d.
——— LITERATURE. By T. B. SHAW, M.A. Post 8vo. 7s. 6d.
——— SPECIMENS of English Literature from the Chief Writers. By T. B. SHAW, Post 8vo. 7s. 6d.
——— HISTORY OF FRANCE; from the Earliest Times to the Establishment of the Second Empire, 1852. By REV. H. W. JERVIS. Woodcuts. Post 8vo. 7s. 6d.
——— MODERN GEOGRAPHY; Mathematical, Physical, and Descriptive. By REV. W. L. BEVAN. Woodcuts. Post 8vo. 7s. 6d.
——— MORAL PHILOSOPHY. By WILLIAM FLEMING, D.D. Post 8vo. 7s. 6d.
——— BLACKSTONE'S Commentaries on the Laws of England. By R. MALCOLM KERR, LL.D. Post 8vo. 7s. 6d.
——— ECCLESIASTICAL HISTORY. A History of the Christian Church from its Foundation to the Eve of the Protestant Reformation. By PHILIP SMITH, B.A. Post 8vo. 7s. 6d.
SPALDING'S (CAPTAIN) Tale of Frithiof. Translated from the Swedish of ESIAS TEGNER. Post 8vo. 7s. 6d.
STEPHEN'S (REV. W. R.) Life and Times of St. Chrysostom. With Portrait. 8vo. 15s.
ST. JOHN'S (CHARLES) Wild Sports and Natural History of the Highlands. Post 8vo. 6s. 6d.
——— (BAYLE) Adventures in the Libyan Desert. Post 8vo. 2s.
STORIES FOR DARLINGS. With Illustrations. 16mo. 5s.
STREET'S (G. E.) Gothic Architecture in Spain. From Personal Observations made during several Journeys. *Second Edition.* With Illustrations. Royal 8vo. 30s.
——— Gothic Architecture in Italy, chiefly in Brick and Marble. With Notes of Tours in the North of Italy. *Second Edition.* With 60 Illustrations. Royal 8vo. 26s.

STANHOPE'S (EARL) England during the Reign of Queen Anne, 1701—13. *Library Edition.* 8vo. 16s. *Cabinet Edition.* Portrait. 2 Vols. Post 8vo. 10s.
———————————— from the Peace of Utrecht to the Peace of Versailles, 1713-83. *Library Edition.* 7 vols. 8vo. 93s. *Cabinet Edition*, 7 vols. Post 8vo. 5s. each.
——————— British India, from its Origin to 1783. 8vo. 3s. 6d.
——————— History of "Forty-Five." Post 8vo. 3s.
——————— Spain under Charles the Second. Post 8vo. 6s. 6d.
——————— Historical and Critical Essays. Post 8vo. 3s. 6d.
——————— Life of Belisarius. Post 8vo. 10s. 6d.
——————— Condé. Post 8vo. 3s. 6d.
——————— William Pitt. Portraits. 4 Vols. 8vo. 24s.
——————— Miscellanies. 2 Vols. Post 8vo. 13s.
——————— Story of Joan of Arc. Fcap. 8vo. 1s.
——————— Addresses Delivered on Various Occasions. 16mo. 1s.
STYFFE'S (KNUTT) Strength of Iron and Steel. Plates. 8vo. 12s.
SOMERVILLE'S (MARY) Physical Geography. *Sixth Edition*, Portrait. Post 8vo. 9s.
——————— Connexion of the Physical Sciences. *Ninth Edition*. Portrait. Post 8vo. 9s.
——————— Molecular and Microscopic Science. Illustrations. 2 Vols. Post 8vo. 21s.
——————— Personal Recollections from Early Life to Old Age. With Selections from her Correspondence. *Fourth Edition*. Portrait. Crown 8vo. 12s.
SOUTHEY'S (ROBERT) Book of the Church. Post 8vo. 7s. 6d.
——————— Lives of Bunyan and Cromwell. Post 8vo. 2s.
SWAINSON'S (CANON) Nicene and Apostles' Creeds; Their Literary History; together with some Account of "The Creed of St. Athanasius." 8vo.
SYBEL'S (VON) History of Europe during the French Revolution, 1789—1795. 4 Vols. 8vo. 48s.
SYMONDS' (REV. W.) Records of the Rocks; or Notes on the Geology, Natural History, and Antiquities of North and South Wales, Siluria, Devon, and Cornwall. With Illustrations. Crown 8vo. 12s.
TAYLOR'S (SIR HENRY) Notes from Life. Fcap. 8vo. 2s.
THIELMAN'S (BARON) Journey through the Caucasus to Tabreez, Kurdistan, down the Tigris and Euphrates to Nineveh and Babylon, and across the Desert to Palmyra. Translated by CHAS. HENEAGE. 2 Vols. Post 8vo.
THOMS' (W. J.) Longevity of Man; its Facts and its Fiction. Including Observations on the more Remarkable Instances. Post 8vo. 10s. 6d.
THOMSON'S (ARCHBISHOP) Lincoln's Inn Sermons. 8vo. 10s. 6d.
——————— Life in the Light of God's Word. Post 8vo. 5s.
TOCQUEVILLE'S State of Society in France before the Revolution, 1789, and on the Causes which led to that Event. Translated by HENRY REEVE. *2nd Edition.* 8vo. 12s.
TOMLINSON (CHARLES); The Sonnet; Its Origin, Structure, and Place in Poetry. With translations from Dante, Petrarch, &c. Post 8vo. 9s.
TOZER'S (REV. H. F.) Highlands of Turkey, with Visits to Mounts Ida, Athos, Olympus, and Pelion. 2 Vols. Crown 8vo. 24s.
——————— Lectures on the Geography of Greece. Map. Post 8vo. 9s.

TRISTRAM'S (Canon) Great Sahara. Illustrations. Crown 8vo. 15s.
———— Land of Moab; Travels and Discoveries on the East Side of the Dead Sea and the Jordan. *Second Edition.* Illustrations. Crown 8vo. 15s.

TWISLETON (Edward). The Tongue not Essential to Speech, with Illustrations of the Power of Speech in the case of the African Confessors. Post 8vo. 6s.

TWISS' (Horace) Life of Lord Eldon. 2 Vols. Post 8vo. 21s.

TYLOR'S (E. B.) Early History of Mankind, and Development of Civilization. *Second Edition.* 8vo. 12s.
———— Primitive Culture; the Development of Mythology, Philosophy, Religion, Art, and Custom. *Second Edition.* 2 Vols. 8vo. 24s.

VAMBERY'S (Arminius) Travels from Teheran across the Turkoman Desert on the Eastern Shore of the Caspian. Illustrations. 8vo. 21s.

VAN LENNEP'S (Henry J.) Travels in Asia Minor. With Illustrations of Biblical Literature, and Archæology. With Woodcuts. 2 Vols. Post 8vo. 24s.

WELLINGTON'S Despatches during his Campaigns in India, Denmark, Portugal, Spain, the Low Countries, and France. Edited by Colonel Gurwood. 8 Vols. 8vo. 20s. each.
———— Supplementary Despatches, relating to India, Ireland, Denmark, Spanish America, Spain, Portugal, France, Congress of Vienna, Waterloo and Paris. Edited by his Son. 14 Vols. 8vo. 20s. each. *_{*}* *An Index.* 8vo. 20s.
———— Civil and Political Correspondence. Edited by his Son. Vols. I. to V. 8vo. 20s. each.
———— Despatches (Selections from). 8vo. 18s.
———— Speeches in Parliament. 2 Vols. 8vo. 42s.

WHEELER'S (G.) Choice of a Dwelling; a Practical Handbook of Useful Information on Building a House. *Third Edition.* Plans. Post 8vo. 7s. 6d.

WHITE'S (Henry) Massacre of St. Bartholomew. 8vo. 16s.

WHYMPER'S (Edward) Scrambles among the Alps. With the First Ascent of the Matterhorn, and Notes on Glacial Phenomena. *Second Edition.* Illustrations. 8vo. 21s.
———— (Frederick) Travels and Adventures in Alaska. Illustrations. 8vo. 16s.

WILBERFORCE'S (Bishop) Essays on Various Subjects. 2 vols. 8vo. 21s.
———— Life of William Wilberforce. Portrait. Crown 8vo. 6s.

WILKINSON'S (Sir J. G.) Popular Account of the Ancient Egyptians. With 500 Woodcuts. 2 Vols. Post 8vo. 12s.

WOOD'S (Captain) Source of the Oxus. With the Geography of the Valley of the Oxus. By Col. Yule. Map. 8vo. 12s.

WORDS OF HUMAN WISDOM. Collected and Arranged by E. S. With a Preface by Canon Liddon, D.D. Fcp. 8vo. 3s. 6d.

WORDSWORTH'S (Bishop) Athens and Attica. Plates. 8vo. 5s.
———— Greece. Pictorial, Descriptive, and Historical. With 600 Woodcuts. Royal 8vo.

YULE'S (Colonel) Book of Marco Polo. Illustrated by the Light of Oriental Writers and Modern Travels. With Maps and 80 Plates. 2 Vols. Medium 8vo. 42s.

ZINCKE'S (Rev. F. B.) Winter in the United States. Post 8vo. 10s. 6d.

BRADBURY, AGNEW, & CO., PRINTERS, WHITEFRIARS.

www.ingramcontent.com/pod-product-compliance
Lightning Source LLC
Chambersburg PA
CBHW020525300426
44111CB00008B/543